Asia
THE BEAUTIFUL
COOKBOOK

AUTHENTIC RECIPES FROM JAPAN, KOREA, CHINA, THE PHILIPPINES,
THAILAND, LAOS AND KAMPUCHEA, VIETNAM, SINGAPORE AND MALAYSIA,
INDIA, BURMA, INDONESIA AND SRI LANKA

JAPANESE *YAKITORI,* recipe page 37

AUTHENTIC RECIPES FROM JAPAN, KOREA, CHINA, THE PHILIPPINES, THAILAND, LAOS AND KAMPUCHEA, VIETNAM, SINGAPORE AND MALAYSIA, INDIA, BURMA, INDONESIA AND SRI LANKA

Asia
THE BEAUTIFUL
COOKBOOK

JACKI PASSMORE

S T O N E H E N G E

Conceived and produced by Weldon Owen Pty Limited
43 Victoria St, McMahons Point, Sydney,
NSW 2060, Australia
Phone (02) 929 5677 Fax (02) 929 8352
A member of the Weldon International Group of Companies
Sydney • San Francisco • Paris • London

This edition published in 1992

Weldon Owen
President: John Owen
General Manager: Stuart Laurence
Co-Editions Director: Derek Barton
Editorial Director: Elaine Russell
Project Coordinator: Jane Fraser
Editor: Pat Connell, Susan Tomnay
Index: Dianne Regtop
Production: Sue Tickner, Kate Smyth

Design and art direction: John Bull, Bull's Graphics
Food photography: Mike Hallson Photography
Maps and illustrations: Stan Lamond
Calligraphy: David Wood

Manufactured by Mandarin Offset, Hong Kong
Printed in Hong Kong

ISBN 0-86706-625-3

This series is published in association with
STONEHENGE PRESS, Alexandria, Va.

Associate Publisher: Trevor Lunn
Marketing Director: Regina Hall
Editorial Director: Donia Ann Steele

Stonehenge Press is a division of Time-Life Inc.
For more information on and a full description of any
of the Time-Life series, please call 1-800-621-7026
or write:
Reader Information
Time-Life Customer Service
P.O. Box C-32068
Richmond, Virginia 23261-2068

A Weldon Owen ◆ Production

RIGHT: FLOATING MARKETS IN BANGKOK· AUSTRALIAN PICTURE LIBRARY
PAGES 2-3: FISHING IN SRI LANKA IMAGES PHOTO AGENCY
PAGES 8-9: CHINATOWN, SINGAPORE R. IAN LLOYD, SINGAPORE
ENDPAPERS: WINTER SERENITY, JAPAN KAZUYOSHI NOMACHI/PPS

HOT CHILI BEEF AND ONION SOUP *(TOP),* AND COLD CUCUMBER SOUP
FROM KOREA, *recipes pages 54-55*

Contents

INTRODUCTION 12

JAPAN 18
Simplicity and elegance

KOREA 46
Warm and sustaining

CHINA 58
From the beginning of time

PHILIPPINES 86
East meets West

THAILAND 98
Titillating, tantalizing

LAOS AND KAMPUCHEA 118
Unforgettable foods

VIETNAM 130
Herbaceous overtones

SINGAPORE AND MALAYSIA 146
A blending of cultures

INDIA 172
Southern fire, northern serenity

BURMA 200
Exotic offerings

INDONESIA 212
Symphony of flavors

SRI LANKA 240
Gems from an enchanted isle

GLOSSARY 252

ACKNOWLEDGMENTS 254

INDEX 255

The Culinary Heritage

Like the countries themselves – many-faceted, exotic, intriguing – so are the manifold cuisines of Asia: a mosaic of styles as different as the social customs and age-old traditions that have shaped them; cuisines created by human ingenuity and influenced by religion, geography and climate, by friendly visitors and aggressive occupation. The world that is Asia is undeniably fascinating. Beauteous in its diverse terrain: from lush tropical rainforests to icy windswept plains; from towering snow-capped mountains to mangrove-fringed fertile delta flats; from jagged grey ranges to coral-ringed emerald islands. Powerful in its deep-felt beliefs for which wars have been fought and won. Wondrous in its colourful traditions and myriad unique customs. Tantalizing in the scope and complexity of its cuisines. Each cuisine, by its style, its cooking methods and its ingredients, is a record of the evolution of the country, telling its own story of land, history and people.

Dominating them all, in history and magnitude, is the cuisine of China, the vast continent occupying the very heart of Asia. Through archeological discoveries, much is known of this ancient land from its earliest times, and prodigious recordings were kept from as early as the Chou Dynasty in the twelfth century BC. The Chinese cuisine we enjoy today was born in these far-off times. A phrase, *ko p'eng*, recorded then, states clearly that the 'cut and cook' method we now call stir-frying was already in use in family kitchens, together with many of the common seasonings – soy sauce, native *chiao* (Szechuan pepper/fagara) and the coarse cinnamon-like bark of the cassia. Sweet flavors were mixed with sour and, although vinegar was in common use, a small sour native plum was more commonly used in these precursors to the modern sweet and sour dish. So too the staple of wild millet. Although to a large extent it was replaced by rice and breads made with wheat flour, a bland millet gruel is to this day the basis of the warming foods cooked by the peasants of the far north.

The Chinese penchant for exotica probably originated from necessity rather than an early blossoming of gourmet tendencies, with frogs, turtles, pheasants and peacocks heading an extraordinary array of wildlife at the Chinese table. But after attaining a height bordering on decadence during the Sung Dynasty (960–127 AD), when emperors and dignitaries dined and entertained with abandoned extravagance, the serving of exotica lost much of its fascination. Today its preparation is restricted to a few select restaurants under special licence – and hawkishly watched from afar by wildlife preservationists.

By contrast, the food enjoyed by the Japanese is almost austere in its simplicity, a clear reflection of the Buddhist philosophy and strongly held convictions of these tradition-bound people. Although Japanese culture had its origins in China, little evidence remains of this historic link. Purity of form, restraint and modesty, and a strict code of social ethics dictate not only the Japanese way of life, but also the direction of Japanese cuisine. Cooking methods are simple, seasonings uncomplicated, and primary ingredients limited to what is absolutely fresh and locally available. But from this apparent lack of complexity has evolved a cuisine which is unique in style and flavor.

Soy bean products are a prime source of seasoning, either as a clear light *shoyu* (soy sauce) – for which the Japanese enjoy a worldwide reputation of producing the very best – and *miso*, a thick, often salty seasoning paste used in sauces, as a topping or glaze, and in soups and stews. The soy bean, with its high yield of vegetable protein, is of major importance in balancing a diet which includes little animal protein. Some pork and chicken are eaten, but seafoods are the main culinary ingredient. Although the milk or beer-fed, hand-massaged beef from Kobe is prized as the epitome of gourmet fare, this and even beef of lesser quality is prohibitively expensive, and therefore out of the reach of most Japanese consumers.

Sandwiched between Japan to the east and northern China to its west, one might expect the Koreans would simply have borrowed from these cuisines. But the Yellow Sea and the Sea of Japan have proved to be more than aquatic boundaries. There is little evidence of culinary influence from either side, save for a Korean penchant for barbecued meats in the Mongolian tradition and the inclusion of seaweed in their diet as is favored in Japan. The latter, though, is a tenuous connection, for edible seaweed is a major primary product in Korea and would naturally be an important food in a country where fresh vegetables are in short supply. Korean cuisine, although limited in scope, lacks nothing in ingenuity, and its robust flavors reveal the passion and strength of this proudly independent people. Chili and sesame combine to give the biting hot and appetizingly nutty taste the Koreans enjoy. The same ingredients occur in many of the palate-stimulating side dishes which often accompany a meal. And there is always a dish of crunchy hot and sour *kim chee*, a spicy vegetable pickle.

To the southeast is the Philippines with its melting pot cuisine marrying traditional Spanish with local and Chinese elements. The combined effect is strangely bland, with a lack of distinction untypical for such an ebullient race. But the curious custom of the *merienda*, a kind of late afternoon siesta-breaking meal in a tradition adopted from Spain, brings a degree of interest. So too does the variety of tempting local sweets – cakes, biscuits, puddings, sweet and sugary snacks based on local tropical fruits, coconut and rice. Most are ostentatiously overcolored in gaudy pinks, greens, purples and yellows. Rarely are they made at home, but purchased from streetside stalls where they are made by specialists from recipes handed down over the generations.

The cuisines of Malaysia and Indonesia overlap in many areas; both have developed through an overlaying of many other styles of cooking. The Indians taught curry making and the use of spices, with which Indonesia is liberally blessed. The Malays and Indonesians themselves had their own culinary ideals, and the Chinese influence did not go unnoticed. In Indonesia, Dutch intervention resulted in some decidedly European touches, most notably the creation of the *rijstaffel* which the Indonesians devised to impress their visitors. This banquet, traditionally served by a line of sarong-clad waiters each carrying a different course, was originally of gargantuan proportions and incomparably impressive. Today, albeit scaled down in size and grandeur, the *rijstaffel* is a drawcard in many fashionable restaurants and a must for tourists.

Curiously, as the West turns its attention more and more to the discovery of Oriental cuisines, so have the cuisines themselves begun a revival of many age-old gastronomic traditions which earlier had been under threat of extinction through lack of interest. Nonya cuisine, a unique offshoot of the cuisines of Malaysia and Singapore, which developed through the intermarriage of Malays and

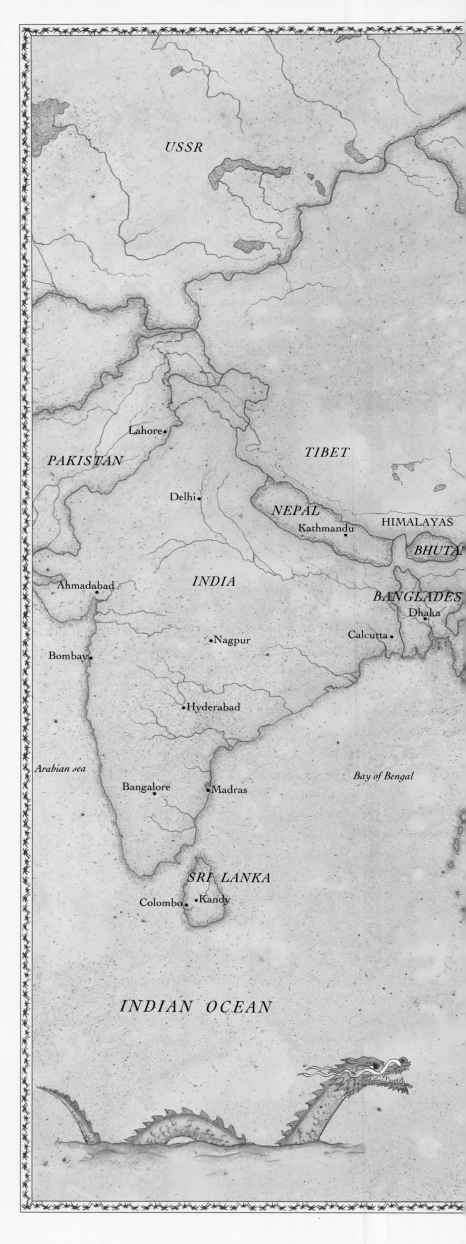

14

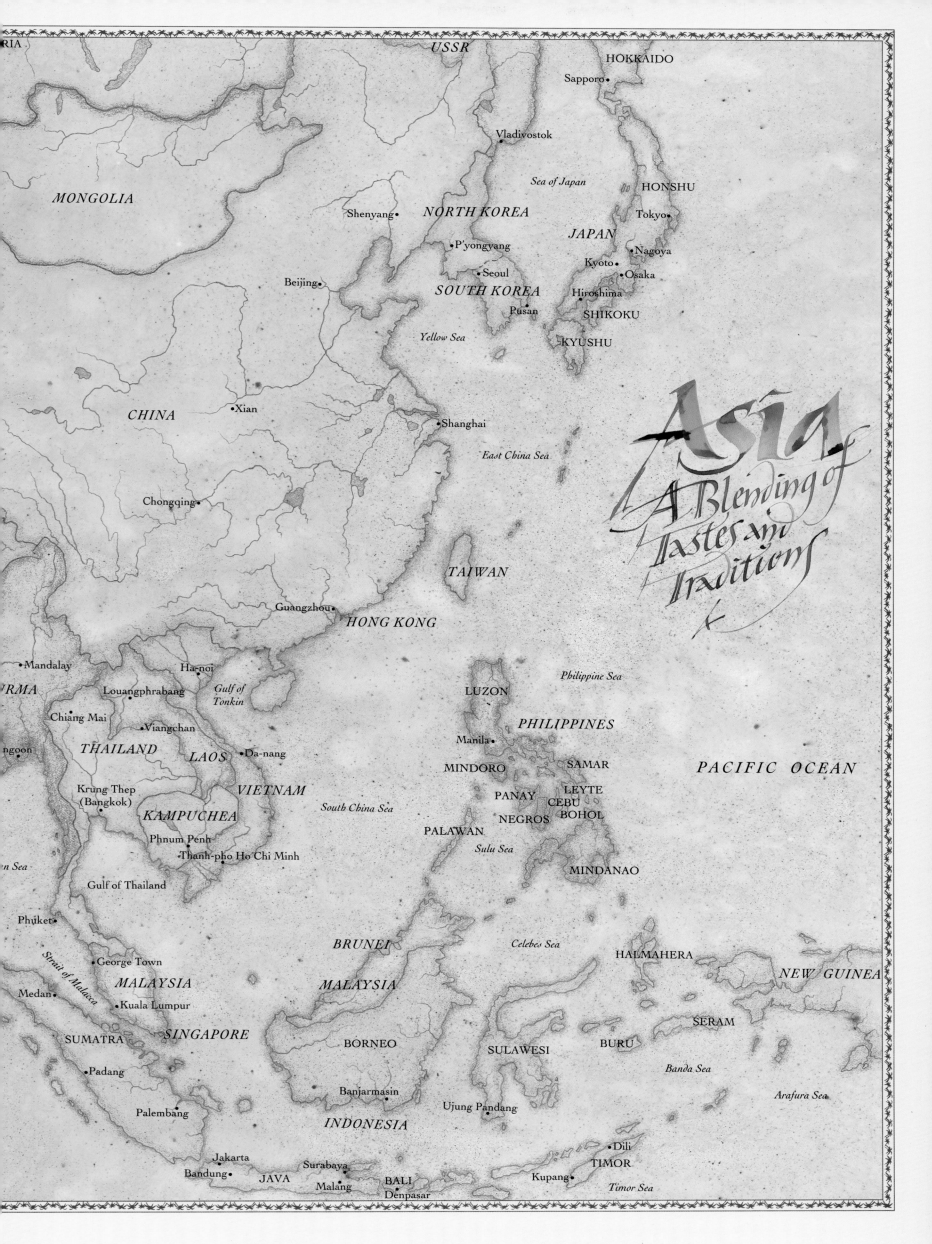

DANCERS IN TRADITIONAL COSTUME, KOREA

JANE MONT

Chinese several centuries ago, is one such cooking style which has returned to vogue.

The dominant element in Thai cooking is undoubtedly the chili. Like their own vibrant culture and their country of violent extremes – rich and poor, supreme beauty and depressing squalor, smog-enshrouded cities and languid country villages – the Thais have evolved a cuisine that demands a passionate response. When a dish is labeled *prik*, then beware. Layered between the multiple ingredients that make up one of their many salads, or reposing in apparent innocence in clear sour soups and in thick, brightly colored curry gravies will be chilies: miniature chilies called *prik keenu* or bird's eyes which sear the senses; shreds of red or green *prik yuak* or slices of *prik chee fa* that bring tears to the eye and sweat to the brow. And then, to surprise and soothe, come extra-mild, almost bland dishes, and a myriad jelly-like sweets to cool the palate and ease the exquisite pain.

As it is throughout Asia, the basic peasant cuisine in Thailand is modest: large bowls of rice, brightened with a few dabs of curry to flavor it and stimulate the appetite; shredded salad greens and herbs interspersed with a few meager shreds of meat; tidbits of spicy grilled meats or fish. At the other end of the scale is the elaborate royal cuisine which had its beginnings in the Sukhotai period (1238–1378 AD) when Thai culture reached its highest stage of development. Glorious in their magnitude, rich, ostentatious, the royal banquets outshone even the sumptuous feasts given by Chinese emperors and mandarins. Today some traces of this past magnificence linger, with the original ornate gold and silver bowls and heavily carved wooden trays and tables being brought out from vaults or museums for a special state occasion. The royal family remains the authority on Thai haute cuisine.

Overlapping Thai cuisine, and drawing slightly from its ideals, are the cuisines of its eastern neighbors, Laos, Kampuchea and Vietnam. In landlocked Laos, where Buddhist ethics direct the way of life, a meager cuisine uses indigenous plants, game meat and buffalo and the large soft-fleshed fish *pa boeuk* caught from the swirling muddy waters of the Mekong. Rice grows wild or under cultivation on sloping hills and is cooked by steam in woven reed cone-shaped containers. Unlike other parts of Asia, where rice is served in the eating bowl to be topped by other foods, the nutty, slightly dry textured Laotian rice is served separately in little covered baskets. Diners break off chunks to nibble as one might a piece of good French *baguette*. The latter in fact can be found in some restaurants in Laos to this day, a legacy of French occupation more than a century ago.

Like the Laos, the Vietnamese often serve an abundance of freshly picked local greenery and herbs with a meal. Occasionally composed into formal salad dishes, the greenery is more often simply stacked together on a lettuce leaf or sheet of edible rice paper together with a meatball or two, a crisply fried stuffed roll, or a couple of slivers of grilled meat. This is rolled up into a cylinder and dipped into a sauce before eating. When the French colonized Vietnam in the nineteenth century, aspects of French cuisine came with them; even today varieties of terrine and compressed sausage can be bought from Vietnamese food stands and restaurants. The Chinese in Vietnam have a long history for they overtook what was already a well-developed culture in the first century BC and remained in control for over a hundred years. Naturally they introduced their own food preferences, which were not far removed from some of the Vietnamese tastes. The Chinese population has now been noticeably depleted by emigration, but the bland stir-fry cooking style of southern China will no doubt remain.

Migrants from Indonesia were among the first settlers in Kampuchea. But here too southern Chinese hilltribes had probably the most profound effect on local culture, which developed into a highly stratified social system. During the reign of Jayavarman II in 809–850 AD the ancient city of Angkor and the famed temple Angkor Wat were built, proclaiming it one of the most influential centers in Asia. Today all that remains are the crumbling, battle-scarred ruins of this great civilization, still regarded as one of the world's greatest architectural achievements. The slow work of their reconstruction, sadly interrupted by war, was begun some years ago. What remains of the once-opulent Kampuchean cuisine reflects the same painstaking skill the people applied to their brilliantly elaborate architecture. It has been said that the traditional cuisine in Kampuchea is the most demanding to prepare but that the splendid results are full justification of the arduous dedication of these fine chefs.

The wide sweep of the Irrawaddy delta cuts through the lower regions of Burma, dumping its yearly load of rich silt during the monsoon season and constantly adjusting boundaries with its teeming flow. So long has Burma held itself apart from outside dealings that an aura of mystery

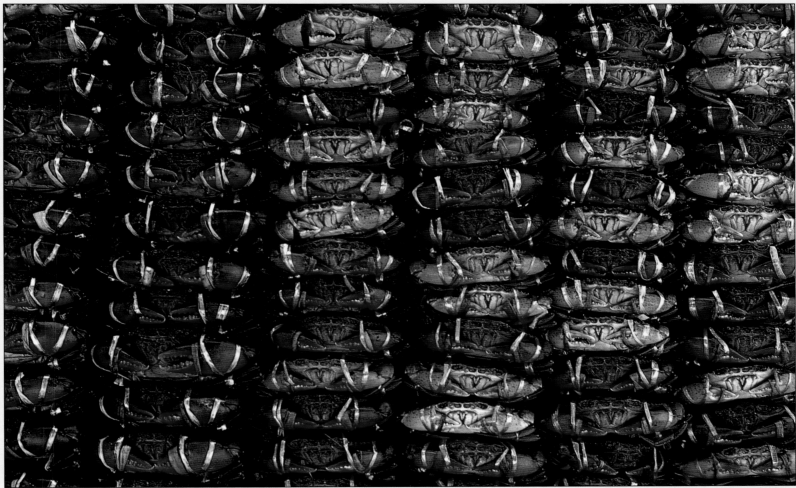

MUD CRABS STACKED IN A BANGKOK MARKET

surrounds this small country. The Burmese are racially akin to the Tibetans, in the main, but there are also several indigenous minority groups, in particular the Thai-related Shan who inhabit the eastern border country close to Thailand.

Burma's history has been made by the succession of people who migrated down along the Irrawaddy. But there is also much evidence of influence from both East and West. Indian and Sino-Tibetan precepts can be distinguished in Burmese food.

Hypnotic India offers a captivating variety of cultures and cuisines. Reaching northward to mountainous Kashmir, hemmed protectively by the towering Himalayas, spreading widely east and west, and tapering to a southern point pressing into the Indian Ocean, it experiences a range of climatic conditions, which in their own way affect the cuisine. Religion has an even more profound influence than either climate or location, for in this diverse country there are several major religions, each with its own convoluted patterns of social ethic, culinary etiquette and food preferences. Lower caste Hindus are primarily vegetarian, although this practice is due more to necessity than religious doctrine. Because vegetarianism is so widespread, from it has developed a comprehensive cuisine worthy of recognition. High-caste Brahmans find their lives tightly restricted by social codes which affect their way of eating: there are rules on everything, from what one eats, to when, with whom, how, in what and by whom it may be prepared, cooked or served.

Other groups enjoy a more liberal approach to food, although ancient traditions are upheld and enjoyed. The Parsis, of Aryan ancestry, were early settlers around the area of Bombay. From Persia they brought culinary skills akin to those of their Middle Eastern cousins. In Kashmir, shades of Tibet and Afghanistan and of the European steppes diffuse the Indian overtones. In Goa on the western coast, Portuguese touches remain from over three centuries of occupation, relinquished only in quite recent times. During the sixteenth and seventeenth centuries Mughlai cuisine made its impact on Indian cooking. Rich, extravagant, highly decorated, it reflected the past glories of the Mongol domination of the Islamic countries which brought about a great flowering of art and architecture.

Sri Lanka, suspended like a teardrop from the southern tip of India, has been known by many names. Most romantic is no doubt "The Pearl of the Indian Ocean." A tiny country fringed by coconut palms, its high ranges are colored jade with tea plantations. It has had a turbulent history, throughout which it has managed to retain an aura of serenity. In the fifteenth and sixteenth centuries it was an important center for spice traders; from this heritage, and from the Dutch who occupied Sri Lanka during these times, has the local cuisine developed. Abundantly spiced, fiercely hot Sri Lankan curries have a distinct style and flavor; juxtaposed with them are the meat dishes and superlative cakes which proclaim Dutch origin.

Within these pages we have gathered together the best each country has to offer, its special favorites and those dishes which we feel most ably illustrate, explain and represent the many cuisines which are collectively known as Asian.

Japan

GRILLED BEAN CURD ON SKEWERS *(RIGHT)*, *recipe page 31*,
SASHIMI (CENTER), *recipe page 33*, CHICKEN BALLS
SIMMERED IN SAUCE *(TOP RIGHT)*, *recipe page 37*, RICE
SERVED WITH BAMBOO SHOOTS *(TOP LEFT)*, AND CLEAR
SOUP WITH CRAB *(BOTTOM LEFT)*, *recipe page 40*   WELDON TRANNIES

PREVIOUS PAGES: SUNRISE, MOUNT FUJI   CLIFF FEULNER/IMAGE BANK

Japan

SIMPLICITY AND ELEGANCE

The Japanese cuisine is one of simplicity bordering on the austere. It has evolved from a singular and original ideology which borrowed little from its neighbors and still less from the outside world. It epitomizes perfection in preparation, cooking and presentation, with the artistic skills of the cook ranking almost as importantly as his knowledge of seasoning and the combining of ingredients.

Elegance is encountered in every aspect: the use of garnish, the arrangement of the food, the selection of tableware, the choice of ingredients. All seek to express the joy of life, of the open air and of all things natural. For the Japanese revere nature, and strive always to incorporate an element of nature into their meals.

But while the aesthetics of a dish requires the highest consideration, it, like the choice of seasonings and sauces, is never allowed to become the main element of the dish; it serves merely to highlight and complement it.

Only the best and freshest is good enough for the Japanese cook; for it is the pure, natural taste of foods that is paramount. Sauces are never thick and coating, but may glossily glaze or float in a thin, unobtrusive pool around the ingredients. Batter is light, airy and crisp, never completely enveloping the food. Seasonings emphasize rather than disguise the true taste of the food.

The Japanese cook has the confidence to present, for instance, as the centerpiece of a meal, *yu-tofu,* a simple iron pot of plain "silk" tofu simmering in a clear seaweed-flavored stock. He will boldly decorate a dish with a single sprig of bamboo leaves. He will show almost poetic inspiration in his arrangement of translucent pink-white slivers of raw fish on a hand-molded fish-shaped plate of white and deep sea blue.

IZU-HANTO PENINSULA IN SOUTHERN HONSHU   NICK BROKENSHA/HORIZON

And just as the choice of a russet-colored maple leaf to decorate a dish heralds the approach of autumn, so too does the choice of the food itself make a statement of time and place. For food in season is naturally the best, and when served in its region of origin it should be infinitely superior.

Of necessity in all parts of the world, the cuisine is born of available produce, and so in Japan we find dishes of tender abalone and crayfish originating from the southern coastal fishing villages. The finest *katsuobushi* is produced in Kochi from the excellent bonito caught in the Tosa Bay. This rock-hard dried fish, the vital ingredient in *dashi,* the stock that flavors most soups and savory dishes in Japanese cooking, is transported all over Japan. A special sharp-bladed grater – *katsuo-bushi kezuri* – is used to shave paper-thin slivers of the fish.

The Kyoto region still retains much of the graciousness of the ancient court days, as well as strongly Buddhist beliefs. Vegetarianism is a continuing tradition here, exemplified by simple yet elegant dishes made with vegetables or with the fine *kinu-goshi tofu* or "silk" bean curd.

In contrast to Kyoto's refined approach, cooks in Osaka, the business capital, offer food in plenty, with hearty flavors and little ceremony.

Another important ingredient is *kombu,* the giant tangle kelp gathered off the coast of Hokkaido. This adds its rich taste and mineral nutrients to stocks, soups and casseroles and lends an intrinsically Japanese flavor to the food.

Sendai, on the eastern coast, is famed for the production of superior *miso.* This is a thick seasoning paste varying in color – and hence in intensity of flavor and saltiness – from light creamy yellow to deep burnt orange-brown. Dishes like *kake dote-nabe,* oysters stewed in a clay pot spread with a thick

layer of *miso,* include two of the important products from this area in a classic form, one-pot cooking.

It is said that the chickens from Nagoya have a finer texture and better taste than from any other area of Japan. One of the most succulent ways to serve them is in *kashiwa no sashimi,* in which wafer-thin slivers of raw chicken fillet are served with a lime-based sauce and marinated onion.

Without the fiery *wasabi* from Hotaka, *sushi* (rice and fish balls) and *sashimi* (raw fish) would not be the same, nor would a *teppan-yaki* of beef be as enjoyable without the fine-textured, marbled beef of Matsuzaka.

Tempura began its history in Nagasaki, where Spanish and Portuguese settlers recreated a version of their *gambas fritas,* and the Japanese adaptation has now become an internationally popular dish.

The food in Tokyo, as in most of the world's large cities, offers a mélange of dishes from all over the country, but with its own idiosyncrasies: the crumbed and fried pork cutlet, *tonkatsu,* which often comes with potato salad and coleslaw; the grilled chicken *yakitori;* the tabletop party dishes *sukiyaki* and *teppan-yaki,* and probably Tokyo's most spectacular specialty, the artfully prepared *nigiri-zushi.*

The seasons, too, dictate eating patterns and availability of ingredients. In the heat of summer, menus may feature cooling chilled *tofu* and *soba* (buckwheat noodles), and light-tasting steamed dishes. Autumn brings flavorful *matsutake* mushrooms, chestnuts and fried foods, while winter menus offer warming and sustaining *nabemono* (one-pot) dishes, hot noodles, tabletop cooking and broiling (grilling), and thick *miso*-impregnated soups.

With the coming of spring, cherry blossoms and *shincha* tea come tender young bamboo shoots to accompany light, clear soups, *sashimi* and seafoods.

Japanese cooks use several main cooking methods, and a meal will usually be made up of a selection of dishes cooked by different methods and featuring different main ingredients and seasonings. Clear simmering, often in a stock flavored with *kombu,* soy sauce, or the ubiquitous *dashi,* produces *nimono* dishes; steaming (*mushimono*) is applied to seafood, pork and poultry and to a number of delicately textured bean curd and egg dishes. *Yakimono,* or broiling (grilling), is done over charcoal – often a miniature broiler in the kitchen or on the tabletop – or in a pan with a richly colored and flavored seasoning sauce that forms a glossy glaze on the food.

Deep-frying (*agemono*) is employed infrequently at home, although it is enjoyed at restaurants and for entertaining. *Sunomono* (vinegared foods) and *aemono* describe cold dishes and salads which are served as side dishes.

One or several dishes prepared by these methods may appear at a single meal. Accompaniments will include a clear or *miso*-flavored soup, served in a covered bowl to be sipped throughout the meal; *sashimi, sushi* or another of a range of tasty little tidbits as appetizers; a small dish of *tsukemono*

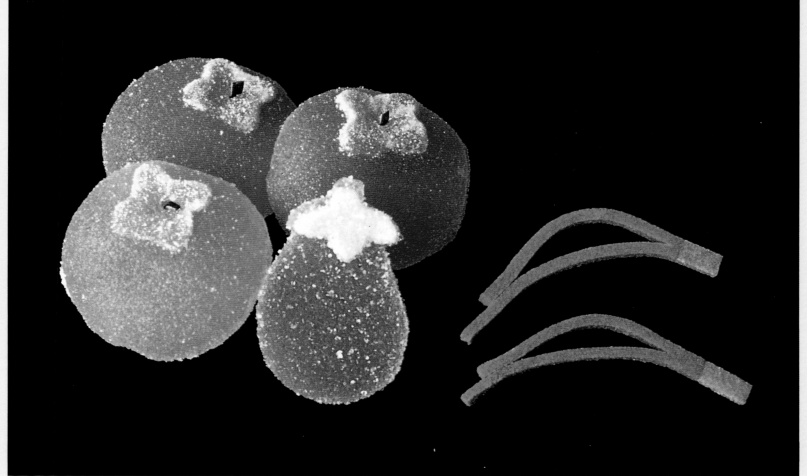

JAPANESE SWEETS, A STUDY IN CULINARY ARTISTRY

(pickled vegetables), a bowl of *gohan* (plain steamed rice) and a cup of *bancha* or other Japanese green tea. Dishes may all be served at once on a tray or presented as various courses, as dictated by the particular etiquette afforded to the occasion and the type of food.

Throughout Japan there are many small specialist restaurants serving just one or two dishes, such as *sushi* or *sashimi; tempura* or the quick meal of *tempura soba* (buckwheat noodles topped with batter-fried ingredients); *yakitori* and *teppan-yaki,* the latter offering an incomparable entertainment in the person of a chef whose lightning movements as he slices, peels, tosses and seasons the food on the grill quite amaze the diner.

While the intricacies of Japanese table etiquette are far too involved to be included here, presentation is another matter. The Japanese believe in symmetry, but their idea of harmony and balance is different from the standard Western concept. Therefore they may not present a meal on a matching dinner set of round plates, but will compose the food on dinnerware which best matches the shape, size, color and mood of the food, so that each dish stands in its own right. Porcelain, raw or lacquered wood and sturdy pottery may all appear within a single meal in complete harmony.

Food is eaten with pointed chopsticks, usually made of lacquered wood. *Sake,* the traditional Japanese rice wine, is warmed to about 108°F (42°C) and is served in tiny porcelain cups.

Nutritionally, the Japanese diet has many points to recommend it. Little in the way of dairy products is included; protein is instead derived from vegetable sources, in particular from *tofu* (bean curd) and its many byproducts. Seaweed, in the form of *kombu* (used as a flavoring agent), *wakame* (the curly-leaf seaweed that appears in salads and as a vegetable), and *nori* (the edible-seaweed food wrapper), offers a rich source of dietary minerals.

Quick and gentle cooking methods do not destroy the natural nutrients of the food, and many dishes are served with the liquid in which they were cooked, thus retaining the vitamins. The average salt intake, however, is higher in Japan than elsewhere in the world owing to the use of salt-preserved *miso* and soy sauce, and to the inclusion of salted pickles with most meals. This, along with the above-average amounts of sugar appearing in many dishes, can be moderated without unduly altering the taste.

A number of ingredients are indispensable to cooking Japanese food. Most are now readily available in Oriental food shops; others can be substituted satisfactorily. *Kombu* and *katsuobushi,* the seaweed and dried bonito flakes used to make the classic *dashi* stock, are available in dried form, and a powder or granule form of the stock, usually labelled *dashi no moto,* is also marketed. *Nori* can be found in Chinese stores along with a range of dried mushrooms. Canned products include a variety of mushrooms, lotus root and bamboo shoots, as well as gingko nuts and pickled garlic and green onions. *Wasabi,* the searing hot green horseradish, is sold in powder or paste form, and very hot mustard or common horseradish will provide a suitable alternative if necessary.

The giant white *daikon* radish is sold by many greengrocers and even supermarkets. It can also be found in Chinese and Japanese food stores, along with *tofu,* which also comes in make-it-yourself kits. *Negi,* the Japanese leek, tastes similar to a young Western leek, although large green onions can be substituted. And *yuzu,* the fragrant citrus used for garnish and flavor, can be replaced by limes or tangerines.

DASHI STOCK

A well-flavored stock can be made by mixing 1 teaspoon dashi no moto *granules or powder into 2-3 cups water. Dashi no moto dissolves easily in cold water.*

But making dashi *by the traditional method gives a fresher taste. The first extraction is called* ichiban dashi. *The ingredients can be used for a second time to make* niban dashi, *which is used in casseroles and one-pot cooking.*

ICHIBAN DASHI

6 cups (1½ liters) water
1½ oz (45 g) *kombu* (kelp)
1½ oz (45 g) *katsuobushi* (dried bonito flakes)

Wipe the kelp with a damp cloth, then slash at regular intervals on one side to release the flavor. Place in a saucepan with 5 cups of the water and bring to the boil. Remove the kelp and set aside to make *niban dashi*.

Add the remaining water, then the bonito flakes; return to the boil. Immediately remove from the heat and strain, reserving the bonito.

NIBAN DASHI

Add the reserved bonito and kombu to 6 cups cold water and bring to the boil. Reduce heat and simmer very gently for 15–20 minutes. Add another 1 oz (30 g) dried bonito to the pot and immediately remove from the heat. Let stand for no longer than 1 minute, then strain.

MAKES 6 CUPS

SUSHI

Japanese fishermen discovered that fresh fish fillets stored on cooked rice that had been sprinkled with vinegar remained fresh and acquired a subtle pleasing flavor. Soon various types of vinegared rice dishes appeared on tables in the fishing villages, and it was not long before they were adapted and embellished to the refined *sushi* we know and enjoy today. A *sushi* chef must now dedicate several years of training to perfecting his preparation techniques, especially the skills required for slicing the raw fish which has become the classic topping for *nigiri-zushi*.

A confident *sushi*-maker assembling "fingers" of *nigiri-zushi* is pure poetry in motion: a squeeze, a flip, a smear, a slice, a pat, a handful of rice and a piece of raw fish are transformed into a two-bite-sized snack of exquisite form, texture and taste.

Sushi is usually sold in small specialty restaurants or at a separate counter in larger restaurants. A refrigerated display case holds the selection of toppings. They usually include several choice cuts of tuna: *chu-toro,* the pinkish half-fat cut; *toro,* the fattiest tuna cut and pale in color; and *maguro,* the red tuna meat. There are also sea bream and yellowtail; *anago,* a type of sea eel that is simmered and broiled (grilled) before using and brushed with a sweet, dark glaze when the *sushi* is assembled; *ikura,* fat red pearls of salmon roe; and *uni,* the sticky orange roe of the sea urchin; boiled or raw shrimp (prawns); squid and abalone; clams and *akagai* or ark shell, a type of red clam. Other fish, such as flounder, shad and fresh trout, may be included; and fatty, strong-

RICE FIELDS AT TWILIGHT   GRANT V. FAINT/THE IMAGE BANK

tasting fish such as mackerel are also used, although these are first marinated in vinegar. *Tamago,* a type of sweet omelet, is also a favorite *sushi* topping, and nowadays we may also see sliced raw sea scallops and smoked salmon.

Decoration on *sushi* is minimal or nonexistent, but the chef will take time to dress the platter on which the *sushi* are presented quite elaborately, using the traditional gifts of nature — leaves, blossoms and twigs. Paper-thin slices of ginger, marinated in a vinegar and sugar solution, are always served with *sushi,* the ginger acquiring a light pinkish color in the marinade. With most *sushi,* soy sauce or a specially prepared mix of soy sauce, sweet cooking wine *(mirin)* and bonito flakes will accompany the platter. *Sushi* are usually eaten with the fingers — without ceremony, but with sheer enjoyment.

There are several different types of *sushi.* From the Tokyo Bay area comes *nigiri-zushi,* literally "handful sushi," requiring the most skill in preparation. In Osaka, "pressed sushi" or *oshi-zushi* is favored: the vinegared rice is packed into wooden molds with removable bases and tops and when unmolded is cut into rectangles. *Maki-zushi* or *nori-maki* are rolled *sushi* encased in paper-thin sheets of *nori* seaweed with fillings varying from pickled vegetables to omelet or seafood, and more recently even avocado and crabmeat. *Chirashi-zushi* is simply vinegared rice "scattered" with toppings of seafood or vegetables, and *fukusa-zushi* is the same kind of rice and extras bundled into thin sheets of omelet. Variations of fish and rice parcels include *saba-zushi,* a square loaf of vinegared rice encased in thin slices of vinegared mackerel, and *kamasu-zushi,* grilled pike or similar fish prepared in a loaf in the same way and cut into slices.

SUSHI-MESHI

Vinegar-Flavored Rice

Rice for sushi *is of the short-grain white variety, cooked by absorption and cooled by fanning. It is flavored with a mixture of Japanese rice vinegar, sugar and salt to give it its unique taste and the necessary stickiness to hold together for molding.*

3 cups (21 oz/655 g) raw short-grain white rice
3¾ cups (30 fl oz/950 ml) water
2½-in (7.5-cm) square piece *kombu* (kelp)
⅓ cup (2½ fl oz/75 ml) rice vinegar
⅓ cup (3 oz/90 g) sugar
3 teaspoons salt

Thoroughly wash the rice with cold water and drain well. Pour into a heavy-based saucepan and add the water.

❧ Wipe the *kombu* with a damp cloth and score several times on one side to release the flavor. Place on top of the rice, cover and bring to the boil over high heat.

❧ Reduce the heat to the lowest setting and let the rice simmer gently for 10 minutes. Remove the *kombu* and continue cooking for a further 8–10 minutes, until the rice is tender and has absorbed the water. Remove from the heat and cover with a folded kitchen towel. Let stand for a further 10 minutes to allow the rice to become plump and tender, and to dry a little more.

❧ Mix the vinegar, sugar and salt, stirring until the sugar dissolves. Transfer the rice to a large mixing bowl. The technique for adding the vinegar to the rice takes practice and is best done by two people as the rice must be simultaneously fanned to cool it and tossed with the vinegar. Trickle on a little of the vinegar and lightly toss and stir the rice with a flat wide spoon to aerate the rice as much as possible; at the same time it must be energetically fanned to cool it quickly. This technique produces the required stickiness as well as giving each grain a shiny gloss and distributing the vinegar evenly. Continue until the rice is at room temperature and is sticky enough to hold together without becoming too damp. It may not be necessary to use all of the vinegar mixture.

❧ *Sushi* rice must be used on the same day it is prepared, and should not be stored in the refrigerator. Cover with a damp cloth and leave in a cool part of the kitchen if not using immediately.

❧ This recipe provides enough rice for approximately 50 *nigiri-zushi* or 10 rolls (60 pieces) of *nori-maki*. A half recipe will suffice for *oshi-zushi* or *chirashi-zushi*.

NIGIRI-ZUSHI

Hand-formed Sushi

1 recipe *Sushi-meshi* (vinegared rice)
2 lb (1 kg) assorted fresh seafood
1½ tablespoons *wasabi* (horseradish)
1 tablespoon rice vinegar
shreds or shavings of vinegared ginger
1 cup (8 fl oz/250 ml) light soy sauce

Choose the very freshest saltwater fish available (freshwater fish can harbor certain parasites that make them unsuitable for *sushi*). Sea bream, tuna, yellowtail and flounder are ideal, and for variety try abalone, shrimp (prawns), clams, salmon and sea urchin roe, and raw squid wrapped with strips of *nori*.

❧ Thick slices of sweetened omelet may be prepared and cut into rectangles as an alternative topping.

❧ A smear of *wasabi* horseradish is spread over each *nigiri-zushi* before adding the topping, and there should be plenty of vinegared ginger and soy sauce to accompany them. The soy sauce may be straight from the bottle, or a heavier brew made by simmering soy sauce with *sake* or *mirin* and bonito flakes for added flavor.

❧ Prepare the vinegared rice and set aside. Skin the fish and cut into neat, thin slices approximately 2½ x 1½-in (7.5 x 4-cm). Prepare the other toppings, as selected, cutting into pieces that will fit on top of the sushi rolls. Mix the rice vinegar with cold water in a bowl.

❧ Keeping your hands well moistened with the vinegar water, take up a golfball-size portion of rice and squeeze it gently into an oval wad by curling the fingers around it, keeping it situated towards the top of the palm of the hand. If necessary, use the index and middle fingers of your other hand to help form the correct shape with an alternating pressing and rolling action.

❧ When the rice has been shaped, select a piece of topping and smear a little *wasabi* along the underside, then press it firmly onto the rice, again using the two fingers of the other hand to press it into shape. The topping should slightly overlap the ends and sides of the rice. Arrange these sushi "fingers" in pairs on a plate with vinegared ginger. Dip each one lightly into the soy sauce before eating with the fingers. (Dip the topping only; the rice will fall apart if moistened with soy sauce.)

❧ If shrimp (prawns) are to be used on *nigiri-zushi,* they should be simmered until pink in *dashi* stock lightly flavored with salt. Skewer the shrimp lengthwise with wooden picks (toothpicks) to prevent them from curling during cooking or they will be difficult to use.

❧ To top *sushi* with salmon or sea urchin roe, form the rice into a little ball, then flatten it top and bottom. Wrap it with a strip of toasted *nori* that extends above the height of the ball, forming a boat shape. When the roe is placed in the center it is held in place by the border of *nori*.

❧ Squid should be scored on both sides to tenderize it. Then cut it into pieces, place it on a rice roll, and secure it with a strip of *nori* wound around the center and ending underneath the rice.

SERVES 8

NORI-MAKI

Rolled Sushi

1 recipe *Sushi-meshi* (vinegared rice)
8–10 sheets *nori* (compressed seaweed/laver)
wasabi (horseradish), optional
SUGGESTED FILLINGS
strips of raw white-fleshed fish or tuna
peeled shrimp (prawns), simmered in *dashi* (fish/seaweed
   stock) until pink
julienne of fresh unpeeled cucumber
shredded green onions
shredded packaged *takuan* (yellow pickled giant white
   radish)
slivers of packaged vinegared ginger (*gari/sushoga*)
omelet strips
julienne of pickled carrot (below)
julienne of simmered *kampyo* (dried gourd, below)
shredded simmered *shiitake* mushrooms (below)

PICKLED CARROT

Peel 1 large carrot and cut into thin slices lengthwise, then into narrow strips. Mix together ½ cup (4 fl oz/125 ml) rice vinegar with 1½ tablespoons sugar and 1½ teaspoons salt.

Stir until the sugar has dissolved, then pour over the carrot and leave for 1 hour until softened and well flavored. It can be stored for several weeks in a covered container in the refrigerator.

SIMMERED DRIED GOURD

Soak 1 oz (30 g) dried *kampyo* strips in water with 1 tablespoon salt. Knead lightly then drain, place in a saucepan with water to cover and simmer gently to soften. Drain again and simmer with 1 cup (8 fl oz/250 ml) *dashi*, 1½ tablespoons dark soy sauce and a large pinch of sugar until tender. Drain well.

SIMMERED *SHIITAKE* MUSHROOMS

Soak 6–8 dried *shiitake* mushrooms in warm water for 15 minutes, then squeeze out the water and discard stems. Cut caps into narrow shreds and place in a small non-aluminum saucepan with ½ cup (4 fl oz/125 ml) *dashi*, 1 tablespoon light soy sauce and 1 tablespoon each *mirin* and sugar. Simmer gently for about 12 minutes, then drain well.

Prepare the vinegared rice and selected fillings, draining all pickled or simmered fillings well before use. *Nori-maki* is rolled in a small bamboo mat (*maki-su* or *sudare*); if this is not available, a plastic or other flexible place mat can serve the purpose.

Before assembling *nori-maki*, the *nori* should be passed over a gas flame, or an electric burner on high, in order to crisp the seaweed and bring out its full flavor. The smooth, glossy side is toasted, and it should be placed this side down on the mat so that it will be on the outside of the finished *sushi* rolls. The inner side has a rougher, less attractive appearance. Untoasted *nori* will be tough and lack flavor.

Spread a ⅓-in (1-cm)-thick layer of prepared rice over the *nori*, keeping the fingers well moistened with cold water and vinegar (see *nigiri-zushi* recipe, page 27) to prevent sticking. Leave a small border at the lower edge of the *nori* and a wider border at the upper edge to keep the filling from overflowing. Arrange a variety of fillings along the length of the rice, about ⅓ of the way from the bottom of the *nori*.

Use the bamboo mat to assist in lifting the *nori* and rice up and over the fillings to encase them, then continue rolling to the top edge of the *nori*. Squeeze the roll gently inside the bamboo mat to firm up the roll, then unroll and cut diagonally at one end only of each piece to make attractive shapes. Wipe the knife between each cut, and cut straight through firmly, without sawing.

Horseradish can be added to *nori-maki* rolls when using cucumber and fish, but is not usually used with other fillings. Arrange the *nori-maki* in groups on flat plates with little piles of vinegared ginger on the side. A dipping sauce is not usually served with *nori-maki*.

Nori squares can be used to form cone-shaped *sushi* or "hand rolls," eaten much like an icecream cone, using any of the above fillings.

SERVES 10

CHIRASHI-ZUSHI

Scattered Rice

This is a simplified version of sushi *in which the rice is simply served in a wide lacquered box and is covered with bite-size pieces of seafood, either raw or cooked, or has a variety of simmered vegetables lightly stirred. The former is the kind of* chirashi-zushi *generally served in Tokyo, while the heartier vegetable, omelet and seafood mixture is a specialty of Osaka restaurants and home kitchens.* Chirashi-zushi *is a popular snack and lunchbox food.*

½ recipe *Sushi-meshi* (vinegared rice), see page 27
8 oz (250 g) raw tuna, smoked salmon or raw white-fleshed saltwater fish
1 sheet *nori* (compressed seaweed/laver)
1 tablespoon white sesame seeds

Prepare the vinegared rice and spread in a lacquered box or flat dish. Cut the fish into thin bite-size pieces and arrange attractively in an overlapping pattern on the rice.

Toast the *nori* over a flame until crisp, then cut into fine shreds. Toast the sesame seeds in a dry pan until they begin to pop. Scatter the *nori* and sesame seeds over the fish and serve.

SERVES 4–6

GOHAN

Japanese Steamed Rice

The Japanese cook their rice by a simple absorption technique, but, unlike the method used in other parts of Asia, they rinse the rice thoroughly to remove surface starch, cook it for the shortest possible time and let the pot stand tightly covered for at least 15 minutes so that the retained heat and steam can continue the cooking. Short-grain white rice is always used.

1½ cups (10 oz/315 g) raw short-grain white rice
2¼ cups (18 fl oz/560 ml) water

Put the rice in a large bowl and place it under a slow-running stream of cold water. Rinse thoroughly, stirring up briskly with the fingers, until the water runs clear. Drain well, transfer to a colander and set aside for about 1 hour to allow it to partially dry.

Pour the rice into a medium saucepan with a heavy base and tight-fitting lid. (Rice cooked by the absorption method demands the right pan for perfect results. If it is too large the water will boil away too quickly; if it is too small, the rice will pack too tightly, leaving the grains in the center uncooked and hard. A heavy base will distribute the heat more evenly and eliminate the risk of burning the bottom layers of rice. The lid must fit snugly in order that steam is retained, as this plays a vital role in the cooking. Should steam escape, the liquid will evaporate before the rice is cooked.)

Bring the pot quickly to the boil, then reduce to the lowest possible heat – use an asbestos mat or heat diffuser if the setting on your cooker is not low enough – and cook for about 12 minutes. *Do not open the saucepan at any time during cooking* or precious steam will escape. Remove from the heat and set aside for a further 15–20 minutes, during which the rice will complete its cooking, giving perfectly cooked, plump grains, well separated yet clinging together just enough to be successfully handled with chopsticks.

Japanese rice is served in a small wooden tub with a flat paddle-like spoon made of bamboo or lacquered wood.

SERVES 6

JAPANESE SUSHI

WELDON TRANNIES   CHICKEN AND RICE POT

TORI GOHAN

Chicken and Rice Pot

Tori gohan, or "chicken rice," falls into the category of donburi, *a dish of rice with a meat, egg or vegetable topping – a kind of fast food, Japanese style.*

Donburi restaurants are now popular throughout Japan, offering fast service and economical, sustaining dishes in a limited menu. The word donburi *actually describes the dish in which the food is served, an oversize rice bowl with a prominent round foot or stand.*

Tori gohan can be served as a snack, lunch or supper, but is also often served at the end of a large meal in place of plain white rice.

1 lb (500 g) chicken meat, preferably from thigh, skinned
½ cup (4 fl oz/125 ml) light soy sauce
2 tablespoons *sake*
¼ cup (2 oz/60 g) sugar
2½ cups (1 lb/500 g) raw short-grain white rice
8 dried Japanese black mushrooms, soaked
5 cups (1¼ liters) *niban dashi* (seaweed/fish stock)*
1 cup (5 oz/155 g) frozen green peas, thawed
salt

Cut the chicken into small cubes or strips and place in a dish with the soy sauce, *sake* and sugar. Mix well and set aside for 25 minutes.

❦ Thoroughly wash the rice, then drain well. Place in a medium-large saucepan with a heavy base and tight-fitting lid and set aside.

❦ Drain the mushrooms, place in a dish and steam for 2 minutes to soften, then discard the stems and shred the caps very finely. (Steaming can be omitted, if preferred.)

❦ Place the chicken and mushrooms on the rice, add the stock, then scatter the frozen peas on top. Sprinkle with about 1 teaspoon salt. Cover and bring quickly to the boil, then reduce heat to very low and simmer until the rice and chicken are tender and the liquid has been absorbed.

Or use dashi *powder or granules, slightly more diluted than normal.*

SERVES 6–8

ZARU SOBA

Chilled Buckwheat Noodles

Eating chilled noodles is a peculiarly Japanese habit and one that often provokes passionate debate as to the best way to prepare and enjoy them. They are traditionally served in little bamboo baskets with a variety of tasty garnishes and a cold sauce or broth for dipping, although many enjoy them swimming in a well-flavored sauce.

10 oz (315 g) dried *soba* (buckwheat noodles)
3 cups (24 fl oz/750 ml) *dashi* (seaweed/ fish stock)
¾ cup (6 fl oz/185 ml) dark soy sauce
⅓ cup (2½ fl oz/75 ml) *mirin* (sweet cooking wine)
2 teaspoons sugar
2 oz (60 g) dried bonito flakes
3 sheets compressed seaweed/laver
2 teaspoons horseradish, or finely grated fresh
    ginger
½ cup each finely chopped green onions and finely
    grated *daikon* (giant white radish)

Bring a large saucepan of lightly salted water to the boil. Add the noodles and simmer for 5 minutes. Add a little cold water and bring to the boil again, then simmer until the noodles are tender. Drain well and rinse thoroughly in cold water, kneading lightly with the fingers to remove the surface starch. Drain thoroughly and arrange in mounds in small bamboo baskets or lacquered wood trays.

❦ Bring the *dashi*, soy sauce, wine and sugar to the boil and simmer for 2 minutes. Wrap the bonito flakes in a clean cloth. Place in the stock and remove from the heat. Set aside for 20 minutes, then drain. Cool the sauce by placing the saucepan in a dish of ice.

❦ Hold the seaweed over a flame for about 30 seconds until it crisps and turns bright green. Remove and cut into short, narrow strips. Scatter the seaweed over the noodles, then place a little mound of horseradish or ginger, chopped green onions and radish on each basket beside the noodles. Serve with the chilled sauce in individual bowls.

Mix the horseradish or ginger, the green onions and radish into the sauce at the table. Dip the noodles into it before eating.

SERVES 4–6

CHILLED BUCKWHEAT NOODLES

SIMMERED BEAN CURD

YUDOFU

Simmered Bean Curd

This dish, devised by the monks in a Kyoto temple centuries ago, epitomizes the purity, simplicity and economy of the Zen Buddhist philosophy.

Traditionally, the bean curd is simmered at the table and, as soon as it has warmed through, the pieces are lifted out with a slotted spoon and placed in individual dishes filled with a hot dashi *and soy flavored sauce. Finely minced ginger,* daikon *and green onions are added to give pep to an otherwise bland dish.*

1 cup (8 fl oz/250 ml) *dashi* (seaweed/ fish stock)
½ cup (4 fl oz/125 ml) dark soy sauce
2 teaspoons sugar
1 oz (30 g) dried bonito flakes
3 green onions
1 tablepoon grated fresh ginger
1 cup (4 oz/125 g) *daikon* (grated giant white radish)
5-in (13-cm) square piece kelp
3 cakes *tofu* (bean curd)*

In a small saucepan bring the stock, soy sauce and sugar to the boil. Wrap the bonito flakes in a clean cloth and place in the pot, set aside off the heat for about 5 minutes, then remove the bonito and squeeze. Keep the sauce warm.
❧ Trim and very finely mince the green onions and place them with the ginger and radish in small dishes on the table.
❧ Wipe the kelp with a wet cloth and score on both sides with the point of a knife to release the flavors. Place the kelp

in a flameproof casserole over a portable tabletop cooker set in the center of the table. Pour in enough boiling water to come just over halfway up the sides of the casserole.
❧ Holding the bean curd cakes in the palm of the hand, gently cut each into quarters. Slide them carefully into the simmering stock and cover with a lid. Simmer just long enough to heat thoroughly. Serve straight from the casserole into bowls of the hot sauce; add ginger, *daikon* and green onion to taste.
Firm bean curd is more successful in this dish, being less fragile, but soft bean curd has a superior flavor.

SERVES 6

TOFU DENGAKU

Grilled Bean Curd on Skewers

In ancient Japan, dengaku *was the equivalent of today's country fair, with agricultural displays, entertainments and snacks. There was always a troupe of puppetlike stilt dancers at these fairs. Much later, a roadside snack of broiled (grilled) slices of* tofu *(bean curd) on flat bamboo skewers became popular; it was named after the* dengaku *puppets because of its resemblance to these dancers on their single stilt. Later still, small whole fish and vegetables such as eggplant, mushrooms and green peppers were dressed with* miso *paste colored in reds, yellows and greens, threaded onto skewers and broiled over charcoal. They all take the name* dengaku.

2 lb (1 kg) *momen tofu* ("cotton" bean curd)
12 flat bamboo skewers, or 6 bamboo fork-shaped skewers
1 cup (12 oz/375 g) white *miso*
½ cup (4 fl oz/125 ml) *dashi* (seaweed/fish stock)
⅓ cup (2½ fl oz/75 ml) *sake* (rice wine)
1½ tablespoons *mirin* (sweet cooking wine)
⅓ cup (3 oz/90 g) sugar
2 teaspoons ginger juice*
3 egg yolks
1 tablespoon red *miso*
1 tablespoon sugar
green food coloring
finely slivered lemon or lime rind
edible small leaves or herbs
sansho (Japanese pepper condiment)

Cut the bean curd into rectangular pieces to make 12 portions. Insert 2 skewers or 1 bamboo fork into each piece; set aside.

Mix the white *miso, dashi, sake, mirin,* ⅓ cup sugar and ginger juice in a saucepan. Beat the egg yolks into the mixture, then place the saucepan in another pan of gently simmering water. Cook, stirring constantly, until the mixture is very thick, at no time allowing it to simmer or the eggs will curdle.

Divide into 3 portions, one slightly smaller than the others. To this one add the red *miso* and 1 tablespoon sugar and blend well. Color one portion green with the food coloring (traditionally, powdered green tea is used). Leave the remaining portion natural.

If cooking over charcoal, arrange the bean curd over the coals on a wire rack and cook until small dark brown blisters appear on the surface, then turn and cook the other side. To cook under a broiler, the bean curd should be placed on a heatproof plate and broiled under moderate heat until flecked with deep brown.

Remove the bean curd from the heat and spread the toppings thickly on one side. Smooth the edges with a wet finger. Lightly press a little slivered rind and decorative leaves onto each, choosing complementary colors. Return to the coals or broiler and cook again until the toppings are flecked with brown. Serve at once.

See Ika Goma-Yaki (page 34).

SERVES 6

SASHIMI

Raw Seafood Platter

Although many foreigners have difficulty understanding it, the Japanese have a fondness for raw fish that borders on reverence. Perhaps more than any other dish, *sashimi* epitomizes the Japanese cuisine. Simplicity, freshness and superlative flavor are combined in an artistic presentation.

Preparing *sashimi* is a specialized business, but it is possible to master the skill sufficiently to serve quite passable *sashimi* at home – as long as only the very freshest fish and shellfish are used. Raw fish has a tenderness and delicacy of taste unmatched by any other ingredient. Correctly sliced, elegantly arranged and accompanied by the right blend of dipping sauce, *sashimi* will always impress.

Generally *sashimi* is not served as a main course but at the beginning of a meal, and therefore the quantities needed per person are not great. A maximum of 3 oz (90 g) per serving should suffice.

The way to cut fish for *sashimi* is dictated by the type of fish involved. Tuna and other large fish with thick fillets may be cut in the *kaku-zukuri* style – first into strips about ½-in (1.25-cm) wide, then into small cubes. *Ito-zukuri* is a thread cut that best suits small fish such as whiting or garfish; the cut is either lengthwise or diagonal across the fillet, with the skin left on. Thread cut raw fish is usually served in small molds, but individual strips are sometimes knotted.

Hira-zukuri is the standard cut used on such fish as bream, snapper and sea bass: the skinned fillet is simply cut crosswise in straight medium-thin slices.

For firm fleshed fish such as sea bream and flounder, the *usu-zukuri* method of paper-thin slicing is appropriate. The fillet is placed flat on a board and the knife is held at a sharp angle to the fillet. The thinnest possible slices are removed diagonally from the fillet and are displayed fanned out in an overlapping arrangement. Sometimes the chef may choose to pinch the narrower end of each slice to give the fish a petal-like appearance. This is not done merely for an attractive presentation, but to make it easier to pick up these very thin slices.

Traditional garnishes and accompaniments for *sashimi* are essential to achieve the right balance of flavors and textures. Grated *daikon,* either by itself or as *momiji-oroshi* (see *Gyuniku No Sashimi,* page 39), very finely shredded lettuce or cucumber, strips of carrot curled in ice water, decorative leaves either edible or not, and little mounds of very finely chopped green onion and ginger are all garnishes it is possible to use in the West.

SUNSET, ARIAKE-KAI   MIKE MIRFIN/HORIZON

The more esoteric garnishes used by the Japanese include *benitade,* minute sprouts with a deep ruby red color and a tart, tangy flavor; pungent *shiso* buds, seed pods, sprouts and flowers; and *bofu,* a small, parsley-like plant of which the deep-red stems are used. The stems are split lengthwise and dropped into ice water to curl.

Kinome are delicate, aromatic sprigs from the prickly ash tree, from which the peppery spice/condiment *sansho* is derived. *Hanatsuki kyuri* are miniature flowering cucumbers; they are used whole and partially peeled, or the flowers alone are used. They resemble flowering zucchinis (courgettes) which could be substituted. *Kiku* is an edible chrysanthemum flower, used fresh or reconstituted from dried form.

Apart from the attractive garnishes, there are several vital condiments that accompany *sashimi.* The most prominent and indispensable is *wasabi,* a bitingly strong green horseradish which in Japan is served fresh, the gnarled root being scraped, finely grated and pinched into a little cone shape. Dried *wasabi* is not quite as smoothly flavored and not as pungent but is a good substitute if made immediately before use.

Other condiments are *shoga,* or grated fresh ginger; *sarashi-negi,* very finely chopped green onions, and *momiji-oroshi,* "red maple" radish, made by inserting hot red chili peppers into holes made in the center of *daikon* (giant white radish), then grating to give a pink-and-white-mixture that is at once tangy, refreshing and bitingly hot. All these condiments are usually served in small mounds on the *sashimi* plate.

Dipping sauces vary according to the type of fish, with stronger, darker sauces accompanying the richer-flavored fish and lighter, more citrus-tasting sauces complementing thin slices or threads.

Allow 2–3 oz (60–90 g) of fish or other seafood per person, using either one kind, or an assortment of different fish and/or shellfish. They must all be absolutely fresh.

12–18 oz (375–550 g) fresh seafood
1½ tablespoons finely shredded fresh ginger
1 cup (3 oz/90 g) finely shredded giant white radish or *momiji-oroshi* ("red maple" radish), see *Gyuniku No Sashimi,* page 39
assorted garnishes
1½ tablespoons powdered or grated fresh *wasabi* (horseradish)
sauces (below)

Cut the fish into bite-size pieces according to type. Shellfish can be dipped quickly into boiling water, then plunged into ice water to arrest cooking. This neutralizes the slightly fishy taste and firms up their texture.

Arrange the seafood on a large single platter or on individual plates, adding a little mound of ginger and radish to each plate, and garnishing as interestingly as possible.

Mix the *wasabi* with enough cold water to form a paste, then shape a little mound for each serving and place on the platter.

Serve the platter/s of *sashimi* with a sauce or sauces. A little of the *wasabi* and the shredded ginger or radish is mixed into the sauce before dipping the *sashimi.*

SASHIMI DIPPING SAUCE

🍴 Mix dark soy sauce and *mirin* (sweet cooking wine), first boiling the *mirin* to burn off the alcohol. Heat the two together, then steep a handful of *katsuobushi* (flaked dried bonito) in the liquid for a few minutes. Strain before using.

SESAME SOY SAUCE

To the above add enough toasted and ground white sesame seeds to make a thin sauce.

SERVES 6

IKA GOMA-YAKI

Grilled Squid with Sesame Seeds

6 fresh medium squid
½ cup (4 fl oz/125 ml) *mirin* (sweet cooking wine)
¼ cup (2 fl oz/60 ml) dark soy sauce
1 teaspoon ginger juice*
salt
white sesame seeds
cucumber sticks and lime wedges

Clean the squid by pulling away the head, entrails and quill. Wash thoroughly under cold running water, then pull off the skin and fins and wash again.

🍴 Cut squid open and lay flat on the work surface. Use a sharp knife to score along the insides in parallel lines, then turn over and score diagonally, cutting as deeply as possible without cutting through. Turn and score in the opposite direction to give a criss-cross effect. This helps to tenderize the squid as well as giving it an attractive appearance when cooked.

🍴 Heat the wine in a small saucepan until almost boiling, then add the soy sauce and ginger juice and pour into a wide, flat dish. Arrange the squid in the marinade, cover with plastic wrap, and let stand for 30 minutes, turning once during marination.

🍴 Thread each squid onto 2 or 3 thin skewers in a fan shape to hold it flat during cooking. Lightly salt the insides. Prepare a charcoal fire and brush grill lightly with vegetable oil to prevent sticking.

🍴 Grill the squid for about 2 minutes on one side, then turn and quickly cook the other side. Remove from the skewers, cut crosswise into slices and sprinkle with sesame seeds. (If preferred, the squid can be cooked in a skillet; when done, the remaining marinade can be poured into the pan to cook briefly, then served as a sauce.) Garnish with sticks of cucumber and wedges of lime and serve at once.

Ginger juice is made by placing minced or grated fresh ginger in a piece of clean cheesecloth and squeezing firmly to extract the juice.

SERVES 6

GRILLED SQUID WITH SESAME SEEDS AND
SHELLFISH IN VINEGAR DRESSING

UNAGI KABAYAKI

Glazed Grilled Eel

Fillets of eel, glazed with a rich brown salty-sweet glaze of sake and soy sauce, are eaten mainly in August when the health-giving properties of eel are believed to ensure against the debilities caused by summer heat. Unagi kabayaki is usually served on rice with a dusting of sansho, *the fragrant ground pepper from the prickly ash tree.*

2–3 small freshwater eels
¼ cup (2 fl oz/60 ml) light soy sauce
¼ cup (2 fl oz/60 ml) *sake* (rice wine)
¼ cup (2 oz/60 g) sugar
cooked rice
sansho (Japanese pepper)

Discard the eels' heads, cut the eels open lengthwise and scrape away the entrails. Wash thoroughly in cold water and rub the skin with coarse salt. Rinse well.

🍴 Remove the meat from the backbone in two or three long strips, then cut crosswise into 4-in (10-cm) pieces.

🍴 Insert thin bamboo skewers through the fillets crosswise, skewering several pieces on each. Place in a

ABALONE STEAMED IN *SAKE (LEFT)* WITH GLAZED BROILED/GRILLED EEL *(RIGHT)*

steamer, propping the skewers against the side so the eel will not touch the base of the steamer or it will stick. (The steaming partially cooks the eel, making the finished dish delicate and tender, as well as drawing off some of the excess oils. If preferred, this step can be omitted; the dish will be just as tasty, but the eel will have a firmer texture.)

Prepare a small charcoal fire and allow the coals to burn down until glowing red. Mix the soy sauce, *sake* and sugar, stirring until the sugar has dissolved. Grill the eel skin side down. Brush generously with the glaze, turn and cook the other side briefly. Glaze the skin side. Continue turning and glazing until the eel has developed a rich red-brown surface. Remove from the heat and gently ease the skewers out of the fillets. Arrange on rice, sprinkle with *sansho* and serve.

SERVES 4

Awabi No Saka-mushi

Abalone Steamed in Sake

Sake is often added to seafood and meats before steaming to impart its subtle taste and to act as a tenderizer. Traditionally this dish is served with a bright green sauce made from undigested seaweed removed from the stomach of the abalone, but we have chosen to make a different sauce.

6 fresh abalone in their shells
salt
¼ cup (2 fl oz/60 ml) *sake* (rice wine)

SAUCE

½ oz (5 g) dried seaweed
1 tablespoon mayonnaise
1 teaspoon light soy sauce
¾ cup (6 fl oz/180 ml) water

Discard the top shells from the abalone, then remove each abalone and trim away the frilled inedible part. Rub with salt, then rinse thoroughly in cold water. Score the top surface lightly and return the abalone to the shells.

Arrange the abalone, shells down, in a rack over steaming water. Pour the *sake* evenly over the abalone, cover the dish tightly and steam for about 2 hours until very tender, replenishing the water as necessary. (Cooking time can vary, depending on the size and quality of the abalone.) Remove the abalone and discard the liquid in the shells. Thinly slice each abalone and return to its shell.

To make the sauce, place the seaweed in a small saucepan and add the water. Allow the seaweed to soften and expand, then simmer gently about 6 minutes until tender. Force the seaweed through a sieve with enough of the liquid to make a thin paste, then add the mayonnaise and soy sauce and mix well. Spoon a little of the sauce over each abalone.

SERVES 6

Sunomono

Shellfish in Vinegar Dressing

Sunomono or "vinegared food" is often served as a kind of appetizer before a meal, or with other main courses as a counterpoint to the menu. Typical sunomono dishes combine cucumber with other vegetables, in particular spring-fresh young wakame (lobe-leaf seaweed), with shellfish.

The dressing combines rice vinegar with dashi and/or light soy sauce, and a hint of sweetness is added with sugar or mirin. Sunomono is served either at room temperature or very slightly chilled.

12 fresh sea scallops, or raw clams, in their shells
12 large uncooked shrimp (prawns), in their shells
1 large cucumber
½ teaspoon salt
2 teaspoons minced fresh ginger, optional
lime slices for garnish

VINEGAR DRESSING (Sambai-zu)

¼ cup (2 fl oz/60 ml) rice vinegar
⅓ cup (2½ fl oz/75 ml) *dashi* (seaweed/fish stock)
2½ teaspoons *mirin* (sweet cooking wine), or 2 teaspoons sugar
1 tablespoon light soy sauce

35

Scrub the scallops or clams with a brush under cold running water, rinse well and place in a steamer. Steam for 3–4 minutes, then add the shrimp in their shells and continue to steam for 7–10 minutes until the scallop or clam shells open and the shrimp are bright pink and cooked through. Remove from the steamer, cover and cool.

Peel the cucumber or score the skin with a fork. Cut in half lengthwise. Scrape out the seeds with a teaspoon or melon scoop and discard. Slice into very thin crescents and place in a dish. Add the salt and enough water to just cover, mix lightly and let marinate while the shellfish cools. Drain cucumber thoroughly, pressing out as much water as possible.

Mix the dressing ingredients together in a small nonaluminum saucepan and bring to the boil, then immediately remove from the heat and pour into a pitcher to cool. Open the scallop or clam shells and remove the meat. Peel the shrimp, leaving the tail sections intact.

Arrange the shellfish and cucumber in dishes or on small plates. Place the minced ginger in a small square of clean cheesecloth and squeeze a few drops of ginger juice over the shellfish. Pour on the dressing and garnish with slices of lime. Serve at once.

SERVES 6

SABA NITSUKE

Mackerel Simmered in Sake and Soy Sauce

An otoshi-buta, *a wooden disc that fits inside a cooking pot, is often employed in the cooking of simmered dishes. This "drop-lid" keeps the food below the surface of the simmering liquid to ensure even cooking. If an* otoshi-buta *is unavailable, use a smaller*

saucepan lid or a plate that fits easily inside the cooking pot.

Nimono, or "simmered foods," come in varying guises and are named according to the method of simmering and the ingredients used to give flavor. Nitsuke applies usually to fish dishes that are simmered first in sake, *then in* mirin *and soy sauce.*

Sake, as well as lending its particular taste, acts as a tenderizer, and is therefore usually added to the pot before the other ingredients. Strongly flavored, oily fish like mackerel respond well to the nitsuke *style of simmering. They are also delicious cooked in* miso-ni *style with salty* miso *paste.*

½ lb (750 g) fresh mackerel
1 cup (8 fl oz/250 ml) *sake* (rice wine)
½ cup (4 fl oz/125 ml) *mirin* (sweet cooking wine)
½ cup (4 fl oz/125 ml) dark soy sauce
3 tablespoons finely slivered fresh ginger
1 tablespoon sugar
cooked rice

Clean the fish, wash thoroughly and remove the head and tail. Lay on a work surface and remove the fillets from both sides. Cut crosswise at an angle to give 6 pieces from each side.

Choose a saucepan with a wide, heavy base. Pour in the *sake* and bring just to the boil. Arrange the fish in the pan skin side up, increase the heat and bring the *sake* back to the boil. Add the wine and heat briefly, then add the soy sauce. Arrange the slivered ginger over the fish and bring to the boil again. Sprinkle the sugar evenly over the top.

Weight the fish with the *otoshi-buta* or other lid and simmer briskly for 11 minutes.

Remove the pan from the heat and remove the *otoshi-buta.* Use a flat spatula to transfer the fish to plates skin side up. Pour a few teaspoonfuls of the sauce over the fish, adding several slivers of ginger. Serve at once with rice.

SERVES 6

MACKEREL SIMMERED IN *SAKE* AND SOY SAUCE

GRILLED CHICKEN

YAKITORI

Grilled Chicken

The ultimate fast food, Japanese style. These skewers loaded with succulent morsels of chicken are sold by street vendors and in small specialty restaurants. They are also often a feature of family meals at home. Small green peppers, mushrooms, quail eggs and onion can accompany the chicken, which itself is prepared in various ways: strips of skin alone are pleated along the skewer, cubes of breast or leg meat are threaded alone or with lengths of naganegi *onion, the meat may be finely ground and formed into balls, and even the gizzards are enjoyed in this way.*

YAKITORI CHICKEN BALLS WITH QUAIL EGGS

2 lb (1 kg) boneless chicken leg meat
1 egg
2 tablespoons light soy sauce
2 teaspoons ginger juice*
1 teaspoon salt
1 tablespoon sugar
10 oz (315 g) canned quail eggs, drained

YAKITORI OF CHICKEN, ONION AND PEPPERS

1½ lb (750 g) boneless chicken leg meat
salt
1 lb (500 g) chicken livers
6 small green or red peppers (capsicums)
6 green onions

YAKITORI SAUCE

½ cup (4 fl oz/125 ml) *sake* (rice wine)
½ cup (4 fl oz/125 ml) dark soy sauce
¼ cup (2 fl oz/60 ml) light soy sauce
¼ cup (2 fl oz/60 ml) *mirin* (sweet cooking wine)
2 tablespoons sugar
sansho (Japanese pepper)

Skin the chicken for the meatballs, cut it into small cubes and place in a food processor. Add the remaining ingredients, except the quail eggs, and process until very smooth. Use wet hands to form the mixture into walnut-sized balls.

For the other style of *yakitori,* skin the chicken and cut into long, narrow strips or little cubes. Sprinkle lightly with salt. Cut the livers in half and trim off connective tissue and sinews. Seed the peppers and cut into quarters. Trim the *naganegi* and cut into 1-in (2.5-cm) lengths.

Thread the meatballs onto bamboo skewers, 3 or 4 at a time. Thread the quail eggs similarly and set aside.

Thread the livers onto bamboo skewers. Pleat the strips of chicken and thread these or the chicken cubes onto other bamboo skewers, alternating with pieces of *naganegi,* threaded crosswise. Thread several pieces of pepper onto other skewers.

Mix all the *yakitori* sauce ingredients, except the *sansho,* in a saucepan and bring to the boil, then remove immediately from the heat. Let cool before using. Grill the skewers over glowing coals, turning frequently, until half cooked. Brush with the *yakitori* sauce and return to the heat. Continue to grill and baste with the sauce until they are done; do not overcook.

Arrange on a platter and serve *sansho* pepper as a dip, or sprinkled lightly over the skewers.

* Grate fresh ginger onto a piece of clean cheesecloth, then squeeze firmly to extract the juice.

SERVES 6

TORIGAN-NI

Chicken Balls Simmered in Sauce

These supremely tender balls of chicken meat can be served in two ways: as a soup in dashi *or as a main course with rice in their tasty soy-and-sake-flavored sauce.*

1 lb (500 g) chicken meat
¼ lb (125 g) white fish fillet
2 egg whites
1 whole egg
¼ cup (2 fl oz/60 ml) *sake* (rice wine)
2 tablespoons dark soy sauce
1½ tablespoons ginger juice*
2 tablespoons sugar
1½ teaspoons salt
4-in (10-cm) square piece kelp
green onion

SAUCE

3 cups (24 fl oz/750 ml) *dashi* (seaweed/fish stock)
¾ cup (6 fl oz/180 ml) *sake* (rice wine)
½ cup (4 fl oz/125 ml) *mirin* (sweet cooking wine)
¼ cup (2 fl oz/60 ml) light soy sauce
2½ tablespoons cornstarch (cornflour)

Skin the chicken and chop coarsely. Dice the fish. Place both in a food processor or blender and add the egg whites, whole egg, *sake,* dark soy sauce, ginger juice, sugar and salt.

Process until the mixture is very smooth, then add about 3 tablespoons of iced water and process again to make the mixture lighter and more voluminous. Traditionally this is prepared in a pottery bowl which has a roughly scored inner surface *(suribachi)*, using a thick wooden pestle *(surikoga)*.

❧ Bring a large pot of water to the boil. Wipe the kelp with a wet cloth, then score on both sides with the point of a knife to release the flavor. Place in the pot, then reduce the heat so that the water simmers gently.

❧ Pinch portions of the chicken paste into small balls and drop into the simmering water. Cook gently for about 5 minutes or until they float to the surface.

❧ If serving as a soup, remove with a slotted spoon and transfer to soup bowls. Strain on the *dashi* and garnish with finely shredded green onion.

❧ Alternatively, drain the chicken balls and set aside, discarding the water. Pour the *dashi, sake,* wine and light soy sauce into a saucepan and bring to the boil. Add the meatballs and simmer gently for 4–5 minutes. Lift out and set aside. Mix the cornstarch with a little cold water and stir into the sauce. Simmer, stirring, until thickened and clear. Pour over the meatballs and serve at once with rice.

Grate fresh ginger onto a piece of clean cheesecloth, then squeeze firmly to extract the juice.

SERVES 6

TORI SAKA MUSHI NO GOMA

Sake-Steamed Chicken with Sesame Seed Sauce

The subtle flavors of sake (rice wine) and goma (sesame seeds) combine to season tender chicken breasts. Ground toasted sesame seeds or Middle Eastern tahini paste are used to make the sauce, although a smooth peanut butter is equally good, if somewhat less authentic.

SAKE-STEAMED CHICKEN WITH SESAME SEED SAUCE

2 whole chicken breasts, boned
    (about 1¼ lb/625 g altogether)
⅔ cup (5 fl oz/155 ml) *sake* (rice wine)
salt
¼ cup (1½ oz/45 g) toasted white sesame seeds, or
    3 tablespoons smooth peanut butter or *tahini* paste
¼ cup (2 fl oz/60 ml) *dashi* (seaweed/ fish stock)
1¼ tablespoons dark soy sauce
¾ teaspoon sugar
1 teaspoon rice vinegar
¼ teaspoon salt
lemon rind

Use a sharp knife to slash through the chicken skin at close intervals. Set the chicken, skin side up, on a dish and place in a steamer. Sprinkle on the *sake* and salt and steam over gently simmering water for about 20 minutes.

❧ Grind the sesame seeds to a fairly smooth paste in a spice grinder or mortar. Stir in the remaining ingredients (except lemon rind) to make a thick sauce. Remove the chicken from the steamer and cool, then cover with plastic wrap and chill.

❧ Cut the fillets diagonally into narrow strips. Arrange on a serving platter or individual plates and spoon on the sauce. Garnish with a strip of lemon rind, or white radish, cut attractively.

SERVES 4

TON-NEGU NO TERIYAKI

Teriyaki Pork Rolls

There are several popular variations on this dish, which is made of paper-thin slices of meat wrapped around vegetables and then pan-fried with teriyaki *sauce. Gyuniku no yawata-maki (thinly sliced beef fillet wrapped around slender burdock roots) is one version, while* gyuniki no namba-maki *(beef with* naganegi, *the long Japanese onion resembling a cross between green onion and leek) is another.*

Made with slices of pork cut from the leg and enclosing green onions or naganegi, *this is always a favorite.*

6 large, thin slices fresh ham (pork leg), approx. 1 lb/500 g
6 *naganegi,* or use thick green onions or young
    small leeks
2 tablespoons vegetable oil
1 large cucumber
½ teaspoon salt

TERIYAKI SAUCE

¼ cup (2 fl oz/60 ml) *sake* (rice wine)
⅓ cup (2½ fl oz/75 ml) light soy sauce
⅓ cup (3 oz/90 g) sugar

Trim the pork, removing skin, fat and connective tissue. Cover the work surface with a piece of heavy-duty plastic wrap and place the pork on it, with spaces between the pieces to allow for spreading. Cover with another piece of plastic wrap, then pound firmly with a rolling pin or the flat side of a meat mallet to flatten and spread the meat as much as possible. It should be almost transparent when ready, but not broken through.

❧ Trim the onions, cutting them to 6½-in (16-cm) lengths. Wrap a piece of pork around each to enclose the onion, leaving a short length exposed at each end. Secure with wooden picks or tie with thread.

❧ Heat a wok or wide flat skillet and add the oil. Sauté the pork rolls until evenly colored.

TERIYAKI PORK ROLLS

GYUNIKU NO SASHIMI

Beef Sashimi

Beef tenderloin (fillet) served raw in paper-thin slivers is a popular sashimi dish. It is given an appetizing appearance and aroma by generously coating with garlic, then lightly grilling over charcoal. The selection of accompanying condiments includes a tasty lime-flavored sauce.

1 lb (500 g) choice beef tenderloin or lean sirloin/
   porterhouse steak
¾ teaspoon salt
2 teaspoons crushed garlic
1 medium cucumber
1cup (or a small bunch) spearmint or basil leaves

CONDIMENTS

Momiji-oroshi ("red maple" radish)
Peel a 4-in (10-cm) piece of *daikon* (giant white radish). Push a chopstick through its length in 2 or 3 places to make holes right through. Into these holes insert a thin, seeded, fresh red chili, using the chopstick to push the pieces into place. Grate the radish and chili onto a piece of clean cheesecloth, gather up and squeeze to remove excess liquid.
Sarashi-negi
Trim a *naganegi* or small leek, or 2 green onions, and mince very finely. Place on a piece of cheesecloth, gather up and swish through cold water to rinse. (This removes the slight sliminess.) Wring out.
Daikon Oroshi
Peel and grate a portion of *daikon* (giant white radish) onto a piece of cheesecloth. Wring out.
Shoga
Grate a knob of peeled fresh ginger onto a piece of cheesecloth. Wring out.
Lime Sauce
Mix ¼ cup (2 fl oz/60 ml) fresh lime juice with 1 tablespoon *tamari* or light soy sauce. Pour 1 tablespoon *mirin* into a saucepan and bring to the boil to burn off the alcohol. Immediately remove from the heat, swirl in the saucepan until slightly cooled and mix with the other ingredients. Add 1 teaspoon rice vinegar.

Trim the beef, removing all fat. Rub with the salt, then the crushed garlic. Quickly sear the surface evenly in a hot skillet or over glowing charcoal. Remove from the heat and place in the refrigerator to cool quickly.

❦ Mix the sauce ingredients together and stir until the sugar has almost dissolved. Pour into the skillet and simmer gently until the sauce is reduced to a shiny, deeply colored glaze on the pork rolls. Gently turn the rolls from time to time during cooking, using two spoons.
❦ Meanwhile, peel the cucumber and cut the flesh into long strips, discarding the seed core. Cut into 2-in (5-cm) lengths, then into sticks. Place in a dish and sprinkle with the salt. Cover with cold water and set aside for 20 minutes. Drain well and pat dry.
❦ Remove the pork rolls from the pan and cut each into 3 or 4 pieces. Remove the wooden picks/thread. Arrange on rectangular plates with several cucumber sticks and serve.

SERVES 6

SPINACH WITH SESAME DRESSING *(BOTTOM), recipe page 42, AND BEEF SASHIMI (TOP)*

Cut into very thin slices. Place several spearmint or basil leaves on each plate and arrange the sliced meat in rosette fashion on these.

Peel and seed the cucumber and cut into crescents or sticks. Place beside the beef. Serve the sauce and condiments in small dishes.

SERVES 4–6

MISO-SHIRU

Miso-Flavored Soup with Bean Curd

2-in (5-cm) square piece kelp
3 cups (24 fl oz/750 ml) *dashi* (seaweed/fish stock)
2 Japanese dried black mushrooms, soaked for 25 minutes
½ cup (1¾ oz/50 g) red *miso* (red fermented soybean paste)
½ square firm bean curd
1 green onion
4 small sprigs watercress or trefoil*

Wipe the kelp with a damp cloth and score on one side to release its flavor. Pour the stock into a deep saucepan and add the kelp. Heat the stock to just warm, then transfer about ½ cup (4 fl oz/125 ml) to a small bowl and continue to heat the remaining stock until boiling. Remove the kelp.

Drain the mushrooms and discard the stems. Finely shred the caps and add to the soup.

Whisk the *miso* with the reserved ½ cup of stock (this step ensures that the *miso* will mix evenly into the soup; if added undiluted to the boiling stock it will break into small lumps instead of amalgamating).

Cut the bean curd into small dice. Trim and diagonally slice the green onion. Slowly add the *miso* mixture to the soup and simmer for a few minutes, then add the bean curd and green onion. Warm through, then transfer to soup bowls and garnish with the watercress or trefoil. Serve immediately.

A delicately flavored and attractive leaf that is extensively used in Japan as a garnish. If unavailable, substitute continental flat-leaf parsley.

SERVES 4

KANI SUIMONO

Clear Soup with Crab

1¼ lb (625 g) hard-shell crab (sand crab)
2 green onions
6 *shiitake* (dried Japanese black mushrooms), soaked for 25 minutes
3½ cups (28 fl oz/875 ml) *dashi* (seaweed/fish stock)
2 tablespoons finely shredded fresh ginger
1 tablespoon light soy sauce
1 tablespoon *mirin* (sweet cooking wine)
2 oz (60 g) soft bean curd

Wash the crab thoroughly under cold running water. Cut the body into four parts, each with legs or claws attached. Remove the undershell and discard, then scrape away the inedible parts. Rinse the crab quickly in cold water. Crack the claws with a heavy cleaver or nutcracker and cut lengthwise along each claw, but do not remove the shell.

CLEAR SOUP WITH CHICKEN AND LEEKS *(TOP)* AND *MISO-FLAVORED SOUP WITH BEAN CURD*   WELDON TRANNIES

Trim the green onions and cut the white parts into thin diagonal slices. Cut the green parts in the same way, setting them aside for garnish. Drain the mushrooms, squeeze out excess water and then trim off the stems. Use a sharp knife to cut a decorative pattern in each mushroom cap.

Bring the *dashi* to the boil in a deep saucepan. Add the shredded ginger, soy sauce and *mirin* and simmer for 2–3 minutes. Add the whites of the green onions and the crab pieces and simmer again for about 6 minutes, until the crab is bright pink and cooked through.

Place the bean curd in the palm of your hand and gently cut into neat dice, then slide into the soup. Simmer for about 40 seconds. Ladle soup into covered serving bowls and garnish with the green onion tops.

HAMAGURI-SU

Substitute 16 small clams for the crab. Rinse them very well and simmer them in the stock just long enough for them to open.

SERVES 4

TORI NO MIZUDAKI

Clear Soup with Chicken and Leeks

Soups are collectively known in Japan as shirumono, *but they come in two main forms. The light and clear soups, which are not unlike the* nimono *or simmered dishes, are called* suimono. *Thick soups are most often flavored with* miso *which turns them a milky ochre color.*

Soup is served at an early stage in the meal, always in a covered bowl which is usually made of lacquered wood. The soup is meant to be sipped throughout the meal.

5 oz (185 g) boneless chicken breast or thigh meat
3 *naganegi* or young leeks
4 cups (1 liter) light chicken stock
1½ tablespoons light soy sauce
1 tablespoon *mirin* (sweet cooking wine)
salt to taste
lime or lemon juice
6 slivers lime or lemon rind

Cut the meat into 12 even-sized pieces. The skin is usually left on, but can be removed if preferred.

Trim off the roots and loose green tops of the *naganegi* or leeks, leaving lengths of about 6 in (15 cm). Rinse very thoroughly in cold water and drain well. Cut each in half crosswise then into quarters, and cut through the center diagonally to give two pieces each with one diagonally pointed end. Set aside.

Bring the stock to the boil in a deep saucepan. Add the chicken and simmer gently for 15 minutes. Add the leeks, soy sauce, wine and salt and continue to simmer gently until the chicken and leeks are tender.

Use a slotted spoon to transfer the chicken and leeks to soup bowls. Skim the soup, then place a double layer of paper towel on the surface to absorb excess fat; lift off and discard. Add lime or lemon juice to taste (it should be just slightly tart), then strain into the soup bowls. Add a sliver of decoratively cut rind to each dish and serve.

SERVES 6

KANI CHIRI

Crab Hotpot

3 lb (1½ kg) fresh crab
4 squares soft bean curd
½ lb (8 oz/250 g) leafy green vegetables such as spinach, mustard greens or Chinese cabbage
1 medium carrot
6 *shiitake* (dried Japanese black mushrooms), soaked for 25 minutes
12 button mushrooms (champignons)
6 green onions
6 cups (1½ liters) *dashi* (seaweed/fish stock)

SAUCES AND DIPS

6-in (15-cm) piece *daikon* (giant white radish)
1 fresh red chili

Peel the radish; seed the chili. Insert a chopstick into the end of the *daikon* to form a cavity. Push the chili into the cavity, then grate them together into a paste.

1 large white onion
1 teaspoon salt

Mince the onion and mix with the salt.

¾ cup (6 fl oz/180 ml) lemon or lime juice
¾ cup (6 fl oz/180 ml) *dashi* (seaweed/fish stock)
½ cup (4 fl oz/125 ml) light soy sauce

Mix the lemon, stock and soy sauce in a small saucepan and bring almost to the boil, then allow to cool.

Cut the crab in half. Remove the undershell and discard, then scrape out the inedible parts. Rinse the crab quickly in cold water, then cut into smaller pieces, each with a leg or claw attached. Cut lengthwise along each leg with a sharp cleaver; crack the claws with the back of the cleaver.

WELDON TRANNIES   CRAB HOTPOT

Holding the bean curd in the palm of your hand, carefully cut into squares, then slide onto a plate. Wash the greens carefully in cold water, drain and chop coarsely.

Peel the carrot and cut lengthwise into a five-sided shape. Make a lengthwise groove in the center of each flat side, then carefully pare away the remaining points, to give five rounded petal shapes. Cut into thin slices to make "plum blossoms." Drain the *shiitake,* discard stems and cut a deep cross into each cap. Drain the button mushrooms. Trim the onions and slice diagonally into 1½-in (4-cm) lengths.

Bring the stock to the boil in a flameproof earthenware pot. Add the vegetables and simmer for 3–4 minutes, then add the crab and simmer 3–4 minutes more before carefully sliding in the bean curd. Prepare the sauces and serve in small dishes.

The hotpot should be placed on a small portable cooker on the tabletop, where it can continue to simmer gently while each diner helps himself.

SERVES 4–6

WAKAME TO KYURI NO SUNOMONO

Lobe-Leaf Seaweed and Cucumber Salad

The lobe-leaf wakame *seaweed, harvested through spring and early summer in Japan's southwestern Naruto Channel, is low in calories and high in nutritional value, making it an excellent salad ingredient. Sold in dried form, this tender curly-leafed seaweed, a member of the brown algae family, is soaked until softened and the firm central rib or spine is removed before use. Kyuri, the slender Japanese cucumber, and a tangy* sunomono *vinegar dressing make perfect companions for* wakame. *Serve very slightly chilled* as a salad, or with rice at the end of the meal in place of pickles.

The seaweed can be found in 1-oz "salad packs" at some Japanese food suppliers; otherwise it comes in larger packs. Once opened, unused wakame must be stored in an airtight container.

1-oz (30-g) pack *wakame* (lobe-leaf seaweed)
⅓ cup (2½ fl oz/75 ml) rice vinegar
¼ cup (2 fl oz/60 ml) light soy sauce
2–3 teaspoons sugar
3 Japanese cucumbers, or 1 English cucumber
large pinch of salt

Place the *wakame* in a bowl and cover with warm water. Let stand for about 30 minutes until the seaweed expands and softens, then remove and drain. Use kitchen scissors to trim away any hard ribs. Rinse the seaweed thoroughly under cold running water, then drain and pat dry. Chop coarsely and place in a dry bowl. Cover with plastic wrap.

❧ Combine the vinegar, soy sauce and sugar in a small saucepan and bring to the boil, stirring to dissolve the sugar. Immediately remove from the heat and pour into a jug. Refrigerate until cool.

❧ Wash the cucumbers and peel if desired). Cut into very thin slices. If using a standard cucumber, cut in half, scoop out the seeds with a teaspoon or melon scoop and cut into crescents. Place the cucumber in a dish, sprinkle with salt and then cover with cold water. Let stand for 15–20 minutes to soften slightly. (The salt also draws off the slight bitterness which is usually present in cucumbers.) Drain well, then pat dry with a paper towel.

❧ Toss the cucumber and seaweed together, adding the dressing when they are well mixed.

SERVES 4

HORENSO NO GOMA-AE
Spinach with Sesame Dressing

Sesame seed (goma) dressing has a delightfully nutty taste that particularly complements green beans and spinach. The seeds are toasted to bring out their fullest flavor, then ground finely before being mixed with the other ingredients to make a sauce.

Aemono, which loosely means "dressed things," covers dishes of this type, which are the Japanese equivalent of the salad or vegetable side dish. They are usually served in small portions on little plates or in small bowls. In some instances a selection of aemono may be served before the meal with drinks, usually warmed sake.

Dressings for aemono, unlike the companion salad dishes known as sunomono or "vinegared things," tend to be thick with a base of puréed bean curd, sesame seeds or miso. Occasionally raw egg yolk is also used as the thickener.

1 large bunch fresh spinach (approx 1¼ lb/625 g)

DRESSING

⅓ cup (2 oz/60 g) *goma* (white sesame seeds)
½ cup (4 fl oz/125 ml) *dashi* (seaweed/fish stock)
2 teaspoons dark soy sauce
2 teaspoons light soy sauce
1½ teaspoons sesame oil
1½ teaspoons sugar

Thoroughly rinse the spinach in several changes of cold water, then drain well and discard the stems. Place the leaves in a saucepan, cover tightly and cook gently for about 6 minutes until tender.

LOBE-LEAF SEAWEED AND CUCUMBER SALAD, *recipe page 41*

TEMPURA JAPANESE BATTERED FOOD

Pour the sesame seeds into a dry wok or skillet and cook over medium heat, stirring frequently, until they turn a light golden color and begin to pop. Grind in a spice grinder or mortar until fairly smooth, then transfer to a small mixing bowl, add the remaining dressing ingredients and whisk briskly until the dressing is smooth and creamy.

Drain the spinach thoroughly, pressing to remove as much water as possible. Pick up a handful of the leaves and cylinder tightly together into a roll of about 1-in (2.5-cm) diameter. Repeat this with the remaining spinach, then cut the rolls crosswise into ¾-in (2-cm) lengths. Stand the spinach rolls on end in small dishes. Pour on the dressing and serve.

An alternative way to serve the salad is to simply toss the cooked spinach leaves with the dressing until all the leaves are well coated. Serve in little mounds.

SERVES 6

TEMPURA

Battered Foods

Although it had its origins in Nagasaki as an adaptation of the Spanish/Portuguese gambas fritas, tempura was welcomed into the Japanese cuisine to such an extent that today most non-Japanese consider it one of the most typical dishes, and flock to specialist tempura restaurants around the world.

Essentially, tempura is food that is coated in an air-light batter, quickly deep-fried and served crisp and piping hot with a dipping sauce of soy flavored with ginger and grated daikon (giant white radish). Getting tempura just right is difficult, so although it is popular dinner party food, it is problematical for the home cook and should perhaps not be undertaken for large groups. Practice does make perfect, though, and once the batter is mastered the rest is easy enough.

4 large uncooked shrimp (prawns) in their shells
4 small whiting or trout fillets
8 fresh green beans
2 medium onions
4 *shiitake* (dried Japanese black mushrooms), soaked for 25 minutes
1 medium-size sweet potato
1 small eggplant (aubergine)
8 cups (2 liters) vegetable oil
½–1 cup (4–8 fl oz/125–250 ml) sesame oil

DIPPING SAUCE

1 cup (8 fl oz/250 ml) *dashi* (seaweed/fish stock)
2 tablespoons *mirin* (sweet cooking wine)
⅓ cup (2½ fl oz/75 ml) light soy sauce
6 slices fresh ginger
4-in (10-cm) piece giant white radish
2 teaspoons sugar

BATTER

2 large egg yolks
2 cups (16 fl oz/500 ml) ice water*
2 cups (8 oz/250 g) all purpose (plain) flour

Peel the shrimp, leaving the tails on. Make 3 lengthwise cuts along the underside of the shrimp to prevent them from curling up during cooking. Insert a small skewer beneath the dark vein in the center back and gently ease out the vein through the incision. Rinse the shrimp in cold water and drain well.

The fish fillets may be left unskinned. Check for the small row of bones running along the center of each fillet and pluck these out with tweezers. Remove the tips of the beans. Peel the onions and cut 2 medium-thick slices from each, removing the remainder for another use. If you wish, divide the slices into rings.

Drain the mushrooms, squeezing out as much water as possible; discard the stems. Peel and slice the sweet potato. Slice the unpeeled eggplant, sprinkle with a little salt and set aside for a few minutes to draw off the bitter juices. Wipe before using.

Pour the liquid sauce ingredients into a small saucepan and bring just to the boil. Remove from the heat and cool slightly, then add the very finely shredded ginger, the radish and the sugar.

Heat the vegetable oil in a wide pan or wok and add the sesame oil. Have ready near the work area a pair of long-handled chopsticks, a draining rack over a drip tray, a mixing bowl for the batter and the platter of ingredients, plus a dish of extra flour.

Fold pieces of attractive paper towel or paper napkins, and arrange them on a serving platter or individual plates.

Beat egg yolk briskly into half the water. Sift half the flour into the mixing bowl. Quickly blend in the egg/water mixture without overstirring. (The secret of good *tempura* is to undermix the batter; the sides of the bowl should still be lined with flour and there can be plenty of little lumps of dry flour in the batter. If overworked, it becomes flat and hard.)

Dip the ingredients several pieces at a time into the extra flour; shake off the excess thoroughly. Coat with the batter and slide into the oil. Fry for about 3 minutes or until the pieces rise to the surface and the batter is crisp and golden, turning occasionally. Once all the batter has been used, make a second batch, using the remaining ingredients.

Do not overcrowd the pan, and do not cook all the *tempura* at once; serve each batch as it is cooked. Serve the sauce in small dishes for dipping.

* *The water must be icy cold to achieve the right results.*

SERVES 4

TEPPAN-YAKI JAPANESE BARBECUE

TEPPAN-YAKI

Japanese Barbecue

Like tempura, teppan-yaki *has become an international favorite. Restaurants specializing in this casual form of dining offer seating around a central bench in which a hotplate or* teppan *has been installed. The cook deftly slices, tosses, seasons and serves the food with flat metal paddles, often making an entertaining display with such exaggerated movements and antics that dining out* teppan-yaki-*style becomes an incomparable occasion.*

At home it can be cooked at the table in an electric skillet or on a griddle over a portable cooking unit.

6 large uncooked shrimp (prawns) in their shells
1 lb (500 g) sea scallops
1 lb (500 g) chicken breast meat
1 lb (500 g) beef tenderloin or sirloin (fillet or rump)
2 medium onions
small piece of fresh suet
10 oz (315 g) fresh bean sprouts
18 large oysters or clams on the half shell (optional)
black pepper

ACCOMPANIMENTS

Ponzu Sauce
light soy sauce
grated giant white radish
minced green onion
fresh limes or lemons
coarse salt, sea salt, kosher salt
black pepper

Peel the shrimp, leaving the tails on. Insert a skewer beneath the vein in the center back and gently ease out the vein through the incision. Rinse the shrimp in cold water and dry thoroughly.

Rinse the scallops in cold lightly salted water. Cut the chicken into narrow strips or small cubes, leaving the skin on. Prick the skin. Cut the beef into narrow strips. Peel the onions. Cut in half and then into thick slices.

Heat a griddle suitable for *teppan* cooking. Grease with a few drops of vegetable oil, then rub the suet briskly over the surface until well greased.

Cook the food in separate groups, stirring, tossing and turning it on the griddle until just done; cook the seafood first, then the meats and onion, and finally the bean sprouts. Grind on plenty of black pepper during cooking. If using oysters, place them at the side of the griddle on the shells to heat through gently. Serve with a few drops of lemon or lime juice and a sprinkle of salt.

For garlic lovers, add whole peeled cloves to the side of the *teppan* to cook until tender. Serve the food in batches as it is cooked, along with the accompaniments.

SERVES 6

MOCHI

Glutinous Rice Balls with Red Bean Filling

Azuki, a small red-skinned bean, and glutinous white rice are the two main ingredients in Japanese confections. Mochi, like most Japanese sweets, are not so much a dessert as a sweet snack for nibbling between meals. They are particularly popular in spring, when the rice is tinted pink and the dumpling is wrapped in a cherry leaf. Salt-packed grape leaves have a similar taste and can be used instead, as it is unlikely that the prepared salt-soaked cherry leaves would be available in other countries.

2¼ cups (15 oz/470 g) glutinous white rice
½ teaspoon red food coloring
¼ cup (2 oz/60 g) sugar
¼ teaspoon salt
3 cups (1½ lb/750 g) cooked *azuki* (red bean) paste (see *Dora Yaki*, page 45)
1–2 packs salted cherry or grape leaves, optional

Place the rice in a dish under cold running water. Briskly stir with the fingers, rinsing until the water runs clear. Drain and cover again with cold water. Add the red coloring and set aside for 3–4 hours until the rice becomes lightly tinted, then drain off most of the water.

Set the dish in a steamer or over a saucepan of simmering water and steam for about 45 minutes or until tender; four times during cooking sprinkle on 2 tablespoons hot water to moisten the rice.

Transfer to a mixing bowl and stir in the sugar and salt, then mash the rice by pounding lightly with the end of a rolling pin or a large pestle.

Form the bean paste into balls the size of a walnut. Spread the hot rice evenly in a tray with wet hands; roll each bean paste ball across the rice until it is thickly coated. Squeeze gently in a wet hand to firm up the ball shape, then wrap in one of the washed and dried leaves.

When all of the *mochi* have been made, arrange side by side on a plate and steam over briskly simmering water for 12 minutes. Serve at room temperature.

MAKES ABOUT 30

RICE BALLS WITH RED BEAN FILLING AND PANCAKES FILLED WITH RED BEANS

Dora Yaki

Pancakes Filled with Red Beans

These delicious little sweet snacks are named dora *or "gong" because of their resemblance to brass gongs. Simply a matching pair of pancakes with a red bean filling, they are popular between-meal snacks to nibble with Japanese green tea. Made and sold by streetside vendors,* dora yaki *are cooked in round iron molds on a skillet, deftly sandwiched and served in a wrapper of waxed paper. Red bean paste can be used in a number of other desserts. It is delicious as an ice cream topping or served on crushed ice, and is solidified with* agar-agar *to make* muzu-yokan, *or red bean jelly.*

Azuki Paste

1½ cups (9 oz/280 g) *azuki* (red beans)
1¼–1½ cups (9–11 oz/280-345 g) sugar
½ teaspoon salt

3 eggs
2 tablespoons light corn syrup or treacle (golden syrup)
½–¾ cup (4–6 oz/125–185 g) sugar*
2 cups (8 oz/250 g) self-rising flour
¾ cup (6 fl oz/185 ml) milk or water
salt
vegetable oil or melted butter
1½ cups (12 oz/375 g) cooked *azuki* (red bean) paste

First make the *azuki* paste. Thoroughly wash the beans and place in a large saucepan. Cover generously with cold water and bring to the boil, then drain. Cover again with water and bring to the boil.

🐝 Simmer over medium-low heat until the beans are tender and the liquid is almost completely absorbed; at this point drain off any excess water, as the final paste should be quite thick. Stir in the sugar and salt and continue to cook over low heat, stirring constantly, until the mixture is thick and the beans are partially crushed. Set aside to cool before using.

🐝 Beat the eggs and corn syrup together, then add the sugar and continue beating until the mixture is light and the sugar has dissolved. Sift in the flour and add half the milk or water and a large pinch of salt. Mix well, then set aside for 10 minutes before adding the remaining milk or water. If necessary, add extra water to make the batter the consistency of heavy cream.

🐝 Rub a wide, heavy skillet with a piece of paper towel dipped in vegetable oil or melted butter. (Or use an ungreased, non-stick pan.)

🐝 Drop in large spoonfuls of the batter and cook until golden brown underneath and bubbles appear across the top surface. Flip over and cook the other sides, then remove from the pan and cover with a cloth until all are cooked.

🐝 When ready, spread half the pancakes thickly with the red bean paste, cover with the remaining pancakes and pinch the edges together. Wrap in little squares of waxed paper and serve just warm.

Japanese sweets are invariably quite sweet, so the amount of sugar can be adjusted to taste.

SERVES 8–10

Korea

KOREAN BARBECUE WITH *BULGOGI* SAUCE, COOKED CUCUMBER SALAD,
CHILI PICKLED CABBAGE, TOASTED DRIED SEA LAVER AND SPICED WHITEBAIT
recipes page 56-57

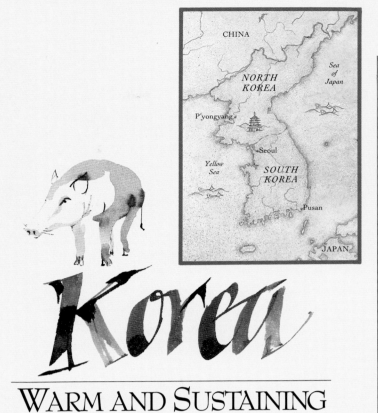

Korea

WARM AND SUSTAINING

The extreme climate of Korea has dictated warming and sustaining food. Chilies and pepper are used in abundance, with garlic and sesame — seeds, oil and paste — combining with them to produce strong, dominant flavors. In one particular beef and onion soup, *yukkai jang kuk,* there is so much chili powder that the soup is stained bright red, and the impact of a single mouthful can be overwhelming.

Beef, seafood and beans are the main ingredients used by the Korean cook, supplemented by eggplant, cabbage in profusion, the giant white *daikon/loh buk* radish, and cucumbers. Limited range, but enough to create some unique flavor combinations.

Economy cuts are often preferred to the more tender muscle meats — as witness the menu in even quite upscale Korean restaurants, where ox tongue, tripe, tail, liver, kidneys and heart all feature prominently. Cooking is by the *kui* method — that is, barbecuing, broiling (grilling) — or *cheegay* (thin stews, halfway between a soup and a casserole).

Seafoods are diverse. Tiny silver whitebait are seasoned and crisp-cooked to serve as *joet khal,* a spicy side dish. Some of the world's best abalone are found here; crabs and crayfish, scallops and clams of several species, and shrimp are all used extensively. Squid and cuttlefish are braised, simmered or stuffed; octopus is stewed with strong seasonings into a quite incomparable dish (ask any fisherman what dish it is that he eats most of). Tangle kelp, curly green and red-purple seaweeds, and compressed sea laver formed into crisp, dry, purple-green sheets provide extra nutrients in a limited cuisine, and lend their distinct fresh-from-the-sea tastes. *Keem kui,* served as a side dish, is toasted sea laver seasoned with sesame oil and salt.

The Koreans have an inordinate fondness for beans — fortunately, as they are a good source of proteins that can be in short supply in their diet. Mung beans are cooked whole, sprouted into short silver needles or ground into a flour to make the popular snack *bindae duk,* rather starchy fried pancakes seasoned with chopped *kim chee.* Soybeans, similarly, are cooked whole, sprouted into long golden slivers or used to make bean curd, while the small red *azuki* bean, which is popular in Japan and China, makes the base of many Korean desserts.

A Korean meal is not complete without white rice, which is served even if noodles are a main course. Soup is also on the menu daily – either a rich and fiery beef- and chili-based type or the cool, quenching *naing kuk,* cold cucumber soup. But perhaps even more indispensable to a meal is *kim chee.* Throughout the fall, when the large *wom bock* (Chinese cabbage) is sweet and tender, *kim chee* is made in every household. The cabbage is cut up, salted and seasoned with chili, salt, pepper and garlic and packed down in gigantic stone jars to ferment into the robust-flavored *kim chee* so loved throughout the country. *Daikon/loh buk* (the giant white radish), green cabbage, spinach and cucumbers are also made into *kim chee,* and occasionally the brew is made more pungent by adding dried shrimp or fish.

Everyday Korean food is simple: rice, *kim chee* and perhaps another small side dish, with a *cheegay.* A banquet to celebrate a wedding, christening or similar occasion, by contrast, is always as lavish as possible. Important state dinners may offer as many as thirty main courses, with a mass of little *na mool* (side salads) and a varied assortment of *kim chee.* Traditionally guests are seated on soft cushions around low tables, while *kisaeng* girls, those trained in the fine art of serving and entertaining, much like the *geisha* of Japan, offer food with silver chopsticks, entertain with song and dance, and ensure that the wine glass is never empty.

Korean cuisine has not yet achieved worldwide acclaim. One dish, however, is always sought after by those who have tried it. The Korean barbecue, *bulgogi,* is a masterpiece of flavor combinations and an enjoyable way to entertain informally. *Bulgogi* is cooked at the table on a conical hot plate mounted over a portable gas ring or charcoal fire. Wafer-thin strips of beef – thoroughly marinated in sesame oil, soy sauce, minced green onions, garlic and ginger, with ground sesame seeds adding their particular nutty flavor – are quick-grilled and dipped into an accompanying sauce. White rice, bowls of soup, several *na mool* dishes and *kim chee* complete the gamut of flavors and textures that make *bulgogi* irresistible.

Guchul pan is an interesting dish of pancakes boasting nine different fillings. Tiny pancakes are wrapped around egg, shredded black mushrooms, grated carrot or radish, chopped *kim chee,* sautéed beef, diced green onions and ground toasted sesame seeds.

Shinsulro is a filling tabletop hotpot of meats, vegetables and nuts simmered together, and eaten with a tart vinegar and soy sauce dip.

The local wines are potent enough to compete with the strong flavors of Korean food. *Jungjong,* similar to *sake,* is brewed from fermented rice, while *suju* is a vodka-style spirit made from grain or potatoes. Koreans rarely drink tea, preferring a rejuvenating red ginseng infusion or a roasted barley "tea" similar to that enjoyed by the Japanese.

Red beans, rice and nuts are the prime ingredients of desserts and sweets. Honey is often preferred to sugar for sweetening, and a number of Korean dessert dishes lean towards a salty rather than sweet flavor. An unusual innovation is the fresh fragrance of pine introduced into simple rice cakes by steaming them over bundles of fresh pine needles.

DANCERS IN TRADITIONAL COSTUME

JANE MONT

MUNG BEAN PANCAKES *(RIGHT),* AND STUFFED SQUID, *recipe page 55*

BINDAE DUK

Mung Bean Pancakes

Little crunchy pancakes, based on ground mung beans with diced ham and kim chee, *make a tasty appetizer served with chili and soy sauce dips. They are eaten hot or cold.*

1¼ cups (8 oz/250 g) hulled split mung beans*
1½ cups (about 5 oz/155 g) finely diced raw ham or salt
   pork
1½ cups (about 3 oz/90 g) chopped *kim chee* (chili pickled
   cabbage)
3 tablespoons chopped green onions
2 teaspoons crushed garlic
1 teaspoon salt
½ teaspoon black pepper
2 large eggs
vegetable and sesame oils

Soak the mung beans overnight in cold water, then drain well. Place in a food processor, blender or mortar and grind to a fairly smooth paste, adding about 1 cup (8 fl oz/250 ml) cold water.

❧ Stir in the remaining ingredients except the oils, beating until well mixed. If you don't have any *kim chee* you can use finely chopped Chinese cabbage. In this case, add a little chili powder to the pancake batter.

❧ Heat a heavy skillet (frying pan) and oil lightly with a mixture of vegetable and sesame oils. Drop spoonfuls of the batter onto the skillet and cook until golden underneath, with small bubbles appearing on the surface. Flip over and cook the other side. As they cook, stack the pancakes under a cloth until the remainder are done. Serve hot or cold with chili and soy sauce dips.

* Mung beans which have been peeled and split in half. Substitute soy beans, canned chickpeas (garbanzos), or yellow lentils.

MAKES 18

GUCHUL PAN

Pancakes with Nine Fillings

This delightful dish is an innovative and economical way to serve a do-it-yourself-style appetizer or main dish. It is usually presented in a special lacquered wood or china tray with the requisite number of compartments. But it is just as effective served on a tray in small bowls or dishes. The pancakes can be made in advance and kept refrigerated until needed, and many of the fillings can also be prepared ahead of time for convenience.

The selection here is representative, but other fillings, such as the accompaniments on pages 56 to 57, could also be used.

PANCAKE BATTER

1½ cups (6 oz/185 g) all-purpose (plain) flour
1 large egg, well beaten
1 cup (8 fl oz/250 ml) cold water
1¼ cups (10 fl oz/310 ml) milk
⅓ teaspoon salt
large pinch each of white pepper and chili powder
oil, butter or lard

NINE FILLINGS

8 large dried black Chinese mushrooms, soaked
1 large carrot
4-in (10-cm) piece giant white radish (Japanese *daikon*/
   Chinese *loh buk*)
8 green onions
3 egg whites
4 egg yolks
1 cup (about 4 oz/125 g) *kim chee*
10 oz (315 g) lean beef rump or fillet
sesame oil
vegetable oil
light soy sauce
salt, pepper and sugar
2–3 tablespoons white sesame seeds

PANCAKES WITH NINE FILLINGS, *recipe page 53*

SAUCE DIP

¾ cup (6 fl oz/185 ml) light soy sauce
2½ tablespoons Chinese brown vinegar
2 tablespoons finely minced green onions
1 tablespoon white sesame seeds, toasted and ground
large pinch each of sugar and chili powder

Sift the flour into a mixing bowl and make a well in the center. Add the beaten egg, water, milk and seasonings and beat until smooth, then set aside for 20 minutes.

❧ Drain the Chinese mushrooms, reserving the liquid. Discard the stems, then squeeze out as much water as possible from the caps and shred them very finely. Place in a small dish and simmer for 6 minutes with 2 tablespoons soy sauce, 2 teaspoons sugar and enough of the reserved water to just cover. Drain well.

❧ Peel the carrot; cut lengthwise into thin strips, then into fine shreds. Cut the shreds into 1-in (2.5-cm) lengths. Heat a small pan, add a very little vegetable oil and a few drops of sesame oil and stir-fry the carrot until softened but still uncolored. Add a little salt, pepper and soy sauce and remove from the heat. Rinse out the pan.

❧ Peel and grate the radish and cook in the same way as the carrot, omitting the soy sauce. Trim the green onions, cut into short lengths and shred finely. Stir-fry briefly in vegetable oil until just softened.

❧ Beat the egg whites until slightly frothy, adding a very small pinch of salt and pepper. Rub a small omelet pan or a well-seasoned wok with oil and pour in the egg. Tilt the pan so that the egg runs thinly over as wide an area as possible. Cook until firm but not colored on the underside, then flip over and cook the other side briefly. Repeat this with the egg yolks, taking care to cook them gently so they do not burn. Cut into narrow shreds, then cut crosswise into short lengths.

❧ Very finely shred the *kim chee,* squeezing to remove as much liquid as possible. Cut the beef into paper-thin slices (having it partially frozen will make this easier), then cut crosswise into very fine shreds. Heat a little vegetable oil and sesame oil together in a pan or wok and stir-fry the beef until it changes color, then splash in 1 tablespoon soy sauce, a sprinkle of salt, pepper and sugar and a little extra sesame oil.

❧ Toast the sesame seeds in a dry pan over moderate heat until they turn golden and begin to pop. Remove, cool slightly and grind to a fairly fine powder.

❧ Mix the sauce ingredients together and divide among several small dishes. Rub the omelet pan or wok again with oil. Pour in a large spoonful of the batter and cook until

underside is golden and small bubbles appear on the surface. Flip over and cook the other side. Continue to cook pancakes over medium heat until batter is used up, stacking the pancakes under a cloth.

❧ Serve the pancakes and fillings at room temperature on a tray with the dipping sauce.

SERVES 6 AS AN APPETIZER

NAING KUK
Cold Cucumber Soup

2 medium cucumbers, each about 6 in (15 cm) long
2 tablespoons light soy sauce
1½ tablespoons white vinegar
1 tablespoon chopped green onions
½ teaspoon sugar
½ teaspoon chili powder
1½ teaspoons sesame oil
5 cups (1¼ liters) chicken stock
2 teaspoons white sesame seeds

Peel the cucumbers and slice very thinly. Place in a dish and add the soy sauce, vinegar, green onions, sugar, chili powder and sesame oil. Set aside for 1 hour, then add the chicken stock.

❧ Toast the sesame seeds in a small pan over medium heat until they turn golden and begin to pop, then grind finely.

❧ Transfer the soup to a tureen and sprinkle on the sesame seeds. Serve at room temperature or slightly chilled.

SERVES 4–6

YUKKAI JANG KUK

Hot Chili Beef and Onion Soup

This chili-red soup is exceptionally hot. It is said that the time to serve it is in the hottest months, when the perspiration it induces has a cooling effect on the diner. It is equally effective ammunition, however, against winter cold.

1 lb (500 g) braising beef
8 cups (2 liters) water
1½ tablespoons hot chili powder
2 tablespoons sesame oil
12 green onions
2 teaspoons crushed garlic
1 tablespoon white sesame seeds, toasted and ground
1 teaspoon sugar
½ teaspoon white pepper
1½ tablespoons dark soy sauce

Cut the beef into cubes and place in a saucepan with the water. Bring to the boil, then reduce heat and simmer gently for 1½–2 hours until the meat is falling apart.

Mix the chili powder with the sesame oil. Trim and shred the green onions. Heat the chili powder and sesame oil in a pan and fry the green onions with the garlic for 2 minutes. Add the sesame seeds, sugar, pepper and soy sauce and fry for 2–3 minutes over medium heat.

Lift out the meat, drain well and toss in the pan for a few minutes. Return the contents of the pan to the stock and bring to the boil, simmering until the soup is well flavored.

SERVES 6

BEEF AND ONION SOUP *(TOP)* AND COLD CUCUMBER SOUP *(BOTTOM)*

OJINGU CHIM

Stuffed Squid

2 lb (1 kg) small squid
2 tablespoons vegetable oil
4 oz (125 g) lean ground (minced) beef
1 cup (3 oz/90 g) chopped cabbage
1 cup (3 oz/90 g) chopped fresh bean sprouts
3 tablespoons finely chopped green onion
1 teaspoon crushed garlic
3 dried Chinese black mushrooms, soaked
1¼ tablespoons light soy sauce
2 teaspoons sesame oil
salt and white pepper

Clean the squid under running water. Remove clear inner quill, pull away the head and tentacles, then cut off the tentacles just above the head. Pull off the skin, discarding the little flaps. Wash squid thoroughly. Very finely chop the tentacles and sauté in the vegetable oil with the meat, cabbage, bean sprouts, green onion and garlic.

Drain the mushrooms, squeeze out as much water as possible, remove the stems and chop the caps finely. Add to the pan and stir-fry for 1 minute, then add the soy sauce, sesame oil, salt and pepper.

Fill the squid with the prepared stuffing, securing the opening with small wooden picks. Set in a lightly oiled dish, sprinkle on a little extra sesame oil and steam over rapidly boiling water for about 20 minutes. Remove from the steamer, cut the squid into thick slices and serve with Vinegar/Soy Dip (see page 56).

Alternatively, the squid can be steamed for 10 minutes, then deep-fried until crisp and golden on the surface in a mixture of 4 parts vegetable oil to 1 part sesame oil.

SERVES 6

SHIN SUL RO

Korean Hotpot

Ever economical, the Korean cook has devised a wide range of tasty and winter-warming dishes using the less expensive meat cuts combined with vegetables and nuts. This cook-at-the-table one-pot dish is served with a biting vinegar/soy sauce dip. The meat and vegetables are eaten first; then the stock, well flavored by the ingredients and pepped up with chili, is served as a soup with a sprinkling of diced green onions.

8 oz (250 g) beef or calves' liver
salt and black pepper
vegetable and sesame oils
8 oz (250 g) prepared tripe
4 oz (125 g) lean beef rump or fillet
4 oz (125 g) lean ground (minced) beef or pork
1 egg
light soy sauce
1 small carrot
6 dried Chinese black mushrooms, soaked
8 cups (2 liters) rich beef stock
3 oz (90 g) canned bamboo shoots, drained
12–18 canned gingko nuts, drained
2 tablespoons pine nuts, optional
1 fresh red chili, shredded
2–3 green onions, shredded or diced

Very thinly slice the liver, sprinkle with salt and pepper and fry lightly in a little vegetable oil with a few drops of

KOREAN HOTPOT, *recipe page 55*

sesame oil until colored and sealed on the surface. Set aside.

Boil the tripe for 8 minutes in lightly salted water; drain and cut into narrow strips.

Cut the beef into thin slices. Pound with a meat mallet or the side of a cleaver and cut into small squares.

Mix the ground (minced) meat with the egg, adding salt, pepper and a few drops each of sesame oil and soy sauce. Form small meatballs with wet hands. Fry in a half-and-half mixture of sesame and vegetable oils until lightly browned.

Peel and slice the carrot. Drain the mushrooms and remove the stems. Bring the stock to the boil in a suitable vessel in the center of the table. Add the meat, vegetables and nuts and simmer gently for about 15 minutes. Spoon straight from the pot into small bowls with the vinegar/soy dip.

When the meat and vegetables have been eaten, add the finely shredded chili and green onions to the remaining stock and serve in soup bowls.

VINEGAR/SOY DIP

¾ cup (6 fl oz/185 ml) light soy sauce
¼ cup (2 fl oz/60 ml) white vinegar
¼ cup (2 oz/60 g) white sesame seeds, toasted and ground
2 teaspoons finely chopped green onions

Mix all ingredients. The sauce keeps for several days in the refrigerator without the green onions, one day with the green onions added.

SERVES 6

BULGOGI

Korean Barbecue

Bulgogi or Bulgalbi, *broiled (grilled) beef strips and ribs of beef respectively, exemplify an age-old tradition of cooking on a curved iron hotplate – a tradition that is matched in northern China and neighboring Mongolia as introduced by the Manchurians. Today this has been streamlined for table service, with specially built cone-shaped hotplates fitted over tabletop burners, to provide an enjoyable and intimate eating experience. Meats of all kinds, including mutton, pork and poultry, offal and seafood, are cooked in this way, being first marinated in a spicy mixture encompassing the characteristic seasonings: soy sauce, sesame oil, garlic, ginger, pepper or chili, toasted sesame seeds and green onions. The meat is marinated well in advance so that the flavor is intense. Cooking*

time is minimal – just enough to cook through and seal the surface. Serve Bulgogi *with white rice and* yangnyum kanjang *sauce (below), together with a selection of accompaniments such as* kim chee *and* jeot khal *(see page 57).*

2 lb (1 kg) lean beef or tenderloin (rump or fillet)
½ cup (4 fl oz/125 ml) light soy sauce
¼ cup (2 fl oz/60 ml) dark soy sauce
½ cup (4 fl oz/125 ml) water
3 tablespoons finely chopped green onion
2–3 teaspoons crushed garlic
2 teaspoons finely minced fresh ginger
½ teaspoon black pepper
1 tablespoon sugar
2 tablespoons white sesame seeds, toasted and ground
1 tablespoon sesame oil

Cut the beef across the grain into very thin slices, then cut into narrow strips. In a glass or stainless steel dish mix all remaining ingredients together. Add the beef and stir thoroughly. Cover and let marinate for at least 3 hours.

Preheat a tabletop broiler (griller), protecting the tabletop with an asbestos mat or other suitable heat shield.

Each diner, or the host/hostess, places a portion of meat on the broiler (griller) and cooks it quickly on both sides. The meat is dipped into the sauce before eating. Use wooden chopsticks or small forks/fondue forks.

SERVES 6

YANGNYUM KANJANG

Sauce for Bulgogi

¼ cup (2 fl oz/60 ml) light soy sauce
1½–2 tablespoons water
1 tablespoon rice wine or Chinese brown vinegar
1 tablespoon finely chopped green onions
½ teaspoon crushed garlic
½–1½ teaspoons chili sauce
1½ teaspoons white sesame seeds, toasted and ground

Mix all ingredients and divide the sauce among several small dishes. It can be prepared up to a day in advance and stored in a covered container in the refrigerator.

SERVES 6

KOREAN GARNISHES AND ACCOMPANIMENTS

*Korean food is traditionally simple, earthy and sustaining. Fanciful garnishes are the preserve of chefs in charge of elegant banquets; day-to-day foods receive little more embellishment than a sprinkling of toasted ground sesame seeds, a little chopped green onion, some shreds of dried toasted sea laver, or some needle-fine shreds of dried chili (*silgochu*). The interest is brought to meals via an array of little full-flavored side dishes featuring pungent* kim chee, *the hot and spicy cabbage pickle without which no Korean meal would be complete.*

Accents like crisp keem kui *(slivers of toasted dried sea laver),* jeot khal *(little crisp spicy fish resembling whitebait) and the variety of salad dishes known as* na mool *– which include marinated cabbage and eggplant, seasoned spinach and bean sprouts, and cooked cucumber salad,* oi bok kum na mool, *below – are always on hand.*

KEEM KUI
Toasted Dried Sea Laver

Tissue-thin sheets of dried and compressed sea laver (keem) are toasted lightly until they turn bright green, then cut into small pieces to serve as a side dish with main courses, rice or vegetables.

Throughout the waters surrounding Korea, Japan and northern China, this type of laver is harvested and processed to be put to many uses in cooking – as a garnish, a vegetable, an edible food wrapper or as part of a mixed condiment.

6 sheets dried compressed sea laver
1 tablespoon sesame oil
½ teaspoon salt

Brush the sea laver sheets on one side with the sesame oil, then sprinkle lightly with salt.

Suspend over a gas flame or place under a hot broiler for about 8 seconds, until the laver turns bright green; do not let it burn or catch fire.

Cool slightly, then cut into small squares and arrange on a serving plate.

SERVES 8

OI BOK KUM NA MOOL
Cooked Cucumber Salad

1 large cucumber
1¼ teaspoons salt
1½ tablespoons sesame oil
2 tablespoons finely chopped green onion
2 tablespoons light soy sauce
1–2 teaspoons chili powder
1½ teaspoons sugar
1 tablespoon white sesame seeds, toasted and ground

Peel the cucumber and cut into wide strips, discarding seed core, then cut crosswise into sticks. Place in a colander and sprinkle with the salt. Set aside for 10 minutes to drain, then rinse and dry thoroughly.

Heat the sesame oil in a pan and fry the cucumber with the chopped green onion over medium heat until it begins to soften. Add the soy sauce, chili powder and sugar and toss until the seasonings are evenly distributed. Transfer to a serving dish and sprinkle with the sesame seeds. Serve warm or slightly chilled.

SERVES 4

JEOT KHAL
Spiced Whitebait

8 oz (250 g) whitebait or other very tiny whole fish
3 egg whites
¾ teaspoon salt
1 tablespoon white sesame seeds, finely ground
1½ teaspoons chili powder
oil for deep-frying
2 tablespoons sesame oil

Wash the fish and dry thoroughly. Beat the egg whites, then blend in the salt, ground sesame seeds and chili powder.

Heat the oil to moderately hot. Dip the fish into the egg-white mixture, then drop into the hot oil and deep-fry until golden brown and crisp. Lift out with a slotted spoon and drain well on paper towels. (The fish can be stored, when cool, in an airtight container.)

Just before serving, heat the sesame oil in a wide skillet to very hot. Add the fish and fry, stirring frequently, until heated through and crisp. Serve at once.

SERVES 4–6

KIM CHEE
Chili Pickled Cabbage

Traditionally kim chee is made months in advance and laid down in large stone jars to mature. It is readily available, in varying degrees of chili-intensity, in stores specializing in Oriental produce. But this simplified recipe for a use-within-a-week version of kim chee is practical and tasty.

2 lb (1 kg) Chinese cabbage
1 tablespoon salt
2 tablespoons chopped green onion
2 teaspoons crushed garlic
1 tablespoon chili powder
2 teaspoons finely chopped fresh ginger
½ cup (4 fl oz/125 ml) light soy sauce
½ cup (4 fl oz/125 ml) white vinegar
2 teaspoons sugar, or more to taste
sesame oil

Chop the cabbage coarsely and place in a glass dish. Sprinkle with the salt and let stand for 3–4 hours; the cabbage will wilt. Mash with the fingers until the cabbage is still softer, then drain off excess liquid and add the remaining ingredients, except the sesame oil.

Transfer to a large jar, seal and leave in a cool place for at least 24 hours before using. It will keep for up to a week in the refrigerator. Sprinkle with a few drops of sesame oil before using.

KOREAN CHILDREN, CHANGG YONG PALACE

TRANQUIL FISHING IN THE PEARL RIVER, GUANGXI PROVINCE
JAN WHITING SUBIACO

China

CRISP CRABMEAT BALLS *(TOP LEFT), recipe page 69,* SHREDDED CHICKEN WITH BEANSPROUTS *(TOP RIGHT),* STEAMED WHOLE FISH *(BOTTOM LEFT), recipes page 74,* WINTER MELON AND HAM SOUP *(FAR RIGHT), recipe page 70,* AND CHINESE VEGETABLE WITH OYSTER SAUCE *(BOTTOM RIGHT), recipe page 82*

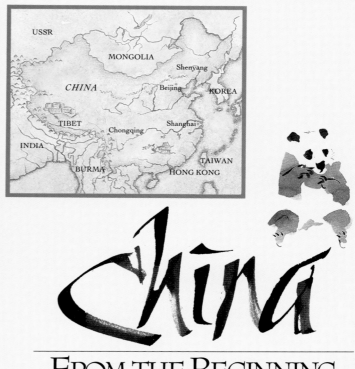

China
FROM THE BEGINNING OF TIME

Because of its vast size and age-old culinary heritage, China boasts a cuisine unmatched in its breadth and scope. With a terrain ranging from fertile river flats to arid wastelands, from inhospitable mountain ranges to a rich coastal strip; and with a climate ranging from subtropical to tundra, the Chinese have evolved a cuisine which encompasses many cooking styles.

While each small region has its own specialty dishes based on deep-rooted traditions and the availability of ingredients, the cuisine can be dissected for convenience into four major styles corresponding roughly to geographical divisions: southern, eastern/coastal, western/central and northern.

Cantonese (Guangzhou) food, that cuisine of southern China which has long been known and enjoyed in the West, is, at least on the surface, the least complex. The underlying ideology of the Guangzhou cook is skilful preparation, a well-honed knowledge of the use of seasonings, and an unfettered imagination.

There is an old saying, "A Cantonese will eat anything with four legs except a piece of furniture, and anything that flies except a kite" – or perhaps, in more modern translation, an airplane. It well applies. For this food-loving people there is scarcely anything that cannot in some way be made to taste absolutely delicious.

Cantonese food is characterized by thin clear sauces, subtle flavors and light seasonings, by brightly colored crisp vegetables, by the restrained use of meat – pork is most popular – and by its variety of fresh fish and shellfish. Rice is the accompanying staple, for the abundant rice crops harvested in this fertile region have made Kuangtung the rice bowl of China.

ON THE WAY TO MARKET, XIAN

The *chao* method of cooking – quick stir-frying in a minimum of oil over super-high heat (gas or flame from charcoal or wood chips, never electricity) – is the chosen cooking method, with a minimum of seasonings judiciously added to enhance the fresh natural tastes, never to envelop or mask them. *See yau* (soy sauce), a dash of *jiu* (rice wine) and a sprinkle of salt, pepper and sugar are added to the wok along with shreds of fresh *geung* (ginger), shredded green (spring) onion, the occasional shredded chili and perhaps a few minced *dow see* (salted black beans). All are bound together with a thin film of near-transparent sauce created out of fresh stock and cornstarch (cornflour).

Chao cooking is done in a flash, so the foods need to be cut small to cook through quickly. A caring Guangzhou chef ensures that the ingredients for a particular dish are cut to the same size and shape – shreds, dice or small strips – and he coordinates colors and selects textures with the skilled eye and instinct of an artist. These nutritious stir-fried dishes are meant not only to satisfy the palate, but also to please the eye.

One of the most popular of the Kuangtung eating traditions, and one that has traveled to other parts of China as well as to the Western world, is that of *yum cha*. In specialty restaurants, diners are served tiny cups of fragrant or green tea to sip while nibbling the offered choice of *dim sum*, by passing waiters. Bite-size steamed stuffed dumplings encasing shrimp, diced pork, chicken and peanuts; vegetables with diced fungi; little baked or fried pastries with a wealth of tasty fillings; mouthfuls of fresh-tasting steamed or spicy braised meats; little filled steamed buns and so on – a good *dim sum* house offers up to fifty choices.

The coastal strip from southern Fukien, bordering Kuangtung, to north of the Yangtze River basin offers a diverse range of foods – naturally with the emphasis on seafoods and Yangtze River fish. The southernmost region, Fukien province, has a distinct cooking style that has been borrowed by neighboring Taiwan. Here a thin rice *juk* (gruel) accompanies meals instead of plain rice. Dishes are lightly seasoned but rich in taste from the use of strongly flavored stocks, and many meat dishes are given the particular *chiu chou* taste by being marinated in a fermented grain mash, the residue left from winemaking. Amoy, the central city, is famed for its quality soy sauce, but much of it is exported, as soy sauce is used sparingly here. For dipping crisply fried foods, a spicy ground pepper and salt mixture or a thickened, sweetened soy sauce are often preferred.

A potent tea accompanies the Fukien meal. So powerful that even moderate excess can cause instant heart palpitation, it is served in thimble-size porcelain cups to be downed in one sip.

This eastern/coastal region encompasses the

major city centers of Hangchow and Soochow as well as Shanghai, all three having played an important role in the development of Chinese cuisine in the past. They were wealthy centers in which important families entertained often and lavishly, vying with each other to present the most creative and opulent meals. The foods therefore are still imaginatively conceived, richly flavored and well seasoned, though not hot.

Dishes cooked by the ancient *keng* method of braising and stewing, or by red-stewing *(hong shao)*, are favored, the sauces being rich and deep brown in color. Vegetables are abundant and are used in many recipes as well as served separately with most meals. The liberal use of sugar gives many dishes a sweetness not found in other parts of China. *Sha* (deep-frying), *bao* (explode-frying, in which the foods are quickly cooked in intensely high heat) and steaming round out techniques. These methods result in crisp-textured seafoods and vegetables and tender braised meats. An array of steamed dumplings, meatballs and thick, round wheat-flour noodle dishes are highlights of this tasty and sustaining cuisine.

The food from the central/western region, of which the provinces of Hunan and Szechuan are the major partners, is power-packed and stimulating. Intense flavors, the unsparing use of chili, garlic, onions and ginger, with *lot yau* (chili oil), *ma yau* (sesame oil), *see jeung* (bean pastes and sauces), and aromatic Szechuan pepper *(fagara)* from the prickly ash tree make this a cuisine with impact.

Fertile Hunan province has a wide range of local produce to call upon and its specialty dishes are diverse and interesting. But the food of Szechuan province has developed along a singular route – that of making do with what is available. And in this area, that has meant chilies and peppers of all kinds; garlic and onions; soybeans aplenty to transform into soy sauce, bean pastes and bean curd; pork and poultry, eggplants, cabbage and peanuts.

Foods tend to be braised, crisply fried or dry-cooked, the seasonings and resultant flavors complex and intense. Textures are dryish to the point of being chewy, or tender-moist from simmering and braising as characterized by one of the most famed dishes of the region, *ma po dofu.*

Northern food, in comparison, is of almost severe austerity. It includes plainly cooked meats, done by the *kao* method of roasting, baking or grilling; wheat-flour breads instead of rice; millet gruel in the average household as the staple; some poultry and a limited variety of vegetables, cabbage being the most predominant.

Seasonings are minimal – garlic and onions, a little soy sauce, lashings of *jiu* (rice wine) for marinating and sauces. Chilies and bean paste are used sparingly and only occasionally, the latter being served as a dip rather than used as a seasoning ingredient; its best-known role is in the famed Peking Duck.

Wheat-flour breads come in many shapes and sizes, either steamed in bun or small loaf shapes, or roasted as hollow sesame buns (see page 82) which,

A CHILD POSES WITH HER BOWL AND CHOPSTICKS   LEO MEIER/WELDON TRANNIES ·

when cooked are filled with shredded meats, or crisply fried to snack on or nibble throughout a meal. There are wheat-flour noodles served in savory broths, or with shredded meats or vegetables and a strong, tasty sauce.

During the season, *bok choy* and *wom bock* are packed down in stone jars with salt and chili to be served throughout the year as a side dish. Much like the Korean *kim chee,* they contribute valuable vitamins to an otherwise limited diet.

Neighboring Mongolia has left its imprint on the cuisine of northern China in several notable instances. The use of lamb in the local cooking is a practice adapted from the Mongols, and one which has not been taken up in other Chinese regions. Mongolian barbecue, a dish of ancient origin attributed to Kublai Khan's marauding warriors, comprises slivers of marinated meat – usually beef cut paper-thin – quickly fried on a hot iron griddle. Originally, it is believed, these griddles were the iron shields of the warriors. The Mongolian hotpot is a communal meal of slivered meats, noodles and vegetables simmered in a tabletop cauldron.

The classic Peking Duck dominates as a pinnacle of culinary achievement with its lacquer-red crisp skin, succulent tender meat, and the original concept of wrapping the duck in one-mouthful-size pancakes with *dow sa* (sweet sauce) and onion. This dish alone has brought the food of northern China to world prominence.

FRIED SPRING/EGG ROLLS *(TOP)*, STEAMED PORK DUMPLINGS *(CENTER)*, *recipe page 69,* AND SHRIMP TOAST *(BOTTOM)*

CHA CHUEN GUEN

Fried Spring/Egg Rolls

Crisply fried spring/egg rolls, packed with finely shredded fillings of meat, mushrooms, bean sprouts and bamboo shoots, epitomize the taste of China t) the westerner. The fillings are many and varied according to taste. Wrappers also vary from thin egg-based crêpes and wafer-thin rice flour rounds to the commercially prepared frozen square wrappers that are now readily available and simple to use. Suitable accompaniments are light soy sauce, chili sauce and ketchup for dipping.

Traditionally, these tasty treats were prepared as a spring festival snack and were filled with the freshest of bamboo shoots.

12 8-in (20-cm) prepared frozen spring roll (egg roll)
    wrappers
4 oz (125 g) lean pork or chicken
1 oz (30 g) pork fat
2 oz (60 g) canned bamboo shoots, drained
2 oz (60 g) fresh bean sprouts
2 dried black mushrooms, soaked
2 green onions
1½ tablespoons vegetable oil
1 tablespoon light soy sauce
1 teaspoon sugar
salt and white pepper
2 teaspoons cornstarch (cornflour)
oil for deep-frying

Thaw the wrappers under a clean cloth and leave covered until needed; they very quickly dry out and become un-usable if exposed to the air. Thinly slice the pork or chicken and the pork fat and cut into very fine shreds. Shred the bamboo shoots and halve the bean sprouts. Drain the mushrooms, squeeze out excess water and discard the stems. Cut the caps into fine shreds. Trim the green onions, discarding the green tops (these can be reserved to use as decoration for another dish). Cut the white parts into 1½-in (3-cm) lengths, then shred finely lengthwise.

Heat the 1½ tablespoons oil in a wok. Add the pork or chicken and pork fat and stir-fry for 1 minute, then add the vegetables and stir-fry briefly. Sprinkle on the soy sauce, sugar, salt and pepper and stir together for 30 seconds over high heat.

Mix the cornstarch with 2 tablespoons cold water. Pour into the wok and stir until the filling clings together. Remove from the wok and spread on a plate to cool.

To assemble, place a wrapper diagonally on the work surface so that there is a corner pointing away at each side. Place a portion of the filling a little below the center, towards the bottom corner. Fold up the lower corner, pinching the filling into a tubelike shape, then fold in the two sides and roll up towards the top corner. Moisten the corner with a little cold water, pinch tightly closed and set aside.

When all are prepared, heat the deep-frying oil over medium-high heat. Deep-fry the rolls until crisp and golden. Lift out and drain well. Serve in a dish or basket lined with folded paper towels.

MAKES 12

HA TO SIE

Shrimp Toast

Although shrimp (prawn) toast is a rather recent innovation, it quickly became one of the most popular of dim sum. Minced ham or cilantro (fresh coriander) can be substituted for the sesame seeds. Serve the shrimp toast with sweet and sour sauce or a spicy tomato ketchup.

6 slices white sandwich bread
8 oz (250 g) peeled fresh shrimp (prawns)
2 tablespoons finely chopped green onions
2 tablespoons finely chopped canned water chestnuts
1 oz (30 g) pork fat, very finely chopped
2 teaspoons ginger juice
¾ teaspoon salt
2 egg whites, lightly beaten
2 tablespoons cornstarch (cornflour)
black and white sesame seeds
oil for deep-frying

Cut each slice of bread in half or quarters (triangles or squares) and remove the crusts. Arrange on a work surface and let stand for about 2 hours to dry out slightly.

Combine the shrimp and the remaining ingredients except the sesame seeds and oil in a food processor and grind to a smooth paste. Use a wet knife or spatula to spread the mixture thickly over each piece of bread, smoothing the edges. Cover half of each piece with black and half with white sesame seeds, in a diagonal design; or use white on half the shrimp toasts, black on the remain-der.

Heat the oil to the smoking point. Slide in the bread, filling down, and fry until the surface is golden. Turn and cook the other side, then lift out and drain well.

Arrange on a paper napkin-lined platter and serve at once. A sweet and sour sauce or a spicy tomato ketchup are good accompaniments.

MAKES 12 OR 24

CHING CHIAO TZE

Shanghai Dumplings

Plump little dumplings, stuffed with chopped pork and cabbage and steamed on cabbage leaves in large bamboo steaming baskets, are one of the joys of the Shanghai cuisine. Warming and filling, they are virtually a meal in themselves. They are given added spice by a dip of Chinese red vinegar – vaguely sweet and peppery-flavored – mixed with finely shredded ginger.

WRAPPER DOUGH

2 cups (8 oz/250 g) all purpose (plain) flour
1 teaspoon baking powder
½ teaspoon salt
2 egg yolks
¾ cup (6 fl oz/185 ml) warm water

FILLING

3 medium cabbage leaves
8 oz (250 g) lean pork, finely ground (minced)
1 tablespoon finely chopped green onion
¼ teaspoon crushed garlic
1 tablespoon light soy sauce
1 tablespoon ginger juice
2 teaspoons sesame oil
1 teaspoon sugar
large pinch of cracked black pepper
1 tablespoon cornstarch (cornflour)

additional 3–4 large cabbage leaves
3–4 slices fresh ginger
Chinese red vinegar

Combine the flour, the baking powder and salt in a mixing bowl and mix well. Make a well in the center. Beat the egg yolks and water together and pour into the well, working in lightly with a pair of chopsticks. When well mixed, remove to a work surface and knead for 3–4 minutes. Cover with a damp cloth and set aside while preparing the filling.

🦐 Blanch the medium cabbage leaves in boiling water. Drain well, then chop very finely. Mix all the filling ingredients, adding about 2 tablespoons cold water to make the mixture smooth and light.

🦐 Roll the dough out into a sausage shape and cut into about 24 equal pieces. Roll each out into a 4½-in (11.5-cm) round on a lightly greased surface using a dry rolling pin; do not let the top surface of the dough become greasy. Place a spoonful of the filling in the center of each round. Gather up the edges, pinching them into a point in the center, then twist the point around gently to give them their characteristic shape and to ensure that the filling is firmly enclosed.

🦐 Pour boiling water over the remaining cabbage leaves and place them in a steaming basket or on a lightly oiled plate. Arrange the dumplings on top, set on a rack in a steamer and steam for 18 minutes.

🦐 Very finely shred the ginger and mix with the vinegar. Pour into small dishes. Serve the dumplings in the basket with the dips.

MAKES ABOUT 24

SHANGHAI DUMPLINGS *(TOP),* AND STEAMED BEEF BALLS
WITH CILANTRO LEAVES, *recipe page 68*

SALT AND PEPPER CRISPY SQUID

JIEN YIM SIEW YAO

Salt and Pepper Crispy Squid

1¼ lb (625 g) fresh small squid
1 tablespoon rice wine, dry sherry or *sake*
1½ teaspoons grated fresh ginger
1½ teaspoons five spice powder
½ teaspoon ground Szechuan or black pepper
2 teaspoons fine table salt
1½ cups (6 oz/185 g) cornstarch (cornflour)
oil for deep-frying

Clean the squid and pull off the skin and flaps. Cut off the heads just above the eyes, leaving a ring of small tentacles. Remove the clear inner quills and cut the squid tubes into lengthwise strips or rings. Rinse thoroughly in cold water, drain and dry. Place in a dish, sprinkle on the wine and the ginger and set aside for 20 minutes. Drain again and pat dry with paper towels.

Mix the five spice powder, pepper and salt and sprinkle evenly over the squid, then coat with cornstarch. (To do this easily, place the cornstarch in a paper or plastic bag. Add the squid, hold the top closed and shake vigorously for 1 minute. Pour the contents of the bag into a colander and shake over a tray to sift off excess flour. The squid should retain a thin but even coating.)

Heat the oil until a haze forms over the top of the pan. Slide in the squid and deep-fry for 3–4 minutes until very well colored and slightly crisped. Lift out, drain well and serve on folded paper napkins.

SERVES 6

NGAU YUK MAI

Steamed Beef Balls with Cilantro Leaves

Little beef balls atop fronds of fresh cilantro (coriander) leaf are steamed in small bamboo baskets to serve with other dim sum, or as a delicately textured and flavored interlude between courses of a Chinese dinner. Serve these with dips of very hot mustard or chili sauce, and light soy sauce.

1 lb (500 g) lean beef steak (rump/sirloin)
¼ cup (2 fl oz/60 ml) cold water
¼ cup (2 fl oz/60 ml) vegetable oil
½ teaspoon crushed garlic
2 tablespoons chopped green onions
2 teaspoons sugar
½ teaspoon salt
¾ teaspoon baking soda (bicarbonate of soda)
1½ teaspoons sesame oil
2 teaspoons finely grated lemon rind
½ cup (about 1½ oz/45 g) finely diced pork fat
1 medium bunch of cilantro

Cut the steak into small cubes, place in a food processor, blender or meat grinder and grind until smooth. If using a food processor or blender, add the water, oil, garlic, green onions, sugar, salt, baking soda and sesame oil and continue processing to a very smooth paste. Stir in the lemon rind and pork fat, processing briefly. If preparing with a grinder, transfer the meat to a mixing bowl and thoroughly blend in the remaining ingredients, except the cilantro.

Cover the mixture with plastic wrap and chill for about 4 hours; this allows the baking soda time to tenderize the meat.

Use wet hands to form the meat into small balls about the size of golf balls. Lightly grease a plate that will fit inside a Chinese steamer basket (or on a rack in a steamer). Cover the plate with the cilantro and arrange the meatballs on top.

Steam, tightly covered, over rapidly simmering water for about 12 minutes. Serve hot on the same plate.

SERVES 4–6

SUNG CHOI HAI KOU

Crisp Crabmeat Balls with Sweetened Soy Sauce

Delicately textured and subtly flavored crabmeat balls, crisp-fried and accompanied by a thick sweet soy sauce, are a chiu chou specialty. They are served at the beginning of a meal or as a main course, arranged on a bed of crisp-fried vegetable leaves. Variations on this theme include rolls of prepared crabmeat wrapped in bean curd "skins" (the thick skin that forms on soy milk during the process of preparing bean curd) and shrimp or squid balls (or rolls) prepared in the same way.

The traditional method employed for pulverizing the seafood is to pound it on a work surface with the side of a heavy cleaver until reduced to a smooth paste. A food processor eliminates the tedium.

12 oz (375 g) crabmeat, shrimp or cleaned squid
3 oz (90 g) shrimp (prawn) meat or white-fleshed fish
2 oz (60 g) pork fat
2 large egg whites
1½ tablespoons chopped green onions
1 tablespoon light soy sauce
1 teaspoon sugar
2 teaspoons rice wine, dry sherry or *sake*
2 teaspoons ginger juice
1 tablespoon cornstarch (cornflour)
oil for deep-frying
Chinese pepper-salt, see below
sweetened soy sauce, see below
2–3 bean curd skins, optional

Flake the crabmeat and place in a food processor with the shrimp or fish and the diced pork fat. Process with the steel blade until the mixture is very smooth and sticky. Add the egg whites, green onions, soy sauce, sugar, wine and ginger juice, then add about ⅓ cup water, processing until the mixture is smooth and fluffy. Add the cornstarch and blend again briefly.

Heat the oil in a large wok until a haze appears over the pan, then reduce the heat slightly.

Remove a handful of the mixture and squeeze a small knob of it out from between the thumb and curled forefinger. Scrape it off with a Chinese porcelain spoon; it should be an almost perfect ball shape. Drop into the hot oil. Repeat the process, cooking about 8 balls at a time.

When they rise to the surface and are golden brown, lift out and drain well. Cook all of the mixture in this way, keeping the crabmeat balls warm. Arrange on a platter on folded paper towels or shredded lettuce. Serve with little dishes of sweetened soy sauce and Chinese pepper-salt.

To make crabmeat rolls, wipe the bean curd sheets with a damp cloth until they soften. Spread a thick layer of the mixture in the center of each sheet and roll up, keeping the mixture in the center. Deep-fry the rolls until the skin is crisp and the crabmeat cooked through.

Seafood balls prepared in this way have other uses: They can be added to soups (see Fish Ball Soup, page 70), stir-fried with sliced meats and vegetables, or simmered in spicy sauces.

CHINESE PEPPER-SALT

Heat 2 tablespoons fine table salt in a wok. Add 1½ teaspoons finely ground Szechuan pepper, mix well and remove from the heat. Cool before using.

SWEETENED SOY SAUCE

Mix equal parts dark soy sauce and dark corn syrup, adding brown sugar to taste and a few drops of sesame oil.

SERVES 6

SIEW MAI

Steamed Pork Dumplings

These little open-face dumplings are among the most popular of the dim sum *snacks. They are steamed and served in slatted steaming baskets. Round wrappers of the kind used for wonton are ideal for making* siew mai. *These are readily available fresh or frozen, but an alternative wrapper can be made using flour and egg, as below. Serve* siew mai *in the Chinese manner, with little dishes of hot chili sauce and mustard, and light soy sauce.*

3 dozen prepared *wonton* wrappers (or dough, below)

WRAPPER DOUGH

1¼ cups (5 oz/155 g) all purpose (plain) flour
1 egg, beaten with enough water to make ⅓ cup (2½ fl oz/75 ml)
glutinous rice flour

FILLING

6 oz (185 g) lean pork
4 oz (125 g) peeled shrimp (prawns)
1½ oz (45 g) canned water chestnuts, drained
4 dried Chinese black mushrooms, soaked
2 tablespoons very finely chopped green onions
½ teaspoon finely grated fresh ginger
1 tablespoon light soy sauce
½ teaspoon salt
1½ teaspoons sugar
2 hard-cooked egg yolks

To make the wrappers, place the flour into a mixing bowl and make a well in the center. Pour in the egg mixture and work with the fingers until it is thoroughly amalgamated, then knead firmly until dough is smooth. Cover with plastic wrap and set aside for at least 3 hours, in which time the flour will soften, making the dough more elastic.

Dust a work surface with the glutinous rice flour and roll out the dough into a large square. Dust the top with more rice flour, fold the dough in half and continue to roll. Repeat this process until the dough is paper-thin. (The glutinous rice flour will prevent the layers from sticking together; ordinary flour cannot be substituted as it will simply mix with the dough, causing it to become too dry.)

Cut the dough into 2¾-in (7-cm) squares. Keep covered until ready to use, as they dry out quickly. The wrappers can be frozen.

Cut the pork into small cubes and place in a food processor with the shrimp. Grind with the steel blade until smooth, then add the water chestnuts and process again briefly. Drain the mushrooms, discard the stems and chop the caps very finely. Mix the mushrooms, green onions, ginger, soy sauce and seasonings into the pork mixture.

Use a sharp knife to cut the points off the wrappers, leaving rounded shapes. To assemble in the traditional manner, curl the forefinger of the left hand to meet the thumb. Drape a wrapper over them and top with a generous teaspoon of the filling. Press the dumpling down through the hole between finger and thumb so that the wrapper is forced up the sides of the filling in a tiny cup shape; the top of the filling will remain exposed. Tap the dumpling gently on the work surface to flatten the bottom so it can stand upright in the steamer. Sieve the egg yolks and sprinkle over the top of the dumplings.

Rub the inside slats of a bamboo steamer with oiled fingers and arrange the prepared dumplings in the basket. They can be placed close together as they will not expand. Cover the basket with its lid, then stand on a rack in a steamer or large wok over simmering water. Cover and steam for about 12 minutes over high heat. Serve at once in the basket.

MAKES ABOUT 36

AN ELEGANT FEAST IN A CANTONESE RESTAURANT   MICHAEL COOK

TUNG GUA JUNG
Winter Melon and Ham Soup

At the market, the giant, pale green winter melon could easily be mistaken for a watermelon; but when cut, it reveals crisp jade-green flesh. Much prized for both its delicate texture and reputed medicinal qualities, winter melon is most often used in soup rather than vegetable dishes. Chayote (choko) makes an excellent substitute, having quite similar taste, texture and color.

8 oz (250 g) winter melon
4 oz (125 g) unsmoked ham
2 chicken livers
6 dried Chinese black mushrooms, soaked
2 slices fresh ginger
5 cups (1¼ liters) chicken stock
1½ teaspoons rice wine, dry sherry or *sake*
1 tablespoon light soy sauce
salt and white pepper
1½ teaspoons vegetable oil or sesame oil

Peel the melon and cut into small cubes. Very thinly slice the ham, then cut into matchstick strips.

Slice the chicken livers, place in a dish and cover with boiling water. Set aside until needed.

Squeeze the water from the mushrooms and discard the stems. Shred the ginger.

Bring the stock to the boil in a deep saucepan. Add the ginger, mushrooms, melon, ¾ of the ham and the drained livers and bring to the boil. Skim the surface, then simmer gently for about 12 minutes or until the melon is very tender. Skin again and add the wine, soy sauce and seasonings to taste. Pour into a tureen, sprinkle with the oil and garnish with the reserved ham.

SERVES 6

YU DOU T'ONG
Fish Ball Soup

Tender little balls of minced fish, shrimp, crab or squid feature frequently in Chinese dishes. In Chinese cities they can be purchased ready-made to add to soups, stir-fried or braised dishes. But they are easily prepared at home – a food processor making them very light work. The traditional method is to reduce the seafood to a pulp by pounding with the flat side of a cook's cleaver; when completely smooth, it is kneaded, squeezed, lifted from the bowl and slapped down again until it is smooth, sticky and light in texture. When mixing, the action must always be in one direction only or the texture will be spoiled.

The Chinese have a unique and very effective way of making perfectly round balls with this smooth, wet mixture: A handful of the paste is lifted from the bowl, then a portion is squeezed between the curled thumb and index finger. A little Chinese porcelain spoon is used to scrape away the resulting ball, which, with practice, is always a perfectly round shape.

11 oz (345 g) fillets of white-fleshed fish
1 tablespoon rice wine, dry sherry or *sake*
1 tablespoon grated fresh ginger
2 tablespoons very finely minced green onion
½ cup (4 fl oz/125 ml) cold water
¾ teaspoon salt
1 egg white
2 teaspoons softened lard or vegetable oil
1¼ tablespoons cornstarch (cornflour)

5 cups (1¼ liters) fish or chicken stock
1 green onion
1½ oz (45 g) pickled mustard greens
2 tablespoons very finely shredded salted ham

Cut the fish into small cubes and place in a food processor. Add the wine. Place the ginger and minced green onion in a piece of clean cheesecloth and squeeze over the fish to extract as much of the juice as possible. Add the cold water and salt and process until the mixture is smooth and fluffy. Add the egg white, lard or oil and cornstarch and blend again.

Bring a large saucepan of water to the boil. Form the fish balls as explained above and drop into the water. Simmer until they float to the surface, then cook for a further 2 minutes. Lift out on a slotted spoon and discard the water.

Pour the fish or chicken stock into the same pan and bring to the boil. Trim and finely shred the green onion and pickled greens. Add to the stock with the ham and the fish balls and return to the simmer. Serve immediately.

SERVES 6

COLD CHICKEN AND SESAME DRESSED NOODLES *(BOTTOM)*, CHICKEN OMELET *(TOP), recipes page 83,* AND FISH BALL SOUP *(CENTER)*

Dai Gee Ha Dung Woo

Scallops and Shrimp with Three Kinds of Mushrooms

Wild mushrooms and a variety of different types of edible fungi are used extensively in Chinese cooking. The most prized are mushrooms with thick dark brown caps and pale cream undersides. They are regarded as particularly good for the health, and their exorbitant price also means that to serve them to guests is to honor them.

In this dish, fresh woody-tasting straw mushrooms, slippery button mushrooms (a test for chopsticks users!) and dried black mushrooms combine their distinct flavors with fresh seafood.

12 large scallops with their coral
6–7 oz (185–220 g) small peeled raw shrimp (prawns)
2 teaspoons rice wine, dry sherry or *sake*
2 teaspoons light soy sauce
6–8 small dried Chinese black mushrooms, soaked
6–8 canned or fresh straw mushrooms
12 canned or fresh button mushrooms
4 slices fresh ginger
3 green onions
2½ tablespoons vegetable oil
⅔ cup (5 fl oz/155 ml) fish or chicken stock
1½ teaspoons cornstarch (cornflour)
salt, sugar and white pepper
½ teaspoon dark soy sauce

Rinse the scallops in cold water, rubbing them gently with a little salt and cornstarch to remove any fishy smell and to whiten the meat. Prepare the shrimp in the same way, then place them together in a dish and sprinkle with the wine and soy sauce. Set aside for 15 minutes.

Drain the dried mushrooms and squeeze out excess water. Trim off the stems close to the caps and discard. Drain the canned straw mushrooms, or trim the base of fresh mushrooms and cut each in half from top to stem to reveal the tender second mushroom inside. Drain the canned button mushrooms, or trim the stems of fresh ones flat against the caps. Finely shred the ginger and trimmed green onions.

Heat 1½ tablespoons of the oil in a large wok. Add the mushrooms and toss over high heat for 1½ minutes, then splash in about 2 tablespoons water, cover and allow the mushrooms to steam for 2–3 minutes until completely tender.

Pour the mushrooms and pan liquids into a dish. Reheat the wok with the remaining oil and sauté the ginger briefly. Add the scallops and stir-fry until the meat is beginning to firm up and turn white. Add the shrimp and green onions and continue to stir-fry until the shrimp are pink.

Mix the stock and cornstarch. Return the mushrooms to the pan and add the stock. Season to taste with salt, sugar and white pepper and add the dark soy sauce. Stir over high heat until the sauce thickens, then transfer to a dish and serve at once.

SERVES 4–6

SCALLOPS AND SHRIMP WITH THREE KINDS OF
MUSHROOMS *(RIGHT)*, AND CRYSTAL SHRIMP *(LEFT)*, recipe page 75

WESTLAKE FISH

Sai Wu Chou Yu

West Lake Fish

The city of Hangchow is situated on the famed West Lake, one of China's most picturesque tourist attractions. Hangchow has always had a reputation for culinary excellence. Couple the skill of a Hangchow chef with the tender-fleshed carp fished from the lake, and you have a dish that deserves its accolades as one of the most important in China.

3-lb (1½-kg) fresh silver carp or freshwater trout
2 tablespoons rice wine, dry sherry or *sake*
1 tablespoon grated fresh ginger
1 teaspoon crushed garlic
oil for deep-frying
cornstarch (cornflour)
3 tablespoons chopped green onions
1–2 fresh red chilies
3 tablespoons sugar
3 tablespoons Chinese red vinegar
1 tablespoon dark soy sauce
1 cup (8 fl oz/250 ml) fish stock or water
salt and pepper
sesame oil

Slit open the cleaned and scaled fish, cutting from the underside through to the backbone without severing the fish completely in two. Cut through the head as well so that the fish can be laid out flat. Place in a dish and rub with a mixture of half the wine and ginger and the garlic. Set aside for 20 minutes.

Heat the oil in a wide pan or large wok to the smoking point. Coat the fish thickly with cornstarch, then brush off the excess. Slide into the oil and cook over high heat for about 5 minutes, or until the surface is crisp and the fish is cooked through. Lift out, drain and place on a large platter.

Pour off the oil and wipe out the wok. Return about 3 tablespoons of the oil. Stir-fry the remaining ginger with the green onions and finely chopped chili. Push to one side of the pan. Add the sugar and cook until it melts and turns a light golden color. Add the vinegar, soy sauce and remaining wine and boil briefly, then add the stock or water and bring to the boil. Simmer for 3 minutes.

Mix about 1 tablespoon of cornstarch with a little cold water and stir into the sauce. Boil until the sauce thickens, then add salt, pepper and sesame oil to taste. Pour over the fish and serve at once.

SERVES 8

CH'ING CHENG HSIEN LI YU

Steamed Whole Fish

Steaming brings out the best in fresh fish, accentuating its delicate taste and texture, retaining its natural moisture and preserving vital nutrients.

The classic steamed fish with five shreds has a mix of finely shredded bamboo shoots, ginger, green (spring) onions, black mushrooms and carrot or omelet as its dressing. Use all of these, or a trio of ginger, green onions and mushrooms, when cooking a whole fresh fish in this way.

1¼-lb (625-g) whole fresh sea bass/snapper
5 slices fresh ginger
2 large dried Chinese black mushrooms, soaked
2 green onions
1½ tablespoons vegetable oil
1 tablespoon rice wine, dry sherry or *sake*
2 tablespoons light soy sauce
½ teaspoon sugar
fresh cilantro/coriander

Scale and clean the fish and rinse thoroughly under cold running water. Drain well and wipe dry. Make several deep diagonal slashes on each side to decorate the fish and to allow the flavors of the seasonings to penetrate.

Place on a lightly oiled plate that will fit inside a steamer or on a rack inside a large saucepan.

Very finely shred the ginger. Drain the mushrooms and squeeze out as much water as possible. Discard the stems and shred the caps finely. Trim the roots and dark green tops from the green onions. Cut into 2-in (5-cm) lengths, then shred finely lengthwise.

Sprinkle the vegetable oil, wine, soy sauce and sugar evenly over the fish, then arrange the shredded ingredients on top.

Place in the steamer or saucepan over 2-in (5-cm) of simmering water. Cover tightly and steam for about 20 minutes; the fish is ready when it flakes easily at the thickest part.

Lift out, surround with cilantro and serve at once with rice to absorb the tasty juices on the plate.

SERVES 4–6

GAI NGA CHOY

Shredded Chicken with Bean Sprouts

8 oz (250 g) boneless chicken breasts
¾ teaspoon sugar
3½ teaspoons rice wine, dry sherry or *sake*
2½ tablespoons vegetable oil
1 teaspoon cornstarch (cornflour)
pinch of salt
2 large green onions
1 slice fresh ginger
5 oz (155 g) fresh bean sprouts
1 small carrot
1 tablespoon light soy sauce

Cut the chicken into thin slices, then stack the slices together and cut crosswise into narrow shreds. Place in a dish and add sugar, 1½ teaspoons of the wine, 2 teaspoons of the vegetable oil, cornstarch and salt. Mix well, cover and leave for 15 minutes.

Trim the green onions, cut lengthwise into quarters, then cut into 2-in (5-cm) lengths. Shred the ginger. Pick off roots and pods from the bean sprouts, rinse in cold water and drain well. Peel and trim the carrot, cut into 2-in (5-cm) lengths, then thinly slice lengthwise and cut into matchstick strips.

Heat the remaining oil in a wok over high heat. Add the chicken and stir-fry for 1½ minutes, until it changes color, then remove and set aside. Add the carrot and stir-fry for 1½ minutes, until it begins to soften slightly, then add the green onions, ginger and bean sprouts.

Sizzle the remaining wine and the soy sauce onto the sides of the pan, stir in and return the chicken. Toss together quickly over high heat for 30 seconds, then serve.

SERVES 4

HAINAN GAI FAARN

Hainan-Style Chicken Rice

The island of Hainan off the coast of southern China boasts a few regional specialties. One of the best known is this simple meal of white rice, green vegetables and poached chicken, served with a soup made from the stock in which the food was cooked and a little dipping sauce of minced green onions and ginger with salt and oil.

3-lb (1½-kg) fresh chicken
2 green onions
4 slices fresh ginger
¾ teaspoon salt
2 cups (12½ oz/400 g) short-grain white rice
2¾ cups (22 fl oz/645 ml) water
2 tablespoons rendered chicken fat*
1¾ lb (625 g) kale or other Chinese green vegetables
1½ teaspoons sesame oil
3 tablespoons ginger dip, see below
salt
light soy sauce

Rinse the chicken and wipe dry. Place in a saucepan with water to just cover. Trim the green onions and add to the pan with the ginger and salt. Bring to the boil, then reduce the heat to very low and simmer for about 45 minutes until the chicken is completely tender. Lift out and set aside until chicken skin is dry to touch.

Meanwhile, combine the rice and water in a pan, cover and bring to the boil. Turn the heat down to very low and cook for 15–18 minutes, until all the water has been absorbed and the rice is tender and fluffy. When almost ready, stir in the rendered chicken fat.

Trim the kale and add to the stock. Simmer for about 8 minutes until very tender. Lift out and drain well.

Brush the chicken skin with the sesame oil, then place chicken on a cutting board and use a sharp cleaver to cut in half, cutting through on each side of the backbone. Discard the backbone. Spread the chicken open and cut through the breast to divide in half, then remove the wings and drumsticks. Diagonally slice the two sides of the chicken, cutting straight through the bones.

Arrange the chicken on a serving plate, reassembling it approximately in its original shape. Surround with the drained vegetables, also brushed with a little sesame oil. Serve the chicken and vegetables at room temperature with the rice and prepared dip.

Boil up the stock in which the chicken and vegetables were cooked. Add salt and soy sauce to taste and serve in small bowls as a soup.

HAINAN-STYLE CHICKEN RICE

GINGER DIP

Pound 2 tablespoons of chopped green (spring) onions and 1½ tablespoons of grated fresh ginger to a paste, adding 3 tablespoons of vegetable oil. Season with 1–1¼ teaspoons of salt and mix well.

Remove the deposits of fat from inside the cavity of the chicken. Place in a small saucepan and cook gently, partially covered, until the fat has been drawn off.

SERVES 4–6

CH'ING CH'AO HSIA JEN

Crystal Shrimp

24 peeled medium shrimp (prawns) (about 1¾ lb/750 g)
1 tablespoon ginger juice
1 tablespoon cold water
¼ teaspoon white pepper
4 green onions
4 slices fresh ginger
1 medium carrot
1 medium cucumber
3 tablespoons vegetable oil
1½ teaspoons cornstarch (cornflour)
½ cup (4 fl oz/125 ml) chicken stock
1½ teaspoons rice wine, dry sherry or *sake*
½ teaspoon sugar
1 teaspoon light soy sauce

Rinse the shrimp under cold running water, rubbing alternately with salt and cornstarch; this whitens the meat and removes any fishy odor. Make a slit in the center back of each shrimp, then open up and flatten slightly by pounding with the side of a cleaver. Pass the tail of each shrimp through the slit to curl them attractively. Place in a dish and sprinkle with the ginger juice, cold water and pepper.

Trim the green onions, using only the firm white end of each one. Cut in half and use the point of a sharp knife to shred the ends. Place in a dish of ice water to curl up.

Very finely shred the ginger. Peel the carrot and cucumber and thinly slice lengthwise. Cut into 2-in (5-cm) lengths, then into matchsticks. Place in ice water until needed.

Heat the vegetable oil in a wok and stir-fry the shrimp and ginger until the shrimp are half cooked. Gradually mix the cornstarch into the stock. Add the wine, sugar and soy sauce to the wok and stir over high heat for a few seconds, then add the stock and cook quickly until the sauce thickens and turns transparent.

Drain the carrot and cucumber and arrange on a serving dish. Top with the shrimp and sauce, then surround with curls of green onion.

SERVES 4

SAUTÉED ABALONE WITH LETTUCE IN OYSTER SAUCE

HAO YU PA CHIN TS'AI

Sautéed Abalone with Lettuce in Oyster Sauce

10 oz (315 g) canned abalone
2 tablespoons finely chopped green onions
1 teaspoon finely chopped fresh ginger
2½ tablespoons lard or vegetable oil
¾ cup (6 fl oz/185 ml) chicken stock
1 teaspoon sugar
2½ tablespoons oyster sauce*
1 head lettuce
1 tablespoon cornstarch (cornflour)
white pepper
1 tablespoon finely minced ham

Drain the abalone thoroughly. Place flat on a work surface and hold firmly in place; cut horizontally into thin slices.

❧ Sauté the green onions and ginger in the lard or oil for about 30 seconds over high heat, then add the sliced abalone and sauté for 1 minute. Add the chicken stock, sugar and oyster sauce and bring to the boil. Simmer for 5 minutes over low heat, then remove the abalone with a slotted spoon and pile in the center of a serving dish.

❧ Rinse the lettuce, separating the leaves. Drop into the pan, cover and cook for about 45 seconds, then turn and continue to cook, covered, for another 45 seconds to 1 minute, until tender. Lift out and arrange around the abalone.

❧ Mix the cornstarch with a little cold water. Stir into the sauce and bring to the boil, stirring. Simmer until thickened, then pour over the abalone and lettuce. Season generously with pepper and garnish with the ham. Serve at once.

Some brands of oyster sauce are very salty and may require additional sugar to taste.

SERVES 6

SAN HSIEN KWO PA

Sizzling Seafood on Crisp Rice Cakes

The Chinese chef cooks his rice by the absorption method. Therefore he is left with a layer of rice adhering to the bottom of the pan. This can be easily soaked off and discarded, and in most rural Chinese households, the chickens or ducks enjoy this daily treat. But the ever-enterprising and economical Chinese cook has, in his inimitable way, found a use even for this potential discard. The layer of rice is cooked until it is golden and crisp-hard, then served with a tomato-red sauce filled with diced meat, vegetables or, most popularly, shrimp (prawns) and chili.

6 oz (185 g) peeled small shrimp (prawns)
6 oz (185 g) fillets of white-fleshed fish
4 oz (125 g) cleaned squid
1 tablespoon rice wine, dry sherry or *sake*
2 teaspoons cornstarch (cornflour)
½ teaspoon salt
2 oz (60 g) canned bamboo shoots, drained
1 medium carrot
2 oz (60 g) canned small button mushrooms
2 oz (60 g) frozen or half-cooked fresh peas
2 green onions
4 slices fresh ginger
10–12 2-in (5-cm) pieces crisp rice, see below
2–3 tablespoons vegetable oil
oil for deep-frying

SAUCE

3 cups (24 fl oz/750 ml) water
½ cup (4 fl oz/125 ml) tomato ketchup
1 teaspoon dark soy sauce
2 tablespoons white vinegar
1½ tablespoons sugar
2–3 teaspoons chili sauce with garlic
2–3 drops red food coloring, optional
2½ tablespoons cornstarch (cornflour)

Cut the shrimp in half lengthwise and scrape out the dark vein. Rinse shrimp quickly in cold water, pat dry with paper towels and place in a dish. Cut the fish into 1-in (2.5-cm) cubes and the squid into fine rings. Place in the dish with the shrimp; add the wine, cornstarch and salt, stir and set aside for 10 minutes.

❧ Cut the bamboo shoots into small cubes or slices. Peel and slice or cube the carrot to match the bamboo shoots. Cut the mushrooms in half. Thaw the peas. Trim the green

SIZZLING SEAFOOD ON CRISP RICE CAKES

onions and cut into thin diagonal slices. Finely shred the ginger.

✵ Prepare the crisp rice in advance, by cooking 1¾ cups (12 oz/375 g) short-grain rice in 2½ cups (20 fl oz/625 ml) water slowly over low heat until tender. Press into a layer in a greased baking dish. Bake in a medium-low oven until dry and crisp. Break into 2-in (5-cm) squares. Set aside.

✵ Heat the vegetable oil in a wok. Stir-fry the carrot for 1 minute, then add the seafood and stir-fry over high heat until firm, about 2 minutes. Add the bamboo shoots, mushrooms, peas, green onions and ginger and stir-fry for 1 minute. Transfer to a plate.

✵ Mix the sauce ingredients and pour into the wok. Bring to the boil, then simmer for 2–3 minutes, stirring frequently, until the sauce is thick and clear. Return the seafood and vegetables and leave over low heat while the rice cakes are fried.

✵ Heat the deep-frying oil in a large wok or deep skillet until a haze forms over the pan. Place the rice cakes in a frying basket, lower into the oil and fry until crisp and golden. Drain and place in a serving bowl.

✵ Bring the rice and sauce to the table separately. Pour the sauce over the rice and serve.

SERVES 6

Peh Ching K'ao Ya

Peking Duck

The magnificent lacquered red of a Peking Duck is a masterpiece in culinary achievement. The lengthy preparation means that it is not a dish prepared in the home kitchen. The plump-breasted ducks, specially bred for the purpose, are coated with a malt sugar solution and hung until the skin is glazed and dry, resembling parchment. Then air is forced between meat and skin so that the skin cooks dry and crisp, for serving as a separate course. When ready to cook, the carcass is filled with hot water and the duck suspended within a special oven so that the water inside cooks the meat moist and tender, while the dry heat applied to the exterior ensures that the outer appearance will be just right.

Peking Duck, which is usually served as the centerpiece of a special banquet, is presented and carved in front of the guests with elaborate ceremony. First the whole duck is displayed to the host and guests. Then a gloved and aproned cook wields cleaver swiftly and deftly, removing only the shiny crisp skin, which he arranges in overlapping rows on a wide platter.

This is served with small wheat-flour pancakes, sticks of cucumber or green onion and a sweet bean paste, the meat and accompaniments being wrapped neatly in the pancakes to be held with the fingers.

The cook returns to the bird to carve the second course, this time the most tender parts of the meat from breast and thigh, which are served in the same way.

Finally the carcass, with its remaining meat, is returned to the kitchen to be cooked into subsequent courses – shredded meat with bean sprouts and green onions, and a thin creamy soup with onions.

This recipe, while not authentic, is simple to prepare and a delicious substitute.

5-lb (2½-kg) plump duck
⅓ cup malt sugar, honey or treacle
⅓–½ cup (2½–4 fl oz/75–125 ml) boiling water
8 green onions
1 cup sweet bean paste or *hoisin* sauce
1 recipe Peking Duck Pancakes (see page 82)
shredded fresh ginger and shredded fresh chili
light soy sauce

Clean and rinse the duck, then hang in an airy place for 3–4 hours until the skin is dry. Mix the malt sugar, honey or treacle with the boiling water. Place a drip tray beneath the duck and then pour on several cups of boiling water. Drain and pat dry.

✵ Brush on enough of the syrup to coat evenly and let stand 1 hour to dry. Coat once or twice again until all of the syrup has been used.

✵ Place the duck on a rack in a roasting pan and roast in a preheated 400°F (200°C) oven for 45 minutes, then turn the duck and roast a further 45 minutes–1 hour until the skin is deeply colored and the meat cooked through. If the duck begins to darken too early, decrease the oven temperature to 375°F (190°C) and continue roasting, then increase to 475° (250°C) for the final 10 minutes to crisp the skin.

✵ Slice and serve as described above, with sticks of green onion, sweet bean paste or *hoisin* sauce and pancakes for wrapping.

✵ Stir-fry the remaining meat with shredded green onions, ginger and a few shreds of hot chili, adding a splash of light soy sauce.

SERVES 6

PEKING DUCK AND PEKING DUCK PANCAKES, *recipe page 82*   WELDON TRANNIES

CRISP-FRIED SHREDDED BEEF WITH VEGETABLES

KAN PIEN NIU JOU SSU

Crisp-Fried Shredded Beef with Vegetables

For extra flavor, add 1 tablespoon hot bean paste in place of 2 tablespoons of the soy sauce. Garlic enthusiasts will enjoy this dish with the addition of 6–8 cloves of finely chopped garlic.

1 lb (500 g) beef rump steak
⅓ cup (2½ fl oz/75 ml) light soy sauce
1 tablespoon rice wine, dry sherry or *sake*
1¼ teaspoons sugar
1 teaspoon minced fresh ginger
6 tablespoons vegetable oil
8 oz (250 g) young celery
1 medium carrot
1 medium onion
1 medium-size green pepper (capsicum)
1–3 fresh red chilies
1½ teaspoons sesame oil
salt

Cut the beef into very thin slices, then cut across the slices into fine shreds. Place in a dish and add the soy sauce, rice wine, sugar, ginger and 1½ tablespoons oil. Mix well, cover with plastic wrap and set aside for 2 hours.

Trim the celery, carrot, onion, pepper and chili and cut into long fine shreds.

Heat 2 tablespoons of the oil in a wok and stir-fry the chili over high heat for 1 minute. Add the other vegetables and stir-fry for 2 minutes. Transfer to a plate and set aside.

Add the remaining oil to the wok and heat to the smoking point. Slide in the meat and stir-fry quickly over high heat until the meat is quite dark and crisped at the edges; do not let the slices stick together. Return the vegetables to the wok. Add the sesame oil and a little salt, if needed. Toss together briskly and serve.

SERVES 6

MU SHU PORK

Pork and Mushrooms with Egg

A popular Peking home-style dish, mu shu *pork combines an array of local wood mushrooms with tender pork, the dish being bound with beaten egg. It is often served sandwich style in little crisp sesame buns (see page 82), but goes just as well with plain white rice.*

8 oz (250 g) pork tenderloin (fillet)
½ teaspoon sugar
2½ tablespoons light soy sauce
2 teaspoons rice wine or dry sherry/*sake*
1 tablespoon cornstarch (cornflour)
½ oz (15 g) dried 'cloud/wood ear' fungus, soaked
6 small dried Chinese black mushrooms, soaked
1 oz (30 g) canned button mushrooms (champignons)
2–3 fresh oyster mushrooms
1½ oz (45 g) canned bamboo shoots
3 green onions
3 slices fresh ginger
3 large eggs
1 teaspoon salt
3 tablespoons vegetable oil
¾ teaspoon crushed garlic
½ cup (4 fl oz/125 ml) chicken stock
½ teaspoon sesame oil

Slice the pork very thinly, then cut into small squares. Place in a dish and add the sugar, ½ tablespoon soy sauce and half the wine and cornstarch. Mix well and let stand for 20 minutes.

Drain the fungus and cut into narrow shreds or small squares. Drain the black mushrooms, remove the stems and cut the caps into quarters. Drain the button mushrooms or champignons and cut in half. Slice the oyster mushrooms. Drain the bamboo shoots and cut into thin slices. Trim the green onions, cut into 1¼-in (3-cm) lengths and cut each in half lengthwise. Shred the ginger.

Beat the eggs with half the salt. Heat 1 tablespoon of the oil in a wok. Pour in the beaten egg and cook over medium heat, lifting the egg as it firms on the bottom to allow the uncooked egg to run beneath. When just holding together, transfer to a plate.

Wipe out the wok and add the remaining oil. Stir-fry the pork until it changes color, then remove with a slotted spoon. Add the mushrooms, bamboo shoots, green onions, ginger and garlic and stir-fry over high heat for 3 minutes. Add the remaining soy sauce, wine and salt. Stir the remaining cornstarch into the stock, pour into the wok and stir over high heat until the mixture thickens and the ingredients hold together. Lightly stir in the egg, sprinkle with the sesame oil and serve.

SERVES 6

PORK AND MUSHROOMS WITH EGG, AND SESAME BUNS, *recipe page 82*

RICE FIELDS NEAR GUIYANG, HUNAN PROVINCE

Au Larm

Spicy Braised Beef

The harsh climate in central-western China calls for warm, sustaining food. Here, an inferior cut of meat is transformed into tasty tenderness by the judicious use of local seasonings – in this case brown peppercorns, a sweet bean paste, dried tangerine peel and star anise. Serve with plenty of white rice.

2 lb (1 kg) flank or shank (shin) beef
2 medium onions
12 slices fresh ginger
10 cloves garlic
2–3 pieces dried tangerine peel or the peel of 1 fresh mandarin
3 whole star anise
2 tablespoons vegetable oil
2 teaspoons Szechuan peppercorns
2 teaspoons cracked black peppercorns
¼ cup (2 fl oz/60 ml) rice wine, dry sherry or *sake*
¾ cup (6 fl oz/185 ml) dark soy sauce
3 tablespoons *hoisin* sauce or sweet bean paste
rice

Cut the meat into 2-in (5-cm) cubes and place in a deep saucepan. Add water to cover. Peel and quarter the onions and add to the pot with the ginger slices, 3–4 cloves of peeled garlic, the tangerine peel and star anise. Cover and bring to the boil. Skim the surface, then reduce heat and simmer for 2½ hours.

Peel and chop the remaining garlic. In a wok or small saucepan fry the garlic in the oil with the Szechuan and cracked black pepper for 1 minute over medium heat. Add the remaining ingredients and cook together, stirring, for about 2 minutes, then pour into the pot and return to the boil. Skim the surface again, cover and simmer 45 minutes – 1 hour, until the meat is tender enough to break up with a fork. Remove the star anise and tangerine peel before serving with white rice.

SERVES 6

SPICY BRAISED BEEF *(BOTTOM)*, AND SPICY BRAISED EGGPLANT *(TOP), recipe page 82*

TWICE-COOKED PORK *(LEFT)* AND BRAISED PORK WITH TARO *(RIGHT)*

HUI KWO JOU

Twice-Cooked Pork

To achieve supreme tenderness, Szechuan chefs cook this popular dish in two stages. The layered "five-flower" pork, with its rind still attached, is first simmered until partially tender, then sliced and stir-fried wirh red and green pepper and a selection of seasoning pastes and sauces.

Meat is a rare treat for many Chinese, so when it is prepared for a family meal, great care will be taken to ensure perfect results.

12 oz (375 g) fresh bacon or pancetta
    (belly pork)
1 small fresh red chili or pepper (capsicum)
1 large green pepper (capsicum)
6–8 garlic chives or 2 green onions
3 tablespoons vegetable oil
1 teaspoon sesame oil
½ teaspoon crushed garlic
2 teaspoons hot bean paste
2 teaspoons *hoisin* sauce or sweet bean paste
2 teaspoons light soy sauce
2 teaspoons rice wine, dry sherry or *sake*
2 tablespoons chicken stock or water
1 teaspoon sugar

Rinse the pork with cold water, place skin up in a saucepan and add water to cover. Bring to the boil slowly, then reduce heat and simmer for about 30 minutes. Lift out, drain very well and use a sharp knife to closely score the skin in a criss-cross design. Cut into thin slices, then cut each slice into 2½-in (6.5-cm) lengths. Set aside.

Cut the chili and/or pepper in half; remove the seeds and inner ribs. Chop the chili finely and cut the pepper into small squares. Trim the garlic chives or green onions and cut into 2-in (5-cm) lengths, cutting thicker shoots in half lengthwise as well.

Heat the vegetable oil in a wok with the sesame oil. Stir-fry the pork over high heat until it is colored and crisp in places. Set aside. Stir-fry the chili and peppers for about 30 seconds, then add the garlic and garlic chives and stir-fry for another 30 seconds.

Mix the remaining ingredients together and pour into the wok. Stir well, then return the pork and toss together until the sauce evenly coats the pork and peppers. Serve at once.

SERVES 4–6

WU TAU MAN JIEW YUK

Braised Pork with Taro

2-lb (1-kg) piece fresh ham (pork leg)
2 tablespoons dark soy sauce
oil for deep-frying
4 green onions
5 slices fresh ginger
1½ lb (750 g) fresh taro
½ cup (4 fl oz/125 ml) light soy sauce
1 tablespoon rice wine, dry sherry or *sake*
1 tablespoon sugar
2 teaspoons sesame oil
black pepper
salt, optional
cooked rice

Pour boiling water over the pork skin, then wipe dry. Rub with half the dark soy sauce and allow to dry.

Heat the deep-frying oil in a wide pan or large wok until a haze of smoke forms over the pan. Add the pork, skin side down, and fry until it is a rich golden brown with little bubbles over the skin. Lift out and place in a saucepan with cold water to cover. Bring slowly to the boil.

Trim the green onions and cut in half. Shred the ginger. Peel the taro and cut into 1-in (2.5-cm) cubes. Place in a saucepan and cover with plenty of cold water. Set aside.

Add the green onions and ginger to the pork with the remaining dark soy sauce, the light soy sauce, wine and sugar. Simmer for about 1½ hours, until tender.

About 20 minutes before the pork is ready, bring the taro to the boil and simmer until almost tender. Drain.

Lift the pork from the pot, put in the drained taro and place the pork on top. Continue to cook until the pork and taro are both very tender and well flavored with the seasonings. Sprinkle with the sesame oil and black pepper and add a little salt if needed. Serve with rice.

SERVES 6

SHA KWO SHIH TZU T'OU

Braised Pork Meatballs

These super-sized meatballs are affectionately referred to as "Lions' Heads." A hearty meal-in-a-pot, "Lions' Heads" must be tender enough to cut with a single chopstick. They are placed in the center of the table and everyone tucks in, cutting off pieces of the meatball, retrieving a piece of cabbage leaf to accompany it and washing it down with a spoonful of the rich broth from the dish. Add white rice and a dish of hot pickled vegetables and an everyday dish becomes noteworthy.

1½ lb (750 g) lean ground (minced) pork
2 tablespoons minced green onions
2 tablespoons minced bamboo shoots
1 teaspoon minced fresh ginger
1½ teaspoons salt
⅓ teaspoon white pepper
1 tablespoon rice wine, dry sherry or *sake*
1 tablespoon light soy sauce
2 tablespoons cornstarch (cornflour)
1½ lb (750 g) Chinese celery/cabbage
3 tablespoons vegetable oil
4 cups (1 liter) hot chicken stock
cooked rice

Place the pork in a food processor and add the green onions, bamboo shoots, ginger, half the salt, the pepper, wine, soy

BRAISED PORK MEATBALLS

sauce and cornstarch. Blend thoroughly until the mixture is smooth and pastelike, then use wet hands to form into 4 or 5 large balls. Set aside.

Trim the cabbage and cut into 2-in (5-cm) lengths, separating the stems and leaves. Heat the oil in a large wok and stir-fry the cabbage stems for 3 minutes, then add the leaves and stir-fry briefly.

Transfer half the cabbage to a large flameproof casserole. Arrange the meatballs on top and cover with the remaining cabbage. Pour in the stock and sprinkle with the remaining salt. Cover the pot and simmer over very low heat for about 1½ hours until the meatballs and cabbage are both extremely tender. Serve in the casserole with white rice.

SERVES 6

FAA GU DOFU

Black Mushrooms with Bean Curd

The aromatic earthiness of dried faa gu *(black mushrooms) goes well with the blandness of* dofu *(bean curd), and the two often appear together as a vegetable dish or in a hotpot with meats. Rich brown, salty* ho you *(oyster sauce) is the ideal accompaniment.*

12 oz (375 g) soft bean curd
8 large dried Chinese black mushrooms, soaked
2 green onions
2 tablespoons lard or vegetable oil
1 teaspoon finely chopped fresh ginger
¾ cup (6 fl oz/185 ml) chicken stock or reserved mushroom liquid
2 teaspoons rice wine, dry sherry or *sake*
2 teaspoons dark soy sauce
1½ tablespoons oyster sauce
1 teaspoon sugar
2 teaspoons cornstarch (cornflour)

Cut the bean curd into 1-in (2.5-cm) cubes, place in a dish and cover with boiling water. Set aside for 20 minutes, then drain. Drain the mushrooms, squeeze out excess water and discard the stems. Steam the caps for 10 minutes or boil in water to cover for 4 minutes, reserving the liquid.

Trim the green onions, cut lengthwise in half, then into 2-in (5-cm) pieces. Heat the lard or oil in a wok. Stir-fry the green onion and ginger for about 45 seconds, then push to one side of the wok. Add the mushrooms and stir-fry briefly.

Mix the stock or mushroom liquid, the wine and soy sauce together and pour into the wok. Boil briefly, then

slide in the bean curd and simmer gently for 3–4 minutes.

Mix the oyster sauce, sugar and cornstarch and a little cold water or extra mushroom liquid to make a thin paste. Pour into the wok and carefully stir into the sauce, taking care not to break up the cubes of bean curd. Simmer for 2 minutes or until the sauce becomes thick and translucent. Serve.

SERVES 4

NAI YU PA CHIN TS'AI

Chinese Cabbage in a Creamy Sauce

The gigantic pale green wom bok *is one of the most popular green vegetables in the Chinese cuisine. In the north and west they enjoy it as a spicy pickle. In the south it is included in many stir-fried dishes – although here a more stalky dark green kale such as* gai larn *and* choy sum *is preferred for vegetable dishes. In the central area, where vegetable dishes are particularly enjoyed,* wom bok *is braised with tasty sauces; the addition of rendered chicken fat gives extra flavor and an appetizing sheen.*

1¼ lb (625 g) *wom bok* (Chinese cabbage), well trimmed
¼ teaspoon salt
1 cup (8 fl oz/250 ml) chicken stock
1½ teaspoons instant chicken bouillon
½ cup (4 fl oz/125 ml) milk
2 tablespoons vegetable oil
½ teaspoon grated fresh ginger
1 teaspoon rice wine, dry sherry or *sake*
1 teaspoon sugar
1 tablespoon cornstarch (cornflour)
white pepper or chopped red chili
1½ teaspoons sesame oil, optional

Rinse the cabbage thoroughly in cold water and drain well. Chop coarsely. Mix the salt, chicken stock and bouillon granules with half of the milk.

Heat a wok with the vegetable oil and fry the ginger very briefly, then add the cabbage and stir-fry for about 2 minutes. Add the wine and sugar, then pour in the milk mixture. Cover and bring to the boil, then simmer gently until the cabbage is tender.

Mix the cornstarch with the remaining milk and pour into the wok. Stir until the sauce thickens and clears. Dust generously with the pepper and stir in the sesame oil, if used. Serve hot.

SERVES 6

BLACK MUSHROOMS WITH BEAN CURD *(RIGHT)* AND CHINESE CABBAGE IN CREAMY SAUCE *(LEFT)*

Ho Yow Gai Larn

Chinese Vegetable with Oyster Sauce

Gai larn is a thick-stemmed vegetable of the kale family. It has a firm texture and a slightly bitter taste, with tiny dark green leaves.

1 lb (500 g) *gai larn*
2 tablespoons vegetable oil
3 slices fresh ginger, shredded
2 teaspoons sugar, or to taste
2–2½ tablespoons oyster sauce

Trim the *gai larn* and cut into 5-in (13-cm) lengths. Drop into boiling water and simmer for about 4 minutes, then lift out and drain well.

Heat the oil in a wok and stir-fry the greens with the ginger for 2 minutes. Lightly stir in the sugar, then transfer to a serving dish and pour on the oyster sauce. Serve at once.

SERVES 4

Yu Heung Kay Chee

Braised Spicy Eggplant

Eggplants (aubergines) and various kinds of peppers (capsicums) are among the most important vegetable crops in the west central regions of China. Braised with plenty of garlic, ginger and bean sauces, plus the inevitable chili, this is one of the most popular Szechuan specialties, served either as a vegetable side dish or as an economical main course with plain rice.

1 lb (500 g) small purple or green eggplants
salt
½ cup (4 fl oz/125 ml) vegetable oil
1 tablespoon sesame oil
5 green onions
2–3 teaspoons crushed garlic
1 teaspoon finely chopped fresh ginger
2 tablespoons dark soy sauce
1 tablespoon *hoisin* sauce or sweet bean paste
1 tablespoon hot bean paste
1½ teaspoons Chinese black vinegar
⅓ cup (2½ fl oz/85 ml) chicken or beef stock
1 teaspoon cornstarch (cornflour)
cooked rice

Remove the stems of the eggplants but do not peel. Cut into 1-in (2.5-cm) cubes and place in a colander. Sprinkle generously with salt and set aside for 15 minutes to draw off the bitter juices. Rinse thoroughly and drain well.

Heat the vegetable oil with half the sesame oil in a wok. Add the eggplant and fry over medium-high heat for about 3 minutes.

Trim and chop the green onions and add most of them to the pan, reserving a little. Add the garlic and ginger and cook, stirring occasionally, for about 2 minutes until the eggplant is tender.

Add the sauces, hot bean paste and vinegar and simmer a further 2 minutes. Mix the stock and cornstarch, pour into the wok and stir on high heat until the sauce thickens. Sprinkle in the remaining sesame oil. Transfer to a serving dish and garnish with the reserved green onions. Serve with white rice.

To make a more substantial dish, add 4–6 ounces coarsely ground (minced) lean pork, frying it until well

colored. Remove from the wok while cooking the eggplant and return to the wok with the sauces.

SERVES 6

Tsi Ma Bow

Sesame Buns

Bread is served with most northern meals. These tasty little baked breads become hollow in the center when cooked, making them ideal for pocketing tasty cooked meats. Seasoned shredded pork, salty with pickled cabbage, or mu shu *pork are the traditional fillings.*

5 cups (1¼ lb/625 g) all purpose (plain) flour
⅓ cup (2½ fl oz/75 ml) vegetable oil
1¼ cups (10 fl oz/310 ml) boiling water
2½ teaspoons salt
2–3 teaspoons white sesame seeds

In a small skillet or saucepan fry 1 cup of the flour with the vegetable oil until it is a light golden color. Remove from heat and cool.

Pour the remaining flour into a mixing bowl and add the boiling water. Mix very quickly, working with a pair of cooking chopsticks or the handle of a wooden spoon. Transfer the dough to a work surface and invert the bowl over the dough. Set aside for 5 minutes.

Knead on an oiled surface for about 7 minutes until the dough is smooth and pliable. Divide into 12 pieces.

Roll each piece out into a square shape. Spread one side with the flour paste and sprinkle with plenty of salt. Fold in two sides to make a rectangle, pinching the edges together at the ends to enclose the flour paste. Roll the dough out a little larger. Moisten the smooth side and sprinkle with sesame seeds.

Arrange on an oiled baking sheet and bake in a preheated 400°F (200°C) oven for 5 minutes, then turn and bake about 5 more minutes until cooked through, crisp on the surface and slightly puffed up. Cut in half to make 2 pockets from each bread.

MAKES 12

Peh Ching K'ao Ya

Peking Duck Pancakes

1½ cups (6 oz/185 g) all purpose (plain) flour
½ cup (4 fl oz/125 ml) boiling water
sesame oil

Sift the flour into a mixing bowl and make a well in the center. Pour in the boiling water and, working quickly with a pair of cooking chopsticks or the handle of a wooden spoon, beat until well mixed. Lift out and knead gently for a minute or two. Cover and set aside to cool slightly, then knead vigorously for about 8 minutes. Cover with a piece of plastic wrap or a damp cloth and let stand in a warm place for about 15 minutes.

Roll dough out into a long sausage shape and cut into 18–20 pieces. Work with 2 pieces at a time, keeping the others covered to prevent them from drying out. Roll each into a ball and flatten slightly. Brush one side of each piece with sesame oil; press the oiled sides of the pieces together. Roll out the resulting piece of dough on a very lightly floured surface until almost transparent. Repeat with the remaining dough.

🎬 Heat a heavy griddle or nonstick skillet and rub with an oiled cloth until the surface is smooth and shiny. Cook the pancakes until both sides are flecked with brown, then remove from the pan and peel apart. Fold into quarters. Keep covered while the remaining pancakes are cooked. Serve warm with Peking Duck.

🎬 Precooked pancakes can be wrapped in aluminum foil and reheated in a 350°F (175°C) oven, or on a rack in a steamer.

MAKES 18–20

TS'UNG YU PING

Crisp Green Onion Pastries

In the northern regions of China, bread in varying guises – usually steamed – tends to be preferred over rice as the staple starch food. This recipe for crisply fried coils of bread, with a salty filling of diced green onions, is popular as a between-meal snack as well as a meal accompaniment. It is delicious on a wintry day with a warming soup.

2 cups (8 oz/250 g) all purpose (plain) flour
½ teaspoon sugar
1½ teaspoons salt
2 tablespoons vegetable oil
½–¾ cup (4–6 fl oz/125–185 ml) cold water
vegetable and sesame oil for frying
1 cup chopped green onions (about 12)
2 tablespoons white sesame seeds

Sift the flour into a mixing bowl with the sugar and ½ teaspoon of the salt. Make a well in the center and pour in the vegetable oil, then work in enough cold water to make a smooth, soft dough.

🎬 Knead lightly, then divide into 6 portions. Roll each out to ¼-in (¾-cm) thickness. Spread a little sesame and vegetable oil lightly over one side of each piece of dough, cover evenly with the chopped green onions and sprinkle with the remaining salt.

🎬 Roll each piece of dough up into a tight roll, stretch out into a rope, then shape into a coil. Sprinkle lightly with a little extra flour and roll out to ½-in (1¼-cm) thickness.

🎬 Heat a wide flat pan and wipe with a thin film of vegetable and sesame oils. Brush the top of each pastry with cold water, then coat with the sesame seeds. Place unseeded surface down in the pan and cook until the underside is golden. Flip over and cook the other side, then cook the first side again briefly, keeping the temperature at medium-high so the pastries cook through without burning. Add more oils to the skillet with each batch of pastry. Cut pastries into quarters and serve at once.

MAKES 6

CRISP GREEN ONION PASTRIES

FU YUNG GAI

Chicken Omelet

The Cantonese have a particular love for omelet dishes, which they often serve with a strongly flavored oyster sauce.

4 oz (125 g) chicken breast meat
1 teaspoon rice wine, dry sherry or *sake*
½ teaspoon sugar
2 tablespoons vegetable oil
2 tablespoons finely chopped green onion
½ teaspoon grated fresh ginger
5 large eggs
salt and white pepper
chopped fresh cilantro/coriander

SAUCE

¼ cup (2 fl oz/60 ml) chicken stock
1½ tablespoons oyster sauce
½ teaspoon sugar
½ teaspoon cornstarch (cornflour)

Cut the chicken into small dice and season with the wine and sugar. Set aside for 10 minutes. Heat half the oil in a wok. Stir-fry the chicken with the green onion and ginger until the meat is white, then remove from the pan and set aside.

🎬 Wipe out the wok, add the remaining oil and heat thoroughly. Lightly beat the eggs, adding salt and pepper. Pour into the hot pan and fry until the underside begins to firm up, then lift a corner of the omelet to allow the uncooked egg to run underneath.

🎬 When the underside is lightly colored but the top of the omelet is still soft, spread the cooked chicken and onion evenly over the surface of the omelet.

🎬 Use the wok spatula to cut the omelet into quarters, then flip each piece and cook this side until golden brown. Invert onto a serving plate.

🎬 Wipe out the wok. Mix the sauce ingredients, pour into the wok and stir over high heat until bubbling. Pour over the omelet, garnish with the cilantro and serve at once.

SERVES 2–4

E FU MIEN GAI

Cold Chicken and Sesame Dressed Noodles

The coastal province of Fukien boasts many specialty dishes distinctly different from those in other parts of the country. This combination of cold cooked noodles, shredded chicken and vegetables and a creamy sesame dressing has an almost Japanese flavor.

8 oz (250 g) uncooked thin egg noodles*
6 oz (185 g) chicken breast meat
4 oz (125 g) fresh bean sprouts
1½ stalks fresh celery
2 tablespoons vegetable oil
2 tablespoons sesame oil
3 tablespoons Chinese sesame paste or *tahini*
1½ tablespoons dark soy sauce
1–2 tablespoons lemon juice or white vinegar
1 fresh red chili
2 tablespoons chopped green onions
½ teaspoon finely chopped fresh ginger
sugar and salt
2–3 teaspoons toasted white sesame seeds

Drop the noodles into a large pot of lightly salted water and simmer gently until tender. Place the chicken breast on a plate and steam for about 12 minutes until cooked through. Lift out and slice thinly, then cut into narrow shreds. Blanch the bean sprouts and finely shredded celery in boiling water. Drain and refresh with cold water.

Drain the noodles and cool under cold running water. Drain again very thoroughly and pour into a serving bowl. Sprinkle with the vegetable oil and 1 tablespoon of the sesame oil. Top with the shredded chicken, bean sprouts and celery.

Mix the remaining sesame oil with the sesame paste, soy sauce, lemon juice or vinegar and enough water to make a smooth, runny sauce.

Slit open the chili and scrape out the seeds; chop the flesh finely. Mix the chili, green onion and ginger into the sauce and season to taste with sugar and salt. Add a little extra soy sauce if desired. Pour over the noodles and chicken and toss lightly. Sprinkle with the sesame seeds and serve.

Bean curd skins, softened in warm water and cut into fine strips, can be sbustituted for the noodles.

SERVES 6

YUK PIN CHAO MIEN

Sliced Beef and Broccoli Stems on Flat Rice Noodles

Jade-green florets of broccoli enhance many Chinese dishes, but the stems have an equally good taste. Their crisp-tender texture and apple-green color go well with beef in an oyster sauce dressing on ribbony rice noodles.

1 lb (500 g) fresh rice flour sheets or ribbon noodles
6 oz (185 g) beef tenderloin (fillet)
1 teaspoon light soy sauce
1 teaspoon rice wine, dry sherry or *sake*
2 teaspoons cornstarch (cornflour)
salt and sugar
3–4 tablespoons vegetable oil
8 oz (250 g) fresh broccoli stems
1 green onion
3 slices fresh ginger
2 teaspoons dark soy sauce
3 tablespoons oyster sauce
1 cup (8 fl oz/250 ml) chicken stock

If using rice sheets, roll up tightly, then cut across the rolls at ⅓-in (1-cm) intervals to make ribbon noodles. Drop noodles into boiling water and let stand for 2 minutes, then drain.

Very thinly slice the beef, then cut into ¾-in (2-cm) strips. Place in a dish and add the light soy sauce, wine, half the cornstarch, a pinch each of salt and sugar and 1 table-spoon of vegetable oil. Mix well and set aside for 20 minutes.

Use a vegetable peeler to peel the broccoli stems. Trim them into 1¼-in (3-cm) lengths, then carve the ends into slightly rounded shapes so the pieces resemble olives. Trim the green onion, cut into 1¼-in (3-cm) lengths, and cut each in half lengthwise. Shred the ginger.

Heat the remaining vegetable oil in a wok and stir-fry the beef for 1 minute. Set aside. Add the broccoli stems to the wok and stir-fry for 1 minute, then cover the wok and cook for an additional 1 minute, stirring once or twice. Remove from the wok. Increase the heat and fry the noodles for 2 minutes, then push to one side of the wok.

SLICED BEEF AND BROCCOLI STEMS ON FLAT RICE NOODLES

Add the green onion and ginger and fry briefly. Add the seasonings and sauces.

Mix the stock and remaining cornstarch together. Return the beef and broccoli to the wok, pour in the stock and simmer, stirring on high heat until the sauce thickens. Check the seasonings, adding more salt or dark soy sauce if needed. Transfer to a serving dish and serve at once.

SERVES 4

FAA SUN WU

Sweet Peanut Cream

Chinese desserts are rare, but when they do appear on a menu they are sure to impress with their originality. Sweet, thick, souplike puddings are popular in most regions. Served warm, they may have peanuts, black sesame seeds, black rice, water chestnut flour or rice flour as their main ingredient.

A warm sweet dish is usually served only after a large-scale dinner of at least 6 courses.

1½ cups (8 oz/250 g) raw peanuts
3 tablespoons white sesame seeds
8 cups (2 liters) water
½ cup (4 oz/125 g) superfine sugar
4 tablespoons cornstarch (cornflour)
½ cup (4 fl oz/125 ml) heavy (double/thickened) cream, optional (or use evaporated milk)

Roast peanuts in a hot oven until golden, then rub in a kitchen towel to remove the skins. Toast the sesame seeds in a dry skillet until they begin to pop.

Transfer peanuts and sesame seeds to a heavy-duty blender and grind to a fine powder. Add a little of the water and continue grinding until the mixture is smooth and thick. Bring the remaining water to the boil, adding the sugar. Add the peanut mixture and simmer for 10 minutes.

Strain to remove any large pieces of peanut or skins. Return to the pan. Mix the cornstarch with a little cold water and add to the peanut mixture. Bring to the boil, stirring, and simmer until thickened. Stir in the cream or evaporated milk, if used, and heat through briefly. Serve warm.

SERVES 8

Lin Jee Ju Chou T'ong Soey

Sweet Birds' Nest Soup with Lotus Seeds

Prized for their delicate taste and reputed beneficial qualities, birds' nests are among the most expensive of ingredients available in China.

They are gathered from the walls and ceilings of enormous caves in cliffs and on islands along the southern Chinese coast and the coast of Thailand. Collecting them is a risky business, which probably accounts in some measure for their special reputation and their cost.

6 oz (185 g) packaged birds' nests
1½ oz (45 g) dried lotus seeds
5 cups (1¼ liters) water
¼ cup (2 oz/60 g) sugar
½ cup (4 fl oz/125 ml) thin coconut milk, optional

Soak the birds' nests in cold water for about 5 hours. Use tweezers to pick out fragments of feather or other impurities. Rinse well, then drain and cover with boiling water. Let stand for a further 1 hour.

Soak the lotus seeds in cold water for 3 hours, then drain. Cover with boiling water and simmer until tender. Drain and cover with cold water until cool. Use a large needle to push out the heart of each seed; these are bitter-tasting and will spoil the dish.

Bring the 5 cups of water to the boil. Add the sugar and stir until dissolved, then add the birds' nests and lotus seeds and simmer for 5–6 minutes. Stir in the coconut milk, if used, and serve hot.

As a cold dessert, birds' nest goes well with diced fresh fruit instead of the lotus seeds.

SERVES 6–8

Hung Yum Cha

Sweet Almond Curd

This delicate dessert was traditionally made with creamy almond milk, prepared by grinding whole almonds on a special grinding stone. This version, using almond extract, gives similar results.

½ cup (4 fl oz/125 ml) boiling water
1½ tablespoons unflavored gelatin
1½ cups (12 fl oz/375 ml) lukewarm milk or almond milk
½ cup (4 fl oz/125 ml) light (single/thin) cream or half and half
2 teaspoons almond extract
1½ tablespoons sugar
1½ cups (8 oz/250 g) diced fresh or canned fruit

Pour the boiling water into a small heatproof bowl and sprinkle on the gelatin. Let stand until softened, then place the bowl in a small saucepan of boiling water and stir until gelatin is dissolved. Add the milk or almond milk, cream, almond extract and sugar and mix well.

Pour into a lightly oiled rectangular dish, cover and refrigerate until firm. Cut into diamond-shaped pieces and divide among glass dessert dishes. Top with diced fruit and serve cold.

SERVES 6

SWEET BIRDS' NEST SOUP WITH LOTUS SEEDS *(LEFT)*, SWEET PEANUT CREAM *(CENTER)* AND SWEET ALMOND CURD *(RIGHT)*

Philippines

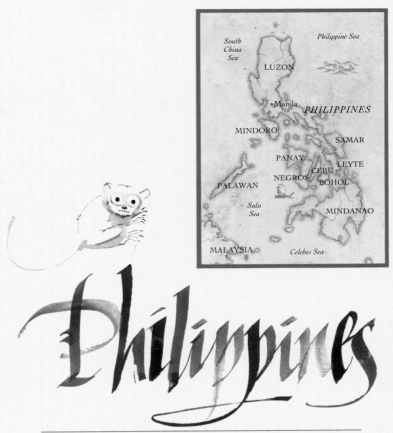

Philippines

EAST MEETS WEST

The food of the Philippines is a homogeneous blending of ideas from many sources. There are *lumpia,* delectable little crêpes filled with sautéed vegetables, lettuce-lined and remarkably like the *popiah* of Malaysia. There is *pancit molo,* a clear soup with *wonton* in the Chinese mode, as well as other *pancit* (noodle) dishes. Then there are *guisado* and *fritata,* Spanish-influenced dishes in which the main ingredients are simmered in a rich tomato sauce, and *adobo,* which is meat simmered with vinegar and garlic before being fried in oil or butter. *Pochero* is another Spanish dish with diced ham, and the pungently flavored *chorizo de bilbao,* sausages of Portuguese and Spanish heritage, are braised with local vegetables. A highly original sauce, based on puréed eggplant or sweet potatoes and flavored with oil, vinegar, garlic and seasonings, accompanies this.

From local sources come such popular Tagalog dishes as *kari kari.* Despite the familiar-sounding name, this is not a Philippine-style curry, but a stew of assorted beef cuts seasoned with local herbs and colored red with *achuete* (annatto) seeds, and thickened with roasted ground rice and peanuts.

Tapa comprises chewy strips of seasoned, sun-dried beef which are fried or broiled to serve with salad. *Paksiw* is a term describing pickled foods; it is usually applied to fish, but sometimes also to pork. It is a strongly flavored, very tart dish that is highly regarded for its stimulating taste as well as for the fact that it can be kept for several days without fear of spoiling.

On festive occasions – and there are plenty in this country that embraces so many different ethnic and religious traditions – there is no dish more enjoyed than *lechon,* a large pig spit-roasted over charcoal or cooked underground in a pit of glowing coals and heated stones. The crisp skin, served separately, is known as *sitcharon.* It is considered a great

COLLECTING SHELLS FROM THE MORO GULF   R. IAN LLOYD, SINGAPORE

PREVIOUS PAGES:
LITTLE SHRIMP PATTIES *(TOP),* CHICKEN IN THE ADOBO STYLE *(CENTER), recipes page 93,* SUN DRIED BEEF *(RIGHT), recipe page 94,* COCONUT PUDDING AND LAYERED CAKE, *recipes page 97*

delicacy and will often accompany cocktails at an important occasion. With *lechon* comes an almost too-rich sauce made from the pig's liver.

There is a wealth of produce to be fished from the surrounding waters. The *lapu lapu,* or spotted grouper, has soft, tender flesh. The *bangus,* or milkfish, which may grow up to 3 or 4 feet in length, is the most commonly used fish. It has, however, a large number of small bones, so among the special skills she must acquire to become a good housewife the Filipina numbers the ability to bone a *bangus.* They can be purchased already pressure-cooked, which renders the bones tender enough to eat with the flesh, but the process somewhat subdues the natural flavor and makes the texture overly soft. *Dilis* (anchovies) are plentiful in the Philippines, a fact that must have been appreciated by Spanish settlers who considered it one of their most important fish. Here, as in the Spanish region of Málaga, several small *dilis* are tied together at their tails, seasoned and battered before being deep-fried.

Bacalhao, the dried salt cod so prized in Spain and Portugal, is used here too, simmered in a hotpot or made into small salty balls. A dish popularized in Central Luzon is *burong dalag:* the tender mudfish is salted and packed down with soft boiled rice colored with *achuete* (annatto) seeds to ferment, after which it is sautéed. The similarity here to the processing of *pa boeuk* roe in Laos is notable.

Vegetables are plentiful in this fertile land and a large number of indigenous vegetables and fruits are used in Filipino cooking. They include taro and yam; the *kangkong,* a kind of wild swamp cabbage; *siguidillas* and *sitaw,* winged beans and long cow peas, both common native vegetables in Thailand; Chinese bean sprouts, bamboo shoots and cabbage; chayote (choko), called *sayote;* beets, eggplant and okra; and of course coconuts and bananas – the giant plantain being the most popular to cook with.

Ubod, the palmetto or coconut heart, has acquired a worldwide reputation and the country enjoys a large trade in its export. But perhaps the most notable local product is the *kalamansi,* a small, bright green citrus with an intense tart-sweet taste. It is like no other citrus fruit; its juice, once tasted, is never forgotten.

Filipinos enjoy a charming custom, that of the *merienda,* a kind of high tea or post-siesta snack. The food, offered with fragrant local coffee or steaming sweet chocolate, may be just a selection of cakes or biscuits – for the Filipino is renowned for his sweet tooth – or almost a full-scale meal.

The range of cakes, biscuits and puddinglike desserts is immense. Once again a choice of unusual ingredients comes to the fore in *bibingka,* a rice flour pudding that can come topped with a mild white cheese. Boiled mashed yam, salted duck eggs, sago and tapioca, grated cassava, condensed milk, banana, coconut and *agar-agar* (seaweed) combine in a myriad of ways to produce colorful, sweet dishes, many of which require the expertise of a professional. Throughout the Philippines one will always find a little shop offering many of the more popular sweets.

A particular type of coconut, the *makapuno,* is filled with a sticky soft white flesh instead of the usual half-inch layer of firm coconut meat and clear water. *Makapuno* is used to make jams and sweets, and it also makes one of the tastiest ice creams ever devised. Here too, avocado, yam and cashew nuts are the original local ingredients for deliciously creamy ice cream.

The Filipino is fun-loving and enjoys living life to the full, and that means good wine. *Tuba* (prepared from coconut sap), *tapoy* (brewed from rice) and *basi,* a sweeter wine made from fermented sugar cane juice, are the national drinks after the local beer, and all pack a powerful punch.

A STREET SCENE IN ZAMBOANGA

R. IAN LLOYD, SINGAPORE

UKOY

Little Shrimp Patties

In Spain, little snack dishes known as tapas *are often served together at the start of a meal – or even to completely replace a meal. The Filipinos have followed this tradition and ukoy patties of shrimp are a popular example. Serve hot with dips of light soy sauce or Chinese black vinegar.*

4 oz (125 g) very small cooked peeled shrimp (prawns)
1¼ cups (5 oz/155 g) all-purpose (plain) flour
1¾ teaspoons baking powder
1 teaspoon salt
½ teaspoon cracked black pepper
1 teaspoon crushed garlic
3 tablespoons very finely chopped green onions
2 large eggs, lightly beaten
oil for deep-frying (half olive oil/half vegetable is ideal)

Finely chop the shrimp. Place in a mixing bowl and add the flour, baking powder, salt and pepper. Add enough water to make a batter of pouring consistency, then beat in the garlic, green onion and eggs. Cover and let stand for about 30 minutes.

Heat deep-frying oil to hot and then reduce the heat very slightly. Drop in small spoonfuls of the batter and cook until they rise to the surface and turn a golden brown. Lift out with a slotted spoon and drain well.

MAKES ABOUT 24

PANCIT MOLO

The Philippine equivalent of wontons in soup.

24 prepared fresh or frozen *wonton* wrappers
3 oz (90 g) lean ground (minced) pork
1½ oz (45 g) peeled shrimp (prawns)
1 oz (30 g) canned water chestnuts, drained
1 tablespoon finely chopped green onions
2 teaspoons light soy sauce
½ teaspoon salt
pinch of white pepper
1 egg white, well beaten

SOUP

6 cups (1½ liters) chicken stock
4 oz (125 g) chicken breast
1 lb (500 g) peeled raw shrimp (prawns)
4 green onions
1 teaspoon crushed garlic
1 tablespoon light soy sauce or fish sauce
salt and black pepper
fresh cilantro (coriander)

Keep the wrappers covered with a damp cloth until needed. In a food processor, combine the pork, shrimp, water chestnuts, green onions, soy sauce and seasonings. Process to a coarse paste, then add the egg white and process briefly.

Place a spoonful of the filling in the center of each wrapper. Fold in half to make a triangle, moistening the edges so that they stick firmly together; seal the edges. Fold the central point over the filling, then lift the two outer points up and pinch together at the top, moistening so that they adhere securely.

Heat a large saucepan of salted water and drop in the dumplings. Bring to the boil and simmer gently for about 4 minutes, then drain and place in a dish of cold water until needed.

WONTONS IN SOUP

Bring the stock to the boil. Cut the chicken into thin slices, then into shreds. Cut larger shrimp in half. Trim and finely chop the green onions. Add to the stock with the garlic, soy or fish sauce and the *pancit molo*. Simmer for 4–5 minutes, then season to taste. Serve garnished with cilantro.

SERVES 6

POLLO ADOBO

Chicken in the Adobo Style

Adobo *dishes, crisply fried pieces of seafood, pork or chicken, with a pungent flavor of garlic and vinegar, are one of the many Spanish-inspired inclusions in the Filipino cuisine. Adobo-style cooking is often given a local touch by the introduction of thick coconut milk or by serving on skewers.*

3-lb (1½-kg) chicken
1½ teaspoons salt
1 teaspoon cracked black pepper
1 tablespoon crushed garlic
2 bay leaves
¾ cup (6 fl oz/185 ml) white vinegar
1 cup (8 fl oz/250 ml) vegetable oil or lard
lettuce
tomato wedges and fresh pineapple (optional)

Cut the chicken into serving pieces. Rub with the salt, pepper and garlic and place in a dish. Tuck the bay leaves between the chicken pieces. Sprinkle on the vinegar. Cover with plastic wrap and let stand for at least 2 hours, turning from time to time. The vinegar tenderizes the meat while giving it an interesting tart flavor.

Transfer the chicken to a wide nonaluminum saucepan, adding the vinegar. Cover and cook gently until the chicken is tender; turn the chicken from time to time and splash in a little warm water once the vinegar has evaporated, to keep the chicken moist and keep it from sticking to the pan.

When done, remove the chicken from the pan and pour in the oil. Heat until very hot, return the chicken and fry on both sides until well colored and crisp. Lift out with a slotted spoon, drain and serve on a bed of shredded lettuce with tomato wedges and cubes of fresh pineapple.

A delicious alternative is to cook the chicken in lard, with pineapple cubes, which will reduce to a thick sauce as they cook.

SERVES 6

SOUR PICKLED FISH WITH VEGETABLES

TAPA

Sun-dried Beef

Sun-dried slivers of beef, marinated in vinegar and garlic with mounds of cracked fresh black pepper, are a tasty treat to serve before a meal or with drinks. In cooler climates, the meat can be dried just as effectively in a low oven.

1 lb (500 g) beef frying steak (rump/sirloin)
10–12 cloves garlic
1 tablespoon salt
1 tablespoon cracked black pepper
1 cup (8 fl oz/250 ml) white vinegar
¼ cup (2 oz/60 g) sugar

Cut the beef across the grain into paper-thin slices, then into narrow strips.

Peel and crush the garlic and mix with the remaining ingredients. Spread over the meat, cover with a double thickness of plastic wrap and set aside for at least 12 hours, turning occasionally.

Remove the meat from the marinade and spread on racks. Place in hot sunlight or in a very low oven to dry until the meat feels firm and dry to the touch. Store in an airtight container until needed.

To serve, heat about 1 in (2.5 cm) of vegetable oil in a wide skillet. Fry several slices of meat at a time until dark and very crisp. Lift out and drain well. Serve hot or warm.

MAKES ABOUT

PAKSIW

Sour Pickled Fish with Vegetables

Paksiw means "pickling": fish or meat is simmered in a strong vinegar solution with ginger and sugar. In this recipe, tart vegetables – eggplant and bitter melon – give added piquancy to the dish. Serve with rice or boiled egg noodles.

1 lb (500 g) white fish fillets or pieces (milkfish is ideal)
1 tablespoon dried shrimp, soaked for 30 minutes
3 oz (90 g) fresh eggplant (aubergine)
3 oz (90 g) canned or fresh bitter melon
2-in (5-cm) piece fresh ginger
2–3 green chilies
½ cup (4 fl oz/125 ml) white vinegar
¾ cup (6 fl oz/185 ml) fish stock or water
salt and cracked black pepper

Cut the fish into pieces about 2 in (5 cm) square. Drain the soaked shrimp, reserving the liquid. Peel the vegetables, cutting them into ¾-in (2-cm) cubes. Peel and slice the ginger. Slit open the chilies, scrape out the seeds and cut into narrow shreds.

Arrange the cubed vegetables in the bottom of a saucepan with the fish on top. Scatter the ginger, shrimp and chili evenly over the fish and pour in the vinegar, stock and reserved shrimp liquid. Season with salt and pepper.

Bring to the boil, then reduce heat to low, cover the pan tightly and cook gently for about 20 minutes until the vegetables and fish are tender.

SERVES 6

SINIGANG

Sour Beef Stew

Sinigang is a sort of stew-soup in which sour fruits and vegetables are boiled with the opaque, slightly starchy water used for boiling rice. Meat or fish is added to this tart stock and simmered until tender. Green mangoes, kalamansis, *tamarind, green guavas or* balimbing *(carambola star fruit) and green tomatoes are used to give the desired tart taste. Serve hot with noodles.*

1 lb (500 g) braising beef
8 oz (250 g) lean pork, or use extra beef
2 tablespoons tamarind pulp
2 *kalamansis* (Philippine citrus) or 1 lime or lemon
2 medium unripe tomatoes
6 cups (1½ liters) rice water*
2 cups (about 5½ oz/170 g) shredded cabbage
2 tablespoons fish sauce or light soy sauce
cracked black pepper

Cut the beef and pork into bite-size cubes.

🦜 Place the tamarind and quartered *kalamansis* or lime in a large saucepan. Add the quartered tomatoes and the rice water and bring to the boil. Simmer for 10 minutes, stirring to dissolve the tamarind. Strain out the tamarind seeds.

🦜 Add the meat, cover and simmer for about 1¼ hours until tender.

🦜 Add the cabbage, soy sauce and pepper and simmer again briefly. Remove *kalamansis* or lime.

The liquid used for boiling rice, reserved after the rice is cooked and drained.

SERVES 8

AT HOME IN THE JUNGLE   LEO MEIER

SOUR BEEF

BRAISED BEEF WITH TOMATOES

TAGALOG STEW

GUISADO

Braised Beef with Tomatoes

East meets West here. Tender steak braised with garlic, onions and tomatoes in the Spanish mode has fresh ginger and soy sauce added as an Oriental touch. Serve with white rice or noodles.

2 lb (1 kg) braising beef
2 large onions
7 cloves garlic
2½ tablespoons butter
4 large very ripe tomatoes
2 slices fresh ginger
2 tablespoons dark soy sauce
salt and cracked black pepper
3½ cups (28 fl oz/875 ml) water or beef stock

Cut the beef into bite-size cubes. Peel and thinly slice the onions and garlic and fry them in the butter for about 3 minutes until soft and lightly colored. Push to one side of the pan and fry the beef until evenly colored.

❧ Coarsely chop the tomatoes; shred the ginger. Add to the pan and simmer until the tomato begins to soften. Add the soy sauce, salt and pepper and pour in the water or stock.

❧ Bring to the boil, then reduce heat and simmer for about 40 minutes until the meat is very tender.

SERVES 6

KARI KARI

Tagalog Stew

4 lb (2 kg) shin of beef
1 cup (8 fl oz/250 ml) softened lard
2 tablespoons annatto seeds
2 large onions
2 tablespoons crushed garlic
2 tablespoons light soy sauce or fish sauce
1 medium celeriac root, turnip or rutabaga
12 oz (375 g) green beans
salt and cracked black pepper
¾ cup (4 oz/125 g) raw peanuts
⅓ cup (2½ oz/75 g) raw short-grain white rice

Have the butcher saw through the shin bone at 1½-in (4-cm) intervals. Drop the shin into a large pot of boiling water, return to the boil and simmer for 5 minutes, then remove and drain on a rack.

❧ In a large saucepan melt the lard, then fry the annatto seeds until the fat is red. Strain off and discard the seeds (or reserve them for a second use as they will still give off some color).

❧ Peel and slice the onions. Return the lard to the pan and fry the garlic and onions until slightly tender and colored. Push to one side of the pan. Fry the meat until evenly colored, cooking it in batches to avoid overcrowding the pan. Add water to cover and the soy or fish sauce and bring to the boil. Cook the meat for about 1¾ hours over medium-low heat, skimming the surface from time to time.

❧ Peel and cube the celeriac, turnip or rutabaga and cut the beans in half. Add the vegetables, salt and pepper to the meat and continue cooking until the vegetables are almost tender.

❧ Meanwhile, spread the peanuts and rice on separate oven trays and roast in a 350°F (180°C) oven until they are both golden. Rub the skins off the peanuts and chop coarsely. Pour the rice into a blender or spice grinder and grind to a fine powder. Add both to the stew and continue cooking until the sauce is thick. Check seasoning and serve hot.

SERVES 8

SAPIN SAPIN

Layered Cake

Yam, coconut milk and rice flour combine in this typical Filipino cake, which is brightly colored in pink, white and green and served with grated coconut.

5 oz (155 g) peeled yam
1¼ cups (5 oz/155 g) rice flour
1½ cups (12 fl oz/375 ml) thick coconut milk
2 cups (16 fl oz/500 ml) thin coconut milk
1¾ cups (14 oz/440 g) sugar
¾ teaspoon salt
green and red food coloring
grated fresh or packaged coconut

Cut the yam into small dice and steam or boil until completely tender. Drain well and mash to a smooth purée.

Combine the rice flour, coconut milks, sugar and salt in a mixing bowl, beating until the sugar has dissolved and the mixture is very smooth. Divide into 3 portions, one slightly smaller than the others.

Beat the puréed yam into the smaller portion and add enough green food coloring to make a light but bright green. Color one of the remaining portions pink/red and leave the other white.

Pour the pink or white portion into a well-greased 8-in (20-cm) round cake pan and cover with a piece of waxed paper. Set on a rack in a steamer and steam over rapidly boiling water for about 18 minutes until firm. Remove the paper and spread the yam batter evenly over this first layer. Cover with the paper again and steam for about 15 minutes until almost firm.

Spread on the final layer and continue to steam until the cake is completely set and firm to the touch. Remove and let cool.

Toast the coconut and spread evenly over the cake, pressing on lightly with the fingers. Chill the cake, and when firm use decorative cutters or a sharp knife to cut into bite-size servings.

SERVES 6–10

BIBINGKA

Coconut Pudding

There are a number of variations of this pudding/cake to be found in Southeast Asian cuisines. In some, it is cooked in several layers, each being browned before adding the next; in others it is composed of pale yellow and deep brown layers – the brown from the rich, dark brown palm sugar known variously as gula jawa, jaggery *and* gula melaka.

This version has melted brown sugar highlighted with caraway seeds on its surface. It is served hot as a pudding or cold as a cake, and is a popular part of the afternoon tea merienda.

¾ cup (6 fl oz/185 ml) thick coconut milk
1¼ cups (12 fl oz/375 ml) thin coconut milk
1¼ cups (5 oz/155 g) rice flour
¾ teaspoon salt
2 large eggs
¾ cup (4 oz/125 g) soft brown sugar
¼ teaspoon finely ground caraway seeds

Mix the coconut milks and rice flour together, add the salt and eggs and beat thoroughly. Stir in all but 2 tablespoons of sugar and continue to beat until the sugar has dissolved.

Pour into a thickly buttered 9-in (23-cm) round or square cake pan and smooth the top. Sprinkle the remaining sugar and caraway seeds over the top, then cover with buttered aluminum foil, pierced in several places.

Bake in a preheated 350°F (180°C) oven for about 35 minutes, until the cake feels firm to the touch. Increase the oven temperature to very hot, remove the foil and return the pudding to the oven to brown the top.

SERVES 8

SAILING ON TRANQUIL PHILIPPINE WATERS

Thailand

A QUIET BAY NEAR PHUKET
AUSTRALIAN PICTURE LIBRARY

OVERLEAF:
MOSLEM CURRY *(RIGHT), recipe page 110,* SALAD OF ROSE PETALS AND MIXED MEATS *(TOP RIGHT), recipe page 113,* FRIED FISH WITH GINGER SAUCE *(CENTER TOP), recipe page 110,* STUFFED CHILIES *(CENTER), recipe page 108,* HEAVENLY CHICKEN *(CENTER), recipe page 106,* DUCK CURRY *(LEFT), recipe page 112,* AND WATER CHESTNUT DESSERT *(TOP RIGHT), recipe page 116*
WELDON TRANNIES

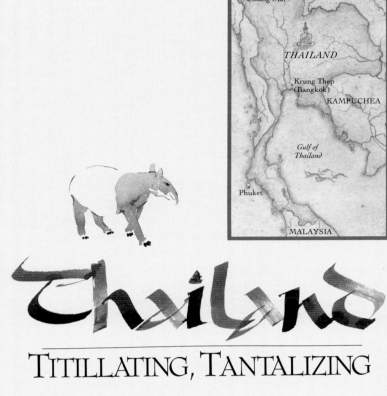

Thailand
TITILLATING, TANTALIZING

Eating a Thai meal is something of an adventure into the unknown. Few flavors are instantly recognizable, save for the unmistakable sting of hot chili. Fresh tastes evocative of lime and mint are ever-present, and perhaps ginger and a suggestion of basil can be singled out. But the salty, fishlike flavors cannot easily be defined, nor can the Western diner identify the aromatic pods, roots, stems and leaves floating in the strongly flavored clear Thai sauces, or the creamy, richly flavored coconut-based curries.

A gamut of flavors, colors and textures are mingled together in most Thai dishes. The cooks of Thailand gather greenery from the garden and *klong* (canal) and combine it with fresh fish and shellfish, poultry, pork, beef and freshly made seasoning pastes spiked with chili.

The leaves, roots, stalks and dried seeds of fresh coriander, otherwise known as cilantro or Chinese parsley; the mild, gingerlike *kha* and *krachai* of the galingale species; fresh turmeric root; *horapa,* a native sweet basil; lemon grass; and local varieties of mint lend their uniquely fresh tastes to many dishes. Cilantro and turmeric are also used as coloring agents – the former to impart a bright emerald green and the latter to bring the rich sun-gold of saffron.

From the canals that criss-cross the land come water chestnuts and lotus plants, whose leaves, roots, stems and seeds appear in many guises in sweet and savory dishes. From gardens, fields and roadsides, tamarind and *rakam* fruit are harvested to acidulate and tenderize. *Makhua khun* and *makhua puong* are tiny, figlike wild fruits with a flavor not unlike a wild gooseberry. The leaves of the *pak krasan* and the aquatic watercress-like *pan puay* and *pak bun* are popular local vegetables; the *makrut* and *som sa* of the citrus family are used whole in some dishes, while their leaves, juice and shredded peel are added as a flavoring and seasoning.

HARVESTERS SORT THE LAMYAI CROP   JOHN EVERINGHAM

TRADITIONAL THAI SWEETS   JOHN EVERINGHAM

Vegetables familiar throughout Asia include the starchy taro and yam bean, tubers whose mild taste and floury flesh can be adapted for sweet and spicy dishes alike; the *luffa,* angled or snake gourd, with its bitter taste and tender flesh; bamboo shoots and mung beans, the latter processed into clear vermicelli and a delicate green flour used for sweets. Cow peas, or snake beans, and the winged bean or asparagus pea also proliferate.

Fruits grow in abundance, and exotic tropical species include the *rambutan* and *mangosteen* as well as several different kinds of banana. When not appearing in the entrée, fresh fruit will be served with or following every meal.

Heavily fragrant tropical flowers find many uses in Thai cooking as flavoring or ingredient. *Mali,* a strong-scented white jasmine; *kadanna, khuichai* and *anjan,* the latter with a bright blue color; and the leaves of the *toey,* from the pandanus family, flavor and color sweet dishes and tidbits.

Processed seasonings center on two flavors – salty and fishy. *Nam pla,* a thin, salty and pungent sauce made from salt-preserved fish, plays the predominant role, while *kapi* – a paste of salt and sun-preserved tiny shrimp – is also frequently used. Then come soy sauce of a stronger, saltier kind than is popular in other parts of Asia, and *pla ra,* a fish preserved and packed in salt and roasted ground rice.

These same tastes combine with the omnipresent chili to produce *namprik phao.* A powerful condiment without which no Thai meal would be complete, it is made of roasted green onions and garlic ground to a paste with softened dried chilies and mixed to a creamy consistency with *nam pla.* A dash of this will liven up any dish, and a good Thai hostess will start the dinner off with pizzazz by serving *namprik phao* with crudités or little triangles of toast or rice crackers.

Last, though by no means least important, we come to chilies and coconut, two ingredients that give Thai food much of its fascination; they are the basis upon which the Thai cook creates her dishes.

Coconut groves proliferate in this steamy tropical land and, as in other parts of Southeast Asia, the byproducts of the coconut palm are a vital factor in maintaining the standard of living. Palm fronds provide roofing, matting, hats and other household items, the sap ferments into a potent wine, and the fruit provides its crisp white flesh to be nibbled, grated for adding to or garnishing food, or ground to a thick, creamy milk that enriches curries, dresses desserts in place of dairy cream, and is used in most sweet dishes.

Chilies come in several forms. The leaves are used as a vegetable, while the fruits add bright green or red colors and searing taste to all spicy Thai dishes. Their potency is in no way reflected by their size, a fact that anyone who has inadvertently bitten into one of the minute "bird's eye" chilies will painfully confirm. Red chilies are sun dried to heighten their flavor and are soaked to soften before being pounded to a paste with water and salt, the beginnings of an aromatic, mouth-searing seasoning paste. Each Thai cook has his or her own special combination of ingredients for seasoning pastes, and guards this formula jealously. Fresh chilies are found resplendent on most spicy dishes as a garnish, being chopped, shredded or carved into decorative floral shapes.

Thai etiquette calls for a gracious but casual approach. There are two main meals of the day – midday and early evening – and these usually consist of a variety of side dishes, a soup (often the classic *tom yam kung* with its hot and sour tastes), several curries and a large bowl of rice. The rice is the centerpiece, and in this hospitable country an invitation to "eat rice" signifies a promise to dine in the best possible manner that the host can afford.

Sweet dishes and fresh fruits are served after the main meal. Food is eaten from plates with a fork and spoon or from bowls with chopsticks; diners may be seated at a table on chairs, or on cushions around a *khan toke,* a low brass tray table. The *khan toke* tradition is most closely observed in northern Thailand, where the meal should comprise five dishes with rice.

As the climate is always torrid and much eating is done in a casual atmosphere out of doors, Thais rarely bother serving food hot, preferring the convenience of advance preparation. Curries and most other cooked dishes are served warm or at room temperature, which does not detract from their impact.

Alcoholic beverages have traditionally not been an important aspect of a Thai dinner, although beer may be served and imported wines may now accompany formal dinner. *Arak,* the local coconut palm wine, is generally reserved for celebratory binges.

The Thai menu is made up of several courses, each of which is usually represented in a meal. *Kaen phed* (curried dishes), *kaen cud* (soups), and *khao* (rice) are the principal parts of the meal, while *yam* (salads), in many forms and tasty little side dishes, provide highlights. Decorative Thai salads bring together a multitude of ingredients: Cold shredded meats and seafoods mingle with fresh vegetables and fruit, strips of omelet, grated unripe fruits such as mango and papaya (pawpaw), flower petals, dried seafoods and crushed roasted peanuts, all of which are flavored with the ubiquitous chili and *nam pla*.

The Thais also enjoy a vast range of delicious cakes and desserts. Making desserts in Thailand is a complex art requiring as much artistic ability as cooking skill. Mung bean flour, rice, coconut, palm sugar and fruit are used to create delightful cakes, or carved to represent blossoms or whole miniature fruits; slivers of fresh fruit are molded in coconut milk jellies; and all are served with a natural flamboyance typical of the Thais.

Flowers decorate tables, and long trains of sweet-perfumed jasmine blossoms hang over doorways and on the necks and wrists of girls waiting on tables.

While the unavailability of many of the more exotic ingredients makes duplication of some of the more esoteric Thai dishes impossible in Western countries, we have managed to compile this workable selection. With a little imagination, improvisation and enthusiasm, you should be able to create your own heady Thai experience.

A THAI FAMILY FROM THE VILLAGE OF KLONG KOW, NORTH OF BANGKOK

MICHAEL JENSEN/AUSCAPE INTERNATIONAL

PORK PARCELS *(LEFT)*, AND CHICKEN WITH BASIL AND CHILI, *recipe page 108*

Rum

Pork Parcels

The original version of this recipe had the egg cooked in a lacy golden net. Today it is more often served as an omelet or crêpe with pork filling. We prefer rum *cooked in the old way.*

¼ lb (125 g) lean ground (minced) pork
½ teaspoon crushed garlic
1 ½ tablespoons vegetable oil
2 teaspoons *nam pla* (fish sauce)
1 teaspoon finely chopped fresh green chili
1 teaspoon sugar
pinch of salt and white pepper
3 eggs
4 sprigs of fresh cilantro (coriander) or basil

Sauté the pork and garlic in 1½ tablespoons vegetable oil until the meat changes color. Add the fish sauce, chili and sugar and cook gently until the pan is dry and the pork is tender. Season to taste with salt and pepper and set aside.

💠 Wipe out an omelet pan, wok or skillet with an oiled paper towel. Heat the pan to moderate. Beat the eggs well. Strain half into a small funnel, holding a finger over the end. Release the egg into the pan in a very thin stream, moving the funnel constantly so that the egg forms a lacy net across the bottom of the pan. Cook until firm and lightly colored underneath, then lift out.

💠 Cook the remaining egg in the same way. Place 2 sprigs of cilantro or basil in the center of each egg net, top each with half the pork and roll up. Serve hot.

SERVES 2

Kai Suan

Heavenly Chicken

This is an incomparably delicate dish of chicken skin spread with a shrimp (prawn) and fish paste, steamed and served with a subtly flavored ginger-soy sauce. It is usually served as a side dish or as a "heavenly" break between more substantial courses.

2½-lb (1¼-kg) chicken
1 ½ cups (7 oz/220 g) peeled baby shrimp (prawns)
1 cup (5 oz/155 g) diced white-fleshed fish
1 teaspoon salt
ice water
½ teaspoon minced fresh ginger

SAUCE

4–5 slices fresh ginger
2½ cups (20 fl oz/600 ml) water
2 tablespoons cornstarch (cornflour)
light soy sauce and/or fish sauce
white pepper
chopped fresh cilantro (coriander) and shredded fresh red chili

Wash the chicken and dry thoroughly. Cut through the skin along the backbone, then remove the skin in one piece. Place on an oiled plate.

💠 Grind (mince) the shrimp and fish together, then pound to a smooth paste, adding salt and ice water slowly until the paste is very thick. Spread it thickly over the chicken skin and scatter with the minced ginger. Set in a steamer and steam gently for 30 minutes.

💠 Meanwhile, combine the chicken carcass and meat trimmings (the meat can be used for the broth or reserved for another use) with the sliced ginger and water and simmer for about 45 minutes, skimming the surface from time to time. Strain the broth into a clean saucepan and boil for 10 minutes longer.

Mix the cornstarch with a little cold water and stir into the sauce; stir until boiling. Return to the boil, then simmer until thickened. Season to taste with soy and/or fish sauce and white pepper.

Cut the stuffed chicken into small squares and arrange on a serving dish. Pour on the sauce and garnish with the cilantro and chili.

SERVES 6

Moo Thod Katiem Prik

Sliced Pork with Several Hot Sauces

Tender slices of pork tenderloin are arranged in a rosette on a large platter; in the center there are three small dishes of hot sauces for dipping. This is usually served as an appetizer, or midway through a meal to tease the palate.

12 oz (375 g) pork tenderloin (fillet)
½ teaspoon salt
¼ teaspoon white pepper
1 tablespoon butter
1½ tablespoons vegetable oil
1½ teaspoons crushed garlic
1 teaspoon minced fresh ginger
1 fresh red chili, seeded and very finely minced
1 lemon grass root, very finely minced

SAUCES (Each to be made to individual taste)

1   Fresh red chilies, fresh ginger, green onion, salt
Seed chilies. Very finely mince the ingredients and pound with the salt to a smooth paste.
2   Tomato, garlic, salt, sugar, chili powder or sauce, fish sauce
Seed and finely chop the tomato. Crush the garlic and mix with the tomato, adding the seasonings and fish sauce to taste.
3   Fresh red chilies, onion, fish sauce, lime juice, crushed roasted peanuts (optional)
Seed and finely shred the chilies. Mince the onion, flavor with the fish sauce and lime juice, and add a sprinkling of peanuts, if desired.

Rub the pork with salt and pepper. Heat the butter and oil together in a skillet, add the pork and sauté, turning frequently, until evenly colored. Lift out.

Add the garlic, ginger, chili and lemon grass to the pan and fry briefly. Return the pork and roll in the seasonings until thickly coated. Continue to cook over moderate heat, with the pan partially covered, for about 8 minutes or until the pork is cooked through and tender.

Remove from the pan and allow pork to cool and firm up. Cut into paper-thin slices. Arrange the slices on a platter overlapping in rosette fashion. Pour the sauces into small dishes and set in the center of the platter.

SERVES 4–6

SLICED PORK WITH SEVERAL HOT SAUCES

KAI PAD BAI GRA PROU

Chicken with Basil and Chili

The very tiny "bird's eye" chilies give potency to this innocuous-looking side dish – definitely to be taken in small doses.

12 oz (375 g) chicken breasts
4 oz (125 g) chicken giblets, or use extra chicken breasts if preferred
3 tablespoons vegetable oil
1 small bunch *horapa* (sweet basil), about 1 cup of tightly packed leaves
¼ cup (2 oz/60 g) "bird's eye" chilies
1 green onion, minced
2 tablespoons fish sauce
½ teaspoon minced cilantro (coriander) root or ground coriander, optional
1 teaspoon sugar

Skin and bone the chicken and cut the meat into very small dice. If using the giblets, trim them, then blanch the hearts and gizzards in lightly salted boiling water until they change color. Drain and rinse in cold water, then drain again and cut into small dice.

Heat the oil in a wok or large saucepan and sauté the chicken giblets (except the liver) for about 3 minutes. Add the chicken meat and liver and sauté a further 3 minutes. Lift out and set aside.

Shred half the *horapa* leaves and add to the pan with the chilies and green onion. Sauté for 1 minute, then add the fish sauce, cilantro and sugar, and return the chicken and giblets.

Sauté together until well mixed and aromatic. Pile onto a serving plate and cover with the remaining *horapa* leaves. Serve at once, with a word of caution.

SERVES 6

PRIK YUAK

Stuffed Chilies

Bite-size foods are ever-present on the Thai table, served as a between-meal snack or an appetizer. These piquant stuffed chilies, with an unusual covering of foi t'on (golden threads), make the kind of exotic dish that was once favored by the upper classes.

12 fresh *prik yuak* (mild yellow/green chilies)
4 oz (125 g) lean ground (minced) pork
2 tablespoons crushed roasted peanuts
nam pla (fish sauce)
¼ teaspoon crushed garlic
2 teaspoons finely chopped cilantro (coriander)
1 small egg
salt and white pepper
oil for deep-frying
½ cup (2 oz/60 g) all purpose (plain) flour

FOI T'ON

3 large eggs

Use the point of a sharp knife to make a slit along one side of each chili, then carefully scrape away the seeds and stem without splitting the chili.

Mix the pork with the peanuts, 2 teaspoons *nam pla,* garlic, cilantro and egg and season sparingly with salt and pepper. Use a teaspoon to stuff the mixture into the chilies,

then smooth the filling with a wet finger. Heat the deep oil to moderately hot.

Mix the flour (½ cup (2 oz/60 g) flour with enough ice water to make a thin batter. Lightly coat the stuffed chilies with extra flour, then coat with the batter. Slide them carefully into the oil and fry for about 3 minutes, turning once or twice, until crisped and golden on the surface. Lift out with a slotted spoon and drain well. Set aside.

To make *foi t'on,* beat the eggs well. Strain ⅓ of the egg into a small funnel, holding a finger over the end. Release the egg into the oil in a very thin stream, moving the funnel so that the egg forms a lacy design. Carefully turn with two spatulas and cook the other side briefly, then lift out and drain on paper towels. Cook the remaining egg in two batches in the same way. (If preferred, cook the egg threads in a lightly oiled omelet pan or nonstick skillet instead of the deep-frying oil.) Divide each bundle of "golden threads" in four and wrap a portion around each chili. Serve at once with additional fish sauce for dipping.

SERVES 6–12

TOM YAM KAENG

Sour and Hot Shrimp (Prawn) Soup

Tom yam kaeng is probably the most famous of Thailand's typical hot and sour soups. Makrut (lime) leaves and lemon grass, lime juice, fresh chilies and nam pla (fish sauce) combine to produce a unique tart taste that is intensely hot.

In many Thai homes and restaurants, this soup is cooked at the table in a charcoal-heated clay pot.

6 cups (1½ liters) fish stock*
2 limes
4 lime leaves, or rind from 2 limes
2 stalks lemon grass
1 teaspoon crushed garlic
2 fresh red chilies, seeded and shredded
1 tablespoon fish sauce
2 teaspoons ground coriander
salt and white pepper
chili sauce or cayenne pepper to taste
1½ lb (750 g) unpeeled medium-size raw shrimp (prawns)
extra lime juice
chopped fresh cilantro (coriander) leaves and green onions

Pour the stock into a large pot. Cut the limes into quarters; bruise the lime leaves and lemon grass. Add to the stock with the garlic, chilies, fish sauce, coriander, salt and pepper and simmer for about 15 minutes. Check the seasoning, adding chili sauce and cayenne if needed; the soup should be extremely hot.

Slit the shrimp along their backs and remove the dark veins, then rinse shrimp in cold water. (The shrimp can be peeled, if preferred, leaving only the tail section intact.) Add to the soup and simmer for about 8 minutes, until they are cooked through.

Add extra lime juice to taste and scatter the chopped cilantro and green onion on top. If desired, the lime and lemon grass can be removed before serving.

* Made by simmering fish heads and bones in water with fresh ginger and green onions, or by simmering the heads and shells of the shrimp. Strain through a fine nylon sieve before using.

SERVES 6

Yam Pla

Marinated Fish

12 oz (375 g) white-fleshed fish fillets
2 medium tomatoes
6 garlic chives (or green onions)
1 fresh red chili
12 sweet basil leaves
lettuce

MARINADE

¼ cup (2 fl oz/60 ml) lime or lemon juice
¼ cup (2 fl oz/60 ml) coconut milk
salt and black pepper
sugar
nam pla (fish sauce)

Place the fish fillets skin side downwards on a worktop and hold firmly by the tail end. Use a narrow-bladed sharp knife to separate the fish from the skin by cutting from the tail end.

❧ Slice the fish into narrow strips and place in a glass dish. Mix the lemon or lime juice and coconut milk, then flavor to taste with salt, pepper and sugar, adding a generous amount of *nam pla.*

❧ Pour over the fish, mix well and then cover with plastic wrap and refrigerate for at least 8 hours. The citric acid in the marinade will turn the fish white and very tender, making cooking unnecessary.

❧ Drop the tomatoes into a saucepan of boiling water, leave for 10–15 seconds, then remove and skin. Chop the flesh, discarding the seeds. Finely snip the garlic chives, or chop the green onions. Cut the chili open and scrape out the seeds, then cut into fine shreds. Rinse the basil leaves and shred finely.

❧ Arrange the lettuce leaves in a salad bowl or glass dish. Add the tomatoes, chives or onion, chili and sweet basil to the fish and mix in evenly. Pile onto the lettuce and serve.

SERVES 4

MARINATED FISH

SOUR AND HOT SHRIMP SOUP *(TOP), recipe page 108,* AND DUCK AND WATER CHESTNUT SOUP *(BOTTOM)*

Pet Tom Kap Kaolot

Duck and Water Chestnut Soup

1¼-lb (625-g) duck
1 stalk lemon grass
8 cups (2 liters) cold water
2 tablespoons vegetable oil
3 shallots or 1 Spanish onion
1–2 cloves garlic
2 teaspoons minced fresh cilantro (coriander) root*
2 teaspoons chopped fresh cilantro (coriander) leaves
½ teaspoon ground coriander
salt and white pepper
1 tablespoon fish sauce
5 oz (155 g) canned water chestnuts, drained

Cut the duck meat into small cubes. Bruise the lemon grass with the side of a cleaver to release its flavor. Place in a large saucepan with the duck and the cold water. Bring to the boil, then reduce heat and simmer for about 45 minutes until the duck is tender.

❧ Heat the oil in a small skillet. Mince the shallots and garlic and fry in the oil until lightly colored. Add the cilantro root and leaves and the ground coriander, and fry lightly. Stir into the soup adding the salt, pepper and fish sauce and simmer a further 10 minutes.

❧ Slice the water chestnuts thinly and add to the soup; heat through. Skim off any fat, garnish the soup with extra fresh cilantro or shredded green onions and serve.
* *If unobtainable use extra cilantro leaves, or omit.*

SERVES 6

SQUID IN HOT SAUCE

PLA MUEG PAD PRIK

Squid in Hot Sauce

The Chinese influence is evident in this dish which combines stir-fried squid with onion and chilies. The sauce is flavored with Chinese oyster sauce, rice wine and Thai nam pla *(fish sauce).*

1 lb (500 g) fresh small squid
1 medium onion
2 cloves garlic
1–2 fresh red chilies
2 tablespoons vegetable oil
1 teaspoon finely chopped fresh ginger
1 tablespoon fish sauce
1 tablespoon rice wine, or dry sherry
1 tablespoon oyster sauce
salt and pepper
2 tablespoons chopped green onions
1 tablespoon chopped fresh cilantro (coriander)

Pull away the heads and tentacles from the squid, then trim off the tentacles just above the head so that they remain in one piece. Skin the squid and remove the transparent quill inside. Rinse squid thoroughly in cold running water, then drain well and cut into rings or small squares.

Peel and chop the onion and garlic. Slit open the chilies and scrape out the seeds; chop the flesh finely.

Heat the oil in a skillet or wok and stir-fry the onion and garlic. Add the chopped ginger and squid and stir-fry over high heat for 1½ minutes, until they change color.

Drizzle the fish sauce and rice wine down the sides of the pan so that they begin to cook before they reach the food, giving it a better taste. Add the oyster sauce, chilies, salt and pepper and chopped green onions. Stir-fry together for 1 minute, then transfer to a serving plate and garnish with the chopped cilantro. Serve at once.

SERVES 4

KAENG MASAMAN

Moslem Curry

Thai curry pastes are based on cilantro (coriander) – the seeds, leaves, stems and roots all being used – along with lemon grass, chilies and garlic. Spices are ground and then pulverized with the fresh ingredients and a little kapi *(shrimp paste).*

Seasonings of nam pla *(fish sauce), tamarind pulp or juice,* som sa *(citrus) juice and palm sugar are added to the finished dish according to taste.*

CURRY PASTE

7 dried chilies
2 tablespoons coriander seeds
1 tablespoon caraway seeds
1 tablespoon grated fresh ginger
1 tablespoon finely chopped lemon grass root
1 teaspoon salt
5–6 black peppercorns
¼ teaspoon freshly grated nutmeg
½ teaspoon shrimp paste
2 tablespoons vegetable oil
8 shallots or 3 small Spanish onions
6 cloves garlic
2½ lb (1¼ kg) braising beef (or use chicken, duck or pork)
3½ cups (28 fl oz/875 ml) coconut milk
1 cup (5 oz/155 g) roasted peanuts
fish sauce
5 whole cloves
2-in (5-cm) piece cinnamon stick
1 teaspoon cardamom seeds
lime or lemon juice
1 tablespoon tamarind pulp
granulated or palm sugar
cooked white rice

Roast the chilies, coriander and caraway seeds in a dry pan for 2–3 minutes until very aromatic, then grind finely. Transfer to a food processor, blender or mortar, add the ginger, lemon grass root, salt, peppercorns and nutmeg and grind to a smooth paste. Add the shrimp paste and mix in well.

Heat the vegetable oil and fry the whole peeled shallots and garlic until well colored. Add to the other seasonings and grind again until smooth.

Cut the beef into cubes and place in a saucepan with the coconut milk. Grind the peanuts finely and stir into the coconut milk, adding about 1 tablespoon of fish sauce.

Bring to the boil, then reduce the heat and simmer for 1 hour until the beef is almost tender. Add the prepared curry paste, cloves, cinnamon stick and cardamom seeds, and continue cooking until tender. Lift out the meat with a slotted spoon and set aside. Continue to simmer the sauce until well reduced.

Return the meat and simmer gently until reheated. Add more fish sauce, lime or lemon juice, the tamarind pulp and sugar to taste. Heat through briefly and serve with rice.

SERVES 8

PLA KAPONG KHING

Fried Fish with Ginger Sauce

Pla kapong is a meaty fish that proliferates in the klongs *(canals) criss-crossing Thailand. Snapper is a good substitute.*

1½-lb (750-g) whole fish, such as snapper or sea bass
1 cup (4 oz/125 g) all purpose (plain) flour
salt and black pepper
oil for deep-frying
1 large cucumber

GINGER SAUCE

4 Chinese dried black mushrooms, soaked for 25 minutes
4 green onions
1 fresh red chili

3 tablespoons shredded pickled ginger
2 tablespoons vegetable oil
¼ cup (2 fl oz/60 ml) white vinegar
¼ cup (2 oz/60 g) sugar
1 teaspoon salt
⅔ cup (5½ fl oz/170 ml) fish stock or water
2½ teaspoons cornstarch (cornflour)

Clean and scale the fish and rinse under cold running water. Drain and wipe dry, then slash several times on each side to allow the fish to cook evenly and to permit the seasonings to penetrate.

Mix the flour, salt and pepper in a large plastic bag. Put the fish into the bag, close the top and shake it to coat the fish thickly.

Heat the deep-frying oil to the smoking point. Slide in the fish and cook over high heat for 3 minutes, then lift out and cool for a few minutes. Reheat the oil, return the fish and cook a further 3–4 minutes until cooked through. Test by inserting a fork into the thickest part of the flesh; it should flake quite easily. Lift from the oil and place fish on a rack to drain.

Squeeze the water from the mushrooms, discard the stems and cut the caps into narrow shreds. Mince the green onions and seeded chili. Drain the pickled ginger. Heat the oil in a saucepan and sauté the onions and chili for a few minutes, then add the mushrooms and cook briefly. Mix the remaining sauce ingredients. Bring to the boil, then simmer, stirring occasionally, until thickened and clear.

Peel the cucumber and cut in half lengthwise. Scoop out the seeds, then slice the cucumber into very thin crescent shapes. Arrange the fish on an oval platter and surround with the cucumber. Pour the sauce over and serve at once.

SERVES 6

ALONG A TRANQUIL WATERWAY, BANGKOK

R. IAN LLOYD, SINGAPORE

CHICKEN IN COCONUT AND PEANUT SAUCE, AND PAPAYA/PAWPAW SALAD, *recipe page 114*

KAI PHENANG

Chicken in Coconut and Peanut Sauce

3-lb (1½-kg) chicken
2 teaspoons salt
½ teaspoon black pepper
1 teaspoon crushed garlic
1½ cups (12 fl oz/375 ml) thin coconut milk
2 tablespoons cumin seeds
1 tablespoon coriander seeds
3 fresh red chilies, chopped
1 teaspoon dried shrimp paste
1 tablespoon light soy sauce
2 teaspoons sugar
⅓ cup (2 oz/60 g) roasted peanuts
½ cup (4 fl oz/125 ml) thick coconut milk
lemon or lime juice
chopped fresh cilantro (coriander) leaves
finely shredded fresh red chili

Wash the chicken, dry well and season inside and out with the salt, pepper and garlic. Place breast up in a deep saucepan and add the thin coconut milk. Cover and bring to the boil, then reduce the heat and simmer gently for 1 hour, turning the chicken after 30 minutes. Remove the chicken, cut into serving portions and set aside, covered.

Toast the cumin and coriander seeds, chilies and shrimp paste in a dry pan until aromatic, then grind together into a smooth paste. Add the soy sauce and sugar and stir into the coconut sauce. Very finely grind the peanuts and add to the saucepan. Bring to the boil, stirring occasionally, then simmer for 2–3 minutes. Add the thick coconut milk and stir the sauce consistently over moderate heat for 5 minutes. Return the chicken and simmer gently for 10–15 minutes.

Lift out the chicken and transfer to a serving dish. Flavor the sauce with lemon or lime juice and pour over the chicken. Garnish with the cilantro and chili.

SERVES 6–8

KAEN OF DUCK

Duck Curry

6-lb (3-kg) fresh duck
6 cups (1½ liters) coconut milk*
7–8 large dried chilies, soaked
1 teaspoon salt
1 teaspoon black peppercorns
2 teaspoons caraway seeds
1 tablespoon coriander seeds
1 teaspoon dried shrimp paste
2 teaspoons minced cilantro (coriander) root, or use extra cilantro (coriander) leaves
1 tablespoon finely chopped fresh cilantro (coriander) leaves
2½ tablespoons finely shredded lemon grass
1 teaspoon grated lime or lemon peel
2 tablespoons minced shallots or Spanish onion
2 teaspoons crushed garlic
1 teaspoon minced fresh ginger
fish sauce
sweet basil leaves
mahkua puong fruit, optional

Wash the duck, dry thoroughly and cut into serving pieces. Set aside. In a deep saucepan or casserole bring the coconut milk to the boil; simmer for 5 minutes. Pour off half and set aside, then simmer the remaining milk for about 15 minutes. Add the duck and simmer for 10 minutes.

Drain the chilies and pound to a paste with the salt. Grind the peppercorns, caraway and coriander seeds together and pound with the chilies. Add the dried shrimp paste, cilantro root and leaves, lemon grass and lime and pound until smooth. Work in the shallot, garlic and ginger and pound to a smooth paste.

Stir into the duck and coconut milk, at first adding only half the paste; check the strength before adding the remaining seasoning paste. Add the reserved coconut milk, a large splash of fish sauce, basil and *mahkua puong,* if used. Simmer until the duck is tender and the sauce thick and flavorful. Check the seasoning and serve with rice.

Unused seasoning paste can be stored for several days in a covered jar in the refrigerator.

* *The coconut milk should be of medium thickness made by mixing together both thick and thin coconut milk.*

SERVES 8

NUA PAD PRIK

Chili Beef

1 lb (500 g) beef fillet (tenderloin)
1 teaspoon salt
½ teaspoon black pepper
1½ teaspoons crushed garlic
2 fresh green chilies
1 fresh red chili
¼ cup (2 fl oz/60 ml) vegetable oil
1½ tablespoons fish sauce
1½ teaspoons sugar
½ cup (1 oz/30 g) chopped fresh cilantro (coriander)

Slice the beef very thinly. Rub with salt, pepper and garlic and set aside for 5 minutes.

Chop the chilies very finely. Heat the oil in a large wok or wide skillet to the smoking point. Add the beef and fry on both sides until well colored.

CHILI BEEF

WELDON TRANNIES   PEPPERED CHICKEN

Add the chilies, fish sauce and sugar and cook over moderate heat, turning frequently, until cooked through. Mix in the cilantro, transfer to a serving plate and serve at once.

SERVES 6

KAI YANG

Peppered Chicken

Traveling through the Thai countryside can reveal a wonderland of tasty – and invariably fiery hot – snacks and tidbits touted by itinerant cooks with portable kitchens. These kitchens range from the most basic improvised charcoal cookers, in discarded metal cans, to the elaborate brass burners which have now become collectors' items. Piquant peppered chicken is one such specialty which no traveler should miss. It is usually eaten with flavored rice wrapped in young banana leaves.

6 chicken thighs
1 teaspoon crushed garlic
1½ teaspoons minced fresh ginger
2 teaspoons coarsely ground black pepper
1 small bunch fresh cilantro (coriander), including roots and stems, finely chopped
1½ tablespoons sugar
2 tablespoons dark soy sauce
2 tablespoons vegetable oil

Wash the chicken, dry thoroughly and prick the skin and meat with the point of a skewer to allow the seasonings to penetrate. Mix the garlic, ginger, pepper and cilantro and spread over the chicken. Cover with plastic wrap and let stand for at least 2 hours.

Prepare a glaze by mixing the sugar into the soy sauce until dissolved, then adding the oil.

Cook the chicken over a charcoal fire, brushing with the glaze and turning frequently, for about 10 minutes or until the chicken is tender inside and the skin crisp and deep brown.

SERVES 6

ROSE PETAL YAM

Salad of Rose Petals and Mixed Meats

1 boneless chicken breast (approx 9 oz/280 g)
1 lb (500 g) lean pork
8 oz (250 g) peeled shrimp (prawns)
8 oz (250 g) pork crackling, optional
6 shallots or 3 small Spanish onions
4–6 cloves garlic
2 tablespoons vegetable oil or lard
lime juice
fish sauce
sugar
2–3 tablespoons coarsely crushed roasted peanuts
5–6 roses or substitute sections of seasonal fruit
2–3 tablespoons chopped fresh cilantro (coriander) leaves
1–2 tablespoons chopped fresh red chilies

Place the chicken and sliced pork in a saucepan, cover with water and bring to the boil, then simmer gently until just tender. Drain and cool.

Drop the shrimp into a saucepan of gently simmering water and cook until pink. Drain well. Cut the chicken, pork and crackling into long, thin shreds. Halve the larger shrimp, leaving the smaller ones whole.

Finely chop the shallots and garlic and fry in the oil or lard until crisp and well cooked. Drain well.

Make a sauce of lime juice, *nam pla* and sugar to taste. Place the meat and shrimp, peanuts and half the fried shallots and garlic in a dish and pour on the sauce. Toss well, then transfer to a serving plate.

Scatter on the rose petals, stirring in lightly. Garnish with the cilantro and chilies, and the remaining shallots and garlic.

SERVES 6

SEAFOOD SALAD

YAM MA-LA-KAW

Green Papaya (Pawpaw) Salad

This salad of unripe papaya (pawpaw) is one of the most delightful side dishes in the Thai cuisine, and is also enjoyed throughout Laos and Vietnam. The chili and nam pla *(fish sauce) blend with the tart crispness of the green papaya in a combination of flavors that is suitable with other traditional Thai dishes.*

Usually the salad is pounded to a smooth paste, but a simplified version can be made using grated papaya with chili flakes, a little garlic, sugar and nam pla *(pictured page 112).*

1 large unripe papaya (pawpaw)
5–6 dried red chilies, soaked in cold water
½ cup small dried shrimp (prawns), soaked in boiling water
5–6 cloves garlic, peeled
lemon or lime juice
fish sauce
sugar

Peel, seed and grate the papaya. Transfer to a mortar, blender or food processor. Drain the chilies and shrimp. Add to the papaya with the garlic, and a little lemon or lime juice, the *nam pla* and sugar. Pound or process until smooth, adding more juice, fish sauce and sugar to taste. Serve at once.

SERVES 6–8

MIAN PLA THO

Seafood Salad

2–3 white fish fillets (about 12 oz/375 g)
1 large squid
¼ cup (2 fl oz/60 ml) vegetable oil
3 green onions, trimmed and shredded
1–2 fresh red chilies, seeded and shredded
½-in (1.25-cm) piece fresh ginger, peeled and shredded
1 unripe mango or a large slice of unripe papaya (pawpaw)
lime juice
fish sauce
sugar
½ cup (2½ oz/75 g) roasted peanuts, coarsely crushed

Wipe the fish with a piece of paper towel. Clean the squid, cut open and wash well. Dry thoroughly and cut into very fine shreds.

Heat the vegetable oil in a skillet. Lightly fry the fish until slightly colored on both sides and just cooked through. Bring a small saucepan of salted water to the boil and drop in the squid. Poach for 30 seconds, then remove and cool under cold running water. Drain well.

Break the fish into bite-size pieces and mix with the squid shreds. Pile in the center of a serving plate and pour on the oil from the pan. Arrange the shredded vegetables around the seafood. Finely grate the mango or papaya and place on top of the fish.

Drizzle with generous quantities of lime juice and fish sauce; sprinkle with sugar. Cover the salad with plastic wrap and chill before serving. Garnish with the roasted peanuts.

SERVES 6–8

RICE AND NOODLES

Rice (Khao Chao)

In the days of King Chulalongkorn, the ladies of the palace, jaded by the heat, asked their chefs to devise a cooling food for the midday meal. *Khao chao* was the result. Shiny grains of white rice floating in dishes of crushed ice are served with minute tidbits such as the *prik yuak* (stuffed chilies) on page 108, little fish or shrimp balls, crispy morsels of sweetly seasoned meat and pickled radishes.

The rice is first soaked in salted water for several hours, then thoroughly washed, then boiled in two or three stages, each time with a change of water in order to draw off as much of the starch as possible. In the final cooking stage, the rice is spread on a cloth and steamed until tender. When cool it is transferred to dishes and covered with iced water and crushed ice.

Ordinarily, the rice that accompanies Thai food is of the long-grain variety, but *khao niew,* an opaque short-grain sticky (glutinous) rice, is enjoyed by those from northern Thailand, and used in dessert making. Black-grained sticky rice makes quite delightful desserts and has a unique flavor.

There are several different types of noodles used in Thai cooking, reflecting the Chinese influence. *Kuei teow* and *mee* are rice noodles which vary in thickness and shape from thin and round to wide and flat. *Khanon chine* are thick white rice noodles which are sold in little "nest" shapes. They are often served with curries, or simply with *nam prik*. *Ba mee* are thick egg noodles, and *wun sen* are transparent noodles made from extruded mung bean flour.

KHAO TOM GUNG

Rice Gruel with Shrimp (Prawns)

Breakfast in most homes throughout Thailand consists of a steaming bowl of rice gruel, to which one adds an assortment of ingredients and a dollop of the ubiquitous nam prik. *The gruel is simply white rice boiled in plenty of water or stock, bland to the taste and the perfect vehicle for plump boiled shrimp, diced chicken, rings of squid, or just a raw egg, which will become partially cooked by the heat of the gruel.*

A typical recipe is chopped green onions and fresh cilantro (coriander), a splash of lime juice, perhaps a basil leaf or two and enough nam prik *or* nam pla *to give it a bite without spoiling the mild flavor. Garlic oil, made by steeping peeled garlic in vegetable oil for several days, is also favored with* khao tom.

2 cups (10 oz/315 g) raw long-grain white rice
18 cups (4½ liters) water

ACCOMPANIMENTS

fish sauce
nam prik (Thai hot sauce), see page 107
chopped green onions
chopped fresh cilantro (coriander) and/or *horapa* (basil)
8 raw eggs, optional
boiled or steamed shrimp (prawns)*, squid, fish, chicken
    breast, lean pork or beef, or diced Chinese sausage
crushed roasted peanuts, optional
garlic oil, optional

Pour the rice into a large saucepan and add the water. Cover and bring to the boil, reduce heat and simmer for at least 1 hour, until the rice is very mushy. Transfer to large bowls.

❧ Meanwhile, steam or boil the shrimp until they are just cooked through and the shells are bright pink. Let cool slightly, then peel. Place several in each bowl of gruel and add the accompaniments to taste.

❧ If preferred, cook the shrimp in their shells, then drain and peel. Return the shells to the stock and simmer 10 minutes. Drain and discard shells. Use this liquid to cook the rice.

For this recipe, use 2 lb (1 kg) medium uncooked shrimp (prawns) in their shells.

SERVES 8

Tako Haeo

Water Chestnut Dessert

Tako is a popular dish of which there are a number of variations. Essentially, a tako dessert comprises a fragrant sugar syrup that is flavored with jasmine flowers or pandanus, thickened with rice flour and cooked to a jellylike consistency. Various ingredients such as haeo (water chestnuts), sweet corn kernels, tapioca and cassava can be used to make tako. With some the dark palm sugar, nam taan peep, is used instead of granulated sugar. A thickened coconut cream sauce is poured over the dessert before serving.

¼ cup (1½ oz/45 g) rice flour
1½ cups (12 oz/375 g) sugar
2 cups (16 fl oz/500 ml) jasmine scented water*
¼ cup (1½ oz/45 g) water chestnut powder
20 canned water chestnuts, drained

COCONUT CREAM SAUCE

1½ cups (12 fl oz/375 ml) coconut milk
2 tablespoons rice flour
¾ teaspoon salt

Mix the rice flour and sugar into the scented water in a large saucepan. Stir in the water chestnut powder. Bring to the boil, then reduce heat and simmer, stirring constantly, until the mixture is thick and clear.

❧ Remove from the heat. Cut the water chestnuts into thin slices or small dice as preferred. Stir into the mixture, then pour into a lightly oiled serving bowl or individual dessert dishes. Set aside to cool and firm.

❧ Boil the coconut milk with the rice flour and salt over moderate heat, stirring until it thickens. Cool to room temperature. Pour over the dessert and serve.

Flower essences such as mali and rosewater are available where exclusive Oriental produce is sold.

SERVES 6

WATER CHESTNUTS IN COCONUT MILK, AND CHICKEN 'GIZZARDS'

Khanom Sai Kai

Chicken "Gizzards"

The name is hardly appealing, but the dish is superb and akin to Indian jalebis. A batter of glutinous rice flour and coconut milk is passed through a small funnel into a pan of hot oil or lard. It is cooked in little loopy rings until golden, then steeped in palm sugar syrup.

1½ cups (9 oz/280 g) glutinous rice flour
½ cup (4 fl oz/125 ml) thick coconut milk
3 cups (24 fl oz/750 ml) melted lard or clean vegetable oil
1½ cups (8 oz/250 g) *nam taan peep* (palm sugar) or dark
    brown sugar
1¼ cups (12 fl oz/375 ml) water

Sift the flour into a bowl, pour in the coconut milk and mix thoroughly. Set aside for at least 2 hours for the liquid to soften the flour.

❧ Heat the lard or oil to moderately hot in a wide skillet. Pour the batter into a funnel or paper cone with a small hole in the bottom. Hold over the fat and allow a thin stream to run in, forming a circular nest shape; fry two or three at a time. Cook until the cakes rise to the surface and are golden brown. Lift out and drain on paper towels.

❧ Melt the sugar in a saucepan, then stir in the water and simmer for 5 minutes. Place the fried cakes in the syrup long enough to absorb the syrup but without becoming soggy. Lift out and drain briefly on a rack, then serve with sweetened thick coconut milk or by themselves.

SERVES 6

Khan Um Kluk

Coconut Pancakes

2½ cups (20 fl oz/600 ml) coconut milk
¾ cup (3½ oz/100 g) rice flour
3 eggs
½ cup (4 oz/125 g) sugar
1 cup (2 oz/60 g) shredded coconut
pinch of salt
green and red food coloring
vegetable oil

Pour the coconut milk into a mixing bowl. Add the rice flour and well-beaten eggs and blend well, then add the sugar and beat until it dissolves. Fold in half the shredded coconut and the salt, then divide the mixture into three equal parts. Tint one batch green and one pink; leave the remainder plain.

❧ Rub an omelet pan with a paper towel and heat to moderate.

❧ Pour a large spoonful of the batter into the pan and cook until flecks of brown appear underneath. Turn and lightly cook the other side. Cook the remainder of the batter in the same way, keeping the pancakes warm.

❧ Roll each pancake up into a tight cylinder. Arrange side by side on a serving plate and scatter with the remaining coconut. Serve warm or at room temperature.

SERVES 8

TRADITIONAL THAI COSTUME   R. IAN LLOYD, SINGAPORE

WELDON TRANNIES   COCONUT PANCAKES

Tub Tim Krob

Water Chestnuts in Coconut Milk

Possibly the most popular dessert throughout Thailand, tub tim krob *is deliciously refreshing and cooling after a typical searing-hot Thai meal. Fresh water chestnuts, quickly boiled after peeling, are usually used, but the canned type are almost as good and twice as convenient. In fact, with the ready availability of both canned coconut milk and water chestnuts, this dessert is one of the quickest and easiest of all to prepare.*

9 oz (280 g) can sliced water chestnuts, drained
2 cups (16 fl oz/500 ml) thin coconut milk
1¾ cups (14 fl oz/440 ml) iced water
large pinch of salt
⅓ cup (2½ fl oz/75 ml) cooled sugar syrup*
crushed ice

Rinse the water chestnuts in cold water. Place in a serving bowl or divide among 6 parfait/coupe glasses or dessert dishes. Mix the coconut milk, ice water, syrup and salt. Pour over the water chestnuts, top with a little crushed ice and serve at once.

Made by simmering 2 tablespoons sugar with ¼ cup cold water for 5–6 minutes.

SERVES 6

Laos and Kampuchea

ON THE MEKONG RIVER   ALEXANDER BOWIE

LAOTIAN CABBAGE SOUP *(CENTER)*, *recipe page 126*, KAMPUCHEAN GRILLED FISH AND SAUCE DIP *(TOP RIGHT)*, *recipe page 127*, BAMBOO SHOOT SALAD *(LEFT)*, AND TAPIOCA AND RICE BEAN DESSERT *recipes page 129*

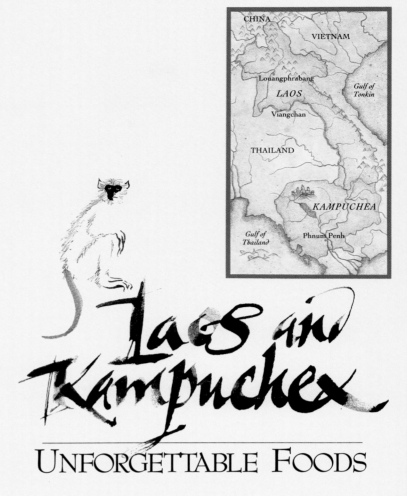

Laos and Kampuchea

UNFORGETTABLE FOODS

The cuisines of Laos and Kampuchea, while quite different in many characteristics, have for convenience been grouped together.

Laos, landlocked and isolated, is unlike any other country in the world – and its food is likewise unique. The differences start with rice, the staple. Here the harvest is not root-soaked *padi*-grown rice, but a glutinous kind grown on the sweeping hillsides. Meat is more likely to be buffalo or venison than beef or pork, and the limited range of ingredients available for cooking are those harvested from the local soil or fished from the swirling muddy waters of the Mekong River.

Eggplants, yam and bamboo shoots are the most common vegetables. Banana groves fringing the Mekong provide not only their soft fruit but tender edible flowers and the delicate inner trunk – as well as leaves to use as food wrappers. From the brushlands and riverbanks come a variety of edible fungi, and at meal preparation time the housewife and cook collect endless types of edible leaves and pods from the trees and shrubs greening the land.

Game from the hills includes venison, wild boar, duck and pheasant. The Mekong yields up *pa boeuk,* a giant of a fish with a delicate roe. A single one of these fish can be large enough to provide a meal for several families, and the roe is salted and packed down to make *som khay,* or Laotian caviar. Other varieties of fish and eels are also plentiful, if somewhat muddy in taste, and soft-textured.

Here rice is not boiled or absorption-cooked as in other parts of Asia, but steamed in a funnel over a pot of water. It is served in baskets with the meal – a single communal basket or small covered individual ones of tightly woven flat cane. The rice is rolled into tight balls to nibble throughout the meal like bread.

A TEMPLE AMID SURROUNDING FARMLAND   ALEXANDER BOWIE

of the purée. It is seasoned to stimulate the palate and again served with the salad ingredients to roll up and dip into a tasty *nam padek*-based sauce.

The Laotians, like the Kampucheans, enjoy a soup with every meal. These *kengs* are usually mildly flavored and based on vegetables with the occasional highlight of meat. *Keng sarama,* however, is a fiercely hot exception that makes a welcome contrast to the other mildly seasoned dishes it will accompany.

Unique again is the Laotian method of using slow-cooked eggplant as the thickening agent for stewed dishes. In the popular national dish *o lam,* cubed buffalo meat and local beans are cooked in this way with several types of edible fungi. Fennel adds a subtle, pervasive anise aroma and taste.

Eggs rarely feature in Laotian cooking. A simple boiled egg is considered a treat and high honor indeed when served to guests. But tender chicken dishes are well loved. They may be simply steamed, the cavity packed with fragrant local herbs, or cooked in a dish borrowed from neighboring Thailand called *phaenang kai,* with a filling of roasted peanuts and a sauce of coconut cream – a touch of luxury in an otherwise austere cuisine.

Kampuchea, on the other hand, enjoys, at least along its narrow coastal strip, a wealth of shellfish and molluscs, and inland a variety of succulent river fish to add to local vegetables and herbs. Seasoning here is fresh and herbaceous, with plenty of hot chili balanced by creamy coconut milk.

Soups are an important aspect of Kampuchean food, and a number of different styles of *samla* (soup) are made. A particularly tart fish soup, *samla mchou banle,* is sharp from tamarind and lemon grass, with tart vegetables adding their own bite.

Tuk trey is this country's version of the indispensable fish sauce used throughout the area. When not actually used in a dish, it is bound to appear on the table to add at will.

Grilling is a popular cooking method, used particularly with seafood, and often the cooked food will be wrapped with herbs, salad vegetables and lettuce as tasty food parcels. The Kampuchean cook is just as fastidious as her Laotian and Vietnamese counterparts in the presentation of her food, ensuring that it is just as visually tempting as it is delicious.

There is one special dish enjoyed throughout the region. *Khao phoune* is ever-ready at roadside food stalls, in markets and at home for a filling and enjoyable meal at any time. Closely related to the Indonesian/Malaysian *laksa* or the Burmese *mohinga,* *khao phoune* similarly is made from cooked rice vermicelli, an assortment of raw salad ingredients, a little pot of fish sauce and perhaps one of pounded fresh red chili, and a steaming hot pot of fish-based thick sauce that is rich with coconut cream and puréed fish, and supplemented with diced meat or meatballs. The tender inner layers of young banana buds or flowers form an important part of the greens that must accompany an authentic *khao phoune.*

The Laotian cook employs few seasonings, for few are available, and imported ones are out of the reach of the average household. Herbs and leaves provide pungent, fresh flavors: *Romdeng,* a type of galingale sometimes known as southernwood, has a mild gingery taste; chilies add a clear hot flavor; and *nam padek* and *prahok* – the former a thin salty essence made from fermented fish, the latter fermented fish itself – are the chief ingredients used to add extra pungency to the otherwise mild, even bland taste of Laotian cooking.

Another unique feature of the food of Laos is its puréed dishes, which are many and diverse. The most notable is *lap,* a luxury dish enjoyed only by those who can afford the extravagance, and then only on auspicious occasions. Tender meat – usually young buffalo or venison, but occasionally imported beef – is pounded to a smooth, soft consistency similar to a Western steak *tartare,* seasoned with chili and herbs and served with lettuce and leafy herbs to wrap into little parcels.

Tom ponh is a similar dish, this one employing simmered fish and soft-cooked eggplant as the base

KHYANG SAMROK KROENG

Oysters with Garlic and Herb Sauce

Kampuchea's narrow southern coastal strip offers an abundance of shellfish and molluscs. Local herbs and aromatic roots such as lemon grass and romdeng/kha *(galingale or young ginger) blend with garlic, chili and refreshing varieties of local mint to transform these succulent oysters into a dish with a kaleidoscope of tastes.*

36 large fresh oysters, in the shell
2 teaspoons crushed garlic
1 teaspoon minced fresh red chili
2 teaspoons minced galingale/young ginger
2 teaspoons very finely minced lemon grass root
¼ cup (2 fl oz/60 ml) vegetable oil
2–3 teaspoons finely chopped Vietnamese or other fresh mint
lime juice
fish sauce
salt, sugar and freshly ground black pepper
fresh fennel or parsley (optional)

Open the oysters over a dish to allow their liquor to drip in. Remove the top shells and discard, then loosen the oysters from the bottom shells.

Place the garlic, chili, ginger and lemon grass in a saucepan or skillet and add the oil. Fry gently for a few minutes until very aromatic, then add the mint.

Make up a generous amount of sauce with lime juice, fish sauce, salt, sugar and pepper in proportions to taste and simmer gently for 1 minute. Drop in the oysters and their reserved liquid and heat gently just long enough to warm the oysters through.

Return oysters to their shells with a portion of the sauce and the fried herbs. Arrange on plates and garnish with sprigs of fresh fennel or parsley.

SERVES 6

TOM PONH

Fish and Eggplant Purée

This dish is a typical example of the ingenuity of Laotian cooks, who have created a delectable dish by combining the tender fish caught in the Mekong with the smooth-textured local eggplants. Gnu mak kheua (eggplant) is boiled until tender, along with the fish. After the fish has been skinned and boned, it is pounded together with aromatics to make a smooth, creamy purée that is spread over salad leaves, topped with herbs and wrapped.

FISH PURÉE

1½ lb (750 g) meaty fresh fish
6 small white or purple eggplants (aubergines), about 3½ oz/100 g each
fish sauce
4 fresh red chilies
2–3 green onions
2 tablespoons chopped fresh mint

SALAD

2–3 heads Boston or Bibb lettuce
1 cup fresh mint leaves
1 cup fresh chervil or fennel leaves
1 cup fresh basil leaves
1 cup fresh Vietnamese mint
2–3 green onions

Place the fish in a saucepan, cover with cold water and drain. Cover again with water and bring to the boil. Reduce heat and simmer the fish for about 12 minutes, until very tender. Drain, reserving some of the poaching liquid.

Bring a large saucepan of lightly salted water to the boil. Trim the stems from the eggplants, drop them into the water and simmer until tender, then drain and scrape off the skin.

Place the eggplant in a mortar, blender or food processor. Remove the flesh from the fish and add to the eggplant, together with 1–2 tablespoons fish sauce and the chilies,

OYSTERS WITH GARLIC AND HERB SAUCE WELDON TRANNIES

FISH AND EGGPLANT/AUBERGINE PUREE WELDON TRANNIES

green onion and mint. Pound/process to a smooth purée, adding a little of the liquid reserved from poaching the fish; the purée should be fairly thick. Check the seasoning, adding extra fish sauce to taste. Transfer to a serving dish.

★ Rinse the lettuce and herbs, separating the leaves. Trim and shred the green onions. Arrange the salad attractively on serving platters.

★ To assemble, arrange a portion of fish purée and several pieces of onion and herbs on each lettuce leaf. Roll up.

★ A dipping sauce based on finely chopped chilies, chopped fresh mint, fish sauce and white vinegar, seasoned with sugar and salt, can be prepared to serve on the side.

SERVES 6

KENG KALAMPI

Laotian Cabbage Soup

No Laotian meal is complete without a soup, which is served in the middle of the meal or at the end, never at the beginning.

The word keng, *which designates a soup dish, is also used in Thailand, and a number of these Laotian soups appear on Thai menus. Cabbage, local mushrooms and bamboo shoots are prime soup making ingredients in Laos, usually coupled with fish and occasionally with meat or potatoes.* Keng kalampi *is a mild-flavored everyday dish that is quickly made using white or Chinese cabbage.*

1 small onion
2 cloves garlic
1 teaspoon grated galingale/young ginger
2 teaspoons ground coriander
2 tablespoons vegetable oil
4 cups (12 oz/375 g) chopped cabbage, trimmed
¼ teaspoon ground black pepper
6 cups (1½ liters) beef stock
2 tablespoons fish sauce
salt

Peel and chop the onion and garlic. Fry the onion, garlic, ginger and coriander in the oil for 1½ minutes on medium heat, then add the cabbage and pepper and fry for 2 more minutes, stirring frequently.

★ Add the stock, fish sauce and a large pinch of salt and bring to the boil. Simmer for 10–12 minutes and serve.

SERVES 6

MOU NEM

Ground Pork with Roasted Rice, in Salad Leaves

White rice is roasted until very dry, ground to a fine powder and mixed with ground pork that has been fried until it too is dry and powdery. The resultant dish is seasoned with romdeng/kha *(galingale or young ginger),* tuk trey/nam padek *(fish sauce) and a little sugar and formed into a paste, which is wrapped in salad leaves. It is not unlike the* nems *of Vietnam, which are similarly wrapped rolls of salad and herbs. Red chilies, cut into flower shapes, and curls of green onion decorate this dish which, when surrounded by young lettuce leaves and sprigs of herbs, has the appearance of a massive bouquet of flowers.* Mou nem *is a dish that appears frequently on the table in Laotian homes, enjoyed equally as a family meal or festive dish. Serve with little bowls of additional* tuk trey/nam padek *with, if liked, finely shredded red chili added.*

10 oz (315 g) glutinous white rice
8 oz (250 g) fresh bacon or pancetta (pork belly)
3 tablespoons vegetable oil
1-in (2.5-cm) piece galingale or young ginger, grated
2 teaspoons sugar
2 tablespoons fish sauce, or to taste
½ teaspoon salt
1 medium iceberg lettuce
1–2 heads Boston or Bibb lettuce
4 fresh red chilies
6 green onions
1 cup loosely packed fresh mint leaves
1 cup loosely packed basil leaves
1 cup Vietnamese mint leaves, fennel or fresh cilantro (coriander)

Wash the rice and allow to dry, then spread in a wide baking dish and place in a 350°F (180°C) oven. Bake until the rice is completely parched, then transfer to a mortar or blender and grind to a smooth fine powder. Set aside. Cut the rind from the pork and place it in a saucepan with water to cover generously. Bring to the boil, then reduce heat and simmer for about 40 minutes until very tender. Lift out and cut rind into very fine shreds.

★ Grind the pork meat and fry in the oil over medium heat until very dry; pour off the oil halfway through cooking so that the pork can dry out.

★ Add the pork to the rice and blend in the pork rind, galingale or ginger, sugar, fish sauce and salt. Spread the mixture in a serving dish.

★ Wash the lettuces, separating the leaves. Use a small, sharp knife to cut lengthwise along the chilies, cutting the flesh into narrow strands from just beneath the stem to the tip. Place in ice water and the "petals" will curl, forming attractive chili flowers. Cut the green onions into 1-in (2.5-cm) lengths. Use the point of a small, sharp knife to shred one end from about halfway down. Place in ice water

GROUND PORK WITH ROASTED RICE IN SALAD LEAVES

to encourage the onions to curl. Rinse the herbs and separate into small sprigs.

🌶 Set the dish of pork mixture in the center of a very large platter and arrange the lettuce and herbs around it. Garnish the pork with the chili flowers and green onion curl.

SERVES 6

TREY AING
Grilled Fish

The Kampuchean word for grilling is aing. *It is a frequently employed method of cooking in home and restaurant kitchens, particularly for fish. The fish are cooked with their scales on, since these act as a natural wrapper to protect the flesh and keep it moist during cooking. As in neighboring Vietnam, the local* tuk trey *(fish sauce) is made into a dip by adding chopped roasted peanuts, chili, garlic, lime juice and sugar. Coconut milk may also be added, with a few shreds of the mild-tasting* romdeng *(galingale), a root of the ginger family.*

2½ lb (1¼ kg) fresh fish of the nonoily kind
2 green onions
2 in (5 cm) piece galingale/young ginger
salt and pepper
1 small bunch fresh spinach
1 head Boston or Bibb lettuce
1 iceberg lettuce
1 bunch fresh watercress
1 medium cucumber
4 oz (125 g) fresh bean sprouts
a selection of fresh herbs such as mint, cilantro (coriander), sweet basil, fennel
1–2 shredded chilies (green or red)

SAUCE DIP

¼ cup (2 fl oz/60 ml) fish sauce
¼ cup (2 fl oz/60 ml) thin coconut milk
2 tablespoons lime juice
1–2 tablespoons sugar
1 tablespoon crushed roasted peanuts
1 teaspoon minced fresh red chili
½ teaspoon crushed garlic
½ teaspoon minced galingale/young ginger
½ teaspoon very finely minced lemon grass root

Gut the fish and rinse thoroughly inside. (The head is usually retained, but may be removed if preferred.) Trim the fins to avoid burning them. Place the green onions and bruised ginger in the cavity, adding a generous amount of salt and pepper.

🌶 Place on a wire rack over a charcoal grill and cook for about 7 minutes on each side. To test for doneness, insert a fork into the thickest part of the flesh near the head; the flesh should appear white and flake easily.

🌶 Thoroughly wash the spinach, lettuce and watercress in cold water. Separate the leaves and shake off excess water. Arrange the leaves on a wide platter. Score the skin of the cucumber with the tines of a fork, then cut into thin slices. Blanch the bean sprouts in boiling water for 30 seconds. Drain and cover with cold water to arrest the cooking, then drain again very thoroughly.

🌶 Rinse the herbs, separate into sprigs and shake off excess water. Add the cucumber, sprouts and herbs to the platter of vegetables.

🌶 Mix the sauce ingredients together, stirring to dissolve the sugar. Pour into small dishes.

KOY TIOUM, LAOTIAN GRILLED FISH

🌶 Remove the fish from the fire by lifting carefully with two wide spatulas. Place on a work surface and scrape away the scales with skin attached. Turn fish onto a serving plate and remove the scales and skin from the other side. Garnish with shredded chili and sprigs of cilantro and serve at once.

🌶 The fish is removed from the bone with two forks, and pieces are wrapped in lettuce or spinach with a selection of the herbs and vegetables. Dip into the sauce before eating.

SERVES 6

Koy Tioum

The Laotian version of this dish uses large freshwater fish from the Mekong, skewered with bamboo rods and grilled/broiled over charcoal. The fish is boned and the flesh pounded to a paste in a mortar. Spoonfuls of the resultant paste are wrapped in salad leaves in cornet shapes, and eaten with the sauce.

PHANENG KAI
Chicken Stuffed with Peanuts

Chickens are scarce and therefore valued in Laos. Eggs are only rarely eaten, the cook preferring to forgo such delicacies as phan khay *(egg pancakes stuffed with raw meat and steamed in banana leaves) in favor of allowing the eggs to hatch into chickens – which can provide more nourishment and variety.*

Phaneng kai, a whole young chicken stuffed with roasted peanuts and seasonings and simmered in coconut milk, is a luxury dish reserved for special occasions.

2½ lb (1¼ kg) chicken
salt and ground white pepper
6 dried red chilies
1 teaspoon fennel seeds
1 cup (5 oz/155 g) roasted peanuts
1 large onion
3 tablespoons vegetable oil
3 oz (90 g) ground pork, preferably slightly fatty
½ teaspoon cinnamon
1 tablespoon finely chopped fresh mint
3 cups (24 fl oz/750 ml) thin coconut milk
fish sauce

CHICKEN STUFFED WITH PEANUTS AND *BAY PHOUM,* A RICE AND PORK MOLD

Place the chilies and fennel seeds in a small heavy skillet or in a hot oven and toast until they are aromatic and crisp, then transfer to a spice grinder or mortar and grind to a powder. Add the peanuts and grind these until reasonably fine.

Very finely chop the onion. Heat the oil in a medium pan and fry the onion until well colored, then add the pork and fry until it changes color. Add the peanuts and ground spices and fry together until well mixed and fragrant. Stir in the mint.

Stuff the prepared filling into the cavity of the chicken and close the openings with skewers or picks. Place in a deep saucepan and add the coconut milk and fish sauce. Bring to the boil, then reduce the heat and simmer gently for at least 1 hour until the chicken is so tender that it is falling from the bones. Lift out, cover and set aside.

Continue to simmer the sauce until well reduced. Check seasonings, adding fish sauce and pepper to taste. Place the whole chicken on a serving dish, pour on the sauce and garnish with fresh herbs.

SERVES 6

Bay Phoum

Glutinous Rice and Pork Mold

In general, Laos and Kampuchea have borrowed little from the Chinese in the culinary sphere; but this one dish is quite similar to a Chinese sticky rice dish that is steamed in lotus leaves. It can be steamed or baked in the oven.

2 cups (12 oz/375 g) glutinous rice
5 cups (1¼ liters) water
4 Chinese pork sausages (about 5 oz/155 g)
6 oz (185 g) fat salt pork or bacon
2 medium onions
3 cloves garlic
6 dried black Chinese mushrooms, soaked
¼ cup (1 oz/30 g) dried shrimp, soaked
¼ cup (2 fl oz/60 ml) fish sauce
½ teaspoon ground black pepper

Wash the rice, drain well and place in a saucepan with the water. Bring to the boil, cover and cook over low heat for about 30 minutes until the rice is tender and has absorbed the water.

Finely dice the sausages, pork or bacon, onions and the garlic. Fry without oil in a wok or skillet for 5 minutes.

Drain the mushrooms, squeeze out excess water and chop the caps finely. Drain the dried shrimp and add with the mushrooms to the pan. Add the fish sauce and season with pepper. Cook over medium heat for 2 minutes, stirring frequently, then add the rice and mix in well.

Transfer to a greased heatproof dish and smooth the top. Cover with aluminum foil and place in a steamer. Steam for 30 minutes, then remove from heat and allow to firm up for 6–7 minutes. Cut into squares to serve.

SERVES 6

Khao Phoune

Laotian Noodle Soup

Soups, especially those containing noodles, are eaten for breakfast throughout Laos. Khao phoune is sold by streetside vendors and most home kitchens have a pot of this sustaining meal ready as soon as the sun rises. Served from a large pot, the soup contains cooked rice vermicelli, chopped banana flowers, bean sprouts, salad greens and an abundance of different local herbs. A large bowl is half-filled with the vermicelli, topped with a selection of the other ingredients and then covered with the hot soup, which is made from beef or pork, fish, chili and creamy coconut milk.

This national favorite is not unlike the laksa *dishes served in Malaysia and Indonesia.*

1 lb (500 g) pork (fresh ham or picnic shoulder)
4 cloves garlic
1 large onion
3 cups (24 fl oz/750 ml) water
1 lb (500 g) white fish, or a whole fish
1 tablespoon vegetable oil
1 teaspoon grated fresh ginger
1 tablespoon finely chopped fresh red chili
8 cups (2 liters) thin coconut milk
2 cups (7 oz/220 g) ground roasted peanuts
salt
fish sauce
2 teaspoons tomato paste (optional)*

LAOTIAN NOODLE SOUP

1 medium cucumber
1–2 banana flowers, optional
1 unripe mango or a slice of unripe papaya
½ giant white radish (Japanese *daikon,* Chinese *loh buk*)
8 oz (250 g) fresh bean sprouts
4 oz (125 g) green or Chinese long beans, sliced
1 medium eggplant
2–3 tablespoons vegetable oil
selection of fresh mint, fennel and basil
6–8 green onions
1 lb (500 g) rice vermicelli

Cut the pork into cubes. Coarsely chop the garlic and onion. Place pork, onion and garlic in a saucepan. Add the water and bring to the boil, then reduce heat and simmer gently for about 1 hour, until very tender, skimming the surface from time to time and adding extra water if needed to keep the meat covered. When tender, lift out meat and add the fish. Simmer until very tender, then remove and bone if necessary. Cut the meat and fish into small pieces, discard the garlic and onion and return the meat and fish to the stock. Simmer again for 5–6 minutes, then set aside.

Heat 1 tablespoon oil in another pan and fry the ginger and chili for a few minutes. Add the coconut milk and peanuts and bring to the boil. Simmer gently for 5 minutes, then add salt and fish sauce to taste and the tomato paste, if used. Pour over the meat and fish and bring to the boil. Simmer together for about 5 minutes, then keep hot.

Peel and thinly slice the cucumber. Wash the banana flowers, slice very thinly and soak in the water. Dice the mango or papaya and radish. Blanch the bean sprouts for 30 seconds in boiling water; drain, cover with cold water and drain again. Parboil the beans in lightly salted water until almost tender; drain, cover with cold water and drain again. Cut the eggplant into very thin slices. Heat 2–3 tablespoons oil in a wide skillet and fry the eggplant on both sides until very crisp. Drain on paper towels. Finely chop the herbs and green onions.

Bring a large pot of well-salted water to the boil. Add the rice vermicelli and simmer until tender, then drain well.

For each serving, place a portion of the vermicelli in a deep dish, add a little of of the prepared vegetables and herbs, then cover with the soup. Serve at once.

* Added mainly for color. Puréed red bell pepper will give even more authentic results.

SERVES 6

THE FORMER ROYAL PALACE, PHNUM PENH   ALEXANDER BOWIE

NJUM
Bamboo Shoot Salad

1 lb (500 g) canned whole bamboo shoots
¼ cup (2 fl oz/60 ml) thick coconut milk
2 tablespoons fish sauce
2–2½ tablespoons lime juice
1 tablespoon minced fresh red chili
1 teaspoon crushed garlic
2 tablespoons finely chopped green onion
1 tablespoon sugar
selection of fresh cilantro (coriander), mint and fennel
    leaves
3 shallots (or 1 Spanish onion)

Drain the bamboo shoots and place in a saucepan with cold water to cover. Bring to the boil, then drain and cover with cold water. Set aside until cold, then drain again and wipe dry. Cut into paper-thin slices.

In a glass measure, mix the coconut milk, fish sauce and lime juice together, then add the chili, garlic, green onion and sugar. Check the flavor, adjusting to taste if needed. Pour over the bamboo shoots, toss lightly and set aside for about 30 minutes.

Rinse the herbs, dry thoroughly and break into sprigs. Very thinly slice the shallots. Pile the bamboo shoots into the center of a serving platter and pour on any remaining dressing. Surround with the herbs and cover with the sliced shallots.

SERVES 6

KHAOLOTE SONG
Tapioca and Rice Bean Dessert

1½ cups (7½ oz/235 g) rice flour
green food coloring
1¼ cups (7 oz/220 g) tapioca
6 cups (1½ liters) water
red food coloring
1 cup (8 oz/250 g) sugar
2½ cups (20 fl oz/600 ml) thick coconut milk
large pinch of salt
shaved ice

Mix the rice flour with enough cold water to make a smooth, thick batter, adding food coloring to make the mixture a bright green. Have ready a large saucepan of lightly salted boiling water. Press the rice batter through the holes in a perforated ladle or skimmer so that it drops into the water in little pellets. Cook until they rise to the surface, then cook for another 2–3 minutes. Lift out and transfer to a dish of ice water to cool.

Separately boil the tapioca in 6 cups water, with red food coloring added to make the tapioca a bright pink color. Cook for about 30 minutes until tender. (If preferred, the tapioca can be cooked in two separate batches, adding food color only to one and leaving the other clear.)

Mix the sugar with at least 1 cup cold water. Bring to the boil and simmer for about 15 minutes to make a thick syrup. Remove from heat and cool.

To assemble the dessert, place a portion of rice flour beans and tapioca in each dessert dish. Add sugar syrup and lightly salted coconut milk, top with a little shaved ice and serve.

SERVES 6–8

Vietnam

SUNSET OVER A VILLAGE, NORTHERN VIETNAM
JOHN EVERINGHAM

BARBECUED BEEF SALAD, *recipe page 138*

Vietnam

HERBACEOUS OVERTONES

From a culinary point of view, Vietnam has remained relatively isolated from its neighbors. The range of dishes is not immense, but the Vietnamese have achieved an impressive and distinctive style of cooking – or more accurately serving – their food which puts to good use their abundance of leafy vegetables and herbs. Fragrant *bac ha* (mint), in many varieties, pungent *can tau* (cilantro), fresh-tasting dill and fennel, and aromatic, stimulating basil are recognized herbs in the West. There are also a number of local herbs – of which *rau ram*/Vietnamese mint is the undisputed leader. All are used frequently both as garnish and as an indispensable cooking ingredient.

The Vietnamese like to serve many of their main dishes sandwich-style in a wrapper of lettuce or *banh trang* (edible rice paper) with leafy herbs, a sliver or two of cucumber, carrot and radish, a small bundle of cooked rice vermicelli and a sauce to dip or dunk the little package into before eating. *Nem nuong* (bite-size charcoal- or griddle-cooked pork meatballs), *bo nuong* (beef balls or stuffed beef rolls), and *cha gio* (little stuffed rolls wrapped in rice paper and crisply deep-fried) are all popular dishes that are served with the accompanying wrappers or lettuce leaves to be rolled up at the table.

Sauces for these dishes can be tart tasting, based on a combination of lime juice and *nuoc mam,* the pungent thin and salty fish sauce that is the basis of Vietnamese seasoning. Or they can be thick, rich and sweet, rather like a cross between the peanut and coconut based *sate* sauce of Indonesia and the sweet *hoisin* sauce of China.

When not wrapped up, salad vegetables are arranged with fastidious precision in layers on flat platters – never piled unceremoniously into a salad bowl – to serve as *goi* (salad) with a varied assort-

JOHN EVERINGHAM

ment of meats. In a single dish these might include shredded cooked chicken, sliced beef or pork, slivers of dried squid and cubes of fried fish. Garnishes are repetitive, though rarely do they become boring. The commonest are chopped roasted peanuts, fine shreds of carrot, chopped or shredded green onion or crisply fried onion, chopped garlic; herbs, of course, particularly cilantro (coriander) and Vietnamese mint, and occasionally cooked rice vermicelli tossed with toasted coconut or shredded omelet.

A meal's attractive presentation is considered almost as important as its taste; in a Vietnamese household the women may devote many hours to the preparation of the evening meal.

Rice is the staple and is served at every meal, except perhaps when the bulk of the meal is one of the popular *mein* (noodle) dishes. These are hearty and sustaining combinations of soup broth, rice noodles in a variety of sizes and shapes, and meat or meatballs. The traditional bowl of *pho,* with tender-simmered beef, broth, rice noodles, bean sprouts, fresh cilantro (coriander) and shredded green onions, is the sort of meal-in-one-bowl that is enjoyed day or night. The broth is enriched by slow simmering with the beef, beef bones and fragrant ginger, star anise and tangerine or mandarin orange peel.

Both beef and pork are popular meats, the former being prepared for special occasions in unique style as a dish – or more accurately, a banquet – called "Seven Styles of Beef." Braised, fried, simmered, sautéed, grilled and barbecued, the meat pieces, slices, balls and cubes are each cooked in a special way and presented one by one in a select sequence each to enhance the other. Pork is generally cooked simply by simmering with soy sauce and pepper or braising as a richly flavored stew; or it may be ground finely to make tender meatballs.

Two dishes displaying the artistry of Vietnamese cooks and epitomizing the delicacy of their seasonings are *chao tom,* in which peeled sugar cane sticks are coated with a layer of pounded shrimp and roasted over a charcoal fire, then served with a mild and sugary *nuoc mam*-based sauce, and *banh phoug tom,* comprising fried shrimp wafers, topped with a square of edible rice paper or a steamed rice flour sheet, a few slivers of barbecued beef and a sprinkling of crushed peanuts and green onions.

The use of seasonings in Vietnamese cooking is restrained. The ubiquitous *nuoc mam* is the Vietnamese equivalent of Chinese soy sauce. Light ochre brown in color, thin and vaguely salty, it has a pungent aroma that is in no way overpowering, and it is the keynote to seasoning foods in the Vietnamese style. The five-pointed star anise and aromatic fresh cilantro (coriander) have been adopted from the Chinese, but otherwise only a dusting of white pepper, fresh red chili, ginger, garlic and lemon grass make up the seasoning repertory. Roasted peanuts, lime juice, and brown sugar and a sparing use of pickled vegetables completes the picture.

COMING HOME WITH THE CATCH   JOHN EVERINGHAM

Vietnamese meals are eaten with chopsticks from a rice bowl in the Chinese way – when not eaten with the fingers. Soups are taken with a spoon for the liquid and chopsticks for the solids. A table-setting would not be complete without a little pot of *nuoc cham* (see page 137), a hot blend of mashed fresh chili, and a jug or shaker bottle of *nuoc mam.*

Excellent coffee and crisp white French-style rolls are two legacies of the French colonial era the Vietnamese have chosen to retain. Otherwise there is little evidence of French influence, save for the occasional flan or *crème caramel* on the menu of upscale restaurants in Ho Chi Minh City.

Sweet tastes are enjoyed by the Vietnamese, but they are most likely to eat a sweet snack – be it cake, cookie or pudding – between meals rather than after a meal. Rice and rich local brown sugar, wedded to coconut meat or milk, form the basis of the sweet dishes in this country.

CHA GIO

Chicken and Crabmeat Rolls with Salad

Finger-sized crisp cha gio *are the Vietnamese version of the Chinese egg or spring roll. But the outstanding difference here is in the way they are eaten. In keeping with their penchant for serving salad with just about everything, the Vietnamese also enjoy their chicken rolls wrapped in salad leaves and herbs. The refreshing, tart bite of* rau ram *(Vietnamese mint) blends with the smoothness of minced chicken and crabmeat, the flakiness of the rice paper pastry and the piquant flavor of the* nuoc cham *dipping sauce.*

WRAPPERS AND SALAD

36 6-in (15-cm) rice paper wrappers
2 tablespoons light corn syrup
¼ cup (2 fl oz/60 ml) water
1 large head iceberg lettuce (or 2 heads Boston or Bibb lettuce)
2 cups tightly packed fresh mint leaves, or
    1 cup tightly packed Vietnamese mint or sweet basil and
    1 cup fresh cilantro (coriander) leaves
oil for deep-frying

FILLING

8 oz (250 g) chicken breast, finely ground (minced)
4 oz (125 g) flaked cooked crabmeat
4 green onions, finely chopped
1 cup (1½ oz/45 g) broken rice stick noodles, soaked to soften
1 medium carrot, finely grated
salt and black pepper
1 egg
1 tablespoon cornstarch (cornflour)

NUOC CHAM (DIPPING SAUCE)

1 fresh red chili, seeded and shredded
1½ tablespoons lime juice
¼ cup (2 fl oz/60 ml) *nuoc mam* (fish sauce)
¼ cup (2 fl oz/60 ml) water
2 teaspoons sugar, or to taste
1 tablespoon crushed roasted peanuts
1 tablespoon finely slivered carrot

Leave the rice papers in a plastic bag until needed.

❧ Mix the filling ingredients, squeezing through the fingers until well mixed.

❧ Dissolve the corn syrup in the water. Brush over one side of each wrapper and leave to soften.

❧ Place the wrappers, glazed side down, on a work surface. Place a spoonful of the filling in the center. Roll up and use a little of the glaze to seal the edge down.

❧ Rinse the lettuce and herbs and separate the leaves. Dry thoroughly and arrange on a serving plate.

❧ Heat the oil to the smoking point, then reduce the heat slightly. Deep-fry the *cha gio* about 8 at a time, until golden brown. Lift out and drain well on a paper towel-lined rack. Arrange the rolls on another serving plate.

❧ Mix the sauce ingredients together and divide between several small dishes. Take everything to the table. To assemble the rolls, place a few sprigs of herbs on the lettuce, add a chicken roll and roll up firmly. Dip into the sauce before eating.

MAKES 36

SHRIMP/PRAWN CRISPS WITH BEEF AND PEANUTS AND CHICKEN AND CRABMEAT ROLLS WITH SALAD

BANH PHOUG TOM

Shrimp Crisps with Beef and Peanuts

This unusual appetizer comprises large fried shrimp crisps – commonly known as kroepuk – *that are topped with a tiny square of moistened rice paper, a few slivers of marinated, barbecued beef and a sprinkling of crushed peanuts and green onions. They are delightful to nibble with drinks.*

4 oz (125 g) beef tenderloin (fillet)
2 teaspoons sesame oil
1 tablespoon *nuoc mam* (fish sauce)
1 teaspoon cornstarch (cornflour)
salt and black pepper
1 teaspoon crushed garlic
1 teaspoon minced lemon grass root
2 cups (16 fl oz/500 ml) vegetable oil
24 *kroepuk* (shrimp/prawn crisps)
3–4 edible rice paper sheets
2 tablespoons crushed roasted peanuts
2 tablespoons finely chopped green onions

Very thinly slice the beef (this is most easily done if it is partially frozen) and cut into 1½-in (4-cm) squares. Mix the sesame oil, fish sauce, cornstarch, salt, pepper, garlic and lemon grass root together in a dish. Add the meat and mix well. Cover with plastic wrap and let stand for 3 hours, turning from time to time.

❧ Heat the vegetable oil in a wok or deep saucepan to the smoking point. Drop in the shrimp crisps several at a time and cook quickly, turning once, until they have expanded; they should not be allowed to color. Lift out on a slotted spoon and drain on paper towels. Dip the rice paper into hot water to soften, then drain and arrange on a rack or cloth to dry out slightly. Cut into squares a little larger than the meat.

Heat a large skillet over high heat with about 2 tablespoons of the vegetable oil from the wok. Fry the meat, about 8 pieces at a time, until just cooked through; the surface of the meat should be well seared while the inside remains tender and moist.

To assemble, place a square of rice paper in the center of each shrimp crisp. Top with a sliver or two of the beef and a little of the oil from the pan. Garnish with peanuts and green onions and serve at once.

SERVES 6

CHAO TOM

Shrimp Paste on Sugar Cane Sticks

Possibly one of the most esoteric dishes in the Vietnamese cuisine, chao tom *comprises a mixture of pounded shrimp (prawns) lightly flavored with* nuoc mam *(fish sauce), wrapped around sections of peeled sugar cane and grilled over a charcoal fire. The dipping sauce is a sweet concoction of sugar cane juice, crushed peanuts and* nuoc mam, *flavored with ground roasted peanuts, garlic and chili.*

It is a popular snack at roadside and market stalls and in most restaurants, but it is rarely made in the home.

6 pieces fresh sugar cane, each about 9 in (23 cm) long
1¼ lb (625 g) peeled uncooked shrimp (prawns)
1 tablespoon fish sauce
2 small egg whites, well beaten
salt and pepper
vegetable oil
2–3 tablespoons minced green onions

SAUCE DIP

1½ tablespoons sugar cane juice (available canned), optional
1 tablespoon soft brown sugar
2 tablespoons fish sauce
1½ teaspoons crushed garlic
1½ teaspoons minced fresh red chili
1 tablespoon crushed roasted peanuts

Use a strong sharp knife to remove the hard outer skin from the sugar cane.

Place the shrimp in a food processor or blender with the fish sauce, egg whites and a large pinch each of salt and pepper. Process to a smooth paste, adding 1–2 tablespoons ice water to increase the volume of the paste and improve its texture.

Use wet hands to mold the shrimp paste around the center section of each cane stick, leaving the two ends exposed. Brush lightly with vegetable oil, then roll in the minced green onions, coating lightly.

Barbecue over glowing coals, turning frequently, until the shrimp paste feels firm to the touch. Brush with extra oil during cooking if necessary.

In the meantime, mix the sauce ingredients, adding a little cold water and a pinch of extra sugar if sugar cane juice is unobtainable. Divide the sauce among several small dishes and place on the table. Cover a serving plate with folded paper napkins, arrange the sugar cane sticks on it and serve immediately.

SERVES 6

SHRIMP/PRAWN PASTE ON SUGAR CANE STICKS   WELDON TRANNIES

BO NUONG GOI

Barbecued Beef Salad

A tiny charcoal-heated iron skillet is brought to the table so diners can cook their own meat, which is then combined with an array of salad and herb ingredients in edible rice paper wrappers. Two sauces provide contrasting tastes.

1 lb (500 g) lean rump or tenderloin (fillet)
2 teaspoons crushed garlic
2 tablespoons minced green onions
1½ tablespoons minced lemon grass root
½ teaspoon salt
1 tablespoon sugar
vegetable oil

SALAD

24 sheets edible rice paper
24 lettuce leaves
4 oz (125 g) fresh bean sprouts
1 cucumber
1 carambola (star fruit)
3 oz (90 g) pickled carrot and radish*
2 oz (60 g) rice vermicelli
3–4 green onions
3 cups tightly packed fresh mint, basil, Vietnamese mint, fresh cilantro (coriander) and chervil

SAUCE 1

¼ cup (2 fl oz/60 ml) thin coconut milk
2½ tablespoons fish sauce
1 teaspoon minced fresh red chili
½ teaspoon crushed garlic
1½ tablespoons finely slivered pickled carrot and radish*
1 tablespoon lime juice
sugar to taste

SAUCE 2

¼ cup (2 fl oz/60 ml) thin coconut milk
2 tablespoons fish sauce
salt, pepper and sugar to taste
1½ tablespoons crushed roasted peanuts

Very thinly slice the beef (having it partially frozen makes this easier), then cut into strips about 1 in (2.5 cm) wide and 4 in (10 cm) long. Mix the garlic, green onion, lemon grass root, salt and sugar together. Rub over the meat and marinate for at least 3 hours.

❧ Prepare the sauces by mixing the ingredients for each. Divide among small dishes.

❧ Dip the rice paper sheets into hot water to soften, then spread on racks until dry enough to handle.

❧ Wash and dry the lettuce, separating the leaves. Blanch the bean sprouts in boiling water for 30 seconds, then drain thoroughly. Peel the cucumber and cut into short sticks, discarding the seeds. Very thinly slice the star fruit. Drain the carrot and radish. Drop the vermicelli into a saucepan of boiling water and simmer gently for a minute or two until almost tender; drain. Place on an oiled plate in a bundle. Cover with another oiled plate and press down firmly until the rice vermicelli is compressed into a cake. Cut into small squares.

❧ Trim and shred the green onions. Rinse the herbs, dry well and separate the leaves. Arrange these ingredients attractively on several large platters.

❧ Have a small table-top charcoal-heated skillet – or an electric frying pan – on the table and heat to fairly hot.

❧ Add a little vegetable oil. Bring the marinated meat to the table along with one pair of wooden chopsticks per person. Have each diner quick-fry a portion of beef, and then assemble it with the other ingredients in a lettuce-lined rice wrapper. Dip into either of the sauces before eating.

* To make pickled carrot and radish, peel the vegetables and thinly slice lengthwise, then cut into narrow sticks about 2 in (5 cm) long. Place in a glass or stainless steel dish and add white vinegar, sugar and salt in proportions to taste; the mixture should be just slightly tart. Let stand for about 3 hours until softened. The pickle will keep for several weeks in the refrigerator in an airtight container.

SERVES 6–8

THIT HEO TAU

Pork Simmered in Coconut Milk

Vietnamese food is characteristically mild in flavor. Coconut milk is used in this classic recipe to provide a creamy sauce whose only seasonings are sugar, nuoc mam *(fish sauce) and white pepper.*

1½ lb (750 g) boneless fresh ham or picnic shoulder (leg/shoulder pork)
2 tablespoons palm sugar, or soft brown sugar
½ cup (4 fl oz/125 ml) cold water
2½ tablespoons fish sauce
¾ teaspoon white pepper
2 cups (16 fl oz/500 ml) thin coconut milk
cooked rice

Pour boiling water over the pork skin, then pat dry. Place skin side down in a saucepan and add enough cold water to cover. Bring to the boil, then reduce heat to medium-low and simmer gently for about 45 minutes, turning several times. Discard the water, set meat aside and drain well. Cut into thick slices, then into strips 2 in (5 cm) wide.

PORK SIMMERED IN COCONUT MILK (TOP), AND HOT FISH SAUCE
(BOTTOM), recipe page 137

❧ Combine the sugar and water in a saucepan and bring to the boil, then reduce the heat and simmer until the syrup is sticky. Pass the pork slices through the syrup to coat each piece, then return to the saucepan.

❧ Sprinkle with the fish sauce and pepper; pour the coconut milk slowly down the side of the saucepan. Cover and bring almost to the boil, then simmer over medium heat until the pork is tender and the sauce is thick and creamy. Serve with white rice.

SERVES 4–6

GA XAO XA OT

Chicken with Lemon Grass and Peanuts

Aromatic lemon grass lends its fresh tasting citrus flavor to many Vietnamese dishes. Here it is combined with roasted peanuts. Serve this hot with boiled rice, or with rice vermicelli that has been deep-fried until crisp and white.

2-lb (1-kg) young roasting chicken
3–4 stalks lemon grass
3 green onions
1 teaspoon salt
large pinch ground white pepper
2 tablespoons vegetable oil
1 fresh red chili, seeded and shredded
2 teaspoons sugar
2 tablespoons fish sauce
½ cup (2½ oz/75 g) roasted peanuts

Cut the chicken in half, then remove the legs, thighs and wings. Cut the remainder into diagonal slices. Divide the wings at the joints; remove the drumsticks and chop in half with a heavy cleaver. Cut each thigh portion into 3 pieces, using a heavy cleaver to chop straight through the bones. Place in a glass or stainless steel dish.

❧ Remove the outer leaves of the lemon grass and trim off the green tops and the roots. Slice the white lower sections, then chop very finely. Trim the green onions and chop finely. Toss the lemon grass and green onions with the chicken pieces, cover with plastic wrap and set aside for 20 minutes. Add salt and pepper, mix well and let stand for 20 more minutes to absorb the flavors.

CHICKEN WITH LEMON GRASS AND PEANUTS, *recipe page 139*

WELDON TRANNIES   BEEF AND BITTER GOURD ROLLS

❧ Heat the oil in a wok or skillet, add the chicken and sauté for about 6 minutes. Add the chili, the sugar and fish sauce and stir over medium heat for about 5 minutes, until the chicken is just cooked through.

❧ Coarsely chop the peanuts and stir into the wok.

SERVES 4–6

BO NUONG KIM TIEN

Beef and Bitter Gourd Rolls

The angled luffa, a thin gourd with deep green, sharply ridged skin, is used throughout Southeast Asia. Although its raw flesh is quite bitter, it has a relatively mild taste when cooked and it is highly regarded for its health-giving properties. The knobby, cucumberlike Chinese bitter melon can be used in its place.

6 oz (185 g) beef tenderloin (fillet) steak
½ bitter gourd, about 8 in (20 cm) long
1 teaspoon salt
2 teaspoons sugar
½ teaspoon Chinese five spice powder
2 teaspoons sesame oil
1 tablespoon cornstarch (cornflour)
vegetable oil
2 heads Boston or Bibb lettuce
1 tablespoon crushed roasted peanuts (optional)
nuoc cham (page 137)

Cut the steak into 12 slices and place on a sheet of plastic wrap allowing space between them. Cover with another sheet of plastic. Use the flat side of a meat mallet or a rolling pin to pound the steaks until quite thin.

❧ Use a sharp knife to trim off the edges of the angled ribs running down the gourd, then peel. Cut into strips, discarding the seed core. Drop into a pot of boiling water and blanch for 1 minute. Lift out, drain, cover with cold water, and drain again.

❧ Mix the salt, sugar, five spice powder and sesame oil and rub over one side of the steaks. Marinate for 20 minutes.

❧ Place a strip of melon in the center of each piece of beef and roll the meat tightly around it. Secure with wooden picks or thread and dust lightly with cornstarch.

❧ Heat a skillet and add about 1 in (2.5 cm) of vegetable oil. When very hot, fry the beef rolls for about 3 minutes until cooked through. Drain off the oil, return the rolls to the pan and continue to cook gently until well colored and crisp.

❧ Arrange washed and dried lettuce leaves on a platter. Remove the rolls from the pan and cut into short lengths. Discard the picks or thread. Pile onto the lettuce and sprinkle with the peanuts. Serve with *nuoc cham* as a dip.

SERVES 4

BUN BO

Beef with Vermicelli

1 lb (500 g) rice vermicelli
salt
1¼ lb (625 g) rump steak
vegetable oil
pepper
2 large onions, thinly sliced
1 large cucumber
4 oz (125 g) crushed roasted peanuts

SAUCE

fish sauce
cold water
white vinegar or lime juice
sugar
chili flakes or chopped fresh red chili

Place the rice vermicelli in a large pot and cover with boiling water. Drain. Bring a large saucepan of water to the boil. Add 2 teaspoons salt and the rice vermicelli and boil for 5 minutes. Drain the noodles and rinse thoroughly with cold water, then drain again. Reheat the noodles by covering with boiling water.

BEEF WITH VERMICELLI *(TOP)* AND NOODLE SOUP WITH ASSORTED SLICED MEATS *(BOTTOM)*

Very thinly slice the steak. Heat a wide skillet and add a thin film of oil. Fry the steak quickly on both sides until well colored and just cooked through; do not overcook. Season with salt and pepper. Transfer to a warm plate, cover and set aside.

Add the onions to the pan and fry until they are well colored and softened. Peel and thinly slice the cucumber.

Drain the vermicelli and divide among 6 deep bowls. Add several slices of the beef, some onion and cucumber to each bowl. Sprinkle the top generously with peanuts.

Place a tray containing the sauce ingredients on the table and hand each diner a small bowl for mixing the sauce to his or her taste. It can be poured over the vermicelli or used as a dip.

SERVES 6

BANH CAHN TOM CUA

Noodles with Assorted Sliced Meats in Soup

4 oz (125 g) fresh bacon or pancetta (pork belly) with rind
4 oz (125 g) chicken breast meat
4 oz (125 g) peeled shrimp (prawns)
4 oz (125 g) cooked crabmeat
4 oz (125 g) cleaned squid
4 oz (125 g) thin egg noodles
6 cups (1½ liters) chicken stock
4 green onions
salt and white pepper
2 shallots or 1 Spanish onion
2 tablespoons vegetable oil
2 tablespoons chopped fresh cilantro (coriander)
nuoc cham (page 137) or
nuoc mam (fish sauce)

Bring a saucepan of lightly salted water to the boil. Put in the fresh bacon and simmer for about 30 minutes, until tender, then add the chicken and cook a further 15 minutes. Lift the meat out and discard the stock. Set the meat aside until cool enough to handle.

Devein the shrimp, using a wooden pick to ease the vein gently through an incision in the centerback. Separate the crabmeat into small chunks. Cut the squid into thin rings, if small, or into small squares if larger, scoring these diagonally at close intervals on one side to tenderize.

Drop the noodles into a pot of simmering salted water and cook briefly, then drain well.

Cut the pork and chicken into thin slices. Bring the stock to the boil and add the meat and seafood. Chop the green onions and add half to the pot with salt and white pepper to taste. Simmer gently for 6 minutes.

Finely chop the shallots and fry in the oil until almost crisp. Pour the soup into a tureen and garnish with the remaining green onions, the cilantro and fried shallots. Serve with *nuoc cham* or *nuoc mam*.

SERVES 6–8

PORK MEATBALLS SERVED IN SALAD ROLLS

Nem Nuong

Pork Meatballs Served in Salad Rolls

Few dishes reach the table in Vietnam without accompanying salad vegetables or a profusion of herbs. Many dishes are made up of a small basic meat dish such as meatballs, tiny stuffed beef rolls, slivers of barbecued beef, or fish purées. These are served with a mix of lettuces, mint and other herbs, bean sprouts, cucumber, radish and carrot and wrapped together in round sheets of edible rice paper. The resultant roll is then dipped in an aromatic sauce based on various combinations of roasted crushed peanuts, fish sauce and garlic.

Nem nuóng are small balls of smoothly ground pork that are first steamed or simmered, then cooked at the table on small portable broilers until crusty and well colored. They are then popped into the rice paper and lettuce roll with a selection of accompaniments and eaten sandwich style.

PORK BALLS

12 oz (375 g) finely ground (minced) lean pork
2–3 green onions, finely minced
1 teaspoon crushed garlic
1 teaspoon minced fresh ginger
2 small egg whites
½ cup (4 fl oz/125 ml) ice water
½ teaspoon white pepper
1 teaspoon salt
1 tablespoon vegetable oil

SALAD

24 iceberg lettuce leaves
2 rice paper wrappers, about 6 in (15 cm) in diameter
5 oz (155 g) rice vermicelli, cooked and thoroughly drained
2 cups tightly packed mixed fresh herbs – mint, Vietnamese mint, spearmint, basil, cilantro (coriander)
5 oz (155 g) fresh bean sprouts
1 small cucumber
1 medium carrot
5-in (12.5-cm) piece giant white radish (Chinese *loh buk*)

SAUCE

⅓ cup (2 oz/60 g) roasted peanuts
2 fresh red chilies, seeded and coarsely chopped
1 teaspoon crushed garlic
1 tablespoon finely chopped fresh mint
2 tablespoons lime or lemon juice
¼ cup (2 fl oz/60 ml) fish sauce
1 cup (8 fl oz/250 ml) thin coconut milk

Place the peanuts and chilies in a mortar and pound to a smooth paste. Add the garlic, mint, lime or lemon juice and fish sauce and mix again, pounding until smooth. Stir in the coconut milk, then transfer to small bowls and set aside.

🎬 Rinse and dry the lettuce. Dip the rice paper into cold water to soften, drain well and spread on paper towels until dry enough to handle. Cut the vermicelli into 2-in (5-cm) lengths. Break the herbs into small sprigs. Steep the bean sprouts in boiling water for 20 seconds, then drain well. Cut the cucumber, carrot and radish into matchstick pieces. Arrange all of these attractively on serving platters and place on the table.

🎬 Mix the pork, green onion, garlic and ginger, squeezing the mixture through the fingers to make it smooth. Add the lightly beaten egg whites and work energetically, then slowly add the ice water, pepper and salt, kneading the mixture until very smooth. Add the vegetable oil and work in smoothly.

🎬 Use wet hands to form the mixture into small balls. Arrange on a lightly oiled plate and set in a steamer. Steam over high heat for 10 minutes. Or drop the balls into a pot of gently simmering, lightly salted water and simmer until they rise to the surface, then simmer another minute and remove with a slotted spoon.

🎬 Have a small portable grill ready on the table. Heat, oil it lightly and cook the pork balls until crisp. Or sauté the pork balls in a skillet and bring to the table on a serving plate.

🎬 Prepare the rolls using a little of each ingredient. Dip into the sauce between mouthfuls.

SERVES 6

BOAT TAXIS AND VENDORS, HUE

JOHN EVERINGHAM

SWEET AND SOUR FISH SOUP

AROMATIC BRAISED BEEF WITH NOODLES IN RICH BROTH

CANH CHUA

Sweet and Sour Fish Soup

This is a popular South Vietnamese dish, in which any type of nonoily fish can be used. The tart tamarind flavor is balanced with sugar. Soybean sprouts, which have a stronger taste and are much larger in size than mung bean sprouts, are used in this dish.

1 lb (500 g) fish fillets
1 stalk celery
1 medium carrot
4 oz (125 g) fresh soybean sprouts
2 tablespoons tamarind pulp
2 tablespoons sugar, or to taste
2 green onions
salt and pepper
mint or Vietnamese mint leaves

STOCK

2 lb (1 kg) fish heads and bones
8 cups (2 liters) water
2 green onions
1-in (2.5-cm) piece fresh ginger, peeled
1 fresh red chili, quartered

Place the fish heads and bones in a deep saucepan and cover with cold water. Set aside for 10 minutes, then pour off the water. Add the 8 cups water, the whole green onions, ginger and chili and bring almost to the boil, then reduce the heat and simmer gently for 18 minutes. At no time should the liquid be allowed to boil or the stock will become cloudy and bitter-tasting. Strain stock into another saucepan.

Cut the fish into bite-size cubes. Diagonally slice the celery and carrot, blanch the bean sprouts in boiling water for 30 seconds and drain well.

Steep the tamarind pulp in a cup of the stock until dissolved, then add the sugar and stir until dissolved.

Add the celery and carrot to the stock and simmer for 5 minutes. Add the fish and simmer a further 5 minutes. Add the tamarind water, green onions and bean sprouts and simmer for 5 minutes longer. Check the seasoning, adding salt and pepper. Transfer to soup bowls and garnish with mint leaves.

SERVES 6

BO BUN HUE

Aromatic Braised Beef with Noodles in Rich Broth

The backbone of the Vietnamese cuisine consists of soup/noodle combinations. Served in deep bowls, they are a meal in themselves and are enjoyed throughout the day. Chicken, pork, shrimp and fish are all served in this way, but perhaps the most common ingredient in these hearty dishes is beef. It comes in varying guises – braised in rich anise-scented broth, thinly sliced and fried with onions, or simply simmered in water with ginger and chilies or fish sauce. It rests atop a generous tangle of tender noodles – rice vermicelli, egg noodles or ribbons of rice noodles. Aromatics and vegetables add to an already hearty meal.

1½ lb (750 g) braising beef
1½ lb (750 g) beef shank (shin) on the bone
6 slices fresh ginger
2 pieces dried tangerine peel, optional
4 whole star anise
1 medium onion
12 cups (3 liters) water
salt
1½ lb (750 g) thick fresh egg noodles
8 green onions
4 oz (125 g) fresh bean sprouts
chopped fresh cilantro (coriander)
nuoc cham (see page 137)
fish sauce

Cut the beef and shank into large pieces. Place in a large saucepan and add the ginger, tangerine peel if used, star anise, halved onion and the water. Bring to the boil. Skim off the froth, reduce the heat and simmer, partially covered, for about 2½ hours until the stock is well flavored. Add salt to taste and keep hot.

Drop the noodles into a large pot of well-salted water and boil for about 2 minutes until tender. Drain and divide between 6–8 deep bowls.

Trim and chop the green onions. Blanch the bean sprouts for 30 seconds; drain. Add a little of each to the bowls. Strain in the hot stock, then add several pieces of beef (the beef should be tender enough to break up with two forks).

❖ Add a sprinkling of chopped cilantro and serve with pitchers of *nuoc cham* and fish sauce.

SERVES 6–8

Xoi Nuoc Dir A

Steamed Sticky Rice in Coconut Cream

Glutinous short-grain white rice, which has a much higher starch content than standard rice, is often used in the East for making sweet dishes. When cooked it acquires a firm jellylike consistency and can be cut into portions for serving. In this recipe coconut milk is used both for cooking the rice and as a sauce.

1½ cups (10 oz/315 g) short-grain glutinous white rice
1 tablepoon salt
3½ cups (28 fl oz/875 ml) thin coconut milk
2 eggs, lightly beaten (optional)
young banana leaves or aluminum foil
vegetable oil

SAUCE

¾ cup (4 oz/125 g) palm sugar, or soft brown sugar
¾ cup (6 fl oz/180 ml) water
1½ cups (12 fl oz/375 ml) thick coconut milk

Rinse the rice in several changes of cold water and drain well. Place in a heavy saucepan with the salt and thin coconut milk. Bring to the boil, then reduce the heat and simmer until the rice has cooked to a thick paste. Cool to lukewarm, then quickly stir in the beaten eggs, if used.

❖ Dip the banana leaves into boiling water to clean and soften. Cut away the thick central rib. Place a piece of leaf in the bottom of a baking pan and brush lightly with vegetable oil. Spread the rice paste thickly over the leaf, then cover with another piece of oiled banana leaf, oiled side down.

STEAMED STICKY RICE IN COCONUT CREAM

❖ Place the dish on a rack in a steamer and steam until firm. Lift out and let cool, then chill thoroughly.
❖ Combine the palm sugar and water in a small saucepan and gently simmer until sugar is dissolved. Cool.
❖ Remove the banana leaf from the top of the rice cake and cut the rice into triangular or diamond-shaped pieces. Place in dessert dishes and add a little of the palm sugar and the thick coconut milk to each dish.

SERVES 6

JOHN EVERINGHAM

A FISHERMAN SECURES HIS BOAT TO THE SHORE

Singapore and Malaysia

A RICKSHAW IN A QUIET
BACK STREET, KUALA LUMPUR

POPIAH SNACKS *(TOP LEFT), recipe page 155;* MILD FISH CURRY, *recipe page 160,* ON FESTIVE RICE *(RIGHT), recipe page 167,* AND VERMICELLI DESSERT *(BOTTOM LEFT), recipe page 171*

Singapore and Malaysia

A BLENDING OF CULTURES

In a region where three nationalities reside together in harmony, there is bound to be an interesting cuisine. Such is the case in Malaysia and the neighboring island republic of Singapore, where Malays, Indians and Chinese have all contributed their own peculiarities to the local cuisine.

Mildly flavored traditional Chinese dishes, based on the Cantonese and Fukienese concept, here include a touch of chili or perhaps a spoonful of curry powder to give them pep. Aromatic Indian spices add fragrance to Malay-style curries, and Chinese ingredients such as *hor fun* (rice vermicelli) or *taucheo* (salted soybean seasoning) make an appearance in Malay dishes.

Possibly the most noticeable instance of the marriage of two culinary traditions is in the Nonya cuisine. Nonyas, or Peranakan Straits-born Chinese, the descendants of intermarriage between Chinese settlers and Malay women, have always prided themselves on their cooking. They have built up an awesome repertory of outstanding dishes, particularly cakes and sweets. Their unique style of cooking is just as respected and envied today as it was from the beginning, four centuries ago, when the first Chinese settlers sought wives from the Malay community.

In the Malay home, daily meals are simple affairs with a large bowl of rice, a curry or two, some vegetables and a choice of *sambals* being offered for lunch and dinner – sometimes even breakfast – with little ceremony. Food is eaten with the fingers from plates, or sometimes from a piece of banana leaf. Once the art of eating with the fingers – the thumb and first two fingers of the right hand – is mastered, it has an enjoyable tactile quality. The rice is formed into a ball, a fragment of curry is picked up with it and the rice is dunked into a sauce and flicked with the thumb into the mouth with rarely a drop spilled.

For special occasions, however, all stops are pulled out to make the *kenduri* (feast) as lavish as is affordable. There are mounds of *nasi minyak*, golden rice, made fragrant with *buah pelaga* (cardamom), *kayu manis* (cinnamon) and *bunga cengkih* (cloves). *Serundeng* (spicy condiments) and other *sambals* (little spicy side dishes) accompany piquant *rendangs*, tasty curried vegetable dishes, extravagantly spiced meat dishes or roasted seafoods. Garnishes are attractive – carved vegetables borrowed from the Chinese cuisine, chili flowers, crisp-fried onion, shredded omelet and plenty of fresh herbs.

Influenced by both Indonesian and Indian cooking, as well as having a noticeable Chinese inclination, the Malay style of cooking has nonetheless developed in its own right and has some notable distinctions. In this hot and humid climate, strong, interesting flavors are necessary to stimulate heat-jaded appetites. Chilies are used with apparent abandon. *Serai* (lemon grass) lends its lemony-peppery undertones, *asam* (tamarind) an invigorating tartness, *blacan* (shrimp paste) its pungent salt and fish taste, *lengkuas* (galingale/galangal) a mild ginger flavor, *kunyit* (turmeric) its bright yellow (*kuning*) color and *santan* (coconut milk) a creamy richness.

From the Indians the Malay adopted the use of spices; from their local gardens comes the distinctive aroma of the *daun pandan* (pandanus leaf), an intrinsic element of their cooking. *Daun ketumbar* (fresh cilantro/coriander), *daun kari pla* (curry leaves), *daun salam* (a type of basil), *daun limau perut* (lime leaves) and *daun kesum* (the leaf of an herb peculiar to this region) all add their definite flavors.

Along the west coast of Malaysia are two regions where the cuisine has taken individual direction. In Malacca, an ancient Portuguese settlement, a cuisine with European overtones has evolved – as in Goa on the west coast of India. The tastes are rich and often sweet, with liberal use of the local dark brown sugar from the *aren* palm, *gula melaka*. The blending of seasonings proclaims both Portuguese and Malay origins, and Malacca's cakes are sweet, light and delightful.

Further north, the island of Penang is now a popular tourist resort, with its own favorite dishes such as crisply fried *inche kabin* (fried chicken) and *popiah* (little snack rolls). Penang, a town of somewhat faded glory, was at one time a prosperous trading post and the retreat of rich rubber planters and tin miners.

Malay cooking styles are simple. A clay or aluminum pot with a rounded base and smaller fluted opening on top is traditionally used for simmering curries, although nowadays a standard

R. IAN LLOYD, SINGAPORE

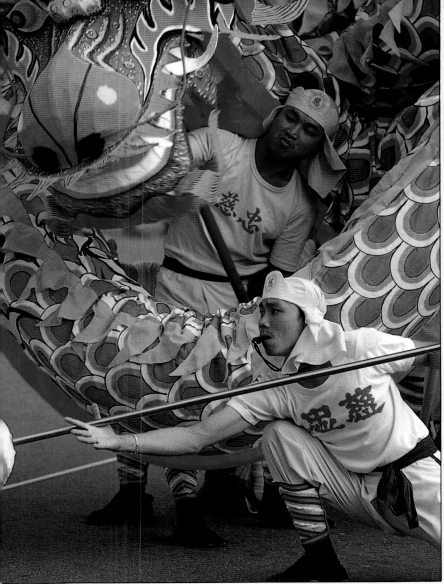

STREET FESTIVAL, SINGAPORE   MICHAEL COOK

saucepan would probably be more in favor. A *kuali* or wok is used for frying, stir-frying or braising, and a *tawa* (flat iron griddle) for grilling. Curries are cooked by slow simmering; rice by boiling or the absorption method; Indian-style breads are cooked on the *tawa*.

There are a number of dishes that always bring back fond memories of countries through which one has traveled. Of this area, I think perhaps that the humble *murtaba* has my vote. Of Indian origin, it consists of a gigantic tissue-thin crêpe made by tossing and stretching an oiled ball of dough over a heated flat metal surface. It is then folded into a square pancake over a tasty curry filling and a sprinkling of fried onions (or simply a well-seasoned beaten egg), fried until the surface is crisp and then cut into quarters to be eaten with the fingers.

Chinese cooking in Singapore and throughout Malaysia is made up of stir-fried or steamed dishes. Most popular, perhaps, are the many types of noodle and rice dishes that make nutritious and filling snacks at any time of day or night. *Cha kway teow* is one of those dishes that both Malays and Chinese might claim as their own. Its preparation by a street-side vendor in his little makeshift stall is a triumph. A heavy iron *kuali* is set over a roaring gas fire and handfuls of *kway teow* (rice ribbon noodles) are tossed into the shallow oil. A little diced meat is added with a handful of fresh bean sprouts, a few slivers of chopped cabbage, some peeled fresh shrimp and rings of fresh squid. For seasoning – chopped garlic and ginger, a splash of soy sauce (both light and dark), perhaps a little oyster sauce, some sugar, salt and pepper – a shower of shredded shallots or green onion and red chili. Toss, flip, stir. An egg or two is broken on top and lightly stirred in, then the wide Chinese ladle brings everything together for a few seconds to crisp at the edges. Then the mixture is scooped out onto a plate, the vendor smiling with delight at his own mastery.

The predominant vegetables used are *bok choy* (Chinese cabbage), bean sprouts, *brinjal* (eggplant/aubergine), okra, yam and a hard-fleshed tuber known as *bangkuang* (yam bean). Bean curd and other soybean products supplement the protein intake deliciously in both Malay and Chinese dishes. *Tofu* or *tauhu* (soft bean curd) and *tukwa* (hard bean curd), as well as *tempe* (compressed cakes of fermented soybeans) and bean curd "skins" are prepared in many guises.

Desserts are important in the Malay and Nonya cuisines. Often oversweet to Western tastes, they are nonetheless highly original in concept. Tapioca, sago, corn, yam and little bean-shaped pellets of dough combine with rich, sweet *gula melaka* and *santan* (coconut milk) as sweets, drinks and puddings.

While the variety of cakes, puddings, biscuits, patties and dumplings available is immense, many require skills or ingredients not readily available to outsiders and are therefore limited in this collection of recipes. We have placed the emphasis on Malay and Nonya dishes, as Chinese dishes are amply represented in the chapter on Chinese cooking.

BEEF SKEWERS WITH PEANUT SAUCE AND ROASTED FISH PARCELS IN BANANA LEAVES

SATE DAGING

Beef Skewers with Peanut Sauce

1¼ lb (625 g) beef tenderloin (fillet) or rump
1 small onion
1 teaspoon crushed garlic
1 teaspoon grated fresh ginger
2 tablespoons dark soy sauce
1 tablespoon sugar
½ teaspoon powdered lemon grass
1 teaspoon chili powder
2 teaspoons ground coriander
1 teaspoon cumin
2 tablespoons peanut oil
½ teaspoon salt
vegetable oil
1 large cucumber

PEANUT SAUCE

⅔ cup (3½ oz/100 g) raw peanuts
2 tablespoons peanut oil
2 tablespoons light soy sauce
1 tablespoon sweet soy sauce or dark
   soy sauce and extra sugar
1 tablespoon sugar
1½ tablespoons ground coriander
⅓ teaspoon turmeric
2 teaspoons garlic and chili sauce
½ teaspoon salt
¼ cup (2 fl oz/60 ml) water
½ cup (4 fl oz/125 ml) thick coconut milk
1–2 tablespoons lemon juice

Cut the beef into ½-in (1.25-cm) slices, then into small cubes. Place in a dish. Finely grate the onion. Mix the

remaining ingredients except vegetable oil and cucumber into the beef, cover with plastic wrap and set aside for 3–4 hours.

Spread the peanuts on a baking sheet and roast in a 350°F (180°C) oven until golden. Spread on a kitchen cloth and rub to remove the skins, then pour into a colander and rinse thoroughly with cold water until the skins have washed away. Grind to a reasonably smooth paste in a food processor or mortar.

Combine all the sauce ingredients in a small saucepan and bring to the boil, stirring. Simmer for 2 minutes, then pour into shallow saucers. Rub bamboo skewers with vegetable oil to keep the meat from sticking. Thread several cubes of meat onto each and grill over glowing charcoal, brushing occasionally with vegetable oil. Serve hot with the sauce as a dip, and with a plate of cubed cucumber.

MAKES 18 SKEWERS (ABOUT 6 SERVINGS)

OTAK OTAK

Little Roasted Fish Parcels

1 lb (500 g) boneless meaty white fish fillets
1 tablespoon coriander seeds
1 cup (3 oz/90 g) shredded coconut
2 tablespoons finely chopped green onions
1 teaspoon crushed garlic
2 teaspoons grated fresh ginger
1 stalk lemon grass, very finely chopped
4–8 dried red chilies, soaked in boiling water
8 candlenuts or macadamias, or
   20 raw cashew nuts
2 tablespoons peanut or vegetable oil
¾ cup (6 fl oz/185 ml) thin coconut milk
salt and black pepper
30 8-in (20-cm) squares young banana leaf, or
   aluminum foil
extra vegetable oil

Cut the fish into thin 2 x ¾-in (5 x 2-cm) slices; alternatively, chop it coarsely, then grind to a smooth paste in a food processor or mortar.

Toast the coriander seeds in a dry skillet until they are very aromatic and lightly colored. Remove and grind finely. Mix with the coconut, green onions, garlic, ginger and lemon grass and grind to a paste.

Drain the chilies and grind to a paste with the nuts and oil. Blend into the coconut mixture, then fry for 2–3 minutes, stirring constantly. Add the coconut milk, salt and pepper and fry until the mixture is very thick.

Place the banana leaves in a large steamer and steam briefly until softened, or drop into a saucepan of boiling water and remove immediately. Wipe dry, then brush one side lightly with oil.

Spread a small spoonful of the seasoning paste over the center of each piece of banana leaf, the same size as the fish slices. Top with a slice of fish (or a little mound of puréed fish) and cover with more coconut paste. Wrap into a rectangular parcel and secure with wooden toothpicks. Roast on a rack over a bed of glowing charcoal for about 15 minutes, turning once or twice, or broil/grill under medium heat, turning several times.

Serve the parcels as they are, to be unwrapped at the table.

MAKES ABOUT 30 PARCELS

POPIAH

Popiah or poh pia are among the most popular snack foods made in Malaysia and Singapore. Some chefs make them in the Chinese way, using commercially prepared egg/spring roll wrappers to enclose a tasty selection of shredded ingredients. These are known as popiah goreng, *or deep-fried* popiah, *being crisply fried in deep oil. The Nonya style of* popiah *come encased in home-made paper-thin egg crêpes (pancakes), while the* popiah *from Penang, different again, are wrapped in soft sheets of edible rice paper.*

For unfried versions of popiah, *the filling ingredients, wrappers and dip sauces are assembled on large platters and diners roll their own according to their taste preferences.*

12 pieces edible rice paper wrappers
12 medium lettuce leaves
1 cup (about 4 oz/125 g) shredded giant white radish
1 cup (about 4 oz/125 g) shredded yam or taro
1 medium carrot, shredded/grated
1 cup (about 3 oz/90 g) shredded cabbage
3 shallots (or 1 Spanish onion), sliced
1 clove garlic, chopped
½-in (1.25-cm) piece fresh ginger, minced
2–3 tablespoons vegetable or peanut oil
1 tablespoon white vinegar
1 teaspoon sugar
1 cup (5 oz/155 g) cooked, peeled small shrimp (prawns)
½ cup (about 2 oz/60 g) fresh bean sprouts, chopped
3 large green onions, shredded
¼ cup (about 2 oz/60 g) compressed bean curd cake, shredded
¼ cup (about 2 oz/60 g) shredded omelet
12 sprigs fresh cilantro (coriander)
3–4 tablespoons sweet soy sauce

Cover the rice paper wrappers with a damp cloth until needed. Wash and thoroughly drain the lettuce.

Sauté the radish, yam, carrot, cabbage, shallots, garlic and ginger in the oil for about 4 minutes. Sprinkle on the vinegar, add the sugar and 2–3 tablespoons water, cover and simmer gently for about 4 minutes, until the vegetables are cooked but still slightly crisp. Turn into a colander to cool and drain.

Arrange the lettuce, shrimp, uncooked vegetables, bean curd, omelet and cilantro on platters with the rice wrappers. Place the drained cooked vegetables in a dish. Pour the soy sauce into a small pitcher. Take all these to the table.

To assemble, line each wrapper with a lettuce leaf. Add a selection of ingredients and a drizzle of soy sauce and roll up firmly.

MAKES 12

NONYA POPIAH

Egg Wrappers

2 large eggs
2 tablespoons vegetable or peanut oil
1 cup (4 oz/125 g) all purpose (plain) flour
½ teaspoon salt

Beat the eggs thoroughly and mix with the other ingredients, adding enough cold water to make a thin batter. Strain through a sieve into a pitcher.

Rub a heavy iron skillet with an oiled cloth, or use a nonstick pan. Pour in sufficient batter to make a thin round wrapper about 7 in (18 cm) in diameter. Cook over medium heat until firm and lightly colored underneath, then flip and cook the other side briefly. Stack the pancakes together, covering with a clean cloth, until needed. Allow to cool before rolling the *popiah*.

FILLING

Prepare in the same way as the previous recipe, adding 2 tablespoons mashed *taucheo* (salted yellow soybeans) in place of the vinegar. Pile the filling into a serving dish. Arrange the wrappers and at least 12 fresh lettuce leaves on another plate.

Prepare little additional dishes of shredded roast pork or sliced *lap cheong* (Chinese sausage), steamed for 5–6 minutes; shredded cucumber; sprigs of fresh cilantro (coriander); thin omelet cut into short strips; crisply fried sliced garlic and mashed fresh red chili.

To assemble, line an egg wrapper with a lettuce leaf. Add a mound of the filling, then a selection of the other ingredients. Roll up tightly and cut each into 2–3 pieces to serve.

MAKES 12

TELURDADA BIASA

Family Omelet

A thin omelet packed full of green onions and red and green chilies is a welcome snack in a Malay household, and is often served with other main courses.

5 eggs
1 teaspoon salt
¼ teaspoon cracked black pepper
4 green (spring) onions
1 fresh green chili
1 fresh red chili
2 tablespoons vegetable oil or ghee (clarified butter)
½ teaspoon crushed garlic
2 tablespoons chopped fresh cilantro (coriander), optional

Beat the eggs with salt and pepper. Trim the green onions and shred finely. Split open the chilies, scrape out the seeds and shred the flesh finely.

Heat a wide skillet and add the oil or ghee. Add the green onions, chilies and garlic to the oil and fry for 2–3 minutes until cooked. Remove and set aside.

Pour the egg into the pan and cook gently until the underside is firm and lightly colored. Spread the onion, chili, garlic and chopped cilantro, if used, evenly over the top while it is still quite wet so that they sink into the egg. Cook a short while longer until firm enough to cut into quarters and turn. When the underside is golden and just firm, lift out. Cut into smaller wedges and arrange on a plate. Serve at once.

SERVES 4

TELURDADA BIASA – A FAMILY OMELET

IKAN BILIS GORENG

Fried 'Ikan Bilis'

Ikan bilis *are tiny silver-skinned fish which proliferate off the Malay coast. They are used both in fresh and dried form for a number of dishes of Malay origin, including some pungent sambals. In this dish, crisp* ikan bilis *and roasted peanuts combine with hot spices to serve with drinks or as an interesting side dish or garnish.*

8 oz (250 g) dried *ikan bilis*
1 large onion
2–3 fresh green chilies
1 tablespoon sugar
2 teaspoons black pepper
salt, optional
oil for deep-frying
½ cup (3 oz/90 g) shelled raw peanuts

Remove the heads from the *ikan bilis*, as these can be bitter when cooked. Rinse fish thoroughly in cold water, then dry well and set aside for about 20 minutes.

In a food processor, blender or mortar, grind the onion and chilies to a paste. Add the sugar, pepper and salt.

Heat the oil to the smoking point, then reduce the heat slightly and fry the *ikan bilis* until crisp. Lift out with a slotted spoon and drain well. Fry the peanuts until golden and drain well. Transfer about 2 tablespoons of the oil to another pan and fry the onion mixture for 3–4 minutes until well cooked and golden brown.

Return the fish and peanuts to the pan and stir over high heat with the seasoning paste until all the liquid has evaporated and the fish are quite crisp. Taste and adjust the seasoning.

SERVES 8–10

AN ITINERANT FOOD SELLER, SINGAPORE — WELDON TRANNIES

FRIED *IKAN BILIS (TOP),* AND SAMBAL CUKA, *recipe page 167*

SPICY MUTTON SOUP

SOP KAMBING

Mutton Soup

Well-flavored and highly spiced mutton soup makes a popular snack or light meal at inexpensive open-fronted restaurants and food stalls. Look for the telltale bright red oil on the surface, indicating that this particular pot of sop kambing *may be searing hot, as the red oil from the chili floats to the surface when it has thoroughly permeated the soup.*

1½ lb (750 g) mutton ribs, neck chops or breast
2 large onions, finely chopped
4 cloves garlic, crushed
2–4 fresh red chilies
1-in (2.5-cm) piece fresh ginger
2 teaspoons black peppercorns
1 tablespoon coriander seeds
12 cups (3 liters) water
salt
1½ tablespoons vegetable oil
4 whole black cardamom pods, partially opened
2-in (5-cm) stick cinnamon
3 tablespoons mild curry paste
3 tablespoons white poppy seeds, ground
½ cup (4 fl oz/125 ml) thick coconut milk
fried onion flakes
2–3 tablespoons chopped green onions
fresh cilantro (coriander) sprigs

Rinse the mutton in boiling water, drain and chop into bite-size pieces. Place in a large saucepan with half of the onion and garlic; add the chilies, ginger, peppercorns and coriander. Pour in the water. Bring to the boil, then reduce heat and simmer gently for at least 2 hours, until the meat is completely tender and the broth is reduced to about 9 cups. Skim the surface from time to time.

Strain the broth into another saucepan. Tear the meat into small pieces, discarding bones. Add salt to taste.

Heat the oil in a small skillet (frying pan) and fry the cardamons and cinnamon stick for a few moments. Add the curry paste and fry briefly, then stir into the soup with the poppy seeds and coconut milk. Bring to the boil. Add the meat and simmer a further 30 minutes. Garnish with onion flakes, green onions and fresh cilantro.

SERVES 8

TA PIN LO

Steamboat

Variations on the basic "steamboat" theme are found in many parts of Southeast Asia. Of Chinese origin, the ingredients and condiments differ according to local taste and availability of ingredients, but the principle remains the same – a pot of simmering water or stock, an array of ingredients to poach in it, a selection of tasty condiments and sauce dips – the elements of an enjoyable cook-it-yourself meal.

6 oz (185 g) lean pork
6 oz (185 g) beef tenderloin (fillet)
6 oz (185 g) chicken breast
6 oz (185 g) cleaned fresh squid
12 medium uncooked shrimp (prawns)
8 oz (250 g) white fish fillets or pieces
2 egg whites
salt and white pepper
1 tablespoon vegetable oil
1 lb (500 g) Chinese cabbage, spinach or lettuce
6 green onions
6 eggs, optional
8 cups (2 liters) chicken stock or water
1-in (2.5-cm) piece fresh ginger
1 fresh red or green chili, optional

Very thinly slice the pork, beef and chicken. Cut the squid into rings or narrow sticks. Peel the shrimp, leaving the heads and tails intact.

Chop the fish coarsely and place in a food processor or blender with the egg whites and a large pinch each of salt and pepper. Add the vegetable oil and 2–3 tablespoons ice water and process to a very smooth paste.

Bring a large pot of lightly salted water to the boil. Form the fish into small balls and drop into the water. Simmer until they float to the surface, then remove with a slotted spoon and place in cold water until cool. Drain well.

Rinse the leafy vegetables and separate the leaves. Drain well and arrange on a platter. Trim the green onions and cut into 2-in (5-cm) lengths. Place the sliced meats and fish balls

on serving plates. Prepare the sauces and divide among several small dip dishes.

🥢 Have ready a large pot on a portable cooker in the center of the table (an electric skillet is suitable). Add the chicken stock or water. Slice the ginger and chili, if used, and add to the pot. Bring to the boil, then reduce heat slightly.

🥢 The eggs can be beaten in small bowls and the ingredients first dipped into the beaten raw egg, if liked.

🥢 Use bamboo or wooden chopsticks, fondue forks or small wire baskets to suspend the ingredients in the hot stock. Cook very briefly, then dip into one of the sauces before eating.

🥢 When the meat and seafoods have been eaten, cook the vegetables and green onions in the hot broth and serve as a soup.

SAUCE DIPS/CONDIMENTS

3 tablespoons chili sauce
3 tablespoons light soy sauce
1½ teaspoons crushed garlic
2 teaspoons minced fresh ginger
2 teaspoons sugar
Mix thoroughly.

3 tablespoons light soy sauce
2 fresh green chilies
2 teaspoons sugar
1 tablespoon vegetable or peanut oil
Slit open the chilies and scrape out seeds. Shred chilies and mix with the remaining ingredients.

SERVES 6

KARI TERUNG KAMBING

Eggplant and Mutton/ Lamb Curry

Kaskas or black poppy seeds, finely ground, are the secret of this mildly flavored curry in the Indian tradition. Serve with rice and sambals, see page 167.

WELDON TRANNIES   EGGPLANT AND MUTTON CURRY

1 lb (500 g) boneless lean lamb or mutton
2 eggplants (aubergines), about 1 lb (500 g) altogether
salt
1½ tablespoons black poppy seeds
1 teaspoon fennel seeds
1 tablespoon coriander seeds
1¼ teaspoons cumin seeds
1½ teaspoons black peppercorns
¾ teaspoon powdered turmeric
6–8 shallots (or 2–3 Spanish onions)
3–4 cloves garlic
1-in (2.5-cm) piece fresh ginger
¼ cup (2 fl oz/60 ml) vegetable oil
3–4 curry leaves
3 whole cloves
1½-in (4-cm) stick cinnamon
2 cups (16 fl oz/500 ml) thin coconut milk
½ cup (4fl oz/125 ml) thick coconut milk
lime juice

Trim the lamb and cut into bite-size cubes. Cut the unpeeled eggplant into cubes of the same size. Place in a colander and sprinkle with about 1 teaspoon salt. Let stand in the sink or on a plate for 20 minutes to drain off the bitter juices.

🥢 In a spice grinder or mortar grind the poppy seeds, fennel, coriander, cumin and peppercorns to a fine powder. Add the turmeric. Separately grind the shallots, garlic and ginger to a smooth paste.

🥢 Heat the oil in a large saucepan and fry the onion paste for 3–4 minutes, until lightly colored, then add the spice powder and fry for 2–3 minutes more, stirring frequently. Add the cubed meat and stir thoroughly until each piece is well coated with seasonings. Cook until evenly colored. Add the curry leaves and whole spices.

🥢 Rinse the eggplant, drain thoroughly and then pat dry with paper towels. Add to the pan and pour in the thin coconut milk. Simmer for 25 minutes, covered, then check the seasonings and simmer a little longer if the meat is not yet completely tender.

🥢 Just before serving pour in the thick coconut milk and add lime juice to taste. Reheat briefly.

SERVES 6

STEAMBOAT

KARI KUBIS UDANG

Shrimp and Cabbage Curry

This is a particularly mild-flavored curry, of the gulai *style, with a simple seasoning of fresh* kunyit *(turmeric root),* lengkuas *(galingale/galangal) and* serai *(lemon grass). Generally served as a side dish, it goes particularly well with crisp or dry-cooked dishes.*

12 oz (375 g) Chinese or white cabbage
1 lb (500 g) medium shrimp (prawns) in their shells
6 shallots (or 2 Spanish onions)
1 clove garlic
2 tablespoons vegetable or peanut oil
1 teaspoon grated fresh turmeric, or ½ teaspoon
   powdered turmeric
2 teaspoons grated fresh galingale/galangal, or
   young ginger
2 teaspoons finely chopped lemon grass
¾ cup (6 fl oz/185 ml) thin coconut milk
¾ cup (6 fl oz/185 ml) thick coconut milk
salt

Rinse the cabbage and chop coarsely. Peel the shrimp, leaving the tail sections intact. Peel and chop the shallots and garlic.

Heat the oil in a saucepan and fry the shallots and garlic for 3 minutes over medium heat. Add the turmeric, ginger and lemon grass and fry for about 3 minutes, stirring constantly. Add the thin coconut milk and half of the thick coconut milk and bring to the boil, stirring.

Put in the cabbage and shrimp and simmer gently for about 6 minutes. Add the remaining thick coconut milk, season with salt to taste and serve.

A little finely shredded red and green chili can be added to increase the taste and hotness. For a more substantial dish, quartered hard-cooked eggs make a welcome addition.

SERVES 4–6

IKAN MOOLEE

Fish Moolee, a Mild Curry

Moolee (or moli *as it is known by the Tamils in southern India) is a mildly flavored curry in which* santan *(coconut milk) forms the sauce. In India, it is sometimes known as "Malay Curry" and in Malaysia it is considered an Indian specialty. Wherever it originated, it is still enjoyed today in both these countries. Steaks of a firm-fleshed fish are ideal to poach in a* moolee *sauce. Serve with plenty of rice.*

6 snapper or mackerel steaks (about 1½ lb/750 g)
2 tablespoons tamarind water
12 shallots (or 4 Spanish onions)
6 cloves garlic
½-in (1.25-cm) piece fresh ginger
1 stalk lemon grass
1–3 fresh red chilies
4 candlenuts or macadamias, or 12 raw cashew nuts
2 tablespoons vegetable oil
¾ teaspoon powdered turmeric
1 teaspoon salt
1¼ cups (10 fl oz/310 ml) thin coconut milk
¾ cup (6 fl oz/185 ml) thick coconut milk

Season the steaks with the tamarind water and set aside. Peel and very thinly slice the shallots and garlic.

In a food processor or blender grind the ginger, lemon grass, chilies and candlenuts to a paste.

Heat the oil in a wide saucepan and fry the shallots and garlic until very soft but not brown. Push to one side of the pan. Add the ground seasonings and fry for 2–3 minutes, then mix in the shallots, turmeric, salt and thin coconut milk. Bring almost to the boil, stirring constantly. Add half the thick coconut milk and bring to the boil again, stirring.

Put in the fish and simmer very gently for about 20 minutes, until the fish is tender. Add the remaining thick coconut milk, transfer to a serving plate and garnish with chili shreds, cucumber and cilantro (coriander).

SERVES 6

ASAM UDANG

The tart taste of asam *(tamarind) adds an interesting accent to crisp, fresh shrimp (prawns). Slivers of marinated carrot, cucumber and radish are served with them.*

1 lb (500 g) peeled fresh shrimp (prawns) of medium size, with tails on
1 cup (8 fl oz/250 ml) boiling water
2 tablespoons tamarind pulp
2 cups (about 9 oz/280 g) slivered mixed cucumber, carrot and radish
¼ cup (2 fl oz/60 ml) white vinegar
1 tablespoon sugar
1½ teaspoons salt
1 fresh red chili
3 tablespoons vegetable oil
1½ teaspoons sugar
tomato wedges and fresh cilantro (coriander), optional

Slit the shrimp down the center back and remove the dark vein. Place shrimp in a glass dish. Mix the boiling water and tamarind together, mashing to extract as much flavor as possible, and strain over the shrimp. Set aside for 20 minutes, then drain and pat dry.

⚙ In the meantime, marinate the slivered vegetables in the vinegar with 1 tablespoon sugar and the salt.

⚙ Slit open the chili, scrape out the seeds and cut the flesh into long narrow shreds. Heat the oil in a *kuali* or wok. Add the shrimp and stir-fry over very high heat for about 1½ minutes or until they turn pink and firm. Add the chili and 1½ teaspoons sugar and stir-fry again briefly.

⚙ Drain the vegetables and spread on a serving plate. Pile the shrimp in the center of the plate and garnish with wedges of tomato and sprigs of fresh cilantro (optional). Serve at once.

SERVES 4–6

TAMARIND SHRIMP/PRAWNS

KUALA LUMPUR RAILWAY STATION

WELDON TRANNIES — SINGAPORE CHILI CRAB

SPICY SQUID

LADAH MERAH KETAM SINGAPORE

Singapore Chili Crab

Changhi Beach, a near-city beachside suburb, boasts rows of giant barnlike restaurants where chefs vie to produce the ultimate chili crab. Succulent, meaty mudcrabs from nearby mangrove swamps cracked and tossed with ginger and chilies in giant-sized kualis *(woks) over roaring gas fires until the meat is tender and the accompanying sauce has a satisfying degree of searing hotness. Eating chili crab is a messy business – there is no ceremony here, and only the most pedantically fastidious would bother with tableware. Instead, dishes of warm water and soap, or plenty of hot moist towels, arrive at the table for after-meal cleanups.*

4 lb (2 kg) fresh meaty crabs
4–6 fresh red chilies
2 teaspoons crushed garlic
2 teaspoons minced fresh ginger
½ cup (4 fl oz/125 ml) peanut or vegetable oil
¼ cup (2 fl oz/60 ml) tomato ketchup
¼ cup (2 oz/ 60 g) sugar
2 teaspoons salt
2 eggs, lightly beaten, optional
2–3 tablespoons chopped green onions

Cut the crabs into large pieces, discarding the undershell and inedible parts. Rinse lightly in cold water and drain very well.

Slit open the chilies, scrape out the seeds and chop the flesh coarsely. Place in a blender or mortar and grind to a paste with the garlic and ginger.

Heat a very large *kuali* (wok) and add the oil. Put in the crab pieces and stir-fry over high heat for about 6 minutes, until the shell is red and the meat has turned white and firm. Push to one side of the pan and add the chili mixture. Fry for 1 minute, then mix with the crab.

Stir the ketchup, sugar and salt together, add a little cold water and pour into the pan. Bring to the boil, stirring into the other ingredients. Simmer for a few minutes, then add the beaten eggs, if using, and cook briefly, breaking up with a spatula. Stir in the onions and serve.

SERVES 6

OPOR SOTONG

Spicy Squid

Small whole squid bodies or tubes, or slim squid rings, are simmered briefly in a thick, heavily spiced sauce, which is very hot from the generous addition of red chili. Accompany with rice.

1¼ lb (675 g) cleaned squid
1 large onion
4 cloves garlic
8–10 dried chilies, soaked in boiling water
¼ teaspoon powdered turmeric
½ teaspoon shrimp paste
2 tablespoons coriander seeds
2½ teaspoons cumin
3 tablespoons coconut or vegetable oil
6 slices galingale/galangal or young fresh ginger
1 stalk lemon grass
3 lime leaves
3 tablespoons shredded coconut
2 cups (16 fl oz/500 ml) thin coconut milk
1 cup (8 fl oz/250 ml) water

Thoroughly rinse the squid. If large, cut crosswise into rings; smaller squid can be left whole. Drain well.

Coarsely chop the onion, peel the garlic and drain the chilies. Place in a food processor, blender or mortar and grind to a paste. Add the turmeric, shrimp paste, coriander and cumin and mix together.

Heat the oil in a medium saucepan and fry the seasoning paste for 2 minutes, stirring constantly. Add the galingale and lemon grass with the lime leaves and shredded coconut; fry together briefly until the coconut begins to turn a light brown. (If needed, splash in a little coconut milk or water to prevent the seasonings sticking to the pan.) Add the coconut milk and water and bring to the boil.

Stir well, then simmer for 5 minutes. Add the prepared squid and simmer for barely 5 minutes; the squid must not be overcooked or it will become tough and chewy. Serve at once.

SERVES 6–8

TAMARIND CHICKEN *(BOTTOM),* AND VEGETABLE SALAD, *recipe page 165*

Asam Ayam

Tamarind Chicken

This is usually served with white rice and cucumber wedges.

2½–3 lb (1¼–1½ kg) fresh chicken
2 cups (16 fl oz/500 ml) boiling water
¾ cup (4 oz/125 g) tamarind pulp
¾ cup (6 oz/185 g) sugar
¼ cup (2 fl oz/60 ml) dark soy sauce
1½ teaspoons crushed garlic
1 large onion, finely minced or grated
2 tablespoons coriander seeds
salt and cracked black pepper

Rinse the chicken and drain well. Pour the water into a deep dish and add the tamarind and sugar. Stir until the tamarind is thoroughly dissolved, then scoop out the seeds and discard. Add the soy sauce, garlic and onion. Put in the chicken and leave to marinate for at least 8 hours, turning from time to time.

🌸 Heat a saucepan large enough to hold the chicken. Add the coriander and dry-fry until the seeds are golden and beginning to pop. Transfer to a spice grinder and grind to a smooth powder, then return to the saucepan. Add the chicken (with marinade), salt and black pepper and bring to the boil. Reduce heat, cover tightly and simmer gently for about 40 minutes until the chicken is very tender. Lift out, drain and cut into serving pieces.

🌸 Bring the sauce to a rapid boil, then continue to boil until well reduced. Pour over the chicken and serve at once.

SERVES 6

CHICKEN LIVER CURRY AND YELLOW 'STICKY' RICE,
recipe page 169

RENDANG HATI AYAM

Chicken Liver Curry

1 lb (500 g) chicken livers
1 large onion
4–5 cloves garlic
3–4 dried red chilies, soaked
1½ teaspoons grated fresh turmeric
1½-in (4-cm) piece fresh galingale/galangal or
   young ginger
1 stalk lemon grass
3 tablespoons vegetable oil
2 tablespoons prepared mild curry paste or powder
¼ cup (2 fl oz/60 ml) thick coconut milk
2 lime or bay leaves
1 medium cucumber
1¾ cups (14 fl oz/425 ml) thin coconut milk
salt
fresh red and green chilies

Soak the chicken livers in cold water for 20 minutes, drain
well and trim away skin and connective tissue. Chop the
livers into large pieces.

Peel the cucumber. Cut the flesh from the seed core in
food processor, blender or spice grinder with the drained
chilies, turmeric, ginger, and lemon grass and chop finely.
Heat the oil in a saucepan and fry the mixture for 5 minutes,
stirring from time to time. Add the curry paste or powder
and fry a further 1–2 minutes, then put in the livers and
toss in the seasonings for 1–2 minutes. Add the thick
coconut milk and lime leaves and cook, stirring, for 2–3
minutes.

Peel the cucumber. Cut the flesh from the seed core in
long, thick strips, then cut crosswise into sticks. Add to the
pan and cook briefly. Add the thin coconut milk and salt to
taste. Bring almost to the boil, then reduce the heat and
simmer gently until the livers are tender and the sauce is
thickened. Pour into a serving dish. Garnish with shreds of
red and green chili.

SERVES 6 AS A SIDE DISH

KARI 'DEVIL'

Devil's Curry

*This recipe is from an old resident of the Portuguese village
on the outskirts of the city of Malacca, where descendants of
Portuguese settlers have congregated. They have retained some of*

culture and traditions their ancestors brought to Malacca in the sixteenth century.

This fiery "Devil's Curry" is an adaptation of the European diable *or deviled dish, and incorporates locally produced spices and seasonings in a unique blending of culinary heritages.*

1½ lb (750 g) fresh ham/picnic shoulder (leg or shoulder/ hand of pork)
2 tablespoons white vinegar
1 tablespoon dark soy sauce
1 large onion
3–4 cloves garlic
1½-in (4-cm) piece fresh ginger
3 tablespoons vegetable oil
8–10 dried red chilies
1 teaspoon mustard seeds
1 teaspoon fenugreek seeds
6–8 candlenuts or macadamias, or 18–24 raw cashew nuts
½ teaspoon powdered galingale/galangal
¾ teaspoon powdered turmeric
1 teaspoon shrimp paste
1¼ cups (10 fl oz/310 ml) chicken or veal stock
salt and pepper
1 stalk lemon grass

Trim the pork and cut into bite-size cubes. Place in a dish and sprinkle on the vinegar and soy sauce. Let stand for 30 minutes to tenderize.

In a food processor or blender grind the onion, garlic and ginger to a paste. Fry in the oil for 3–4 minutes in a large saucepan.

DEVIL'S CURRY

In a spice grinder or mortar grind the chilies, mustard seeds, fenugreek seeds and candlenuts to a powder. Add the galingale, turmeric and shrimp paste and mix well. Add to the pan for 2–3 minutes until very aromatic. Add the pork and stir until each piece is covered with the seasonings, then fry until evenly colored.

Add the stock, seasonings and trimmed lemon grass. Cover and simmer gently for about 45 minutes or until very tender, uncovering the saucepan halfway through cooking so that the liquid evaporates.

SERVES 4–6

PASEMBOR

Vegetable Salad

The Malay version of the Indonesian gado gado *salad with its peanut sauce, this one incorporates slices of* taukua kuning *(compressed bean curd), which have a bright yellow-dyed surface.*

6 oz (185 g) fresh bean sprouts
1 medium cucumber
1 firm pear
1 green apple
1 small yam or taro
1 fresh red chili
1 cake compressed yellow bean curd
2 hard-cooked eggs
4 shallots (or 2 Spanish onions)
1 medium head lettuce
1 cup lightly packed fresh herbs such as mint, chervil, basil, cilantro (coriander)

SAUCE

2 heaping tablespoons roasted peanuts or crunchy peanut butter
4–5 dried red chilies, soaked
1 teaspoon shrimp paste
1 tablespoon tamarind pulp
½ cup (4 fl oz/125 ml) boiling water
1 tablespoon sugar or to taste
salt

GARNISH

1 egg, made into omelet shreds
2 tablespoons fried onion flakes

Blanch the bean sprouts in boiling water for 20 seconds, then drain well. Cover with cold water and drain again. Peel the cucumber. Cut the flesh away from the seed core in long strips, then cut crosswise into sticks. Peel and very thinly slice the pear and apple.

Peel the yam/taro and cut into small cubes. Drop into lightly salted boiling water and simmer for about 8 minutes; drain well. Slit open the chili, scrape out the seeds and then shred the flesh. Cut the bean curd into strips. Peel and quarter the eggs. Peel and slice the shallots. Wash the lettuce, separating the leaves. Wash the herbs, separate into small sprigs and toss in a cloth to dry.

Place the peanuts, drained chilies and shrimp paste in a blender or mortar and grind to a paste. Mix the tamarind, boiling water and sugar together, stirring until sugar dissolves. Strain onto the ground sauce ingredients and mix.

Arrange the lettuce on a platter. Pile the prepared salad ingredients onto the lettuce, tossing lightly together. Pour on the sauce and garnish with omelet shreds and fried onion flakes. Serve at once.

SERVES 6

TEMPE IN COCONUT MILK

TEMPE LEMAK

Tempe in Coconut Milk

Tempe, *cakes of fermented soybeans, are a popular vegetarian ingredient. Having a bland flavor, they are first crisp-fried, then simmered in a hot coconut milk sauce.*

4 cakes tempe, about 12 oz (375 g) altogether
2 medium onions
1 cup (8 fl oz/250 ml) vegetable oil
½ teaspoon crushed garlic
2 tablespoons salted soybeans
4 fresh green chilies
2 slices fresh ginger
2½ cups (20 fl oz/600 ml) thin coconut milk
1½ tablespoons rice flour
salt and cracked black pepper
4 hard-cooked eggs

Cut the *tempe* into bite-size squares. Peel and thinly slice the onions. Heat the oil in a skillet and fry the *tempe* until the surface is crisp and golden. Lift out and drain well.

Pour off all but 3 tablespoons of the oil and fry the onions with the garlic for about 4 minutes, until they are well colored and tender. Add the soybeans and cook briefly.

Slit open the chilies, scrape out the seeds and add the flesh to the dish with the sliced ginger.

Mix the coconut milk and rice flour together, pour into the pan and return the *tempe*. Simmer for 5–6 minutes, stirring from time to time, until the sauce is thick. Season to taste with salt and pepper. Add the halved eggs, heat through and serve.

SERVES 4

Malaysian Sambals and Garnishes

The word *sambal* encompasses the host of little side dishes which are served with Malaysian meals, as well as a number of tasty curry-like dishes which are similarly served with a meal, but not as the main feature. They are intended to add interest and counterpoint to the menu, providing a medley of tastes, colors and textures to complement the larger dishes and to stimulate the appetite.

Some sambals are made fresh for the meal. Others can be kept in sealed jars or in the refrigerator for some time, making it easier for the hostess to present an interesting array of these tiny tastebud ticklers at a moment's notice. A number of little condiment-type side dishes are also served with Malaysian meals. Among these are sliced cucumber; diced pineapple; fried dried fish; Bombay duck; roasted peanuts; sliced onion (plain or marinated in vinegar with sugar); lemon or lime wedges; sliced chili; sliced green (spring) onions or shallots; hard-cooked eggs, sliced or cut into wedges; shredded omelet; and fried onion flakes.

Some of these can double as garnishes, along with finely shredded chili and green onion; "flowers" made from fresh chilies; sprigs of cilantro (coriander), chives and mint leaves; shredded coconut; crisply fried egg or rice noodles; decoratively cut cucumber; onion and radish "chrysanthemums" and thin strips of *taukua* (compressed bean curd cake, deep-fried).

ONION SAMBAL

12 shallots (or 3–4 Spanish onions)
1 teaspoon crushed garlic
½ cup (4 fl oz/125 ml) white vinegar
1 tablespoon sugar
½ teaspoon salt

Peel the onions and slice thinly. Divide into rings. Place in a dish with the garlic. Pour on the vinegar and sprinkle the sugar and salt evenly over the onions. Marinate for at least 30 minutes before serving, stirring several times.

SAMBAL CUKA

8–10 fresh red chilies
½-in (1.25-cm) piece fresh ginger
2 cloves garlic
2½ tablespoons white vinegar
1 tablespoon sugar
1 teaspoon salt

Slit open the chilies and scrape out the seeds. Place the flesh in a blender or mortar with the ginger and garlic and grind to a paste. Add the vinegar, sugar and salt and mix in thoroughly.

SAMBAL BLACAN

5–6 fresh red chilies
1 tablespoon *blacan* (shrimp paste)
½ teaspoon sugar
large pinch of salt

Coarsely chop the chilies, leaving the seeds in. Place with the *blacan* in a blender or mortar and grind to a smooth paste, without breaking the chili seeds any more than necessary. Add the sugar and salt and mix in well. Store in the refrigerator for no more than 2–3 days.

CHILI SAMBAL

3–4 fresh green or red chilies
½ cup (4 fl oz/125 ml) light soy sauce
2 teaspoons sugar
1 tablespoon peanut oil

Very thinly slice the chilies, leaving the seeds in. Mix the soy sauce, sugar and peanut oil; stir in the chilies. Let stand for at least 30 minutes before serving.

ASSEMBLING DISHES IN THE SINGAPORE HILTON

MICHAEL COOK

HOKKIEN MIE

Hokkien Style Noodles

10 oz (315 g) fresh bacon or pancetta (pork belly)
12 (375 g) uncooked shrimp (prawns) in their shells
2 cups (16 fl oz/500 ml) water or chicken stock
1¼ lb (625 g) fresh *hokkien mie* (soft yellow egg noodles)
8 oz (250 g) fresh bean sprouts
4 oz (125 g) fresh spinach or kale
1 stalk celery
4 green onions
1 small cucumber
3 eggs or 2 cakes compressed bean curd
½ cup (4 fl oz/125 ml) vegetable or peanut oil
1 tablespoon crushed garlic, or to taste
1–2 teaspoons fresh red chili, pounded
1 tablespoon salted yellow soybeans
salt and black pepper
dark soy sauce
chili sauce

Place the pork in a saucepan, cover with boiling water and simmer for 20 minutes.

Peel the shrimp and place the shells in another saucepan with 2 cups water. (Omit this step if using chicken stock.) Cover and boil for 20 minutes. Drain and discard shells, reserving the liquid.

Cover the noodles with boiling water and drain in a colander. Blanch the bean sprouts and spinach and kale. Diagonally shred the celery. Trim and shred the green onions. Peel the cucumber and cut into narrow strips, discarding the seeds.

Beat the eggs together, if used. Pour into a lightly oiled pan and cook into a thin omelet, turning when the underside is lightly colored. Lift out, cool and cut into shreds. If using the bean curd, shred finely and stir-fry in a little peanut oil until lightly colored. Set aside.

Heat the oil in a *kuali* or wok and fry the garlic for 1 minute. Add the chili and mashed soybeans. Fry briefly. Drain the pork and cut into narrow strips. Add to the pan and fry until lightly colored. Add the shrimp and half the green onions and stir-fry briefly. Add the bean sprouts and spinach and fry again briefly. Push to one side of the pan. Add the noodles and fry, stirring and tossing constantly, for 3 minutes, then pour in the reserved shrimp or chicken stock and simmer until it has been absorbed. Add salt and pepper to taste.

WELDON TRANNIES   CHICKEN WITH *LAKSA* NOODLES IN COCONUT SAUCE

aside. Add the chopped onion and garlic and fry until soft and lightly colored. Grind the candlenuts to a fine powder. Add to the pan with the coriander and cumin and fry for 1 minute, stirring. Finely chop the tomatoes. Add to the pan with the salt, pepper, chili powder and sugar and fry for 2 minutes, stirring, then pour in the thin coconut milk and bring to the boil. Simmer for 12 minutes, stirring from time to time.

Pour boiling water over the vermicelli, then drain well. Shred the chicken and stir-fry in a little vegetable oil. Add the bean sprouts and stir-fry briefly. Shred the compressed bean curd, add to the pan and stir-fry a further 1½ minutes. Add the fried sliced onion. Transfer the contents of the pan to a bowl.

Trim and shred half the green onions; chop the other half finely. Slit open the chilies, scrape out the seeds and cut the flesh into long, fine shreds. Add half the green and red chili and the chopped green onions to the pan and fry briefly. Add the thick coconut milk and heat through. Stir in the drained vermicelli and transfer to a serving dish. Spread the chicken and bean sprout mixture over the top. Garnish with the shredded green onions and chili and the chopped cilantro. Serve at once.

SERVES 8

NASI MINYAK

Festive Rice

Nasi minyak is another bright yellow rice served on special occasions. This one has the Indian influence of buttery ghee (clarified butter) and sweet spices.

3 cups (1 lb/500 g) long-grain white rice
8 shallots (or 2 Spanish onions)
3 cloves garlic
¾ cup (6 oz/185 g) ghee (clarified butter)
2 sticks cinnamon
3 whole cloves
½ teaspoon cardamom seeds
4 slices galingale/galangal or young ginger
¾ teaspoon turmeric
1 teaspoon cracked black pepper
1½ teaspoons salt
3¼ cups (26 fl oz/810 ml) strong beef stock, or water and
    1–2 beef bouillon cubes

Wash the rice thoroughly, pour into a colander and set aside for 1 hour to drain.

Peel and slice the shallots and garlic. Melt the ghee in a medium-large saucepan. Add the spices and fry for 1 minute. Stir in the shallots, garlic, galingale, turmeric, pepper and salt and cook over medium heat for 1 minute.

Add the rice and stir until each grain is coated with ghee. Pour in the stock and bring to the boil. Reduce heat, cover the pan very tightly and cook gently until the liquid has been completely absorbed and the rice is fluffy. Stir up lightly with the handle of a wooden spoon. Serve hot.

SERVES 8

PULUT KUNING

Yellow Sticky Rice

Glutinous rice, boiled and tinted a bright golden yellow, is served with all festive banquets. It looks particularly attractive if pressed into an ornate jelly or brioche mold and unmolded onto a platter covered with banana leaves.

Serve the noodles with dark soy and chili sauce and the shredded green onions, celery, cucumber and omelet or bean curd.

SERVES 6

LAKSA AYAM

Chicken with Laksa Noodles in Coconut Sauce

Thin rice vermicelli, beehoon, *swimming in a mildly seasoned coconut milk sauce with diced meat, vegetables and bean curd is one of the most popular dishes in Singapore and Malaysia.*

2 large onions
4 tablespoons peanut oil
2 teaspoons crushed garlic
6 candlenuts or macadamias, or 18 raw
    cashew nuts
1 tablespoon ground coriander
1 teaspoon ground cumin
2 large tomatoes
2½ teaspoons salt
½ teaspoon cracked black pepper
1–2 teaspoons chili powder (or 1–3 fresh red chilies,
    pounded)
1 teaspoon sugar
8 cups (2 liters) thin coconut milk
1 lb (500 g) thin rice vermicelli
12 oz (375 g) boneless cooked chicken
vegetable oil
8 oz (250 g) fresh bean sprouts
2 squares/cakes compressed bean curd
6 green onions
1 fresh red chili
1 fresh green chili
¾ cup (6 fl oz/185 ml) thick coconut milk
2 tablespoons chopped fresh cilantro (coriander)

Peel the onions; very finely chop one and thinly slice the other. Heat the oil in a *kuali* or wok and fry the sliced onion until deeply colored. Remove with a slotted spoon and set

Pungent, distinctive daun pandan *(pandanus leaf) is added by tradition to lend its unique aroma and taste, but it can be omitted or replaced with a few drops of* pandan *essence.*

2 cups (1 lb/500 g) glutinous rice
1 teaspoon powdered turmeric
1½ teaspoons crushed garlic
1 teaspoon salt
2 cups (16 fl oz/500 ml) thin coconut milk
1 *daun pandan* (pandanus leaf) or a few drops
    pandan essence

Rinse the rice and drain thoroughly. Place in a bowl and add the turmeric and garlic. Add water to cover and soak for about 4 hours. Drain. Add the salt and coconut milk, then push the pandanus leaf into the center of the rice. Bring quickly to the boil, then reduce the heat to very low and allow to cook slowly for about 20 minutes, until the liquid has been completely absorbed. Discard the pandanus leaf.

Pack the rice into a buttered mold and press it in firmly. Let stand for a few minutes, then invert onto a serving plate and serve at once. Can be garnished with finely shredded shallots.

SERVES 6

CENDOL
Coconut Milk Dessert

Cendol – *a tall glass of iced coconut milk, brightly specked with "beans" of pink and green jelly, with a syrup of rich brown* gula melaka *(palm sugar) in the bottom of the glass – is one of the most refreshing drinks/desserts that has ever been concocted.*

Green pea or mung bean flour is used to make the jelly, although a passable substitute can be obtained using arrowroot. It is boiled with water until thick, colored brightly with green and red food coloring, and then forced through small holes into a basin of ice water, where it sets into the characteristic little bean-shaped lumps. Cendol is unmatched for soothing the throat and mouth after blazing hot curries.

2 oz (60 g) green pea/mung bean flour or arrowroot
1⅓ cups (11 fl oz/345 ml) water
red and green food coloring
1 cup (5 oz/155 g) crumbled palm sugar or dark
    brown sugar
1 crushed *daun pandan* (pandanus leaf, optional) – or use
    a few drops of *pandan* essence
⅔ cup (5 fl oz/155 ml) hot water
shaved ice
7 cups (1¾ liters) thin coconut milk

RIDING HOME FROM MARKET, CENTRAL SINGAPORE

LEO MEIER/WELDON TRANNIES

Mix the flour and water in a small saucepan and bring to the boil, stirring constantly. Cook gently until the mixture is very thick and clear. Divide in half; color one pink, the other green. Transfer to a coarse strainer or colander placed over a dish of ice water. Push the mixture through so that it falls into the ice water in small bean-shaped pellets.

❧ Place the sugar in a small saucepan. Add the *pandanus* leaf and hot water and simmer over low heat until the sugar dissolves. Discard the leaf, strain the syrup and cool.

❧ Pour about 1 tablespoon sugar syrup into each tall glass. Add 2–3 tablespoons of the "beans" and a scoop of shaved ice; top up with coconut milk. Serve with long straws and long-handled spoons.

MAKES ABOUT 12 GLASSES

BURBUR CHACHA
Yam and Coconut Pudding

Burbur *epitomizes the originality of the sweet dishes served in Singapore and Malaysia. Diced cooked yam and little pellets of mung bean flour, sago or tapioca are tossed together over cracked ice. Thick* santan *(coconut milk) is poured over and the dish is given a caramel-like topping of melted* gula melaka *(palm sugar).*

1 recipe green mung bean dough (see *Cendol*)
1 small yam, about 5 oz/155 g
2 tablespoons tapioca or sago
1 teaspoon salt
3 cups (24 fl oz/750 ml) thick coconut milk
5–6 oz (155–185 g) *gula melaka* (palm sugar/dark brown sugar)
1 *daun pandan* (pandanus leaf) or 4–5 drops *pandan* essence, (optional)
⅔ cup (5 fl oz/155 ml) boiling water
shaved or cracked ice

Prepare the pellets of mung bean dough and let stand in a dish of ice water until needed. Peel the yam and boil or steam until tender, then cut into very small dice. Boil the tapioca or sago until clear and tender; drain. Mix the salt with the coconut milk.

❧ Grate the *gula melaka* into a small saucepan. Add the pandanus leaf and boiling water and stir over medium heat until the sugar is completely dissolved. Remove from the heat and stand the pan in a dish of cracked ice to cool.

❧ To assemble the dessert, place a spoonful each of the dough pellets, the diced yam and tapioca or sago in the bottom of glass dessert dishes. Cover with cracked or shaved ice, then add the coconut milk and the cooked sugar syrup. Serve at once.

SERVES 6

SEVIAN
Vermicelli Dessert

Consisting of rice vermicelli in a milky-sweet sauce laden with dried fruit and nuts, sevian *is one dessert that the Malays have happily adopted from the Indians.*

⅔ cup (5 oz/155 g) ghee (clarified butter)
4 oz (125 g) raw cashew nuts or almonds
4 oz (125 g) golden raisins (sultanas)
5 oz (155 g) rice vermicelli
4 cups (1 liter) milk
¾–1 cup (6–8 oz/185–250 g) sugar
¼ teaspoon ground cardamom
1 tablespoon rosewater
1 cup (8 fl oz/250 ml) heavy (double/thick) cream

Melt the ghee in a medium saucepan and fry the cashews or almonds until golden, then add the raisins and fry these until plump. Lift out with a slotted spoon and set aside.

❧ Break the vermicelli into short lengths. Add to the ghee and fry until golden. Add the milk, sugar and cardamom and bring to the boil. Reduce heat and simmer until the vermicelli is almost tender, about 6 minutes. Add the rosewater, nuts and raisins and simmer briefly. Stir in the cream and heat gently until the vermicelli is tender. Serve warm.

SERVES 8

CENDOL (TOP) AND YAM AND COCONUT PUDDING *(BOTTOM)*

171

India

FISHING NEAR SRINAGAR IN NORTHERN KASHMIR

A TRADITIONAL PARSI MEAL OF LAMB AND LENTIL CASSEROLE, BROWN RICE, *DHANSAK* KEBABS, AND *KACHUMBER, recipes pages 190-191*

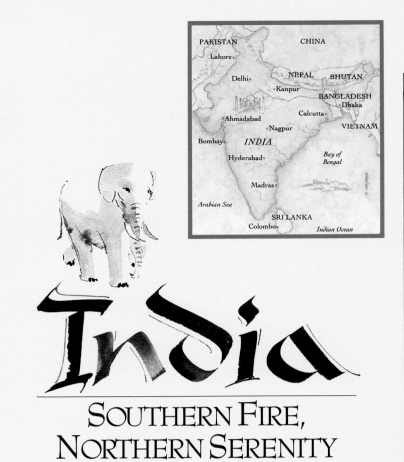

India

SOUTHERN FIRE, NORTHERN SERENITY

To travel through India from subtropical south to ice-capped north is to be introduced to a tantalizing diversity of food styles. Over four centuries ago, Mogul emperors brought to the mountainous north the richness of Persian culinary tradition, blending meats, most often lamb and poultry, with dried fruits and nuts, binding them in sweet, spice-laden creamy sauces made fragrant with essence of lime and rose, and decorating them with gossamer fine sheets of beaten silver. To this day, the Persian influence persists in the food served from Kashmir south to the Punjab, and to a lesser extent in the once-opulent Hyderabad. Curries are intricately seasoned with the sweet spices cardamom, clove, cinnamon, nutmeg and mace, with hints of saffron and many more, and are made creamy-rich with *dahi* (yogurt) and reduced cream.

Religion has had a marked influence on Indian food. Orthodox Hindus have woven a complex set of rules and values governing not only what is to be eaten, but when, how and with whom; religion even dictates who cooks and serves for whom. The eating of beef is sacrilege, but Hindus are also cautious about such foods as domestically reared pigs because they feed on scraps. Fish is eaten in Bengal and in some districts of Assam where it is abundant. In Bombay, where fish is equally plentiful, some high-caste Brahmans may eat it fried; others will not touch it. Those lower on the intricate Indian caste scale are mainly vegetarian, but this is more often from necessity than choice. Most Indians will eat mutton or goat if it is available and affordable.

Education and modern food technology have etched marginally into these long-established ideals, but even today an Indian may choose to go hungry rather than eat beef, or food cooked or served by one of lower caste.

SIMLA, AT THE FOOT OF THE GREAT HIMALAYA RANGE

MICHAEL DILLON

177

The "sacred cow" tradition persists in India, and Indians have a high regard for the value of cow's milk. Although rarely taken in its natural state, milk is used in many different ways throughout India. *Dahi* (curds or yogurt) is made into a nourishing and refreshing drink called *lassi*, it is used in curry sauces and desserts and compressed to make a soft curd cheese, *paneer*. Cream is made into butter, then clarified by boiling to make ghee, which is considered the pinnacle of purity and much venerated. Not only does it give its buttery richness to sweets, rice and meat dishes and desserts, but it is often used in religious ceremonies. As the one food considered totally pure, it is thought to be capable of purifying.

A typical Indian meal comprises a curry or two, a bowl of white rice and a vegetable dish – either curried, as a salad, or a dish of cooked lentils or other dried beans. With this may come a pickle or chutney, perhaps a little dish of *dahi* (curds) and often some kind of bread. Thus, even in a poor vegetarian household there will be a reasonable balance of nourishment – carbohydrates, proteins and fats.

Regional cooking styles are quite distinct. Almost 1300 years ago, Parsis, persecuted in their homeland of Iran, settled on India's west coast. Unhindered by the then-ruling Hindus, they established a way of life similar to the one they had left behind; they practice their religion and many of their old traditions to this day. Over the centuries Parsi food underwent a subtle transition as cooks included more local ingredients. Today coconut, coriander, red chilies and garlic have become the bywords of Parsi cooking. Ritual in Parsi families is the Sunday gathering to enjoy *dhansak*, a substantial dish of several kinds of lentils, diced lamb and vegetables traditionally accompanied by little meat kebabs, an onion salad called *kachumber* and rice made deep brown with fried onions.

Gujarat is perhaps the only state in India where vegetarianism prevails totally, with all castes and creeds following a strict regime. It is not, however, an uninteresting or limited cuisine, as much of the food is taken in the form of *farshan*, tasty little well-seasoned snacks. Gujarati dishes have a unique sweet-sour taste because of the sugar and lime juice which appear in almost every recipe. Local cooks are particularly respected for their chutneys and pickles, as well as their rich sweetmeats.

Lapped by the Arabian Sea, the vast state of Maharashtra has access to a wonderful variety of seafoods, which are often prepared with the state's other major commodity, coconut. Peanuts grow profusely here, and their flavorful oil gives its particular taste to many local dishes. Maharashtrians also enjoy a wide variety of vegetables and include many vegetarian dishes, often prepared with grated coconut or coconut milk, in their menus.

Coastal Kerala state also uses coconut products – milk, shredded or grated coconut, or coconut pounded to a smooth paste – with seafood and vegetable dishes. Cooks here rely for flavor not on spices, but on fresh herbs such as *pudina* (mint), *methi* (fenugreek) and *hara dhania* (fresh cilantro/coriander).

AT PLAY ON A REMOTE RIVER, KERALA, IN SOUTHERN INDIA   MICHAEL DILLON

Goa, with its Portuguese ancestry, reflects yet another aspect of India's complex cuisine. Its fiery curried dishes, using pork and duck or eggs, are seasoned with deeply colored toasted spices mixed with vinegar or other acidulating ingredients to give a strong, tart taste with overtones of European *diable* dishes.

In Bengal, seafoods as well as river fish take precedence over meat dishes. Powerfully flavored mustard seed oil lends a unique and distinctive taste.

Across the southern states of India the mainly Tamil population follows a vegetarian regime. Dishes are usually stingingly hot with chilies. Sauces are generally thin and watery, almost souplike in many instances; an example is *sambar,* a fiercely hot mixture of diced vegetables, split peas and lentils, which accompanies the enormous crisp *dosai* pancakes served at breakfast. Little cakes of steamed semolina, *iddlys*, accompany hot curry dishes.

These breads differ from those served in other parts of India. The *chupati*, an unleavened round flat bread made from finely milled wholewheat flour and cooked on a flat iron griddle (*tawa*), is perhaps the most universal. But there are also *puris*, similar to *chupatis* but deep-fried until they blow up like little edible balloons. *Kulchas* are a soft bread made with a natural yeast leaven produced by a yogurt ferment. *Parrathas* could well be the most luxurious bread served in India. Prepared in a similar way to *chupatis*, they are spread thickly with melted ghee, rolled and folded and rolled again so that the dough becomes interlayered with ghee, then shallow-fried in more ghee.

Towards the central north where the *tandoor* oven dominates the kitchen, soft-textured leavened *naans* accompany other dry-roasted *tandoor* foods such as the famed *tandoori* chicken, whole fish, *tikkas* (little pieces, usually fish or chicken) and kebabs. The *tandoor* resembles a large earthenware plant pot turned upside down. It has thick clay walls and stands over a charcoal fire. Food to be cooked in the *tandoor* oven is first marinated in spices and acidulating ingredients such as lime juice or *dahi* (curds). A bright orange food color is traditionally used to give *tandoori* foods their distinctive orange-red tone. The intense heat inside the oven immediately seals the surface of the food, locking in the natural moisture and keeping the food tender and succulent inside. *Tandoori* roasted foods are usually served with onion rings, fresh or marinated in vinegar, and wedges of lemon or lime.

Curries are the staple of the Indian cuisine, but making a good curry is not a simple task. Curry is made up of several elements, the balance of which must be just right. The seasonings in the meat or vegetables and the liquid to make the sauce are the essentials. In the north, *garam masala* or other aromatic *masala* (spice mixtures) provide the basic flavor. From a minimum of about six to more than twenty spices may be used in a carefully selected combination in a single curry. Cream or curds add smoothness and thickness to the sauce. In the south, fresh seasonings – cilantro, fenugreek, mint, onions, garlic, ginger and chili, combined with turmeric and spices such as mustard seeds – are favored over the sweeter aromatics. Coconut milk provides the sauce in many dishes.

Curries are cooked in the deep, straight-sided *degchi*, while the wok-like *karahi* is used for frying. A flat, thick metal griddle, the *tawa* is used for baking unleavened breads and for broiling or grilling, as well as serving double duty as a heat diffuser under the *degchi*.

Indians rarely drink alcoholic beverages. *Lassi*, plain water, coconut water or milk, fruit juices – mango is a particular favorite – and tea are the liquids that accompany a meal. Tea can be quite a treat here, with such spices as cardamom, cinnamon and mace added to make the drink fragrant and subtly spicy. In Kashmir, the Russian-style samovar has long been in use, brewing up a potent mixture that may be flavored with almonds and spices, with a pinch of baking soda to turn the tea a bright pink-red hue.

AN INDIAN FAMILY AT BREAKFAST
KATE WIMBLE

BEEF PASTRIES AND DEEP-FRIED PEA FLOUR AND VEGETABLE PATTIES

PAKORAS

Deep-Fried Pea Flour and Vegetable Patties

Indian vegetarians enjoy a varied, nourishing and filling diet. Protein obtained from milk, butter and eggs is supplemented by an ample intake of dried beans and peas. Vegetables are usually in plentiful supply; as well as being made into a host of curried dishes, they are cooked up as snacks for daylong consumption.

There are many different kinds of pakoras. A type of deep-fried patty, they range from being little more than a highly seasoned dough of besan *(chick pea) flour, as they are preferred in the northern regions, through finely chopped vegetables suspended in a* besan *dough in central India, to more sizable chunks of vegetable dipped in a* besan-*based batter in the south. No matter how they are done, pakoras are one of those tasty little dishes that are almost impossible to stop eating. Serve with a spicy chili sauce, or with* narial *(coconut) or* pudina *(mint) chutney.*

2 medium boiling potatoes
5 oz (155 g) cauliflower
5 oz (155 g) broccoli
5 oz (155 g) eggplant/aubergine
1 medium onion
3 fresh spinach leaves
½ cup (2 oz/60 g) frozen peas, thawed
oil for deep-frying

BESAN BATTER

1¼ cups (½ pint/315 ml) water
1 teaspoon *garam masala* (curry spices)
1½ teaspoons ground coriander
2½ teaspoons chili powder
¼ teaspoon dried green mango powder
¼ teaspoon turmeric
2 teaspoons salt
1 teaspoon baking powder
1 cup (5 oz/155 g) chick pea flour
⅓ cup (1½ oz/45 g) finely ground white flour

Peel the potatoes and cut into small dice. Place in a saucepan with hot water to cover, bring to the boil and simmer until half cooked. Cut the cauliflower and broccoli into very small florets. Cut the eggplant and onion into small dice. Thoroughly wash and dry the spinach leaves and chop finely.

Mix the batter ingredients, then set aside for 20 minutes. When ready to cook, mix the vegetables thoroughly and evenly into the batter. Heat the oil until a haze of smoke forms over the pan. Slide in spoonfuls of the batter and cook over medium-high heat until the *pakoras* are a rich golden brown. Lift out with a slotted spoon and drain on paper towels; keep warm while the remainder are cooked, then serve at once.

MAKES ABOUT 36

SAMOOSAS
Beef Pastries

While there is less diversity in the range of non-vegetarian snacks in the Indian cuisine, there are still many popular spicy tidbits that are enjoyed as the prelude to a meal or as a between-meals snack. Samoosas are deep-fried parcels of spiced ground meat and peas that go well with fried mint chutney (pudina chutni) and are delicious with cocktails.

PASTRY

2 cups (8 oz/250 g) finely ground white flour
1 teaspoon salt
1 teaspoon *garam masala* (curry spices)
½ teaspoon cracked black pepper
½ teaspoon turmeric
1½ tablespoons vegetable oil
warm water

FILLING

1 tablespoon ghee (clarified butter)
8 oz (250 g) lean ground (minced) beef or lamb
2 teaspoons grated fresh ginger
1 teaspoon crushed garlic
1 large onion, minced
2 teaspoons *garam masala* (curry spices)
1 teaspoon chili powder
½ teaspoon turmeric
½ teaspoon salt
3 oz (90 g) frozen peas
1 tablespoon lemon juice
1½ tablespoons finely chopped fresh cilantro/coriander
   or mint
oil for deep-frying

Combine the flour, salt, *garam masala*, pepper and turmeric in a mixing bowl and mix together thoroughly. Make a small well in the center and pour in the oil, then add enough warm water to make a stiff dough.

Knead for about 10 minutes until the dough is completely smooth and pliable. Cover with a damp cloth and set aside for 20 minutes.

Heat the ghee in a medium saucepan and fry the ground meat until it changes color. Add the ginger, garlic and onion and fry, stirring frequently, for about 5 minutes until cooked. Add the spices, salt and frozen peas, cover the pan and cook gently for about 6 minutes, stirring from time to time, until the peas are tender. Stir in the lemon juice and toss lightly over medium-high heat until there is no liquid left in the bottom of the pan. Add the chopped herbs and transfer to a plate to cool.

Roll the dough into a sausage shape and cut into 15 pieces of even size. Roll each out to a round about 5 in (13 cm) in diameter, then cut in halves.

Place a spoonful of the filling towards one side of each piece of pastry. Run a wet finger around the edge and fold over to give a triangular pastry with one curved side. Pinch the edges together, then press around the edges with the tines of a fork to seal and decorate.

Heat the deep-frying oil in a wide pan until a haze forms over the pan. Deep-fry the *samoosas* several at a time until golden brown. Lift out, drain well and serve hot with *pudina chutni* (see page 194).

MAKES ABOUT 30

PATIR
Cabbage Rolls

An enterprising cook created this tasty dish from a few economical ingredients. Cabbage leaves spread with a spiced batter are rolled and deep-fried, then sliced for serving as a side dish or snack.

24 cabbage leaves
2 tablespoons softened ghee (clarified butter)
½ cup (3 oz/90 g) chick pea flour
3 tablespoons all-purpose (plain) flour
2 teaspoons minced fresh green chili
1 teaspoon crushed garlic
1 teaspoon minced fresh ginger
3 tablespoons very finely chopped fresh cilantro/coriander
   or mint
1–1½ teaspoons chili powder
1 teaspoon *garam masala* (curry spices)
1 teaspoon salt
⅓ teaspoon ground black pepper
1 tablespoon lemon or lime juice
plain yogurt
oil for deep-frying
lime or lemon wedges
chili powder

Bring a large pot of water to the boil. Drop in the cabbage leaves and leave only long enough for them to wilt, then lift out and drain well. Wipe dry and cut away any large central ribs. Brush one side of each leaf with the clarified butter, then place two leaves together, buttered sides in.

Mix the flours with the seasonings and spices, then stir in the lemon or lime juice and enough yogurt to make a thick but spreadable paste. Spread evenly over the cabbage leaves on the upper side only, then roll each into a firm cylinder to enclose the filling. Tie with thread or secure with wooden picks.

Heat deep-frying oil to moderately hot and slide in the rolls about 4 at a time. Deep-fry for about 3 minutes or until slightly crisped on the surface and just cooked through. Lift out and drain very well, then cut into 1-in (2.5-cm) slices and arrange on a paper napkin-lined platter. Serve with plenty of lemon or lime wedges and garnish with a sprinkling of chili powder.

SERVES 6

CABBAGE ROLLS

Jhinga Kachcha Aam Kari

Shrimp and Green Mango Curry

Mangoes (aam) proliferate throughout all but the cooler northern regions of India. Their succulent, sweet orange-red flesh is enjoyed as a fruit, made into thick, sweet juice and used in desserts and pickles. But the flesh of the unripe mango is treated as a vegetable, lending its unique, slightly tart crispness to lightly curried dishes. In this specialty of Kerala state, it is combined with fresh local shrimp (prawns) and freshly grated coconut.

1½ lb (750 g) medium size uncooked shrimp (prawns)
    in their shells
salt
2 large unripe mangoes
⅔ cup (2 oz/60 g) freshly grated coconut
    or 1½ oz/45 g dry shredded coconut
1 tablespoon coriander seeds
6 dried red chilies, soaked in hot water
2 cups (16 fl oz/500 ml) water
2 medium onions
2½ tablespoons coconut or vegetable oil
2 curry leaves or bay leaves
¾ teaspoon turmeric
fresh cilantro/coriander
⅓ cup (2½ fl oz/75 ml) thick coconut milk

Peel the shrimp leaving the heads and tails intact, although these can be removed if preferred. Devein, then rinse the shrimp in cold water, rubbing with a little salt. Drain.
Peel the mangoes and cut into bite-size pieces. Set aside. Combine the coconut, coriander and chilies with a little of the water in a food processor or blender and grind to a smooth paste.
Peel and slice the onions; fry in the oil until softened and very lightly colored. Add the curry leaves and coconut paste and fry gently for about 6 minutes or until the oil floats to the surface.
Add the shrimp and sliced mango, the remaining water, the turmeric and a large pinch of salt. Simmer over medium heat for about 10 minutes until the mango and shrimp are both tender. Check for seasoning, then transfer to a serving dish. Garnish with the cilantro and drizzle on the thick coconut milk.

SERVES 4

SHRIMP IN GREEN MASALA *(TOP)* AND SHRIMP AND GREEN
MANGO CURRY

Jhinga Dhania Masala

Shrimp in Green Masala

Hara dhania, the pungent leafy green cilantro, is otherwise known as fresh coriander or Chinese parsley. Easily cultivated, it is enjoyed throughout Southeast Asia for its strong taste, which is both refreshing and palate-stimulating.

The seeds of the coriander plant dhania *are one of the most important elements in the curry spice blends and are essential to* garam masala. *The fresh green leaves are used mostly as a garnish, but in certain meat and seafood dishes, large quantities of the leaves are used to create bright green flavorful sauces. These* dhania masala *dishes are favored along India's west coast.*

1½ lb (750 g) uncooked shrimp (prawns) in their shells
salt
2 medium onions
2 cloves garlic
1-in (2.5-cm) piece fresh ginger
2 fresh green chilies
1 cup loosely packed fresh cilantro/coriander leaves
1 teaspoon anise/fennel seeds
½ teaspoon cumin seeds
2 tablespoons coconut or vegetable oil
¾ cup (6 fl oz/185 ml) water

Peel the shrimp leaving the heads and tails intact, although these can be removed if preferred. Devein, then rinse the shrimp in cold water, rubbing with a little salt.

Peel the onions and garlic; thinly slice one onion. Chop the other coarsely and place in a food processor or blender. Grind to a smooth paste with the ginger, seeded chilies and cilantro. Grind the spices and add to the seasoning paste with 1 teaspoon salt.

Fry the sliced onion in the oil for about 4 minutes, until softened but only lightly colored. Add the seasoning paste and fry gently for about 4 minutes, stirring frequently.

Pour in the water and simmer until the sauce thickens, then add the shrimp and cook for about 5 minutes until tender. Check the seasonings and serve at once. Cubes or slices of fish can be cooked in the same way.

SERVES 4–6

Pomfret Masaledar

Pomfret in Coconut Sauce

From the state of Maharashtra comes this lightly seasoned fish dish, its sauce thick with fried onion and coconut.

1½ lb (750 g) fillets or steaks of pomfret, John Dory or
    mackerel
2 medium onions
6–8 cloves garlic
½ cup (4 fl oz/125 ml) mixture of melted ghee
    (clarified butter) and vegetable oil
½ cup (2 oz/60 g) shredded (desiccated) coconut
1 teaspoon chili powder
1½ teaspoons ground coriander
1 teaspoon ground cumin
½ teaspoon turmeric
2 teaspoons white poppy seeds, crushed
2 teaspoons tamarind pulp
2 cups (16 fl oz/500 ml) water
1 teaspoon salt

POMFRET IN COCONUT SAUCE

Cut the fish into strips 1 in (2.5 cm) wide. Peel and very thinly slice the onions. Crush the garlic. Heat the ghee and oil in a medium saucepan and fry the onions and garlic for 4 minutes until they have begun to color. Add the coconut and fry for 1½ minutes, stirring to prevent burning. Remove to a food processor or blender and grind to a smooth paste.

Return to the pan, add the spices and poppy seeds and fry briefly. Mix the tamarind into the water, then strain into the pan. Bring to the boil and simmer for 5 minutes, then add the fish and salt and simmer gently until the fish is tender, about 15 minutes.

SERVES 6

Machhli Tamatar

Baked Fish in Tomato Cream Sauce

1½-lb (750-g) whole snapper
1¼ teaspoons fenugreek seeds, finely ground
1¼ teaspoons crushed garlic
1½ teaspoons minced fresh ginger
3 tablespoons ghee (clarified butter)
1 tablespoon ground coriander
2 teaspoons ground cumin
1½ teaspoons chili powder
¾ teaspoon turmeric
4 large tomatoes
¾ cup (6 fl oz/185 ml) fish stock or water
salt and black pepper
lemon or lime juice
½ cup (4 fl oz/125 ml) heavy (double/thickened) cream
¼ cup (2 fl oz/60 ml) plain yogurt

Clean and scale the fish. Rinse thoroughly under running cold water, then drain well and wipe dry. Make several deep cuts across each side to allow the flavors to penetrate and the fish to cook evenly.

Fry the fenugreek, garlic and ginger in the clarified butter in a medium saucepan for 2 minutes, stirring frequently. Add the remaining spices and fry for 2 more minutes.

BAKED FISH IN TOMATO CREAM SAUCE, *recipe page 183*

TENDER CURRIED CHICKEN *(TOP)* AND *SORPOTEL, recipe page 199*

Finely chop the tomatoes, add to the pan and cook for 5 minutes. Add the fish stock or water and bring to the boil. Cover and simmer gently for about 30 minutes until the sauce is thick.

While the sauce is simmering, season the fish with salt, pepper and lemon juice and place in a lightly greased baking dish. Cover with aluminum foil and bake in a pre-heated 425°F (220°C) oven for about 25 minutes. Test by inserting a fork into the thickest part; the fish should flake easily. Remove the foil, increase the oven heat to very high and bake 5 more minutes.

Stir the cream and yogurt into the sauce and simmer for 2–3 minutes. Transfer the fish to a serving dish, pour on the sauce and serve at once.

SERVES 6

MURGH MOELHO
Tender Curried Chicken

Like so many dishes from Goa, this one combines an acid such as vinegar or tamarind juice with hot spices. In this recipe mustard seeds add their piquant taste. Prepare it at least a day before serving to taste it at its best.

2 lb (1 kg) chicken thighs
2 teaspoons cumin seeds
1½ teaspoons white mustard seeds
4–8 dried red chilies
¾ teaspoon turmeric
2 tablespoons white vinegar
1 large onion
1½ teaspoons crushed garlic
3 tablespoons vegetable oil or a mixture of ghee (clarified butter) and oil
1½ cups (12 fl oz/375 ml) water
1 teaspoon salt

Prick the chicken skin thoroughly with the point of a sharp knife to allow the seasonings to penetrate.

Place the cumin, mustard seeds and dried chilies in a small saucepan and heat until the seeds begin to pop, then grind to a fine powder. Mix with the turmeric and vinegar. Pour over the chicken, rub in well and let stand for at least 30 minutes.

Peel and thinly slice the onion. Fry the onion and garlic in the oil and ghee until very deeply colored. Lift out with a slotted spoon.

Fry the chicken pieces 2 at a time until evenly colored. Add the fried onion and the water and bring to the boil. reduce heat to very low, stir in the salt and simmer the chicken, tightly covered, for about 45 minutes, until it is completely tender. Serve with white rice and *dhal* (lentils).

SERVES 4

PAKORA MURGH

Battered Deep-Fried Chicken

The Moti Mahal, *doyen of all Indian restaurants, still enjoys a flourishing trade in Old Delhi. Although its walls are now crumbling and guests occupy rickety furniture in its paved gardens while the fountain rarely emits more than a trickle, it retains much of its original character – and many of the evergreen dishes on which its* fame *was established. For a few rupees, guests can be entertained, embarrassed or receive a good-natured ribbing from the band of itinerant musicians who occupy a stage in one corner of the garden. Pakora murgh, chicken thighs encased in a light crisp batter and bedecked with rings of marinated onion and wedges of fresh lime, is one of the* Moti Mahal *trademarks. The chicken is baked in a* tandoor, *coated with a spiced batter of fine flour and besan (chick pea flour), then quickly deep-fried to crisp perfection.*

6 chicken thighs, 6–7 oz (185–220 g) each
1 teaspoon crushed garlic
1 teaspoon minced fresh ginger
1 tablespoon lemon or lime juice
⅓ teaspoon dried mango powder
1 teaspoon chili powder
¼ teaspoon white pepper
¾ teaspoon salt
½ cup (4 fl oz/125 ml) plain yogurt
small pinch of powdered turmeric or a few drops
    red food coloring (optional)

BATTER

1 cup (4 oz/125 g) finely ground white flour
½ cup (2½ oz/75 g) chick pea flour
½ teaspoon crushed *ajwain* seeds (optional)
½ teaspoon chili powder
1 teaspoon salt
2 teaspoons baking powder
1¼–1½ cups (10–12 fl oz/315–375 ml) cold water
oil for deep-frying

Prick the chicken thighs all over with the point of a sharp knife to allow the seasonings to penetrate. Mix the next 9 ingredients and use to coat the chicken. Let stand for at least 3 hours. Place on a rack in a baking pan and roast in a preheated 375°F/190°C oven for about 25 minutes until almost cooked through. Let cool.

Mix the batter ingredients and let stand for at least 10 minutes before using.

Heat oil to the smoking point. Dip the chicken into the batter, coating evenly. Hold over the dish for a moment to allow excess batter to drip off, then slide into the oil. Deep-fry until the batter is crisp and golden brown. Lift out and drain well.

Serve *pakora murgh* in the traditional way, with wedges of fresh lime or lemon and rings of red onion.

SERVES 6

BATTERED DEEP-FRIED CHICKEN WITH *CHUPATIS*

VINDALOO

A Hot Curry

Vindaloo *curries are prepared in two stages; the meat is first marinated in a strongly acidulated liquid with spices, then slowly simmered with additional seasonings until completely tender. The method gives a particularly pungent taste but also preserves the meat to a certain extent, so that a good* vindaloo *can be safely kept for several days in a hot climate.*

The vindaloo *style of cooking originated on India's west coast, in Kerala and its neighboring states, and the idea spread into Portuguese-influenced Goa. Game meats such as wild boar, venison and duck are inevitably cooked up as* vindaloos, *since their strong taste requires assertive seasonings to do them justice.*

Vindaloos of pork are most likely to appear on menus in India, but this recipe is also successful with beef and domestic or wild duck and venison.

VINDALOO PASTE

¼ cup (1 oz/30 g) coriander seeds
1 tablespoon cumin seeds
6 whole cloves
2-in (5-cm) stick cinnamon
1½ teaspoons black peppercorns
2 teaspoons fenugreek seeds
1 teaspoon anise/fennel seeds
¼ cup (2 fl oz/60 ml) white vinegar

VINDALOO CURRY *(RIGHT),* AND BRAISED TOMATO AND EGGPLANT, *recipe page 193,* WITH YOGURT AND CUCUMBER SAUCE, *recipe page 194*

2 lb (1 kg) fresh ham or beef round steak
  (pork leg/braising beef)
3 tablespoons ghee (clarified butter)
6 dried red chilies, soaked
6–8 cloves garlic
1 large onion
1-in (2.5-cm) piece fresh ginger
2 bay leaves
2 cups (16 fl oz/500 ml) beef stock or water
salt

To make the *vindaloo* paste, combine the spices in a dry skillet and dry-fry for 4–5 minutes over medium heat until very aromatic. (Or spread on an oven tray and roast in a hot oven for 5 minutes.) Pour into a spice grinder or mortar and grind to a fine powder. Mix with the vinegar.

❧ Trim the meat and cut into 1-in (2.5-cm) cubes. Place in a stainless steel or glass dish, add the *vindaloo* paste and stir until the meat is evenly coated. Cover and set aside for 3–4 hours for the flavors to permeate the meat and the vinegar to tenderize it.

❧ Heat the butter in a heavy saucepan and sauté the meat until evenly colored. Drain the chilies, chop the garlic, onion and ginger. Remove the meat, add the chili, garlic, onion and ginger and fry for 2–3 minutes, stirring occasionally. Return the meat, add the bay leaves and stock or water, cover and cook gently for about 1¼ hours, until the meat is tender. Add salt to taste.

❧ *Vindaloo* dishes should preferably be cooked at least a day in advance and reheated before serving. This softens the slightly harsh taste of the freshly cooked dish.

SERVES 4–6

KASHMIRI CURRIED MEATBALLS

RISTA

Kashmiri Curried Meatballs

In Kashmir these lightly seasoned meatballs of tender mutton are served in rich red-brown curry sauce made fragrant with rose essence and saffron.

4 lb (2 kg) leg of mutton
2 tablespoons coriander seeds
½ teaspoon fenugreek seeds
1 tablespoon mild chili powder
1½ teaspoons salt
¼ cup (1½ oz/45 g) chick pea flour
1½ large onions
2 teaspoons crushed garlic
4–5 tablespoons ghee (clarified butter)
½ cup (4 fl oz/125 ml) plain yogurt
4 whole cloves
1 2-in (5-cm) cinnamon stick
1 cardamom pod, broken
1 teaspoon ground ginger
small pinch of asafoetida
3½ cups (28 fl oz/875 ml) water
¼ teaspoon powdered saffron
oil for deep-frying
1 teaspoon rose essence or 2–3 teaspoons rosewater
roasted almond slivers for garnishing

Trim the leg of mutton and cut the meat into small cubes. Place about 2 lb (1 kg) of the meat in batches in a food processor and grind to a very smooth paste. Pour the coriander seeds into a skillet and dry-fry until well colored, then grind finely. Mix half with the ground meat. Dry-fry the fenugreek seeds; grind and add to the meat with 1 teaspoon of the chili powder, the salt and chick pea flour. Mix thoroughly and set aside.

Peel and chop the onions. Heat the ghee in a large saucepan, add the remaining cubed meat and cook until well colored. Remove, add the meat bone – broken in several places if possible – and fry until colored. Lift out. Fry the onions and garlic until deeply browned, then return the meat and the mutton bone.

Add the yogurt, cloves, cinnamon, cardamom, ginger, asafoetida and remaining chili powder and fry, stirring, until the yogurt dries up. Add the water and simmer for 2 hours.

Form the ground meat into meatballs about the size of a golf ball, then flatten them slightly. Heat the oil until a haze forms over the pan. Fry the meatballs until very well colored, lift out and drain well.

Remove the mutton bone from the sauce, add the meatballs and simmer gently for 20–25 minutes, skimming the surface from time to time. Just before serving, stir in the saffron and rose essence.

SERVES 6

LAMB WITH SPINACH SAUCE (*BOTTOM*) AND TENDER LAMB CURRY (*TOP*)

PALAK JHOST

Lamb with Spinach Sauce

Palak or sag dishes, the Indian equivalent of the Western dishes we know as Florentine, combine puréed spinach with tender meats, cheeses and eggs. Palak jhost or sagmeat/sagwala is popular in central and northern India. Palak paneer, cubes of homemade curd cheese in a thick spinach sauce, and anda palak, eggs cooked with spinach, fill the bill for the vegetarian, and in the same vein the Parsi dish of bhaji per eenda, eggs on spinach, and bhajia danama jhinga, fried prawns and peas with spinach, are enjoyed in the southwest.

1½ lb (750 g) lean lamb
1 fresh green chili
1½ teaspoons crushed garlic
1½ teaspoons minced fresh ginger
2 tablespoons ghee (clarified butter)
1 tablespoon poppy seeds
1 teaspoon salt
2 tablespoons plain yogurt
1 black cardamom, broken open and lightly crushed
1 cup (8 fl oz/250 ml) water
1 lb (500 g) fresh or frozen spinach leaves
½ cup (4 fl oz/125 ml) heavy (double/thickened) cream
½ teaspoon freshly grated nutmeg

Trim the lamb and cut into bite-size cubes. Blanch in boiling water and drain well.

Slit open the chili; scrape out the seeds and chop the flesh very finely. Sauté the garlic, ginger and chili in the clarified butter for 1 minute, add the lamb and sauté until lightly colored.

Grind the poppy seeds and salt to a fine powder. Add to the pan and fry lightly, then stir in the yogurt and cardamom. Add the water and bring just to the boil, then reduce heat, cover the pan tightly and cook gently until the lamb is tender.

Thoroughly wash the spinach in cold water. Chop the leaves coarsely, place in a large saucepan, cover tightly and simmer for about 7 minutes. Drain, then transfer to a food processor or blender and purée. Add to the lamb and simmer for 2–3 minutes. Stir in the cream and nutmeg, heat through, check the seasonings and serve.

SERVES 6

ROGANJHOST

Tender Lamb Curry

Although of Kashmiri origin, Roganjhost *is one of those dishes that appears on menus throughout India. Tender lamb cubes in a creamy aromatic sauce, lightly seasoned and with just a hint of chili, illustrates that curries need not be hot to be enjoyable.*

2 lb (1 kg) lean boneless lamb
2 tablespoons ghee (clarified butter)
⅛ teaspoon asafoetida
1½ teaspoons salt
¼ teaspoon cracked black pepper
1 cup (8 fl oz/250 ml) plain yogurt
1½ cups (12 fl oz/375 ml) warm water
1½ tablespoons coriander seeds
⅛ teaspoon powdered cloves
½ teaspoon ground dried ginger
1½ teaspoons mild chili powder
½ teaspoon crushed cardamom seeds
1–2 teaspoons Kashmiri style *garam masala**
¾ cup (6 fl oz/185 ml) heavy (double/thickened) cream
1 teaspoon sugar

Trim the meat and cut into bite-size cubes. Heat the clarified butter in a large skillet and fry the meat in several batches until well colored. Add the asafoetida, salt and pepper and return all of the meat. Add the yogurt and cook over medium-high heat, stirring frequently, until the liquid

FLOATING MARKETS, KASHMIR   REG MORRISON/WELDON TRANNIES

has been absorbed, then add the water and bring to the boil. Reduce heat and simmer gently.

Dry-fry coriander in a small skillet until well colored. Grind to a fine powder and add to the pan with the cloves, ginger, chili powder, cardamom and *garam masala*. Simmer for about 25 minutes, until the meat is tender and the liquid is reduced.

Stir in the cream and sugar and simmer again briefly, then serve. A little extra *garam masala* may be sprinkled over the finished dish.

* *A mild curry spice blend having slightly more cardamom than usual and no turmeric.*

SERVES 6

SORPOTEL

A Pork Dish from Goa

Pork liver is added to this tart pork curry to give it a rich, strong flavor that proclaims its Portuguese connections. If made several days ahead, the meat will be supremely tender.

1½ lb (750 g) fresh ham (lean pork shoulder or leg)
8 oz (250 g) pork liver
1½-in (4-cm) piece fresh ginger
2 tablespoons coriander seeds
1 tablespoon cumin seeds
1 teaspoon turmeric
½ cup (4 fl oz/125 ml) tamarind water, made with
   1½ tablespoons tamarind pulp
3 curry leaves
3–4 tablespoons ghee (clarified butter)
2 large onions
8 cloves garlic
3–5 fresh green chilies
salt
extra tamarind water or lime juice
chopped fresh cilantro/coriander leaves

Remove the skin from the pork and cut the meat into 2–2½-in (5–7-cm) cubes. Blanch the liver in boiling water, drain and cut open. Trim carefully, then cut into 1½-in (4-cm) cubes.

Place the pork and liver in a large saucepan and add water to cover generously. Peel the ginger and cut half into thick slices. Add them to the pan, cover and bring to the boil. Reduce the heat and simmer gently for 1¼–1½ hours until the meat is fairly tender, skimming occasionally.

Dry-fry the coriander and cumin seeds until they turn a deep brown. Remove and grind to a fine powder, adding the turmeric. Mix with the tamarind water in a large bowl, adding the curry leaves. Drain the pork, reserving the cooking liquid. Cut the meat into small cubes.

Heat the ghee in a clean skillet and fry the meat until well colored. Add to the tamarind water and spices and set aside.

Peel and finely chop the onions, garlic, chilies and remaining ginger. Fry in the pan in the remaining ghee for 3–4 minutes, stirring frequently. Pour in the reserved stock and bring to the boil, then simmer for about 15 minutes.

Return the meat with the marinating liquid and continue to simmer for about 20 minutes, until the meat is very tender. Add salt and extra tamarind water or lime juice to taste; the flavor should be quite sharp. Stir in the chopped cilantro. Cool, cover and refrigerate for at least 12 hours. Reheat before serving.

SERVES 6–8

SKEWERED GROUND MEATBALLS AND PUMPKIN CREAM CURRY,
recipe page 192

SEEKH KEBABS
Skewered Ground Meatballs

*These are not meatball-shaped at all, but rather longer in a tradi-
tional sausage or kofta shape. Seekh kebabs, made of finely
ground (minced) meat – in India they would be made with mutton,
but beef will do just as nicely – seasoned with sweet spices and
bound with besan (chick pea flour), are among the many skewered
foods cooked in the tandoor oven. The meat is threaded on long
metal rods that are suspended inside the oven, giving even overall
heat which quickly sears the surface, trapping in the juices to make
the kebabs crunchy on the surface and tender-moist inside. A
heavy stone mortar is used in India for grinding meat. Dry ingredients, such as rice and wheat or spices, are ground with a stone
mortar and pestle or a large masala stone – a slab of stone over
which is rubbed a smaller stone.*

1¼ lb (625 g) lean boneless mutton (or beef)
1 teaspoon crushed garlic
1 small onion, finely grated
½ teaspoon minced fresh ginger
¼ teaspoon powdered cloves
¼ teaspoon crushed cardamom
1½ teaspoons ground coriander
1½ teaspoons salt
½ teaspoon cracked black pepper
1½ tablespoons poppy seeds
1½ teaspoons chick pea flour
½ cup (4 fl oz/125 ml) plain yogurt
1 small onion
1–2 fresh limes or lemons

Cut the meat into small cubes and place in a food processor.
Grind to smooth paste, then work in the garlic, onion,
ginger, ground spices, salt and pepper.

Dry-fry the poppy seeds in a small ungreased skillet
until they begin to pop, then add the chick pea flour and
cook until lightly toasted. Grind to a fine powder, stir into
the yogurt and add to the meat mixture. Blend until very
thick and smooth.

Use wet hands to form the mixture into long, thin
sausage shapes, very slightly thicker in the center. Thread
oiled metal skewers through the center of the *kebabs*.

Cook on a rack in a very hot oven or on a lightly oiled
griddle or skillet (frying pan), turning frequently, until the
surface is crisp and well colored and the kebabs are cooked
through. Remove the skewers and arrange the *kebabs* on a
serving plate.

Peel and slice the second onion; divide into rings. Cut
the lime or lemon into wedges. Arrange over and around
the kebabs and serve at once.

SERVES 4–6

DHANSAK
Parsi Lamb and Lentil Casserole

*Dhansak is the traditional Sunday meal eaten by the Parsis,
descendants of Persian immigrants who settled on the west coast of
India. Their unique style of food, with its European overtones, is
quite distinct from other styles of Indian cooking. This dish, made
up of a variety of lentils, lamb and vegetables, is traditionally
served with rice that takes its color from onions fried until they
turn a deep brown, little meat kebabs, and* kachumber, *an
onion salad dressed with a strongly flavored sauce of* jaggery
(palm sugar) and tamarind.

DHANSAK

1 large onion
3 tablespoons ghee (clarified butter)
2 teaspoons crushed garlic
1½ teaspoons minced fresh ginger
6–8 dried red chilies, soaked in hot water
1 tablespoon *dhansak* curry spices
2 black cardamoms, broken open
2-in (5-cm) cinnamon stick
8 black peppercorns
1½ teaspoons turmeric
1¼ lb (625 g) lean lamb or mutton
3 medium tomatoes
2 teaspoons salt
8 cups (3¼ pints/2 liters) water
⅓ cup (2 oz/60 g) yellow lentils
⅓ cup (2 oz/60 g) red lentils
⅓ cup (2 oz/60 g) green lentils
4 oz (125 g) diced peeled pumpkin
4 oz (125 g) diced peeled eggplant/aubergine
4 oz (125 g) fresh spinach leaves
1 tablespoon tamarind pulp
1 tablespoon crumbled or grated palm sugar or dark
    brown sugar
1 tablespoon finely chopped fresh cilantro/coriander
1 tablespoon fried onion flakes

Peel the onion and slice thinly. Fry in the clarified butter
until well browned, then add the garlic and ginger and
fry briefly.

Drain the chilies and chop coarsely. Add to the onion
with the curry spices and whole spices and the turmeric.
Stir together and fry briefly. Trim and dice the lamb, add to
the pan and stir over medium heat until the meat is lightly
colored and coated with the seasonings.

Coarsely chop the tomatoes and add to the pan with the
salt and water. Bring to the boil, cover and simmer gently
until the meat is half cooked, about 25 minutes. Add the
lentils, diced vegetables and spinach and continue to cook
until the meat is tender and the vegetables and lentils are
cooked through.

Mix the tamarind with a little boiling water, add the sugar and stir to dissolve. Add to the pan and simmer for 5–10 minutes. Taste for salt. Keep the *dhansak* warm while the rice and *kachumber* are prepared. Garnish with fresh cilantro and onion flakes.

BROWN RICE

2 large onions
3 tablespoons ghee (clarified butter)
1¼ tablespoons palm sugar or dark brown sugar
2½ cups (1 lb/500 g) raw short-grain white rice
2-in (5-cm) cinnamon stick, broken
5 whole cloves
1½ teaspoons salt
3½ cups (28 fl oz/875 ml) water

Peel and thinly slice the onions; fry in the clarified butter until they are a deep rich brown. Add the sugar and stir until melted; stir in the rice and spices, salt and water. Bring to the boil, reduce the heat and cook very gently, tightly covered, until the liquid has been completely absorbed and the rice is tender; lift the lid and quickly stir the rice 2–3 times during cooking to distribute the onions evenly.

KACHUMBER

3 medium onions
salt
2½ teaspoons crushed or grated palm sugar or dark brown sugar
1 tablespoon tamarind pulp
2–3 tablespoons boiling water
1 large tomato
⅓-in (1-cm) piece fresh ginger
2 tablespoons finely chopped fresh cilantro/coriander
3–6 fresh green chilies

Peel and thinly slice the onions. Sprinkle with salt and set aside for 1 hour, then squeeze to remove as much water as possible. Mix the sugar, tamarind and boiling water. Finely chop the tomato, grate the ginger and seed and shred the chilies. Add the chopped cilantro.
Combine all ingredients and toss together thoroughly. Set aside for at least 15 minutes before serving.

DHANSAK KEBABS

1–3 fresh green chilies
1 small onion
½-in (1.25-cm) piece fresh ginger
1 lb (500 g) lean ground (minced) beef or lamb
½ cup (about 2 oz/60 g) mashed potato
1 egg, lightly beaten
1 tablespoon chopped fresh cilantro/coriander
1 tablespoon chopped mint
1 teaspoon crushed garlic
½ teaspoon turmeric
½ teaspoon ground cumin
½ teaspoon *dhansak* spices
½ teaspoon *garam masala* (curry spices)

Slit open the chilies and scrape out the seeds; chop the flesh coarsely. Peel and coarsely chop the onion and ginger. Combine all three in a food processor or blender and grind until smooth. Add the meat and process again briefly. Mix in the potato and egg, then the remaining ingredients.
Form into walnut-size balls and fry gently until well colored and lightly crisp. Drain well before serving.

SERVES 8–10

BENARES, ON THE BANKS OF THE SACRED GANGES   KATE WIMBLE

EGGPLANT/AUBERGINE IN SPICY YOGURT SAUCE (*BOTTOM*)
WITH SAVORY BAKED POTATOES (*TOP*)

BRINJAL DAHI

Eggplant in Spicy Yogurt Sauce

1 medium eggplant/aubergine, about 8 oz/250 g
1½ teaspoons salt
½ teaspoon black mustard seeds
1 teaspoon black cumin seeds
½ cup (4 fl oz/125 ml) plain yogurt
1 cup (8 fl oz/250 ml) cold water
2 tablespoons ghee (clarified butter)
2 dried red chilies
¼ teaspoon fenugreek seeds
1 teaspoon sugar
2 tablespoons chopped fresh cilantro (coriander)

Cut the eggplant into lengthwise strips. Sprinkle with the salt and let stand for 20 minutes, in which time the salt will draw off the bitter juices.

❧ Combine the mustard and cumin seeds in a small ungreased skillet and dry-fry until they begin to pop. Grind finely and set aside. Mix the yogurt and water.

❧ Heat the clarified butter in a medium saucepan, add the halved dried chilies and fenugreek seeds and fry for 45 seconds.

❧ Squeeze excess water from the eggplant and fry in the ghee until lightly colored. Add the yogurt mixture and sugar and simmer over medium heat until the eggplant is tender and the sauce is well reduced and thick. Stir in the toasted spices and the cilantro and serve.

SERVES 4

DUM ALU

Savory Baked Potatoes

Dum *cooking is a method of cooking foods tenderly yet without sauce. It is done in a* degchi, *a straight-sided deep pot with a close-fitting lid. To achieve a baked effect, the* degchi *is placed on hot coals, with more coals being heaped on top of the lid so that the heat comes from both beneath and above.*

2 lb (1 kg) medium potatoes
2 cups (16 fl oz/500 ml) mustard oil (or ghee/vegetable oil)
1 teaspoon salt
2 tablespoons boiling water
4 tablespoons ghee (clarified butter)
⅛ teaspoon asafoetida
4 whole cloves
1½ teaspoons cumin seeds
1 fresh green chili
2 teaspoons ground coriander
¾ teaspoon ground ginger
1 teaspoon sugar
1¼ cups (10 fl oz/310 ml) warm water
2 teaspoons mild *garam masala* (curry spices)
1 teaspoon mild chili powder
2 tablespoons finely chopped fresh cilantro (coriander)

Peel the potatoes and leave them whole. (Boiling potatoes should be partially cooked, but the more starchy types will not require this.) Heat the mustard oil in a deep skillet and fry the potatoes in two or three batches until lightly colored on the surface and partially cooked. When all are done, sprinkle with the salt mixed with the boiling water – to ensure that the salt will be more evenly absorbed.

❧ In another pan heat the clarified butter and fry the asafoetida, cloves and cumin seeds for about 45 seconds. Slit open the chili and scrape out the seeds, then chop finely. Add to the pan with the coriander, ginger and sugar and fry briefly. Add the potatoes and the warm water. Bring to the boil and boil briskly for a few minutes, then sprinkle in the *garam masala* and chili powder and cover.

❧ Place in a preheated 350°F/180°C oven and cook, tightly covered, for about 30 minutes or until the water has been absorbed and the potatoes are tender.

❧ Garnish with the chopped cilantro and serve piping hot.

SERVES 6

KADU MALAI KARI

Pumpkin Cream Curry

Malai, *a richly flavored reduced cream, gives this simple pumpkin curry a smoothness and subtle flavor that transforms a humble vegetable into a delectable dish.* Malai *is obtained by simmering fresh milk until the water content is reduced, leaving behind a thick, creamy residue (see page 196 for details of its preparation).*

12 oz (375 g) peeled pumpkin
1½ tablespoons ghee (clarified butter)
½ teaspoon ground cumin
¼ teaspoon turmeric
1–2 fresh red or green chilies (optional)
½ cup (4 fl oz/125 ml) light (single/thin) cream,
    half and half or milk
2 curry or bay leaves
1 tablespoon *malai*, reduced cream, ricotta cheese or heavy
    (double/thickened) cream
salt, sugar and freshly grated nutmeg

Cut the pumpkin into 1-in (2.5-cm) cubes. Heat the clarified butter in a medium saucepan. Add the cumin and turmeric and fry for about 30 seconds, then add the pumpkin and fry for about 2–3 minutes, stirring constantly.

Slit open the chilies, if used, scrape out the seeds and cut each chili into 3 or 4 pieces. Add to the pumpkin with the cream and curry or bay leaves.

Cover and simmer gently without stirring for about 10 minutes, until pumpkin is tender. Stir in the *malai* and season to taste with salt and sugar. Sprinkle on a little grated nutmeg before serving.

SERVES 6

TAMATAR BAINGAN BHUJIA

Braised Tomato and Eggplant

Bhujias are dishes of simply cooked vegetables with a little seasoning, intended as accompaniments to curries or meats.

1 lb (500 g) eggplants/aubergines
2 teaspoons salt
1 large onion
1-in (2.5-cm) piece fresh ginger
4 medium tomatoes
1–2 fresh green chilies
3 tablespoons ghee (clarified butter)
freshly ground black pepper

Cut off the stem ends of the eggplants and discard. Cut the eggplants into ¾-in (2-cm) cubes and place in a colander. Sprinkle with 1½ teaspoons of the salt. Set aside for about 20 minutes to draw off the bitter juices, then rinse thoroughly and drain well.

Peel and thinly slice the onion and ginger. Chop the tomatoes. Slit open the chilies, scrape out the seeds and cut the flesh into thin shreds.

Place the drained eggplant in a kitchen towel and pat dry. Heat the clarified butter in a medium saucepan. Add the sliced onion and ginger and cook over low to medium heat for 3 minutes. Add the eggplant and fry until lightly colored, then add the tomatoes and chilies with the remaining salt and black pepper to taste. Cook gently for about 9 minutes, until the vegetables are tender.

SERVES 6

CHUTNEYS, PICKLES AND GARNISHES

Achars (pickles) are served with Indian meals to stimulate the appetite and aid in digestion. They also add a vibrant taste highlight to an otherwise mildly flavored meal, as is often the case with dishes from northern India where chilies are less frequently used.

There are many kinds of commercially produced achars available, perhaps the most popular being the tart nimbu ka achar *(whole lime pickle) with its strong, salty citrus taste. But mango, fish, whole stuffed lemons and chilies, and even eggs and game meats are made throughout India into bold-tasting pickles that make a welcome addition to meals.*

Chutni, or chutney as it has become known in the West, originated in this part of the world. There are two distinctly different types of chutnis *served with Indian food: preserved chutneys like those obtainable commercially (mango, tomato, brinjal (eggplant), etc.) and a variety of freshly made chutneys or relishes ranging from mild and refreshing to searing hot. Pudina (mint), hara dhania (fresh cilantro/coriander), tomatoes, apples, coconut, chilies, mangoes and ginger are blended in myriad ways with spices, lime juice and vinegars to make fresh* chutnis *to complement main dishes.*

In late summer, when the mango trees are heavy with fruit and the monsoon season has not yet brought its strong winds and pelting rain to do their damage, the women of India spend weeks

FRESH MINT CHUTNEY *(RIGHT),* AND COCONUT CHUTNEY *(LEFT),*
recipes page 194

peeling, slicing and blending spices for aam ka achar *and* aam chutni *(mango pickle and mango chutney). Some of it goes to market, while enough is laid up for use throughout the year with family meals.*

PUDINA CHUTNI

Fresh Mint Chutney

1 cup loosely packed fresh mint leaves
3 small green onions
1–3 fresh green chilies
2 teaspoons sugar
½ teaspoon salt
2–3 teaspoons white vinegar

Wash and dry the mint leaves. Trim the green onions, discarding most of the green tops. Slit open the chilies, scrape out the seeds and chop the chilies coarsely.
Combine the ingredients in a food processor, blender or mortar and grind until fairly smooth.
Set aside for several hours before using. The chutney keeps for up to a week in a sealed jar in the refrigerator.

MAKES ABOUT ½ CUP (3 oz/90 g)

NARIAL CHUTNI

Fresh Coconut Chutney

2–3 fresh green chilies
1 cup (3 oz/90 g) shredded (desiccated) coconut
1 tablespoon water
2 teaspoons crushed garlic
1½ tablespoons lemon or lime juice
¾ teaspoon salt

Slit open the chilies and scrape out the seeds; coarsely chop the flesh. Combine the ingredients in a food processor, blender or a mortar and grind until fairly smooth. Add a little more water to make it a just-moist paste. Set aside for 1–2 hours before using. The chutney keeps for 3–4 days in a sealed jar in the refrigerator.

MAKES ABOUT 1 CUP (4 oz/125 g)

RAITA

Yogurt and Cucumber Sauce

A spicy meal is incomplete without a soothing dish of dahi *(curds/yogurt). It may be served plain, but many cooks like to add flavors that complement the meal and highlight its special features. Grated cucumber, finely chopped chili, mint or cilantro (coriander), fried spices or onion, mashed banana, diced tomato and grated green mango are among the ingredients added to give plain yogurt interest, and these dishes then become known as* raita.

1½ cups (12 fl oz/375 ml) plain yogurt
1 medium cucumber
1 tablespoon finely chopped fresh mint leaves
½ teaspoon salt
1 teaspoon sugar
½ teaspoon black pepper

Beat the yogurt until smooth. Peel the cucumber and rub lightly with salt, then grate into a small dish. Drain off excess liquid. Add the yogurt with the mint and remaining ingredients and mix well. Serve cool.

SERVES 6

SAMBAR

Hot Lentil and Vegetable Curry

Sambar is a thin, very hot curry of vaal dhal *(yellow split peas) and diced vegetables. It is the traditional accompaniment to* dosa, *the large, crisp pancake-like breads enjoyed throughout southern India as a breakfast food. It can also be served as a side dish with meat curries.*

¾ cup (5 oz/155 g) yellow split peas
1 medium onion
1 medium potato
2 medium carrots
1 medium zucchini (courgette)
1 small eggplant (aubergine)
4 cups (1 liter) water
1 teaspoon turmeric
1 teaspoon salt
2 tablespoons tamarind pulp
2 tablespoons ghee (clarified butter)
2 teaspoons ground coriander
1 teaspoon ground cumin
1 teaspoon *sambar masala* (tart curry spices)*
1 teaspoon black mustard seeds
2–3 dried red chilies
3–4 curry leaves

Soak the split peas for about 45 minutes in cold water. Peel and finely chop the onion. Peel and dice the potato, carrots, zucchini and eggplant. Pour the water into a medium saucepan and add the drained peas, onion and diced vegetables. Stir in the turmeric and salt and bring to the boil. Simmer for about 40 minutes until tender.
Mix the tamarind pulp with ½ cup of boiling water, then mash it until the pulp is dissolved. Strain into the saucepan.
Heat the ghee and fry the spices, dried chilies and curry leaves for 1 minute, then add to the saucepan. Continue to simmer for at least 15 minutes. Serve hot.
* *Or use* garam masala *with extra cumin and fenugreek.*

SERVES 4–6

HOT LENTIL AND VEGETABLE CURRY

DHAL

Lentil Purée

Throughout India, family meals are not complete without some sort of lentil or bean dish. Dhal is not only an inexpensive way to bulk up a meal; it also provides valuable protein, making it extra important for vegetarian diets. In the south, it may be quite a thin and watery dish, almost a soup, while it becomes progressively thicker, smoother and richer towards the northern regions.

1¾ cups (11 oz/345 g) red or yellow lentils
2 teaspoons salt
1 teaspoon turmeric
2–3 dried red chilies
4 cups (1 liter) water
1-in (2.5-cm) piece fresh ginger
3–4 cloves garlic
1 large onion
2 tablespoons ghee (clarified butter)
2 medium tomatoes, finely chopped
1½ teaspoons *garam masala* (curry spices) or a mild
   commercial curry powder
2–3 tablespoons heavy (double/thickened) cream
   (optional)
chili powder or chopped fresh cilantro/coriander or mint

Wash the lentils thoroughly, drain and place in a saucepan with the salt and turmeric. Add the whole dried chilies and water, cover and bring to the boil. Reduce heat and simmer for about 12 minutes until softened, skimming the surface from time to time to remove the froth and particles of broken lentils.

Combine the peeled ginger, garlic and onion in a food processor or blender and chop finely. Fry in the clarified butter for 3–4 minutes, then add the chopped tomatoes and curry spices and fry for 2–3 minutes.

Drain the *dhal*, if excess liquid remains, and add the fried onion mixture. Taste for salt and simmer for 2–3 minutes. Add the cream if used, reheat briefly and transfer to a serving dish. Garnish with a sprinkling of chili powder or a little chopped fresh cilantro or mint.

SERVES 8

JHINGA PULAO

Shrimp Rice

2¼ cups (12 oz/375 g) raw long-grain white rice
1 large onion
4 tablespoons ghee (clarified butter)
1 teaspoon crushed garlic
1 teaspoon minced fresh ginger
3 whole cloves
2-in (5-cm) cinnamon stick, broken
2 green cardamoms, broken open
2 bay leaves
1 teaspoon salt
½ teaspoon black pepper
¼ cup (2 fl oz/60 ml) thick coconut milk or heavy
   (double/thickened) cream
3 cups (24 fl oz/750 ml) water
1 lb (500 g) uncooked small shrimp (prawns)
   in their shells
fresh cilantro/coriander or mint
sliced red and green chili

SHRIMP/PRAWN RICE (*TOP*), SPICED CHICK PEAS/GARBANZOS
AND LENTIL PUREE (*RIGHT*)

Rinse the rice and drain thoroughly. Peel and thinly slice the onion. Fry the onion in the clarified butter until lightly colored and softened, then add the garlic, ginger and rice.

Fry, stirring constantly, until each grain of rice is coated with the butter, then add the spices, bay leaves, salt, pepper and coconut milk or cream. Add the water and bring to the boil. Cover tightly and simmer for 15 minutes until the water is partially absorbed.

Peel the shrimp, leaving the heads and tails intact (or remove them if preferred). Devein, rinse quickly in cold water and wipe dry. Add to the rice, stirring in lightly. Cover the pan and cook for about 6 minutes or until the shrimp are pink and cooked through and the rice is tender and the liquid completely absorbed. Transfer to a serving dish and garnish with the fresh herbs and chili.

SERVES 6

KABLI CHANNA

Spiced Chick Peas/Garbanzos

Kabli Channa, or "Bengal Peas," are eaten in different guises throughout India. They are invariably cooked with an abundance of seasonings, as they are bland on their own. In the Punjab, they may be served in place of a dhal dish, or simply cooked with plenty of garlic and garam masala, a dash of aamchur (dried powdered green mango) or a few fresh or dried pomegranate seeds.

The vegetarian Tamils enjoy kabli channa as a unique "sandwich" filling. Tiny fried rounds of bread (pani puris) are slit open and pocketed with some kabli channa, a dab of plain yoghurt and a little tart-tasting sonth, a chutney of mango and ginger.

1 lb (500 g)* canned *kabli channa* (chick peas/garbanzos)
2½ tablespoons ghee (clarified butter)
1¾-in (4-cm) piece fresh ginger
1 large onion
2 fresh green chilies
3 medium tomatoes
1 teaspoon powdered dried pomegranate seeds
2½ teaspoons *garam masala* (curry spices)
1½ teaspoons salt
1 tablespoon lemon juice or ½ teaspoon dried
   mango powder
¼ cup chopped fresh cilantro/coriander

Drain the chick peas, reserving the cooking liquid. Heat the clarified butter in a medium saucepan. Place the peeled ginger, onion and seeded chilies in a food processor or blender and chop finely. Add to the butter and cook gently for 3 minutes. Add the tomatoes and cook briefly, then add the pomegranate seed powder, the curry spices and salt and cook for 1 minute.

Add the drained chick peas and seasonings and stir for 2–3 minutes over medium heat. Add reserved liquid to just cover, cover the pan and simmer for 25 minutes. Add the lemon juice or mango powder and fresh cilantro. Check for salt and serve hot.

Or use 8 oz (250g) dried kabli channa, soaked for 6 hours, then simmered in water for about 5 hours, until tender.

SERVES 4–6

Gajar Halwa

Carrot Cream Dessert

Grated carrot combines with milk and spices in a creamy golden-yellow dessert that symbolizes riches and success. Edible silver leaf (warq), pressed onto the surface or wrapped around whole toasted almonds, recreates the elegance of the Muglai era, when this dessert first came into prominence.

1½ lb (750g) carrots
8 cups (2 liters) milk
½ cup (2 oz/60 g) powdered whole milk
2-in (5-cm) cinnamon stick
¾ cup (4 oz/125 g) raisins, soaked
3 black cardamoms, opened and lightly crushed
½ teaspoon powdered saffron
1 tablespoon boiling water
½ cup (3 oz/90 g) softened ghee (clarified butter) or butter
2 tablespoons honey
¾ cup (6 oz/185 g) sugar, or to taste
¾ cup (3 oz/90 g) slivered almonds
1½ teaspoons rosewater
silver leaf

Peel and grate the carrots. Place in a saucepan and add the milk, milk powder and cinnamon stick. Stir until the milk powder has dissolved, then bring to the boil, reduce the heat to low and simmer, stirring frequently, for about 25 minutes or until the mixture has thickened and the carrot is soft.

Drain the raisins; add to the pan with the cardamons. Mix the saffron with boiling water, pour into the pan and continue to cook gently until the pudding is thick.

Stir in the clarified butter, honey and sugar and cook for a few more minutes until well mixed. Stir in the almonds and rosewater, then transfer to a lightly buttered serving dish and smooth the top. Decorate with the silver leaf and serve warm or cool.

SERVES 6–8

Ras Malai

The Supreme Creamy Dessert

One of the hallmarks of a good Indian cook is her (or his) ability to make the renowned jamons, little balls of infinitely delicate texture made from a carefully balanced mix of flour and milk, sweetened with sugar and made fragrant with gulab (rosewater). A serving of gulab jamons, in sugar syrup, or ras gulla, another version in a slightly thickened sugar syrup, or the creamy ras malai, floating in a sweet cream sauce, is sheer indulgence.

CARROT CREAM DESSERT (*TOP*) AND THE SUPREME CREAMY DESSERT, *RAS MALAI*

1¼ cups (4 oz/125 g) powdered whole milk
¼ cup (1 oz/30 g) self-rising flour
3 cups (24 fl oz/750 ml) milk
1 cup (8 oz/250 g) sugar
1¼ cups (10 fl oz/315 ml) water
½ cup (4 fl oz/125 ml) heavy (double/thickened) cream
1½ teaspoons rosewater
1 tablespoon blanched slivered almonds or pistachios, toasted

Mix the milk powder and flour, adding just enough of the milk (about ⅓ cup) to make a dough that just holds together. Wrap in a damp cloth or a piece of plastic wrap and set aside for 3 hours for the flour to soften and the milk powder to expand.

Break up the dough, crumbling it with the fingers, then with wet hands form it into walnut-size balls.

Bring the sugar and water to the boil in a wide saucepan. Gently add the milk balls and simmer for about 15 minutes, shaking the pan to turn them, rather than using a spoon which might damage them. Splash in 1–2 tablespoons of ice water (this encourages the balls to expand and soften a little). Lift out the milk balls with a slotted spoon and place in a dish to cool.

Bring the remaining milk to the boil and add enough of the sugar syrup to sweeten it to taste. Pour over the milk balls and let stand for 3 hours.

Remove the milk balls with a slotted spoon and set aside. Boil the milk sauce until reduced to about half its original volume, then stir in the cream, rosewater and toasted nuts. Return the milk balls to the sauce and leave to cool. Serve slightly chilled.

SERVES 6–8

GULAB JAMONS
India's Favorite Dessert

Gulab jamons, *little balls of cream floating in a rose-flavored sugar syrup, are one of the highlights of the Indian cuisine. Rich, smooth and very sweet, they are the perfect ending to a spicy curry dinner. It takes much practice and infinite patience to perfect the technique of making them with just the right texture, but the results are worth the effort.*

1⅔ cups (6 oz/185 g) powdered whole milk
2 tablespoons ghee (clarified butter)
1 cup (4 oz/125 g) self-rising flour
1 teaspoon baking powder
pinch of ground cardamom, optional
vegetable oil or ghee (clarified butter) for deep-frying
1¼ cups (10 oz/315 g) sugar
1¾ cups (14 fl oz/440 ml) water
1½ teaspoons rosewater

Pour the milk powder into a mixing bowl. Cut the ghee into tiny pieces and, using the fingertips, rub it lightly into the milk powder until the mixture resembles fine breadcrumbs.

Mix in the flour, baking powder and cardamom, if used, and add just enough cold water to make a very stiff dough. Wrap in plastic wrap or a damp cloth and let stand for at least 3 hours.

Break up the ball of dough, then rub it hard on a lightly floured board until it has broken into crumbs again. Add a sprinkling of water, then form into walnut-size balls.

Heat the oil or ghee over medium heat. Slide in the balls and fry them gently until golden brown, turning them carefully several times. Lift out and drain well.

Meanwhile, bring the sugar and water to the boil in a wide saucepan and simmer for 10 minutes, then remove from the heat. Place the *jamons* in the syrup, sprinkle with the rosewater, and let stand for about 30 minutes to soak up the syrup. Serve warm or cold.

SERVES 6

INDIAN DOUGHNUTS

KHAJOOR
Indian Doughnuts

Almost every cuisine in the world includes a version of this deep-fried sweet dough. The "doughnuts" of Kashmir have the rich, buttery taste of ghee. For a touch of elegance, serve them thickly coated with confectioner's (icing) sugar flavored with very finely ground elaichi (cardamom).

3 cups (12 oz/375 g) finely ground white flour
3 oz (90 g) ghee (clarified butter)
¾ cup (6 oz/185 g) sugar
½–¾ cup (4–6 fl oz/125–185 ml) cold water
extra ghee for frying
confectioner's (icing) sugar, optional
finely ground cardamom seeds, optional

Place the flour in a mixing bowl. Cut the clarified butter into tiny pieces and, using fingertips, rub it lightly into the flour until the mixture resembles fine breadcrumbs. Add the sugar, stirring in evenly. Slowly work in enough cold water to make a stiff dough. Invert the mixing bowl over the dough, and let stand for 2 hours.

Divide the dough into about 30 pieces and roll each into a ball, then elongate into small ovals; twist into crescent shapes if desired. Press a fork into the top of each to make a design.

Heat about 4 in (10 cm) of ghee in a *karahi*, wok or wide saucepan over medium heat. (The heat of the ghee is crucial; if it is too hot, the "doughnuts" will become dark and hard on the surface before the inside is cooked; and if too cool, they will crumble.) Cook until the "doughnuts" are a red-gold color and are cooked through, about 6 minutes. Drain well.

Mix the sugar and cardamon and sprinkle over the *khajoor*. Serve warm or cold.

MAKES ABOUT 30

WELDON TRANNIES INDIAN BREADS, *PARRATHAS* AND *NAANS*

BREADS

Wheat flour breads are an important part of the Indian diet, in many places virtually replacing rice as the staple. Many Indian breads, such as chupaties *and* parrathas, *cooked flat on a griddle, are made with finely ground wholewheat flour, and are unleavened. Others, made with a finer white flour called* maida, *are leavened in the sourdough tradition with a starter called* khamir, *made from flour, plain yogurt and sugar.* Kulchas *and* rotis *are leavened breads that can be either dry-griddle-cooked or shallow-fried in ghee to give them a crisp surface and rich flavor.*

Naans, the large triangular breads traditionally cooked in the tandoor, *are usually leavened with baking powder. Neither leavened nor unleavened breads keep well, so they should be made fresh for each meal.*

Indian breads are used, simply speaking, as edible food scoops. A small piece is broken off, used to dip into the gravy and take up a piece of curry at the same time. It works well, particularly if eating curry in the traditional style with the fingers.

Another kind of bread, the unleavened wholewheat puri, *is rolled out flat and smooth before being deep-fried, which causes it to puff up dramatically and float on the oil. Its resultant hollow center makes an excellent receptacle for curry. Vegetarian Indians in particular prize small* puris *packed full with* kabli channa *(spiced chick peas, page 195).*

PURIS

Fried Unleavened Bread

3 cups (12 oz/375 g) fine wholewheat flour
1¼ teaspoons salt
1¼ tablespoons softened ghee (clarified butter)
warm water
ghee or vegetable oil

Place the flour and salt in a mixing bowl. Add the ghee in small spoonfuls and rub it lightly into the flour until the mixture resembles fine breadcrumbs. Or combine the ingredients in a food processor and blend to fine crumbs. Gradually add warm water to make a smooth, slightly soft, elastic dough. Transfer to a work surface and knead lightly for 5–6 minutes. Roll the dough out into a sausage shape and cut into 16–18 pieces of even size. Shape each into a ball. Use a rolling pin to roll each out into a round about the thickness of a coin.

Heat plenty of ghee or oil until a haze forms over the pan, then turn the heat down slightly. Fry the *puris* one at a time, pushing them quickly under the oil as this encourages them to rise, and splashing the top with oil during cooking. As soon as they puff up, turn over and fry the other side briefly, then lift out, drain well and place on a rack covered with paper towels to drain.

Cook the remainder as quickly as possible, then serve at once; even the best-made *puris* will deflate after a time.

SERVES 4–6 (about 18 *puris*)

NAANS

Leavened Tandoor Bread

While puris *and* chupatis *are enjoyed throughout India, being easily prepared at home,* naans *are the bread of the northern regions, and for perfection are cooked in the clay* tandoor – *a conically-shaped oven, heated from below with wood or charcoal. The soft dough is shaped into long triangles, dampened on one side and slapped onto the side of the oven, where they cling until cooked. They emerge golden brown on one side, crisp and dry on the side that has adhered to the oven wall. Variations on the traditional* naan *are found in better restaurants; they include painting the upper surface with red food coloring and dotting it with chopped nuts (usually pistachios), chopped fresh cilantro (coriander) or spices, and even sliced red cherries.*

3 cups (12 oz/375 g) finely ground white flour
1¾ teaspoons baking powder
1½ teaspoons superfine sugar
¾ teaspoon salt
¾ cup (180 ml/6 fl oz) plain yogurt
1 tablespoon vegetable oil
1 large egg

Place the flour in a mixing bowl and stir in the baking powder, sugar and salt. Make a well in the center and add the yogurt, oil and lightly beaten egg. Mix thoroughly to make a smooth, soft dough. (The dough can also be mixed in a food processor.)

Transfer to a work surface and knead lightly for about 5 minutes. Wrap dough in plastic wrap or cover with a damp cloth and let stand in a warm place for at least 3½ hours. The baking powder will begin to activate, increasing the volume of the dough and giving it a smooth, soft texture.

Roll the dough into a short, thick sausage shape and divide into 6 even pieces. Use wet hands to stretch and pull each piece into a triangle, then pull one corner so that the triangle becomes elongated to the traditional *naan* shape.

An electric skillet is ideal for cooking *naans* (or heat a heavy baking sheet in a 375°F/190°C oven). Moisten one side of each *naan* and place this side down in the pan. Cook for about 2 minutes, then increase the heat slightly and cook a little longer.

Remove the *naans* and place under a preheated broiler until the tops brown and the bread begins to bubble and puff up. When done the *naans* should be slightly springy to the touch. Wrap in a clean, dry cloth until needed.

SERVES 6

CHUPATIS

Griddle-Cooked Unleavened Bread

Indian housewives mix and knead chupati *dough in a shallow wooden dish, which when inverted has a flat surface on which to roll them out. A tawa – a very slightly curved iron griddle over a charcoal or woodchip fire – is used to cook them.*

2 cups (9 oz/280 g) wholewheat flour
½–⅔ cup (4–5 fl oz/125–155 ml) warm water
1 tablespoon ghee (clarified butter)

Place the flour in a mixing bowl or food processor and work in enough of the water to make a slightly firm dough. Transfer to a work surface and knead vigorously for at least 8 minutes until the dough forms an elastic ball that is soft and pliable and comes away cleanly from the worktop. (The more kneading you do, the softer and lighter the *chupatis* will be.) The dough is ready if it springs back when pressed with a finger. Wrap in plastic wrap or a damp cloth and let stand for at least 1 hour for the flour to soften.

Roll into a sausage shape and divide into 12 pieces. Roll the *chupatis* out into thin rounds on a lightly floured surface; they should be about 5 in (13 cm) in diameter.

Heat a flat iron griddle or *tawa* and rub vigorously with a ghee-moistened cloth. Cook the *chupatis* over medium heat until little brown flecks appear on the surface, then turn. Press the cloth firmly over the surface of each *chupati* to encourage it to bubble up. (This ensures that the center is cooked through and makes them lighter in texture.) Keep the *chupatis* warm while the remainder are cooked.

SERVES 4 (about 12 *chupatis*)

PARRATHAS

Buttered Layered Flat Bread

Parrathas *are possibly the most delicious of the Indian breads; they are crisp in texture, golden brown and rich with the buttery taste of ghee (clarified butter). They are prepared from a basic* chupati *mixture, but once rolled – or in this case stretched – out, they are spread generously with ghee, then either folded to enclose the butter or pleated and twisted into a coil before being rolled out flat. The result is layers of crisp dough separated by reservoirs of butter.*

2 cups (9 oz/280 g) fine wholewheat flour
1 teaspoon salt
½–⅔ cup (4–5 fl oz/125–155 ml) warm water
2–3 tablespoons ghee (clarified butter)

Place the flour and salt in a mixing bowl or food processor and add enough of the water to make a smooth, slightly firm dough. Lift out and knead for at least 8 minutes, until the dough is smooth and springs back when pressed with a finger.

Roll into a sausage shape and divide into 9–10 pieces. Roll out into rounds, or stretch into shape in the traditional manner by tossing them from hand to hand, until each piece is about 6 in (15 cm) in diameter.

Melt the ghee and brush some generously over the top of each *parratha*. Fold in the edges to form a square, edges slightly overlapping to enclose the butter, then gently roll out again without allowing butter to escape. Alternatively, gather the edges together on two sides to give a pleated strip, then twist into a coil and roll out flat.

Heat a *tawa* or griddle over medium-high heat and add enough of the remaining ghee to moisten the surface. Cook the *parrathas* on both sides until crisp and golden, adding more ghee as needed.

If desired place the *parrathas* under a preheated hot broiler for a few seconds to puff them up slightly and to crisp them.

SERVES 4–6 (about 9 *parrathas*)

THE TAJ MAHAL IN AGRA, INDIA'S MOST CELEBRATED MONUMENT

JAN WHITING SUBIACO

Burma

MOHINGA, THE BURMESE NATIONAL DISH *(LEFT)*, WITH ACCOMPANIMENTS *(CENTER), recipes page 209,* AND BEAN PATTIES *(RIGHT), recipe page 207*

Burma

EXOTIC OFFERINGS

With India to the west, China on its north-
ernmost borders and Thailand its eastern
neighbor, it is little wonder that Burma's food is
something of a hybrid. There will be pickles and
chutneys in the Indian mode, with *balachuang*, a
strongly flavored relish made of pounded dried
shrimp, and *pazun nga-pi*, a pungent shrimp paste,
on the table with most meals. Curries are spiced in
the Indian way with sweet spices such as cardamom, cinnamon and clove, as well as rich blends of
garam masala (curry powder), but they are always
based on fried onions, garlic and ginger as they are in
Thailand. Sometimes a lighter Chinese-style curry
blend, emphasizing cinnamon or cassia bark and
anise flavors, is preferred.

Rice noodles make their appearance with almost
monotonous regularity in main dishes and soups
and with vegetables. Chinese cabbage, bamboo
shoots and bean sprouts feature prominently, but
then so too do okra, *brinjal* (eggplant) and squash.
Besan, a flour made from ground chick peas, often
used in Indian cooking, also finds a place here – to
thicken curries or to bind *koftas* (meat or vegetable
balls). Coconut milk and cream add a smooth
creamy taste and richness to curry sauces.

Foods are either stir-fried, braised – as for curries
– or deep-fried. Peanut oil is the chosen medium for
deep-frying, but for stir-frying a light sesame oil
adds a special flavor unique to this cuisine. The
Chinese dark sesame oil is too strong in taste for this
purpose and should be diluted with vegetable oil to
give good results.

Rice and soup are the pivotal dishes at a Burmese
meal. Served both at lunch and dinner, they should
always be piping hot, even though the curries and
other accompanying dishes may be at room temperature or at best lukewarm. Long-grain white rice is

SHWEDAGON PAGODA   JOHN EVERINGHAM

dried salted fish that are fried and served as an accompaniment much like the Indian *Bombay duck*. The name *toolee moolee* fits these strong-flavored condiment-style accompaniments, and also encompasses all of the other little side dishes that go to make up a Burmese meal: chutneys, pickles and relishes, fried sliced shallots and garlic cloves served in their oil, ground roasted chick peas, crisply fried pieces of egg noodle, ground dried shrimp (with or without chili), chili powder or paste (in Burma powder is usually preferred), fish sauce and tamarind water to splash on, fried dried chilies and strips of cooked omelet.

There are also a number of little fried snacks, not dissimilar to those enjoyed in southern India by the Tamils – *beya kyaw*, ground lentil patties; patties of peanuts; slices of squash or little bundles of batter-coated bean sprouts or green beans; and *pazun ngabuang kyaw*, patties made of chopped shrimp and bound with egg and *besan* flour.

These varied little side dishes are vital components of the Burmese cuisine, not just as between-meal snacks but as an essential part of many other dishes. *Htamin lethoke*, or "finger-mixed rice," is actually not just a rice dish but a mixture of cooked rice and several different kinds of noodles – usually made from egg and wheat, rice and mung bean flour – plus cooked vegetables, particularly potato, and perhaps salad vegetables like spinach and bean sprouts. These are arranged on a large platter and served with as many of the little side dishes (described above) as the cook can manage. The diner makes up his own meal by helping himself to whatever he fancies.

Mohinga is undeniably Burma's most prominent dish, and one of the tastiest imaginable. Basically a thick, well seasoned fish soup, it is served piping hot to pour over rice noodles, then the diner is free to add as much or as little of the accompanying dishes as he likes. One of the important ingredients of *mohinga* is slices of the trunk of young banana plants.

Burmese vegetable dishes are quite distinctive. Many are made more or less as cooked salads, vegetables being parboiled or stir-fried, then dressed with fried onions and garlic, *sa nwin* (turmeric) to give them a bright yellow color and emphatic flavor, and vinegar, which mingles with the cooking oil to make a dressing. Otherwise, vegetables are simply stir-fried in the Chinese tradition, using sesame oil. Again onions and garlic are fried in oil and seasonings are minimal, salt and pepper with a small splash of fish sauce being all that's required.

Desserts as such are not part of the Burmese meal, but the Burmese enjoy the many little *agar-agar* (seaweed gelatin) jellies that are created by specialist sweets makers, as well as the Indian-influenced puddinglike cakes that are based on semolina, noodles and rice, and enriched with ghee (clarified butter) or coconut milk.

Long, cool, refreshing drinks are also popular. Featuring cooked sago or tapioca or little cubes of *agar-agar* jelly, they combine sweet *jaggery* (brown palm sugar) and coconut milk, Malay style, or rose essence or grenadine in the Indian tradition.

the only type used by Burmese cooks, who prefer the absorption method to achieve the plump fluffiness they like. For special occasions *htamin* may be prepared by adding lemon grass to the rice as it cooks, then stirring in fried onions and garlic, pounded dried shrimp or fish, chilies, fish sauce and lime juice to give it a zesty flavor. Soups are generally mild in flavor, and often have either clear vermicelli or egg noodles added.

Burmese curries are cooked in a particular way, whatever the final seasonings may be, to achieve a thick, well-flavored, reddish brown sauce. Puréed onions, garlic and ginger are cooked in oil until they are tender and have taken on a little color, then seasonings – in particular *sa nwin* (turmeric), and usually chili powder – are added and fried further until the paste is thick and the oil has begun to cook back out of the onions, forming a golden or red pool on the surface. Only then are the remaining seasonings and the main ingredient added to the pot.

Beef, pork, poultry and fish are the principal ingredients used in curry making. The Burmese prefer freshwater fish to those from the sea, but as plenty are available from both sources, this does not present a problem. Tender-fleshed catfish are particularly enjoyed. Shrimp (prawns) anywhere in the world always seem to taste better if caught near the mouth of a river where salt and fresh waters meet and blend. The delta of the Irrawaddy River, therefore, is an ideal breeding place, and shrimp is caught for cooking fresh and for processing into pungent *pazun nga-pi*, a shrimp paste of the Malay *blacan* kind. Fish similarly are salted, dried and processed into *ngan pya ye* (fish sauce) and *nga-pi*, a strongly flavored thick fish paste.

From these comes *balachuang*, with its almost overpoweringly strong taste, and from processed dried shrimp the Burmese make *nga-pi htuang* – a pungent condiment paste to serve with rice and mildly flavored dishes – and *nga chuak*, little cubes of

BEYA KYAW

Bean Patties

An accompaniment for mohinga, *these tiny, crisp patties of ground lentils or split peas are also delicious served on their own with drinks, or as an appetizer with a dipping sauce of chopped fresh chilies mixed with fish sauce. Thinly sliced shallots (or Spanish onion) and lime wedges are the usual garnish if served in this way.*

1 cup (6 oz/185 g) yellow lentils
8 shallots (or 3 Spanish onions), very finely chopped
1–2 fresh red chilies, very finely chopped
1 teaspoon crushed garlic
1 tablespoon finely chopped fresh cilantro (coriander)
½ teaspoon powdered turmeric
¾ teaspoon salt
oil for deep-frying

Soak the lentils overnight to soften, then place in a blender or food processor and grind to a smooth paste. Mix with the shallots, chili and garlic and knead until the mixture is fairly smooth. Add the cilantro, turmeric and salt and knead again until smooth.

Coat your hands with vegetable oil and roll the mixture into small balls. Heat the deep oil until a haze appears over the pan, then reduce the heat slightly. Drop in the balls several at a time and cook until they are golden brown and well crisped on the surface. Lift out with a slotted spoon and drain on paper towels before serving.

SERVES 4–6

PAZUN NGABUANG KYAW

Shrimp Patties

These are enjoyed as a side dish with mohinga *but can be served as a snack or a side dish with other meals. They can also be made with fish.*

8 oz (250 g) peeled small raw shrimp (prawns)
1 teaspoon salt
¼ teaspoon powdered turmeric
½ cup (2 oz/60 g) chick pea flour
½ cup (2 oz/60 g) all purpose (plain) flour
2 egg whites, well beaten but not frothy
ice water
oil for deep-frying

Chop the shrimp finely. Place in a bowl and add the salt and turmeric, then sift on the flours and add the egg whites. Mix together, adding enough ice water to make a fairly stiff batter.

Heat the oil until a haze forms over the pan. Reduce the heat slightly. Drop teaspoonfuls of the batter into the hot oil, pushing each below the surface to seal it before adding another (in this way they should not stick together). Cook in several batches or the oil will cool, and the patties will absorb too much of it. As they turn a rich golden color, lift out with a slotted spoon and drain well on paper towels.

SERVES 6

SHRIMP/PRAWN PATTIES

SHRIMP/PRAWN AND BAMBOO SHOOT CURRY

PAZUN-HMYIT-HIN

Shrimp and Bamboo Shoot Curry

The combination of shrimp (prawns) and bamboo shoots appears frequently in Burmese cuisine. The dish is at its peak midyear when a particular type of tender bamboo shoot is sprouting; known as wahbo, *it should be picked and used on the same day. Serve this curry with rice.*

2 lb (1 kg) fresh unpeeled medium shrimp (prawns)
salt
cornstarch (cornflour)
12 oz (375 g) peeled fresh or canned young bamboo shoots
2 medium onions
8 cloves garlic
2-in (5-cm) piece fresh ginger
3 tablespoons vegetable or peanut oil
1½ teaspoons powdered turmeric
1½ teaspoons dried chili flakes
1 cup (8 fl oz/250 ml) fish stock, or water
1½ cups (12 fl oz/375 ml) thick coconut milk
ngan-pya-ye (fish sauce)

Peel and devein the shrimp. Rinse with cold water, rubbing with a little salt and cornstarch to remove the fishy smell and to keep them white.

If using fresh bamboo shoots boil them in lightly salted water until they are tender enough to pierce easily with the point of a knife. Drain the bamboo shoots and slice thinly, or cut into small cubes. Peel and thinly slice the onions and garlic; shred the ginger.

Heat the oil in a saucepan and fry the onions, garlic and ginger for about 4 minutes, until softened and lightly colored. Add the turmeric and chili flakes and continue to fry until the onions are well colored. Add about 2 tablespoons cold water and simmer this mixture until the liquid has evaporated, then add the fish stock or water and bring to the boil.

Simmer for 2–3 minutes, add the shrimp and bamboo shoots and bring almost to the boil. Cook gently for 5 minutes, then add the coconut milk and simmer again for about 2 minutes, until mixture is well heated through; do not allow to boil. Add fish sauce to taste and serve.

SERVES 6

CHET GLAY HIN

Chicken Curry

The use of spices and garam masala, *a sweet Indian-style curry powder, here underlines the influence that Indian cooking methods have had on Burmese cuisine. But this is not to imply that all Burmese curries follow the Indian style. Their own unique blending of spices, and the moist seasonings with which most curries start, give them a decidedly individual flavor. Serve with rice.*

1½ lb (750 g) chicken parts
½ teaspoon powdered turmeric
1 teaspoon dried chilies, toasted and crushed
½ teaspoon cinnamon
½ teaspoon allspice
salt
3–4 tablespoons peanut oil
6 shallots (or 2 Spanish onions)
1-in (2.5-cm) piece fresh ginger
2 cloves garlic
1 fresh red chili
2–3 curry leaves
2 teaspoons *garam masala* (Indian sweet curry powder)
2½ cups (20 fl oz/625 ml) water or chicken stock
lime juice and *ngan-pya-ye* (fish sauce)

Place the chicken in a dish and sprinkle with turmeric, crushed chilies, cinnamon and allspice. Rub in lightly, adding a little salt. Cover and set aside for 1 hour.

Heat the oil in a heavy saucepan and fry the chicken pieces, several at a time, until evenly colored. Lift out and set aside. Grind the shallots, ginger, garlic and fresh chili to a paste. Add to the pan and fry for about 2 minutes until softened and aromatic. Add the curry leaves and *garam masala* and fry briefly.

Return the chicken to the pan and add the water. Bring to the boil, then reduce the heat and simmer gently for about 45 minutes until the chicken is very tender and the sauce well reduced. Adjust seasoning to taste, adding a splash of lime juice and a little fish sauce.

This dish looks particularly attractive if garnished with "flowers" made from red and green chilies (see page 233).

SERVES 4–6

CHICKEN CURRY AND BURMESE RICE, *recipe page 210.*

PORK CURRY *(TOP)* WITH DRIED SHRIMP AND SHRIMP
PASTE RELISH, *recipe page 210.*

WETHANI KYET

Pork Curry

*This recipe is similar to Indian vindaloos: The meat is first
marinated in a spicy mixture containing vinegar, which acts as an
efficient tenderizer. Serve with rice.*

3 lb (1½ kg) fresh ham or picnic shoulder (pork leg or hand)
1 large onion
12–15 cloves garlic
2-in (5-cm) piece fresh ginger
8 shallots (or 2–3 Spanish onions)
2 tablespoons white vinegar or ¼ cup (2 fl oz/60 ml)
   tamarind water
½ cup (4 fl oz/125 ml) peanut oil
2 tablespoons sesame oil, optional
1½ teaspoons salt
2 fresh red chilies, finely chopped
1 teaspoon powdered turmeric
1 teaspoon shrimp paste
rice

Cut the pork into cubes and place in a dish. Peel the onion
and grate it finely. Pour the accumulated onion liquid over
the pork. Crush 2–3 cloves of the garlic and finely grate half
the ginger. Add this to the pork with the finely chopped
shallots. Add the vinegar and mix in well. Set aside for 2
hours, stirring occasionally.

❧ Heat half the oils in a saucepan and fry the pork for
about 5 minutes until lightly colored. Add the salt and
enough water to cover generously. Bring to the boil and
simmer for about 1½ hours, skimming the surface from
time to time.

❧ Finely chop the remaining garlic and ginger. Heat the
remaining oil and fry the onion pulp, garlic, ginger and chili
for about 4 minutes over medium heat. Add the turmeric
and shrimp paste and fry for 3–4 minutes, adding a little
water to the pan if needed to prevent sticking. Add this
mixture to the pork and cook 8–10 minutes until the meat
is completely tender.

SERVES 6–8

MOHINGA

The National Dish

Essentially a simple dish of rice vermicelli (moh) *in a curried fish
soup* (hinga), *this dish is an inherent part of the Burmese culinary
tradition and is sold at every market and in every small restaurant.
It is a meal in itself and is always consumed with a passion
bordering on reverence. An essential ingredient for the authentic
dish is a section of trunk from a young banana tree. Enjoyed for its
crisp texture, subtle flavor and attractive pale green and pink
coloring, this is often used as a vegetable in Southeast Asia and
other countries where bananas proliferate. No other ingredient will
really do and to leave it out is to rob* Mohinga *of at least one of its
highlights. But I have experimented with celery root and bamboo
shoots, both of which gave passable results, and with a fennel
bulb, which added a pleasant anise flavor and the right texture.*

*If you can obtain a suitable piece of banana tree, slice it very
thinly after removing the outer layers. Place it in a dish with water
to cover. It emits a very sticky sap, which forms into fine strands;
pull these off and discard them. Soak for at least 2 hours, then
drain thoroughly and rinse in cold water.* Mohinga *comes, like so
many other Burmese dishes, with a selection of tasty
accompaniments that are added by each diner to his or her own
taste: hard-cooked duck eggs cut into wedges; lime wedges; fried
garlic and onion; pulverized chili in peanut oil or fish sauce; little
bean patties or tiny cakes made of pulverized fish or shrimp; fresh
cilantro (coriander) leaves; ground roasted chick peas; broken
crisp-fried noodles; sliced green onions.*

1½ lb (750 g) strongly flavored fish or fish pieces
2½ stalks lemon grass
¼ cup (2 fl oz/60 ml) *ngan-pya-ye* (fish sauce)
¾ teaspoon powdered turmeric
2–4 fresh red chilies
2 large onions, chopped
3 tablespoons vegetable or peanut oil
4 cloves garlic
1-in (2.5-cm) piece fresh ginger
2 tablespoons rice flour
2 tablespoons chick pea flour
2 cups (16 fl oz/500 ml) thick coconut milk
8–9-in (20–23-cm) piece young banana tree trunk,
   or 1 medium fennel bulb
salt
1¼ lb (625 g) rice vermicelli

ACCOMPANIMENTS

3–4 duck or hen eggs, hard-cooked and quartered
3 limes, cut into wedges
2–3 tablespoons fresh cilantro (coriander), chopped
peanut oil
10–12 cloves garlic
20 shallots (or 6 Spanish onions)
2–3 fresh red chilies
fish sauce, see below
2–3 tablespoons ground roasted chick peas
1 cup broken rice vermicelli
8–10 green onions, chopped
shrimp (or fish) patties (*pazun ngabuang kyaw*), see page 207,
   or bean patties (*beya kyaw*), see page 207

Cut the fish into pieces and place in a saucepan with water
to cover. Remove the green outer leaves of 2 lemon grass stalks
and use only the pale green root section. Cut in half and
bruise with the side of a Chinese cleaver or a meat mallet to
release the flavor. Add to the fish with the fish sauce, turmeric and half the fresh chilies, sliced in half lengthwise.

Cover and bring to the boil, then simmer gently until the fish is tender.

🥢 Lift out the fish with a slotted spoon, and break the flesh into tiny pieces; set aside. Return the head and carcass to the soup and simmer for 5 minutes, then strain the liquid into another saucepan and add the fish pieces.

🥢 Fry the chopped onions in the oil until very well colored. Grind the garlic, ginger and remaining lemon grass and chilies together and add the onion and the oil. Fry for 2–3 minutes, then mash until smooth. Add to the fish stock.

🥢 Mix the rice and *besan* flours with a little cold water and pour into the stock. Add the coconut milk and at least 6 cups (1½ liters) water. Add the very thinly sliced and soaked banana trunk or fennel bulb, season with salt to taste and simmer about 10 minutes.

🥢 Bring a large saucepan of well-salted water to the boil. Add the rice vermicelli and simmer until tender (cooking time depends on the brand and type of noodles and can vary considerably). Drain well, cover with cold water and drain again to remove any starch, then cover with hot water and set aside until needed.

🥢 Drain the vermicelli and place in another dish. Take to the table with the pot of hot fish soup. Begin with the vermicelli and soup, then add accompaniments to taste.

ACCOMPANIMENTS

Arrange the eggs, lime wedges and chopped cilantro on a platter.

🥢 Heat a little peanut oil in a skillet and fry the whole garlic cloves (or slice them if preferred) with the sliced shallots or onions until they are darkly colored and crisp.

🥢 Discard the chili seeds and grind the chilies to a paste. Place in a small dish and add peanut oil or fish sauce to cover.

🥢 Roast chick peas in a hot oven until very dry and crisp (they can also be purchased in Greek or Middle Eastern stores, or in certain stores where Indian produce is sold). Grind to a fine powder in a spice grinder or mortar.

🥢 Heat oil to the smoking point. Drop in a handful of crisp-fried noodles and fry quickly until they have dramatically expanded and is white; do not allow to color. Lift out, drain well and crush into short pieces.

🥢 Arrange all accompaniments, together with a dish of shrimp or bean patties, on platters.

SERVES 6–8

HTAMIN

Burmese Rice

Although most main courses and the majority of accompaniments are served at room temperature in Burma, rice and soup are always piping hot and are served at every meal, except perhaps when noodles or soup noodles are the main course.

Long-grain rice is always used. It is cooked by the absorption method, in which a carefully measured amount of water – or sometimes thin coconut milk – is added to the rice and cooking is done over low heat so that the liquid is completely absorbed into the rice. The result is plump individual grains; though supremely tender, they cling together just enough to make eating with the fingers, as is usually done in Burma, an easy task.

In this tasty dish, lemon grass is cooked with rice to impart its delicate citrus taste, and after cooking a piquant seasoning paste is stirred in. Crisply fried shallots are used as garnish.

2½ cups (13 oz/410 g) raw long-grain white rice
1 stalk lemon grass
4½ cups (1.06 liters) water
1 medium onion
3 cloves garlic
2½ oz (75 g) dried shrimp or dried salted fish, soaked to soften
1–2 fresh red chilies
¼ cup (2 fl oz/60 ml) vegetable or peanut oil
1½ tablespoons *ngan-pya-ye* (fish sauce)
1 tablespoon lime or lemon juice
salt
3–4 shallots (or 1–2 Spanish onions)
red and green chili "flowers" (see page 233)

Pour the rice into a saucepan with a very heavy base and tight-fitting lid. Trim the green tops from the lemon grass leaving only the lighter-colored root. Cut this in half, then bruise with the side of a Chinese cleaver or a meat mallet to release the flavor. Place on the rice. Pour in the water, cover and bring to the boil. When bubbling briskly, reduce the heat to the lowest possible setting and continue to cook for about 20 minutes until the rice is tender, stirring once or twice to ensure that the rice is evenly flavored with the lemon grass.

🥢 Meanwhile, chop the onion and garlic; drain the shrimp or salt fish and dry well. Grind these together with the chilies to a reasonably smooth paste.

🥢 Heat the oil in a skillet or small saucepan and fry the seasonings for about 3 minutes. Add the fish sauce, lime or lemon juice and about 1¼ teaspoons salt.

🥢 Stir lightly into the rice, cover and cook 4 minutes, then remove from heat and set aside for 10 minutes to absorb the flavors.

🥢 Slice the shallots very thinly. Fry in a little oil until very crisp and well colored. Pile the rice into a serving dish and cover with the fried shallots. Garnish with chili flowers and serve at once.

SERVES 6

BALACHUANG

Dried Shrimp and Shrimp Paste Relish

This pungent preparation is to the Burmese what brinjal pickle is to the Indians, nuoc cham to the Vietnamese or soy sauce to the Chinese. It is eaten with vegetables and salads, with cooked meats and curries, with rice and noodles. Serious enthusiasts of Burmese cooking consider this an absolute essential for the table. Store in the refrigerator in a sealed jar; it keeps for several weeks. White vinegar is sometimes added to the balachuang if it is to be kept for a longer period.

8 oz (250 g) small dried shrimp (prawns) or the same weight of prawn powder, an Indonesian product sometimes sold with chili added
16 cloves garlic
1 medium onion
1-in (2.5-cm) piece fresh ginger
2–3 fresh red chilies
½ cup (4 fl oz/125 ml) sesame oil
½ cup (4 fl oz/125 ml) peanut oil
1 teaspoon powdered turmeric
1¼ tablespoons shrimp paste
salt

Pound the whole dried shrimp, if used, in a mortar – or grind in a blender or food processor – until reduced to minute strands. The prawn powder is already of this texture.

⚜ Very finely mince the garlic, onion, ginger and chilies. They should be just a little coarser than powder.

⚜ Heat the sesame and peanut oils together in a saucepan. Add the minced ingredients and cook gently for about 4 minutes. Strain the oil into another pan, reserving the fried ingredients.

⚜ Add the pounded shrimp and the turmeric to the oil and fry until the shrimp is quite crisp, then strain the oil again, adding the shrimp to the other fried ingredients.

⚜ Return the remaining oil to the pan and fry the shrimp paste for about 2 minutes over medium heat, mashing it with a fork or the back of a wooden spoon to break it up. It will turn from pungent-smelling to aromatic as it cooks. Add the other fried ingredients and mix thoroughly, adding salt to taste.

⚜ Allow to cool, then transfer to jars to store.

MAKES ABOUT 2 CUPS

SANWIHN MAKKIN

Semolina Cake

Pronounced "sinna makin," this famed semolina cake is served, like most Burmese sweets, not after a meal as dessert, but between meals. Unlike those of neighboring Thailand, Burmese cakes and sweets are not oversweet. As a rule, they are not prepared at home but bought from vendors who usually specialize in just one or two different types, made according to age-old recipes. The companion to this rather moist, heavier-texture cake is the featherlight mo sein buong, a rice flour sponge cake, half of which is colored a rich honey brown with jaggery (palm sugar).

1¼ cups (7 oz/220 g) fine semolina
2 cups (16 fl oz/500 ml) fresh milk
2 cups (16 fl oz/500 ml) thick coconut milk
1 cup (7 oz/220 g) granulated or light brown sugar
½ teaspoon salt
⅓ teaspoon ground cardamom

SEMOLINA CAKE

5 oz (155 g) butter
4 large eggs
2 tablespoons white sesame seeds
1 tablespoon extra butter

Pour the semolina into a medium saucepan and toast over low heat for about 5 minutes, stirring constantly, until a light golden color. Stir in the milk and coconut milk, then add the sugar and salt. Bring to the boil and simmer, stirring constantly, until very thick. Add the cardamom and the 5 oz (155 g) butter and continue stirring over low heat until the mixture is very smooth and pulls away from the side of the pan.

⚜ Separate the eggs, add the yolks to the semolina mixture and beat in vigorously. Beat the egg whites to soft peaks and fold into the mixture. Pour into a buttered cake pan or ovenproof dish and smooth the top. Sprinkle with the sesame seeds.

⚜ Bake in a preheated 325°F (160°C) oven for at least 1¼ hours, until the cake is firm and springy to the touch.

⚜ Remove from the oven, dot the remaining butter over the surface and let cool in the pan. Cut into diamond-shaped pieces to serve.

SERVES 8–12

BUDDHIST MONKS, INLE LAKE

BARBARA HALLIDAY/IMAGES

A BEACH VENDOR, BALI
STEVE VIDLER KEY PHOTOS

OVERLEAF:
BAKED WHOLE FISH, *recipe page 222,* MILD CURRIED LAMB, *recipe page 229,*
GOLDEN YELLOW RICE, *recipe page 235.* CUCUMBER PICKLES *(LEFT),*
recipe page 232, AND BEEF AND KIDNEY BEAN SOUP, *recipe page 221*

Indonesia

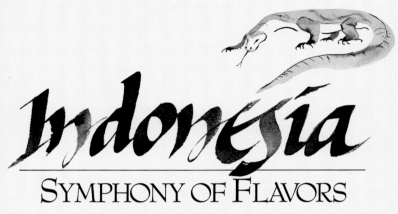

Indonesia
SYMPHONY OF FLAVORS

Indonesian cuisine: the heady, haunting aroma of spices, chilies and coconut; the kaleidoscope of bright colors and the overlay of contrasting textures; the myriad flavors to tantalize the palate; the simplicity of a family meal or the beauty and extravagance of a festive spread. Indonesian cuisine is one in which contrasts create equilibrium – searing chili-hotness is quenched by cooling coconut milk or crunchy cucumber; crisp-fried *krupuk* (shrimp crisps) surround a dish of tender rice; sour tastes offset sweetness; hot *sambals* accompany mildly flavored dishes.

Throughout Indonesia, beguiling aromas fill the air: the acrid promise of a wood fire's smoke; a toasty waft of roasting coconut; the all-pervasive fragrance of *pandan* (pandanus leaf) or the pungency of *trassi/belachan* (shrimp paste); the nutty smell of ground roasted peanuts in preparation for *sate* or *gado gado* sauce; a drift of clove as someone nearby lights up a *kretek* (clove/tobacco cigarette) or the invitation of a thin trail of smoke, suggesting soy, sugar and roasting meat, from the *sate* vendor's charcoal burner.

From Minangkabau, the west coast of the island of Sumatra, comes the food that takes most of the accolades in Indonesia. This is the home of Padang food, named after its capital city. With a wealth of local sweet spices to draw from, creative cooks have produced a memorable cuisine based on thickly sauced and pungently perfumed curries, on tart and strongly seasoned pickled fish dishes, on spicy *sates* and throat-searing little parcels of spiced seafoods, on burning hot dry-cooked dishes.

Necessity has long been the mother of invention, and the food that is known as Padang, like that of other parts of Indonesia, has been dictated by the availability of ingredients. This is the heart of the old

Spice Islands and most types of sweet spices are cultivated here. Nevertheless, for basic ingredients the Indonesian cook has had to make do with such humble organ meats as brains, liver and tripe, supplemented by the occasional piece of beef or buffalo meat. Predominantly Moslem in faith, the Indonesians – except for most of the people on the island of Bali, where Hinduism prevails – have banned the eating of pork. But cooked Indonesian style, organ meats take on a new importance. Pungent Padang *gulai kantjah* combines as many types of organ meats as are available in a potent stew of superlative flavor; *gulai hati* has livers enlivened with the tastes of *sereh* (lemon grass) and *laos* (galingale) in a light, turmeric-yellow sauce based on coconut milk; *hati bumbu Bali* features cubes of liver combined with soy sauce, sugar and ground peanuts and drenched with fried onions.

Javanese dishes, slightly lower on the scale of chili-hotness but no less flavor-packed, are aromatic, often creamy from the use of *santen* (coconut milk) in the sauces and a shade sweeter in taste. From here too come many crisp dry-cooked dishes.

Life in Bali seems to revolve around the temples, with a succession of religious festivals celebrated throughout the year. The *selatan,* or festive feast, is a time when even the poorest family will cook up as lavish a meal as possible and join with its neighbors in a colorful procession through the rice *padis* to the temple. Balanced on the women's heads are foods both for offering and for eating. They are later arranged beautifully on small wooden tables bedecked with flowers and intricately woven decorative structures in palm leaf strips and banana leaves. The centerpoint of the spread is always a towering cone of *nasi kunci* (yellow rice) and perhaps a spit-roasted or cooked-on-the-coals *babi guling* (suckling pig) or *bebek betutu* (spiced duck).

Everyday meals are simpler but nevertheless impressive. A roadside café may offer an array of aluminum or enameled pots containing an assortment of curries in a spectrum of colors: one yellow from *kunci* (turmeric), one a rich brown from a medley of seasonings, one bright red from chili, another ochre brown from fried onions or white from *santen* (coconut milk). Dishes of simmered green vegetables float in salted coconut milk, or a tumble of fruits and vegetables are flavored with tasty sauces – for instance *rudjak* or *gado gado,* the former with *kecap manis,* a sweetish soy and chili sauce, the latter coated in a creamy spiced peanut sauce.

Fruits are abundant in Indonesia and local cooks do not balk at using them in curries, salads or even soups. Bananas and pineapples, and the more exotic *salak* with its crisp flesh and snakeskin-like peel, or juicy *rambutan* and the sappy *belimbing* (carambola/ star fruit) feature in many recipes.

Rice, served either plain or flavored with turmeric or coconut, accompanies every meal. There are always at least two curries to choose from, with a selection of spicy little side dishes *(sambal)* and salads. Snacks of all kinds are readily available from small cafés or roadside vendors where fried bananas *(pisang goreng),* jackfruit fritters, small peanut-filled fritters, *krupuk* (shrimp crisps) and *sate* can be bought to eat on the go.

A BALINESE MASK MAKER

CHRISTINA DE WATER/WILDLIGHT PHOTO AGENCY

Gula jawa, a brown palm sugar, is used in many savory dishes, particularly those from the island of Java. Its main use, however, is as an ingredient in desserts and refreshing sweet drinks. Of these, *cendol,* a mixture of pea flour beans, coconut milk, crushed ice and palm sugar, is the most popular. Desserts in Indonesia, as in surrounding countries, depend largely on this palm sugar, brought together with rice and coconut in infinitely diverse ways. One of the most delightful is *kuah klepon,* little balls of glutinous rice flour coated thickly in flaked coconut, which when bitten reveal a cache of melted *gula jawa.*

Water accompanies most Indonesian meals, although a strong local brew made from coconut sap is enjoyed on some occasions, as is a pleasant sweet pink Balinese wine known as *brem.* Though it is deceptively mild to the taste, it is wickedly potent.

The crowning glory of Indonesian cuisine is the *rijstaffel.* Its Dutch name is a legacy from the opulent days of spice trading, when the Dutch held lavish banquets. Guests were seated at long tables on which elaborate floral and leaf decorations and large bowls of rice were arranged. Lines of sarong-clad servants filed past, offering a selection of up to thirty or forty different curries, meat dishes, vegetables, eggs and salads, accompanied, of course, by many kinds of crisp, hot, spicy or crunchy *sambals. Rijstaffel,* or rice table, it has remained to this day and, although now often served in buffet fashion, it is an outstanding example of the diversity and splendor of Indonesian cuisine.

CHICKEN SATE STALL   GRAHAM MONRO

COLORFUL DISPLAYS AT AN INDONESIAN MARKET   CHRISTINA DE WATER/WILDLIGHT PHOTO AGENCY

SATE BALI, SKEWERED CHICKEN AND PORK WITH PEANUT SAUCE
ACCOMPANIED BY COMPRESSED RICE, *recipe page 237*

SATE BALI

Balinese Skewered Pork and Chicken with Peanut Sauce

The sate *for which Bali has become famous is its tender turtlemeat version, but pork and chicken are also enjoyed. There are many recipes for the smooth peanut-based sauce which accompanies* sate. *It can be mild, thick or thin; redolent of* sambal ulek *and burning hot; dark and sweet with plenty of* kecap manis *(sweet soy sauce); or tasting of peanuts, with just a dash of chili heat and coconut milk for creaminess. The traditional* sate *accompaniment is cubes of cucumber, and on special occasions cubed* lontong *(compressed rice).*

SATES

10 oz (315 g) pork tenderloin (fillet) or chicken breast
1 medium onion, finely grated
1½ teaspoons finely grated fresh ginger
2 teaspoons sugar
½ teaspoon ground chili paste
1 teaspoon ground coriander
2 tablespoons thick coconut milk
¼ teaspoon salt
1 tablespoon light soy sauce *(for chicken only)* OR
  1 teaspoon sweet soy sauce *and*
  1 tablespoon dark soy sauce *and*
  ½ teaspoon ground cumin *(for pork only)*

PEANUT SAUCE

1 cup (5 oz/155 g) raw peanuts
2 tablespoons peanut oil
1 tablespoon ground chili paste
1 tablespoon sugar
1 tablespoon light soy sauce
¼ cup (2 fl oz/60 ml) water
½ cup (4 fl oz/125 ml) thick coconut milk
½ teaspoon lemon grass powder

½ teaspoon ground coriander
pinch each of turmeric and salt
vegetable oil

Cut the pork or chicken (or a mixture of the two) into small cubes and place in a dish. Add the remaining *sate* ingredients and mix in thoroughly. Cover with plastic wrap and set aside for at least 1 hour.

Spread the peanuts on a rimmed baking sheet and roast in a medium oven until golden. Rub in a kitchen towel to remove the skins, then pour into a colander and rinse with cold water until the skins have been washed away. Place in a food processor or a large mortar and grind to a paste. Mix it with the remaining sauce ingredients (except vegetable oil) in a small saucepan and bring to the boil. Simmer, stirring, for 5 minutes, then pour into several flat saucers.

Rub thin bamboo skewers with vegetable oil to prevent the meat from sticking. Thread several cubes of meat onto each skewer.

Grill the *sate* over glowing charcoal, brushing with a little vegetable oil during cooking to keep the meat moist. Serve hot with the sauce.

MAKES 12 STICKS (approx. 4 servings)

PILUS

Sweet Potato Savories

1 lb (500 g) sweet potatoes
1 large egg
1½ tablespoons soft brown sugar
1 teaspoon salt
2½ tablespoons all purpose (plain) flour
oil for deep-frying
hot chili sauce (see page 234)

Peel the sweet potatoes and cut into small cubes. Boil or steam until they are completely tender, then drain thoroughly. Leave the saucepan over low heat while mashing to a smooth purée so that the heat can evaporate any moisture left in the potatoes.

Stir in the remaining ingredients, beating until smooth. (The dough should be dry enough to be worked with the fingers without sticking, but not so dry that it begins to crumble.) Form into small balls.

Heat the oil to moderately hot and deep-fry the balls until golden brown. Lift out with a slotted spoon and drain. Serve hot or cold with a hot chili sauce.

Note: The temperature of the oil is critical. If it is too hot, the balls may split open; if too cool, they may disintegrate.

MAKES ABOUT 18

SWEET POTATO SAVORIES AND HOT CHILI SAUCE, *recipe page 234*

SAYUR ASAM KACANG MERAH

Beef and Kidney Bean Soup

1¼ cups (8 oz/250 g) dried kidney beans
2 teaspoons salt
6 cups (2⅓ pints/1½ liters) beef broth or water
1 large onion
1 teaspoon crushed garlic
2 tablespoons vegetable oil
6 oz (185 g) coarsely ground (minced) beef
2 teaspoons ground chili paste
½ teaspoon shrimp paste
1 teaspoon soft brown sugar
4 candlenuts or 10 raw cashews or macadamia nuts
2 teaspoons tamarind pulp
2 tablespoons chopped fresh cilantro (coriander), optional

Soak the beans in plenty of water overnight to soften, drain and place in a deep saucepan with the salt and beef broth or water. Bring to the boil, skim the surface, then reduce heat and simmer until the beans are tender.

Peel and finely chop the onion. Fry onion and garlic in the oil until they are a rich brown color, then push to one side of the pan and fry the beef until colored. Add the chili paste, shrimp paste and brown sugar and fry for about 2 minutes.

Grind the candlenuts to fine powder and stir into the seasonings, then transfer to the soup.

Remove ½ cup of the hot stock and mix with the tamarind pulp, then strain back into the soup. Taste for seasoning. Simmer for 20 minutes, then serve with a garnish of cilantro.

SERVES 6

FISH IN HOT SAUCE, AND PINEAPPLE SALAD, *recipe page 232*

IKAN SEMUR JAWA

Fish in Hot Sauce

Kecap manis is an ingredient used with enthusiasm in Indonesia. Based on dark soy sauce with spices and caramelized sugar to add sweetness, this rich, thick sauce is used both as condiment and seasoning for cooked dishes. Now readily available in Asian food stores, it can, however, be replaced with a mixture of two parts dark soy sauce to three of dark corn syrup. Both the consistency and taste of this alternative are quite acceptable.

1 lb (500 g) thick firm-fleshed fish
1 teaspoon salt
1 tablespoon lemon or lime juice
2 cups (16 fl oz/500 ml) vegetable or peanut oil
1 large onion, chopped
1 teaspoon crushed garlic
1 cup (8 fl oz/250 ml) thick coconut milk
⅓ cup (2½ fl oz/85 ml) sweet soy sauce
1½-2 teaspoons ground chili paste
½ teaspoon salt
1 tablespoon lemon or lime juice

Cut the fish into pieces about 2 in (5 cm) square. Sprinkle with the salt and lemon juice and set aside for 20 minutes.

Heat the oil in a deep skillet. Wipe the fish with paper towels. Fry several pieces at a time until well colored on the surface and just cooked through. Lift out and drain on a rack.

When all the fish has been cooked, drain the oil, reserving about 2½ tablespoons. Add the onion and garlic and fry until well colored and tender. Add the coconut milk, soy sauce and chili paste and bring to the boil. Simmer for 2 minutes, then slide in the fish and cook gently for 3-4 minutes. Add salt and lemon juice, if needed. Serve with rice and pickled cucumber (see page 232).

SERVES 4–6

GRILLED POMFRET WITH A SWEET SOY SAUCE

PANGGANG BUNGKUS

Baked Whole Fish

A large whole fish, smothered in spices and seasonings and wrapped in a banana-leaf parcel, makes a spectacular centerpiece to an Indonesian meal. The seasonings used here are only moderately hot, as the hot tastes will be provided by an assortment of side dishes and sambals. The counterpart to this is ikan pepes *which translates literally as "hot fish" – little banana-leaf parcels of sliced or ground (minced) fish coated with shredded coconut and chili.*

2½-lb (1¼-kg) whole fresh snapper/sea bass
1½ teaspoons salt
½ teaspoon ground black pepper
2 teaspoons tamarind pulp
1 tablespoon hot water
1 fresh red chili
1-in (2.5-cm) piece fresh ginger
3–4 cloves garlic
1 large onion or 10 shallots
1 teaspoon powdered turmeric
1 teaspoon shrimp paste
8 candlenuts, or 24 raw cashews or macadamia nuts
1 teaspoon sugar
2–3 tablespoons shredded coconut, optional
2 medium tomatoes
2 tablespoons chopped fresh cilantro (coriander) or sweet
　basil
vegetable oil
several young banana leaves or aluminum foil
2 lime or bay leaves

Clean and scale the fish. Make several deep slashes across each side to allow the seasonings to penetrate and the fish to cook evenly. Sprinkle with salt and pepper. Mix the tamarind pulp with the hot water, kneading with the fingers until thoroughly mixed. Smear over the fish.

Slit open the chili and scrape out the seeds. Place the chili, ginger, garlic and onion in a food processor or blender and process until smooth. Add the turmeric, shrimp paste, candlenuts, sugar, coconut and tomatoes and process again until the mixture is smooth and thick. Add the cilantro or basil.

Dip the banana leaves into boiling water to clean and soften. Drain and wipe dry. Cut away the thick central rib. Place several leaves overlapping on a work surface. Brush with vegetable oil to prevent sticking.

Spread half the seasoning paste over the center of the banana leaves or a sheet of aluminum foil large enough to wrap around the fish. Place the fish on top, insert the bay leaves into the cavity, then spread the remaining paste over the fish. Cover with the banana leaves or foil and tie the parcel securely with string. Alternatively, wrap the fish in aluminum foil. Place on a rack over a baking sheet and bake in a preheated 350°F (180°C) oven for about 45 minutes. Test by inserting a fork into the thickest part of the fish. The flesh should flake easily from the bones.

SERVES 6

Panggang Ikan Bawal
Grilled Pomfret

The silver pomfret or bawal putih is prized for its quite delicious flesh. These flat upright, almost round fish, resembling John Dory, are particularly highly regarded by the Chinese. They are usually cooked quite simply so as not to mask their sweet taste.

1 fresh pomfret, about 1¼ lb (625 g)
2 teaspoons crushed garlic
1 teaspoon grated fresh ginger
3 tablespoons sweet soy sauce
1 tablespoon peanut oil
cucumber slices
shredded fresh red chili

SAUCE DIP

1 tablespoon ground chili paste
3 tablespoons fresh lime juice
1 tablespoon sweet soy sauce
sugar and salt to taste

Clean and scale the pomfret and rinse thoroughly in cold water. Wipe dry and make several shallow slashes across both sides, horizontally to the head.

Mix the garlic and ginger with the sweet soy sauce and peanut oil. Brush over the fish and let stand for 2 hours to absorb the flavors. Grill over glowing charcoal, brushing with the marinade several times during cooking.

Mix the sauce ingredients together and divide among several small dishes. Set the fish on a serving plate. Surround with slices of fresh cucumber and garnish with fine shreds of fresh red chili. Serve with the sauce to use as a dip for each mouthful.

SERVES 4–6

Kari Kepiting
Curried Crab

Large-clawed crabs abound in the mangrove swamps that fringe many parts of the Indonesian coast. By tradition, those of the Moslem faith do not eat certain shellfish and crustaceans, however visitors to Indonesia and non-Moslems can enjoy crab cooked in many ways. This santen (coconut milk)-based curry is a favorite. Serve it with white rice.

2 large crabs (about 1½ lb/750 g each)
6 shallots or 2 Spanish onions
8 cloves garlic
1-in (2.5-cm) piece galingale/galangal or young fresh ginger
2–3 fresh red chilies
1 teaspoon shrimp paste
4 candlenuts, macadamias or 12 raw cashew nuts
1 teaspoon salt
¼ teaspoon cracked black pepper
¼ teaspoon turmeric
2-3 tablespoons vegetable or coconut oil
2 stalks lemon grass, root section only
1½ cups (12 fl oz/375 ml) thin coconut milk
2 teaspoons tamarind pulp
½ cup (4 fl oz/125 ml) thick coconut milk
2 tablespoons fresh cilantro (coriander) leaves

Cut the body of each crab into 6 pieces, each with a claw or 2 legs attached. Remove the pieces of undershell and scrape away the inedible parts. Crack the shell and claws with the

CURRIED CRAB

back of a heavy cleaver. Slit open the legs along their length, but do not remove shells.

Peel and halve the shallots, or slice the larger Spanish onions. Peel the garlic and ginger. Slit open the chilies and scrape out the seeds. Place the garlic, ginger, chilies, shrimp paste, nuts, salt, pepper and turmeric in a food processor, blender or mortar and blend to a smooth paste; this gives the "wet seasoning" that is the base of so many Indonesian curried dishes.

Heat the oil in a *wajan,* wok or wide saucepan and fry the prepared seasonings for about 2 minutes, until they are fragrant. Add the onions and fry briefly, then put in the crab pieces.

Fry the crab, stirring constantly, until it begins to change color. (If necessary add a little of the thin coconut milk to prevent the seasonings from burning.) Add the lemon grass and thin coconut milk and bring to the boil, then reduce heat.

Mix the tamarind with a little hot water, stirring until the pulp has dissolved, and strain into the pan. Simmer for about 15 minutes, until the crab is tender and the sauce slightly reduced. Stir in the thick coconut milk and add fresh cilantro. Serve with white rice.

SERVES 6

Ayam Besegnek
Spicy Chicken Besegnek

Besegnek, *pronounced* beh-sen-yek, *is a spice mixture used especially when cooking chicken. Sold commercially as* bumbu besegnek *(spices for besegnek), it contains* ketumbar *(coriander),* jintan *(cumin),* laos *(galingale/galangal) and* lombok *(chili).* Trassi/belachan *(shrimp paste) and* gula jawa *(palm sugar) are added to this dish and the sauce is based on* santen *(coconut milk).*

3-lb (1½-kg) chicken
¼ cup (2 fl oz/60 ml) vegetable or peanut oil
3 medium onions
1 teaspoon crushed garlic
3 tablespoons tamarind water
1½ teaspoons palm or dark brown sugar
4 candlenuts or macadamia, or 8 raw cashew nuts, finely ground
1 cup (8 fl oz/250 ml) thick coconut milk
1 cup (8 fl oz/250 ml) thin coconut milk
3 tablespoons sweet soy sauce
salt

SPICY CHICKEN *BESEGNEK, recipe page 223*

BUMBU BESEGNEK

1 tablespoon ground coriander
1 teaspoon ground cumin
2½ teaspoons powdered galingale/galangal
1 teaspoon dried chili/hot pepper flakes
1 teaspoon shrimp paste

Cut the chicken into quarters. Heat the oil and fry the chicken until evenly colored, then lift out. Peel and finely chop the onion and fry with the garlic until deep brown.

❧ Add the *Besegnek* spices and shrimp paste and fry for 2–3 minutes, stirring constantly. (Add a little of the thin coconut milk if the spices begin to stick to the bottom of the pan.)

❧ Add the tamarind water, sugar and ground nuts, then pour in the coconut milks and bring almost to the boil, stirring constantly. Simmer for 4–5 minutes, stir in the soy sauce and salt and add the chicken pieces. Cover and simmer gently for about 1 hour, occasionally turning the chicken and basting with the sauce.

SERVES 6

OPOR OTAK

Brains in Coconut Curry

Opor is a mild curry dish, white in color from coconut milk, with just a few mild spices to add subtle flavor and aroma. Light-colored meats such as brains and chicken are cooked in this way.

4 sets calves' or lambs' brains
2 teaspoons tamarind pulp
1 cup (8 fl oz/250 ml) boiling water
1 medium onion
2 cloves garlic
1-in (2.5-cm) piece fresh ginger
2 tablespoons vegetable oil
1 tablespoon ground coriander
1½ teaspoons ground cumin
10 candlenuts or macadamia nuts, or 28–30 raw
   cashews
¾ cup (6 fl oz/185 ml) thick coconut milk
1 lemon grass stalk
1 teaspoon salt
¼ teaspoon white pepper
chili powder

Place brains in a saucepan of cold water and soak for 1 hour, changing the water once. Drain, cover with clean cold water and bring to the boil. Remove from the heat and let stand until the water is cool. Drain, pick off surface membrane and return brains to the saucepan, adding the tamarind and boiling water. Simmer gently for 4–5 minutes. Drain again.

❧ Finely chop the onion, garlic and ginger and fry in the oil for about 3 minutes. Add the spices and finely ground nuts and cook briefly over medium heat. Pour in the coconut milk and add the lemon grass, salt and pepper. Bring to the boil and simmer gently for 1–2 minutes. Add the brains and add a little warm water to at least half cover the brains.

❧ Simmer gently for 5–6 minutes. Transfer to a serving dish and sprinkle lightly with chili powder.

SERVES 4–6

GULAI HATI

Curried Calves' Liver

12 oz (375 g) calves' or lambs' liver
black pepper
1 cup (8 fl oz/250 ml) vegetable oil
1 onion, finely chopped
1 teaspoon crushed garlic
1 teaspoon minced fresh ginger
⅓ cup (2½ fl oz/75 ml) boiling water
2 teaspoons tamarind pulp
½ teaspoon powdered turmeric
1–1½ teaspoons chili powder or flakes
1 cup (8 fl oz/250 ml) thick coconut milk
½ cup (4 fl oz/125 ml) beef broth
1 Kaffir lime or bay leaf
salt
shredded red and green chili

CURRIED CALVES' LIVER *(TOP)* AND BRAINS IN COCONUT CURRY *(BOTTOM)*

Soak the liver in cold water for 20 minutes, drain and wipe dry. Slice very thinly and dust with pepper. Heat the oil in a wide skillet and when very hot fry the liver slices on both sides until sealed and lightly colored. Remove from the pan.

❧ Pour off all but 2 tablespoons of the oil and fry the onion, garlic and ginger for 2–3 minutes.

❧ Mix the boiling water and tamarind together, stirring well. Pour into the pan and add the turmeric, chili, coconut milk, broth and bay leaf. Simmer for 3–4 minutes, then return the liver, reduce heat and simmer gently until the sauce is thick and the liver is very tender. Check seasoning, adding salt and pepper to taste.

❧ Pour into a serving dish and garnish with shredded chili.

SERVES 4–6

RICE – A VALUABLE INGREDIENT OF INDONESIAN COOKING

CHRISTINA DE WATER/WILDLIGHT PHOTO AGENCY

ROAST SUCKLING PIG

BABI GULING

Roast Suckling Pig

Roasted with a medley of aromatic spices, bedecked with flowers and perched triumphantly on a carved wooden tray, Babi Guling is a familiar sight in Bali. It will usually be bound for a temple to celebrate a religious occasion, or to the selamatan – the feast and prayer session.

Pork is eschewed by the majority of Indonesians, about 90 per cent of whom follow the Moslem faith. But in the fairytale island of Bali, populated predominantly by Hindus and with a flourishing pig-breeding industry, pork is an important source of protein, as well as a valuable export product. Generally the piglets cooked in this particular way are quite small, the larger beasts being simply roasted over pits of charcoal until the skin is crackling and the flesh succulent.

In keeping with the informality of the island during these festivities, one can inexpensively purchase a banana-leaf cone filled with white rice and topped with a handful of cubes of the tenderest roast pork. It's an innocuous looking parcel of fun "fast food," but the unsolicited bonus of a dollop of chili sambal has sent many an unwary tourist in search of the nearest water vendor.

8- to 10-lb (4- to 5-kg) suckling piglet
4-in (10-cm) piece fresh ginger
2 stalks lemon grass
2 large onions
8 cloves garlic
2–3 fresh red chilies
¼ cup (2 fl oz) vegetable oil
2 teaspoons powdered turmeric
2 teaspoons black peppercorns
4 green cardamom pods, broken
2 tablespoons coriander seeds
8 cloves
1 teaspoon freshly grated nutmeg
2 tablespoons salt
black pepper
1 tablespoon shrimp paste
cooked white rice
chili sambal (see page 234)

Ask your butcher to clean and prepare the piglet, ensuring there is no hair on the skin. Wash thoroughly in cold water and dry well.
Place the ginger, lemon grass, onions, garlic and chilies in a food processor or blender and grind to a paste. Heat the oil in a small pan and fry the paste for 3–4 minutes, then add the turmeric. Remove from the heat. In a spice grinder grind the peppercorns, cardamom seeds, coriander seeds and cloves to a powder. Add to the saucepan with the nutmeg, salt and shrimp paste and fry together for 3 minutes.
Spread this mixture thickly in the cavity of the piglet. Rub salt evenly over the skin, then dust with pepper. Roast in a preheated 375°F (190°C) oven for about 2½ hours, until cooked through inside. Or roast on a spit over a charcoal fire. Test by inserting a skewer into the thickest part; if the liquid that runs out is clear, the pork is done. Slice and serve with white rice and chili sambal.

SERVES 12–18

BEBEK BETUTU

Festive Spiced Duck

A tender duckling coated with aromatic spices is wrapped in young banana leaves and cooked on a bed of coals beneath the ground, or over a fire of coconut husks. This dish, with its tantalizing combination of spices, features at most festive occasions in Bali. Serve it with Nasi Kunci (page 235).

4-lb (2-kg) duck
2 medium onions
4–5 cloves garlic
2-in (5-cm) piece galingale/galangal or young ginger
2 tablespoons coconut or vegetable oil
young banana leaves (or aluminum foil)

SPICES

5 dried red chilies
2 black cardamom pods, peeled
1 tablespoon coriander seeds
1½ teaspoons cumin seeds
½ teaspoon fennel seeds
1–2 blades mace
1½ teaspoons salt
1 teaspoon black peppercorns
1 teaspoon shrimp paste
1 teaspoon grated fresh turmeric root,
   or ⅓ teaspoon powdered turmeric
12 candlenuts or macadamias or 20 raw cashew nuts

Clean the duck, rinse in cold water and drain well. Place the onions, garlic and ginger in a blender or food processor and grind to a smooth paste. Fry in the coconut or vegetable oil for about 3½ minutes. Remove from the heat.
In a dry pan roast the chilies, cardamoms, coriander, cumin, fennel and mace over medium heat for about 5 minutes, until aromatic. Transfer to a mortar or spice grinder and grind to a reasonably smooth powder. Add the salt and peppercorns and grind briefly.

FESTIVE SPICED DUCK

226

❧ Mix the spices with the fried onions, adding the shrimp paste and turmeric. Fry for 2–3 minutes, stirring. Place the nuts in a mortar or spice grinder and grind to a fine powder, then add to the spices in the pan and mix together thoroughly. Spread the seasoning paste evenly over the duck, rubbing a little of it inside the cavity as well.

❧ Rinse the young banana leaves in boiling water to clean and soften. Cut away the thick central ribs. Use several leaves to wrap the duck, first brushing them generously on the inside with coconut or vegetable oil to prevent them sticking to the duck. (There should be several layers of leaves; otherwise the duck may burn.) Make a neat parcel and tie it with thin wire if the duck is to sit directly over hot coals. If using aluminum foil, proceed in the same way.

❧ Place in the prepared fire, or in a preheated 350°F (180°C) oven over a drip tray and roast for about 2 hours.

SERVES 6

BABI KECAP

Pork in Sweet Soy Sauce

This unique dish takes its taste from kecap manis, *the thick, rich-tasting sweetened soy sauce that is an exclusively Indonesian ingredient. Long, slow simmering makes the meat supremely tender. Serve with plain white rice and a sambal well spiked with chili.*

2 lb (1 kg) lean boneless pork (fresh ham/picnic shoulder)
1 teaspoon salt
1 teaspoon black pepper
¼ cup (2 fl oz/60 ml) vegetable oil
1 large onion
2 teaspoons crushed garlic
2 teaspoons minced fresh ginger
1 teaspoon minced fresh red chili, or more to taste
½ cup (4 fl oz/125 ml) sweet soy sauce
1 cup (8 fl oz/250 ml) thin coconut milk

Cut the pork into 1½-in (4-cm) cubes and sprinkle with the salt and pepper. Heat the oil in a large pan until very hot and fry the pork until evenly colored; do not overcrowd the pan or the pork will begin to stew instead of browning. Transfer to a heavy saucepan or baking dish.

❧ Peel and finely chop the onion. Sauté in the remaining oil with the garlic and ginger until softened, then add the chili and sauté again briefly. Add to the pork with the remaining ingredients.

❧ Bring to the boil, then simmer gently over low heat or in a 350°F (180°C) oven for about 1½ hours, until the meat is completely tender and the sauce is well reduced. Add a little more coconut milk during cooking, if needed. Skim the fat from the surface before serving.

SERVES 6

PORK IN SWEET SOY SAUCE

KELIA SUMATERA

Sumatran Beef Curry

Sumatran dishes are heavy with spices, fragrant with fresh herbs, and burning with chili and pepper, for this is food from the original Spice Islands. Beef or young buffalo, poultry, organ meats and seafood are the ingredients mainly used here in curries such as this one.

2 lb (1 kg) shank, flank or chuck (braising) steak
4 large onions
8 cloves garlic
1½-in (4-cm) piece fresh ginger
1 stalk lemon grass
2–3 tablespoons vegetable oil
1 tablespoon ground coriander
2 teaspoons ground cumin
¾ teaspoon powdered turmeric
¾ teaspoon shrimp paste
2 cups (16 fl oz/500 ml) thin coconut milk
2 lime or bay leaves
2–3 fresh red chilies
8 candlenuts or macadamia nuts, or 24 raw cashews
10 small new potatoes
cooked white rice

Cut the meat into cubes. Peel and coarsely chop the onions, garlic and ginger. Trim the lemon grass, using only the lower pale root section; chop roughly. Place onions, garlic, ginger and lemon grass in a food processor or blender and process to a purée.

🐾 Heat the oil in a heavy saucepan and fry the meat until evenly colored, remove and set aside. Fry the onion purée for 5 minutes, stirring frequently. Add the spices and shrimp paste and fry briefly. Add the coconut milk and bay leaves and bring to the boil, then simmer for 5–6 minutes.

🐾 Slit the chilies and scrape out the seeds. Add the flesh to the curry. Grind the candlenuts to a powder and stir into the sauce, adding salt to taste. Return the meat and cook gently for about 1½ hours until very tender. Add extra coconut milk or water if needed during cooking.

🐾 Peel the potatoes, add the curry and cook until they are tender and the sauce is thick. Garnish with chopped green onions (optional).

SERVES 6–8

SUMATRAN BEEF CURRY, WITH TOMATO AND SHRIMP PASTE SAMBALS,
recipes pages 234-235

WORKERS GATHER AT A TEA PLANTATION

NEIL FARRIN/IMAGES

GULAI KAMBING

Mild Curried Lamb

1½ lb (750 g) lean lamb (from shoulder or leg)
salt and white pepper
3 tablespoons vegetable oil
2 large onions
8 cloves garlic
1-in (2.5-cm) piece fresh ginger
¾ teaspoon powdered turmeric
1½ teaspoons powdered galingale/galangal
1 teaspoon shrimp paste
2 teaspoons dark brown sugar
1–2 fresh red chilies
2 cups (16 fl oz/500 ml) thin coconut milk
½ cup (4 fl oz/125 ml) thick coconut milk
fresh cilantro (coriander) and basil
cooked white rice

Cut the lamb into small cubes and dust generously with salt and pepper. Heat the oil in a large pan and fry the meat in several batches until evenly colored. Set aside.

Grind one of the onions, the garlic and ginger to a paste. Peel and very thinly slice the remaining onion. Fry the sliced onion in the oil until very well colored. Push to one side of the pan and add the ground ingredients, frying for about 4 minutes. Add the seasonings and sugar and fry for about 2 minutes, stirring all together.

Slit open the chilies and scrape out the seeds. Place in the pan whole, or cut into several large pieces – they are usually removed before serving – and add the coconut milks. Bring to the boil, then simmer, stirring constantly, for about 8 minutes until oil rises to the surface of the sauce. Add the lamb and simmer gently for about 1½ hours, stirring from time to time.

Check the seasonings, stir in chopped cilantro or basil and serve with rice.

SERVES 6–8

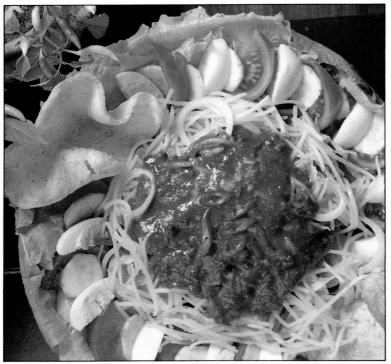

SALAD WITH PEANUT DRESSING

WELDON TRANNIES

GADO GADO

Salad with Peanut Dressing

A thick peanut sauce similar to that served with sate accompanies this salad of cooked and raw vegetables and fruit.

1 small head lettuce
2 large boiling potatoes, cooked in their jackets
1½ cups (about 6 oz/185 g) sliced green (French) beans
1½ cups (about 6 oz/185 g) chopped fresh bean sprouts
1½ cups (about 4 oz/125 g) shredded white or
   Chinese cabbage
2–3 medium tomatoes
1 medium onion
2–3 green onions
1 medium cucumber
2 slices canned or fresh pineapple
1 cup loosely packed fresh herbs (cilantro/coriander, basil,
   parsley)
1–2 fresh red chilies
2–4 hard-cooked eggs
2 eggs, made into omelet shreds (see page 233)

PEANUT SAUCE

1 tablespoon dark soy sauce
2 teaspoons lemon juice
4 tablespoons crunchy peanut butter
1 teaspoon ground chili paste
2 teaspoons dark brown sugar
1 cup (8 fl oz/250 ml) thick coconut milk
½ teaspoon crushed garlic
½ teaspoon minced fresh ginger
½ teaspoon minced lemon grass root
2 tablespoons vegetable or coconut oil

Rinse the lettuce in cold water, drain well and shake or wipe dry. Arrange on a wide platter. Peel the potatoes and slice thinly. Drop the beans into a saucepan of lightly salted water and simmer for about 4 minutes, then drain, refresh with cold water and drain again. Pour boiling water over the bean sprouts and cabbage and drain immediately.

Thinly slice the tomatoes and onion. Trim the green onions and cut into shreds about 2 in (5 cm) long. Peel the cucumber and cut into cubes, discarding the seeds. Cube the pineapple.

Arrange the potatoes in a circle around the edge of the platter, slices overlapping. Place the remaining vegetables and pineapple in a bowl and toss together until well mixed. Remove from bowl and pile into the center of the platter. Surround with the herb sprigs.

Slit the chilies and scrape out the seeds, cut the flesh into fine shreds. Quarter the eggs and arrange on the salad. Cover the salad with omelet shreds and place the shredded chilies on top. Cover and chill.

Mix the soy sauce, lemon juice, peanut butter, chili paste and sugar together in a small saucepan; add the coconut milk. Heat, stirring, almost to the boiling point.

Sauté the garlic, ginger and lemon grass root in the oil for 2–3 minutes until very fragrant. Pour into the sauce and simmer for 4–5 minutes, until the sauce is very thick, stirring constantly to prevent sticking. Allow to cool. Pour into a dish or pitcher and serve with the salad.

SERVES 6–8

SAYUR LODEH

Simmered Vegetables

Vegetables are an important part of the Indonesian cuisine and are served with every meal. They may be made into salads ranging from a simple dish of cucumbers to a multifaceted salad like the popular Gado gado, which combines raw and cooked vegetables in a tasty peanut dressing.

Most cooked vegetables are made into sayurs, the vegetables being quickly cooked to retain the goodness, color and crispness.

Sayurs are soup-like dishes in which the main ingredients are simmered in a thin coconut milk sauce. Beans, cabbage, bean sprouts and cucumber are commonly used vegetables, along with dried red kidney beans and potato. But it is not unusual to find, in a salad or vegetable dish, chunks of fresh pineapple, water chestnuts, or the crisp-fleshed salak, a small fruit encased in a hard "snakeskin." Carambola is often featured too; it is a tart, sappy five-cornered fruit which, when sliced, has a star shape and hence is commonly known as star fruit.

1 large boiling potato
1 medium carrot
1½ cups (about 4 oz/125 g) white or Chinese cabbage
1 cup (about 4 oz/125 g) green (French) beans
1 cup (about 4 oz/125 g) fresh bean sprouts
1 large onion
2–3 green onions
2 tablespoons vegetable oil
1 teaspoon crushed garlic
½ teaspoon finely minced fresh red chili (optional)
1½ teaspoons minced fresh ginger
1½ teaspoons ground coriander
1 teaspoon powdered lemon grass
1 teaspoon powdered turmeric
½ teaspoon shrimp paste
2¼ cups (18 fl oz/560 ml) thin coconut milk
salt

Peel the potato and cut into small cubes. Peel and thinly slice the carrot. Chop the cabbage coarsely, discarding any thick ribs. Trim the beans and slice diagonally into 2-in (5-cm) lengths. Rinse the bean sprouts and pick off the roots and seed pods, if desired. Peel the onion, cut in half and slice thinly from stem to root. Separate the pieces. Trim the green onions and cut into 2-in (5-cm) pieces.

Heat the oil in a saucepan. Add the garlic, chili if used, and the ginger, spices and shrimp paste. Fry for 2 minutes, splashing in a little of the coconut milk if the seasonings begin to stick to the bottom of the pan.

Add the coconut milk and salt and bring to the boil, slowly stirring the sauce. Add the potato, carrot and beans and simmer gently, stirring occasionally, until they begin to soften, then add the remaining vegetables and simmer, covered, until the vegetables are tender but retaining crispness. Serve at once.

Sayurs, like most other Indonesian dishes, are served at room temperature, but do not allow too much time to pass between cooking and serving or the vegetables will become too limp to be enjoyable.

SERVES 6

Rujak Manis

Spiced Fruit and Vegetable Salad

Raw fresh fruits, salad greens and lightly cooked vegetables combine ingeniously with a full-flavored sauce to make this side dish for hot curried dishes.

1 green apple
2 very firm pears
1 unripe mango
1 small fresh pineapple
1 medium cucumber
1 large onion or 6 shallots (or 2 Spanish onions)
1 cup (about 4 oz/125 g) sliced green (French) beans
1 cup (about 4 oz/125 g) diced taro/cassava (yam)
1 medium-size head lettuce

3 teaspoons tamarind pulp
2 tablespoons boiling water
¼ cup (2 fl oz/60 ml) sweet soy sauce
½ teaspoon shrimp paste
2 teaspoons ground chili paste
¾ teaspoon salt
1 tablespoon crumbled palm sugar/dark brown sugar
½ cup (4 fl oz/125 ml) thick coconut milk

Peel the apple, pears, mango and pineapple and cut into small cubes. Place in a mixing bowl. Peel the cucumber, cut lengthwise in half, scoop out the seeds and slice thinly, or cut into matchsticks. Peel and slice the onion or shallots.

Drop the beans into a pan of lightly salted boiling water and simmer for about 4 minutes until crisp-tender. Place the taro in another saucepan of well-salted water and boil until tender, about 18 minutes. Drain well and cool.

Wash and dry the lettuce, separating the leaves. Arrange on a wide serving dish. Toss the prepared fruit and vegetables together.

Dissolve the tamarind in the boiling water. In a small saucepan simmer the sweet soy sauce, shrimp paste, chili paste, salt and sugar together, stirring to dissolve the sugar. Add the tamarind water and coconut milk and stir until cool. Pour over the salad and toss well, then pile onto the lettuce and serve at once.

SERVES 6

SIMMERED VEGETABLES *(BOTTOM),* SPICED FRUIT AND VEGETABLE SALAD *(TOP),* AND *KECAP SAMBAL, recipe page 235*

LOCAL FRUIT, A COOLING INGREDIENT IN A TROPICAL CLIMATE

SELADA NANAS

Pineapple Salad

Hot curries call for something sweet and refreshing to quench the fire. Salads such as this one of fresh pineapple and cucumber are served as side dishes.

1 small, fresh ripe pineapple
1 medium cucumber
1 large green onion
1 fresh red chili, optional
1 teaspoon crushed garlic
1 teaspoon minced fresh root ginger
¼ cup (2 fl oz/60 ml) light soy sauce
1½ tablespoons white vinegar
1½–2 tablespoons palm sugar or dark brown sugar
vegetable oil
½ teaspoon shrimp paste, or 2 teaspoons fish sauce
2–3 tablespoons crushed roasted peanuts

Cut the pineapple in half lengthwise, cutting straight through the leaves as well. Scoop out the flesh, discard the core and cut the pineapple into small cubes. Place in a mixing bowl.

Peel the cucumber. Cut the flesh away from the seed core in several long thick strips, then cut into dice. Trim the green onion and chop finely. If using the chili, slit open and scrape out the seeds, then shred the flesh finely. In a small cup mix the garlic, ginger, soy sauce, vinegar and sugar together, stirring to dissolve the sugar.

Heat a small pan and add 1 tablespoon vegetable oil. Fry the shrimp paste until very aromatic. Add to the dressing with the oil, stirring to mix thoroughly. (The fish sauce has a milder taste than shrimp paste in this dish.)

Pour the dressing over the salad and toss thoroughly. Pile into the pineapple shells and garnish with the crushed peanuts. Serve cool.

SERVES 6

ACAR KETIMUN

Cucumber Pickles

Pickles appear on the Indonesian table with the frequency of side salads in a Western meal. They come in many variations, some even being made with meat and fish. They can be stored in airtight jars in a dark cupboard for several months. Serve with hot curries to temper the fire, and with rice dishes.

1 large cucumber
1 small onion
1 fresh red chili
½ cup (4 fl oz/125 ml) white vinegar
3 tablespoons lime or lemon juice
1 teaspoon sugar
½ teaspoon salt
large pinch of black pepper

Peel the cucumber, then use a teaspoon to scoop out the seeds. Slice the cucumber thinly. Peel and halve the onion. Slice from top to bottom into little wedges and separate the layers. Make a slit in the chili and scrape out the seeds; leave chili whole.

In a small nonaluminum saucepan bring the vinegar, lime juice, sugar, salt and pepper to the boil. Simmer for 2 minutes, then add the onion and chili and simmer for about 30 seconds.

Pack the cucumber into a sterile jar and pour in the vinegar mixture. Let stand until cool, then seal. Shake lightly to ensure that the liquid has coated every slice of cucumber. Set aside until needed. Pickle keeps for several months.

SERVES 6

GARNISHES

Indonesian cooks love to pay particular attention to the decoration of their food, the objective being to present a lavish spread of appetizing dishes. Certain garnishes in particular dress cooked meats, curries, rice dishes and salads.

CHILI

In keeping with their penchant for searing hotness, fresh red and green chilies add both attractive color highlights and a distinct burning taste.

SHREDDED CHILI

Cut off the top (stem end) of the chili and insert a paring knife or bamboo skewer to scrape out the seeds. Use a very sharp knife to cut diagonally into thin rings. Or slit the chili open along its length and scrape out the seeds, then slice across the chili at close intervals to give thin shreds, or lengthwise to give long narrow shreds.

CHILI FLOWERS

Select plump fresh chilies with smooth skin. Use the point of a small sharp knife to cut through the flesh from top to end at close intervals. Carefully scrape any pith from the inside of these "petals" and make sure that the central stamen and seeds are not adhering to any of the petals. Place in a dish of ice water for at least 30 minutes and the petals will curl backwards to make an attractive flower. Shake off water before using.

FRIED *LAKSA* (Rice Vermicelli)

Heat oil for deep frying until a haze appears over the pan, then reduce heat slightly. Drop a small handful of uncooked *laksa* into the oil; it will immediately expand into a voluminous white cloud. Scoop off immediately, as it will quickly burn. Drain well, then crumble lightly and use to scatter over dishes.

FRIED *KRUPUK* (Shrimp Crisps/Wafers)

These are sold in ready-to-fry form and look like small slices of slightly transparent pink or colored plastic. Drop them, several at a time, into hot oil and fry just long enough for them to expand. Drain thoroughly on paper towels. Arrange around salads and over rice and noodle dishes, or serve as a snack.

FRIED ONION FLAKES

Peel small white or brown onions, or better still shallots (or small Spanish onions). Slice very thinly into rings, or cut in half lengthwise and slice crosswise. Drop into deep oil and fry over medium heat until a rich brown. Lift out, drain, and place on paper towels to dry and complete draining. When cool they should be quite crisp. Store in an airtight container until needed.

OMELET SHREDS/STRIPS

Beat one or two eggs very thoroughly; strain if desired to remove any lumps. Heat a dry *wajan/*wok or skillet to moderately hot and pour in a little of the egg. The pan should be nonstick or well seasoned. Slowly move the pan around, forcing the egg to spread thinly over as wide an area as possible. Cook until just lightly colored underneath, then flip over and cook briefly on the other side.

Spread on a kitchen cloth to cool, then roll up tightly and cut crosswise into very thin slices. Unroll to make long thin strips. Pile these on rice, noodles, meat dishes and dry curries.

DELICIOUS GARNISHES – FRIED *LAKSA*, FRIED *KRUPUK*, FRIED ONION FLAKES, OMELET STRIPS, CHILI FLOWERS AND STRIPS AND *SERUNDENG*

SPICY *SERUNDENG* (*TOP*) AND FRIED NOODLES (*BOTTOM*)

SERUNDENG

Spicy Condiment

Toasted and spiced kelapa *(shredded/desiccated coconut) mixed with roasted peanuts is an intrinsic part of the Indonesian meal, and can be sprinkled over virtually any dish to give it added flavor and texture.*

1 tablespoon palm sugar/dark brown sugar
½ cup (4 fl oz/125 ml) tamarind water
2 cups (6 oz/185 g) shredded/desiccated coconut
½ cup (2½ oz/75 g) shelled roasted peanuts
1 large onion, very finely chopped
4 cloves garlic, finely chopped
1 tablespoon coconut oil
¾ teaspoon powdered turmeric
1 teaspoon ground ginger
large pinch each of ground nutmeg, mace and cardamom
2 teaspoons ground coriander
½ teaspoon salt

Dissolve the sugar in the tamarind water, then combine with the remaining ingredients in a mixing bowl.

Heat a *wajan*/wok and fry the mixture over medium heat, stirring slowly and constantly, until the coconut is crisp and well colored and the mixture is dry and aromatic. This is a tedious process, but it should not be accelerated by attempting to cook over a higher heat or the coconut will quickly burn. Spread on a plate or tray to cool completely, then store in an airtight jar and use as needed.

SERVES 6–8

SAMBAL

Spicy Pickles and Relishes

There are many varieties of sambal *made to accompany Indonesian meals. Basically they comprise chili, pounded to a paste and mixed with such other ingredients as soy sauce,* trassi/ belachan *(shrimp paste), shredded (desiccated) coconut, tomatoes and minced dried shrimp. They are served as condiments to pep up a mild dish or to take an already hot one a step further, for the Indonesians relish the fiery, eye-watering, tongue-searing taste of chili.*

SAMBAL SAUS (Hot Chili Sauce)

2 tablespoons ground chili paste
1½ teaspoons crushed garlic
2 tablespoons grated onion
2½ tablespoons brown sugar
2 tablespoons white vinegar
¾ cup (6 fl oz/180 ml) water
1½ teaspoons cornstarch (cornflour)

Mix the chili paste, garlic, onion and sugar together in a small saucepan, then add the remaining ingredients. Bring to the boil and simmer briefly. Serve as a dipping sauce for *bregedel jagung* (sweetcorn fritters) and *lumpia* (spring rolls).

TRASSI/BELACHAN SAMBAL (Shrimp Paste Sambal)

1 tablespoon dried chili flakes
2 tablespoons shredded coconut
1½ teaspoons shrimp paste
½ teaspoon salt

Grind the chili and coconut to a fairly fine powder in a spice grinder. Add the shrimp paste and salt and grind until well mixed. Store in an airtight container. Keeps for several weeks.

TRASSI/BELACHAN LOMBOK SAMBAL (Shrimp Paste and Chili Sambal)

3 tablespoons ground chili paste
2 tablespoons grated onion
1 tablespoon salt
1 tablespoon shrimp paste
2 tablespoons peanut oil
1½ tablespoons lemon juice

Place the ingredients, except the lemon juice, in a small saucepan and cook gently for about 5 minutes, mashing the shrimp paste with a fork to break it up. When heated through and thoroughly mixed, add the lemon juice and cook a further 5–6 minutes, stirring frequently.

SAMBAL TOMAT (Tomato Sambal)

2 medium tomatoes, finely chopped
½ teaspoon ground chili paste
1 tablespoon water
1 tablespoon shrimp paste
½ teaspoon salt

Mix the ingredients together. The shrimp paste has a better flavor if it has been lightly fried in a little peanut oil.

KECAP SAMBAL (Soy Sauce Sambal)

2 tablespoons dark soy sauce
½ teaspoon crushed garlic
1 teaspoon minced fresh red chili
1 teaspoon crushed palm sugar or dark brown
   sugar

Mix the ingredients together, stirring until the sugar has dissolved.

SERVES 6

NASI KUNCI
Golden Yellow Rice

Locally grown kunci, *fresh turmeric, is a rhizome with an orange-yellow color and distinctive taste. It is similar to ginger and* galingale *or* galangal, *a species of ginger used often in Southeast Asia. As well as lending its bright yellow color to dishes both sweet and savory,* kunci *has an agreeably earthy flavor that marries well with rice dishes and lends its particular taste to most Indonesian curries.*

2½ cups (13 oz/410 g) raw long-grain white rice
4 cups (32 fl oz/1 liter) thin coconut milk
1¾ teaspoons salt
2 teaspoons grated fresh *kunci* or 1 teaspoon powdered
   turmeric
2 lime or bay leaves
½ cup (1½ oz/45 g) shredded coconut

GARNISH

2 eggs, well beaten
2 tablespoons fried onion flakes (see page 233)
1 red and 1 green chili flower (see page 233)
2 sprigs fresh cilantro (coriander)

Wash the rice in cold water and drain well. Place in a heavy saucepan and add the coconut milk, salt, turmeric, bay leaves and shredded coconut. Bring to the boil, then reduce the heat to very low and cook, tightly covered, for about 20 minutes until the rice has absorbed the coconut milk completely; twice during cooking briefly lift the lid and stir the contents to evenly distribute the ingredients, then cover again.

Wipe out a *wajan* or wok with an oiled cloth. Heat over medium heat and pour in half the egg. Slowly move the pan back and forth so that the egg spreads into as wide and thin a sheet as possible. Cook just until the underside is firm but has not colored, then turn and briefly cook the other side. Remove and spread on a cloth to cool. Cook the remaining egg in the same way. Roll up the egg sheets and use a sharp knife to cut across the roll to give fine shreds.

Pile the cooked rice into a deep dish, cover with the shredded egg and sprinkle the onion flakes on top. Decorate with the chili flowers and cilantro and serve at once.

SERVES 6–8

BAHMI GORENG
Fried Noodles

In Indonesia, noodles may serve as the entrée – packed full of diced meats, seafoods and vegetables – or they may supplement an already interesting menu. Noodles come in many types. There is laksa *or* su'un, *transparent thin vermicelli, or rice flour vermicelli, used in the dish known as* laksa; *there are the various thicknesses of* mi, *or Chinese-style egg noodles; and there are flat ribbonlike rice sticks.*

Egg noodles or mi, *either thick or thin, are usually used for fried dishes like this one.*

12 oz (375 g) thin egg noodles
4 oz (125 g) small peeled shrimp (prawns)
4 oz (125 g) chicken breast
4 oz (125 g) lean pork
4 oz (125 g) Chinese cabbage, cabbage or spinach
4 green onions
10 shallots (or 2 Spanish onions)
4–5 cloves garlic
3 slices galingale/galangal or young ginger
1–2 fresh red chilies *or* ground chili paste,
   to taste
¾ cup (6 fl oz/185 ml) peanut oil
2 tablespoons light soy sauce
1 teaspoon sugar
1 teaspoon salt
large pinch of cracked black pepper
sprigs of fresh basil or cilantro (coriander)
omelet shreds and fried onion flakes (see page 233),
   optional

Soak the noodles in boiling water to soften and untangle, then bring quickly to the boil. Drain, cover with cold water, drain again and spread in a wire strainer to cool and dry. Thick noodles will require boiling for at least 5 minutes.

Cut the shrimp in half lengthwise. Slice the chicken and pork, then cut into narrow strips. Coarsely shred the green vegetables, and rinse thoroughly.

Trim the green onions. Cut in half lengthwise, then into 1-in (2.5-cm) lengths. Peel and thinly slice the shallots and garlic. Shred the ginger. Slit open the chilies and scrape out the seeds, then cut the chilies into long, narrow strips. Set a little aside for garnish.

Heat the oil in a *wajan,* wok or wide skillet until smoking. Add the noodles and fry until they are crisp on the edges. Lift out and set aside.

Reheat the pan and stir-fry the chicken and pork until they change color. Push to one side of the pan, add the onions, garlic, ginger and chili and stir-fry for about 2 minutes, until the onions are soft. Add the shrimp and cabbage and toss everything together.

Stir in the seasonings and mix thoroughly. Return the noodles, toss lightly to reheat and mix. Arrange on a serving platter. Garnish with the herbs and reserved chili shreds, and with omelet shreds and fried onion flakes in the traditional manner, if desired.

SERVES 4–8

Nasi Goreng

Fried Rice

With an eye also on producing a dish to inspire the tastebuds, economical cooks created nasi goreng, *using up leftover white rice and adding whatever bits and pieces were available, to produce this wholesome family dish. Virtually a meal in itself,* nasi goreng *is delicious with a salad such as* gado gado, *and a dish or two of a tasty sambal or hot sauce on the side.*

¼ cup (2 fl oz/60 ml) vegetable oil
1 large onion, finely chopped
1½ teaspoons crushed garlic
1 teaspoon minced fresh ginger
¾ teaspoon powdered turmeric
½–2 teaspoons ground chili paste, to taste
1 teaspoon shrimp paste, optional
1½–2 teaspoons salt
½ teaspoon black pepper
1 cup (about 6 oz/185 g) cooked meat such as chicken, ham, roast pork, shrimp
1 cup (about 6 oz/185 g) mixed diced peppers (capsicum), diced celery, diced carrot and thawed frozen peas
¾ cup (about 4 oz/125 g) finely shredded white or Chinese cabbage
1 cup (about 4 oz/125 g) chopped fresh bean sprouts
6–8 cups cooked white rice (made from 2–2½ cups raw long-grain white rice)
¼ cup (2 fl oz/60 ml) thick coconut milk
2 tablespoons tamarind water
1 tablespoon sweet soy sauce
2–3 eggs, made into shredded omelet (see page 233)
6 tablespoons fried onion flakes (see page 233)
fresh cilantro (coriander)

NASI GORENG – INDONESIAN FRIED RICE

Heat the oil in a large wok or wide skillet. Add the onion and garlic and stir-fry over high heat by mixing and turning constantly with a wide spatula. Add the ginger, turmeric, chili paste and shrimp paste and continue to stir-fry for 2–3 minutes. Add the salt and pepper, then the meat, diced vegetables and peas. Stir-fry for about 5 minutes, keeping the food constantly moving to prevent it from burning.

 Add the cabbage and bean sprouts and stir-fry all together for a further 2–3 minutes. Add the rice and stir-fry the food briskly over high heat.

 Add the coconut milk, tamarind water and sweet soy sauce. Check seasonings, adding more salt if needed. Pile into a serving plate, shaping the rice into a cone. Cover with the omelet shreds and fried onion flakes. Surround with fresh herbs and serve.

SERVES 6–8

LONTONG
Compressed Rice

White rice cooked in little parcels of banana leaf, or boiled and compressed firmly into cakes, is often served in Indonesian homes in place of the traditional boiled white rice. Little cubes of lontong *may accompany, for instance, a platter of grilled* sate.

2½ cups (1 lb/500 g) raw short-grain white rice
young banana leaves or aluminum foil
sweet soy sauce, optional
fried onion flakes (see page 233), optional

Wash the rice thoroughly. Rinse the banana leaves in boiling water to clean and soften. Dry and brush lightly with vegetable oil. Place a large spoonful of rice in the center of a piece of banana leaf or aluminum foil about 8 in (20 cm) square. Fold over to completely enclose the rice, allowing a little room for expansion. Tie securely with string or thread.

 Have ready a large pot of well-salted water. Drop in the rice bundles and simmer for at least 1½ hours, until the rice is cooked through and well compacted. Drain and unwrap to serve. Garnish with a dribble of soy sauce and fried onion flakes.

 Alternatively, cook the rice by the absorption method (see page 235 for detailed technique). When done, pour into a lightly oiled mold and place a suitable cover on the rice so that it can be weighted to compress the hot rice into a firm cake. Top with a weight and set aside until completely cool and firm.

SERVES 6–10

KUEH KLEPON
Coconut Balls

These little snowy-white, coconut-covered balls have a surprise filling of melted gula jawa *(brown palm sugar), which flows deliciously into the mouth when you bite into them. They can only be made with a special flour of finely ground* ketan *(sweet glutinous rice).*

1 cup (4 oz/125 g) glutinous rice flour
¾–1 cup (6–8 fl oz/185–250 ml) thin coconut milk
½ teaspoon salt
24 small cubes of palm sugar or several tablespoons dark brown sugar
1 cup (3 oz/90 g) shredded coconut

Mix the flour and coconut milk together, adding the salt. The dough should be firm enough to mold without sticking to the fingers. Form into 24 small balls of equal size. Push the point of a finger into each one to form a hollow and press a piece of the palm sugar (or a scant half teaspoon of brown sugar) into each. Pinch the dough up and around the filling to completely encase it, ensuring that the edges are firmly sealed together.

 Bring a large saucepan of water to the boil. Drop in about 8 of the balls at a time and simmer until they float to the surface, then cook for a further 1½ minutes. Lift out with a slotted spoon and drain. When all of the *kueh klepon* are cooked, toss them in shredded coconut until thickly and evenly coated. Serve cold.

MAKES 24

COCONUT BALLS

FRIED BANANAS AND BANANA PARCELS

KUEH PISANG

Banana Parcels

These sweet little parcels of sliced banana set in pea flour require a special flour labeled tepong hoen kwe. *This flour is made from powdered green mung beans; when cooked it turns into a thick, pale green paste. Arrowroot or cornstarch (cornflour) with a few drops of green food coloring can be substituted, or alternatively a few drops of* pandan *essence with rice or water chestnut flour.*

5 large bananas
⅔ cup (4 oz/125 g) green mung bean flour
⅓ cup (3 oz/90 g) sugar
large pinch of salt
2¾ cups (22 fl oz/680 ml) thin coconut milk
1¾ cups (14 fl oz/440 ml) water
banana leaves or aluminum foil
thread or toothpicks

Place the whole bananas in a steamer and steam for about 10 minutes until softened. Set aside.

Combine the flour, sugar, salt, coconut milk and water in a saucepan and bring to the boil, stirring constantly. Continue to cook gently, stirring, until the mixture turns thick and becomes transparent.

Peel and slice the bananas. Cut the banana leaves or aluminum foil into 6-in (15-cm) squares and brush with clean vegetable oil. Place a small spoonful of the mixture on each; top with a piece of banana and another spoonful of the flour mixture. Wrap into small square parcels and secure with cotton thread or wooden toothpicks. Set aside to cool, then refrigerate until they are completely set. Serve as a snack or for dessert.

SERVES 6–8

PISANG GORENG

Fried Bananas

A crisp batter, rich and nutty with coconut milk, makes a delightfully light and crunchy coating for tropical fruits. In travels around Indonesia, one often comes unexpectedly upon a little roadside stand set with a wajan *of bubbling oil and a platter of sliced pineapple, wedges of jackfruit and large, ripe bananas awaiting battering and frying — a delicious and inexpensive snack on the run. Or thick coconut cream and soft brown sugar can be spooned over the fried bananas to make them into a dessert.*

12 ripe bananas
½ cup (2 oz/60 g) rice flour
1 cup (4 oz/125 g) all purpose (plain) flour
2 teaspoons baking powder
½ teaspoon salt
1 large egg, lightly beaten
1 cup (8 fl oz/250 ml) thick coconut milk
1 cup (8 fl oz/250 ml) water
oil for deep-frying

Peel the bananas, cover and set aside. Beat together the remaining ingredients, except the oil. Let stand for about 25 minutes.

Heat the oil to the smoking point, then reduce heat slightly. Dip the bananas one by one into the batter, then slide into the oil. (Do not fry more than three at a time or the temperature of the oil will drop too much, making the batter heavy and oily.) Cook until golden, turning once or twice. Lift out on a slotted spoon and drain. Serve while hot.

MAKES 12

INTENSIVE RICE CULTIVATION, BALI FRITHFOTO/OLYMPUS

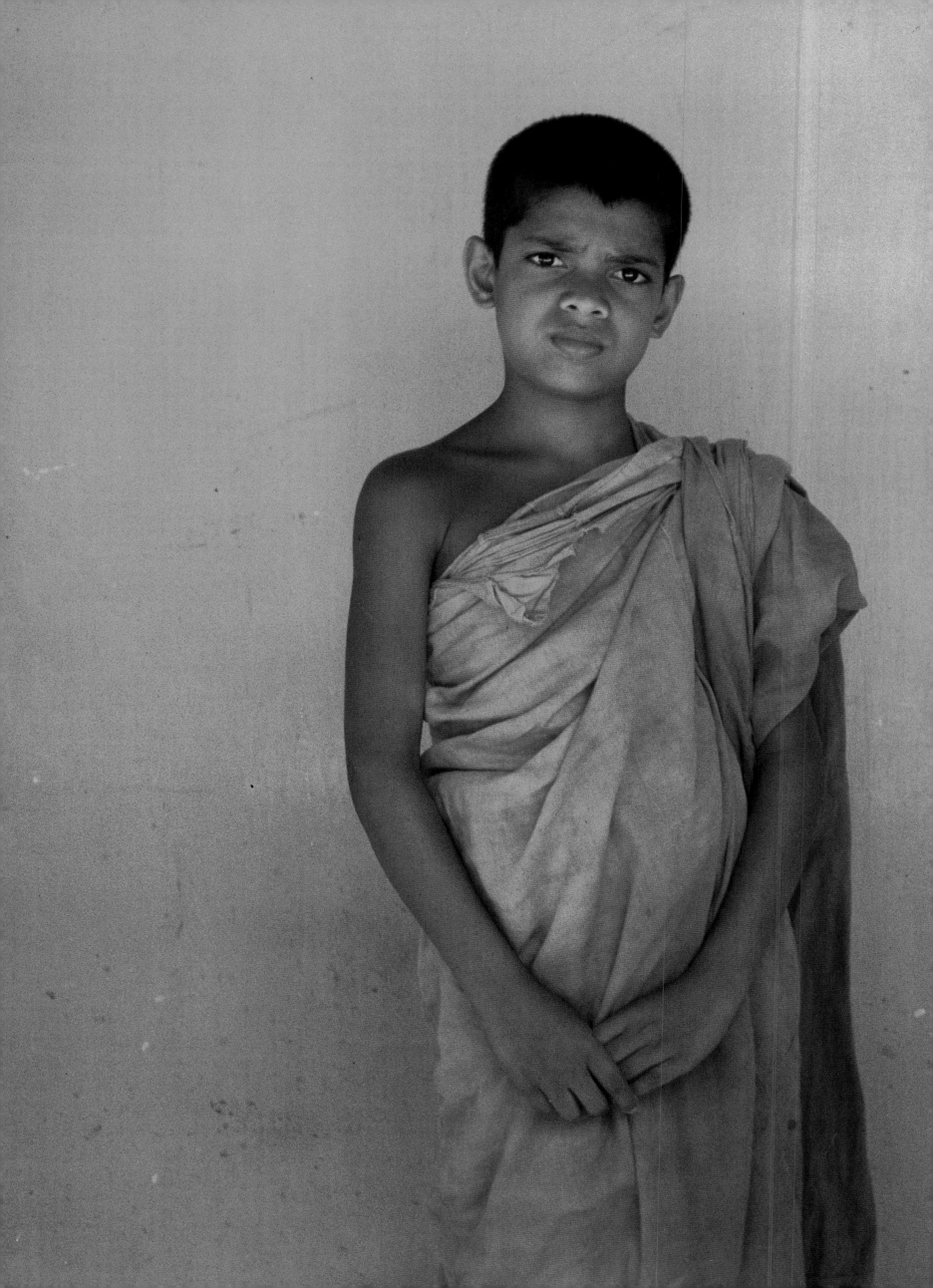

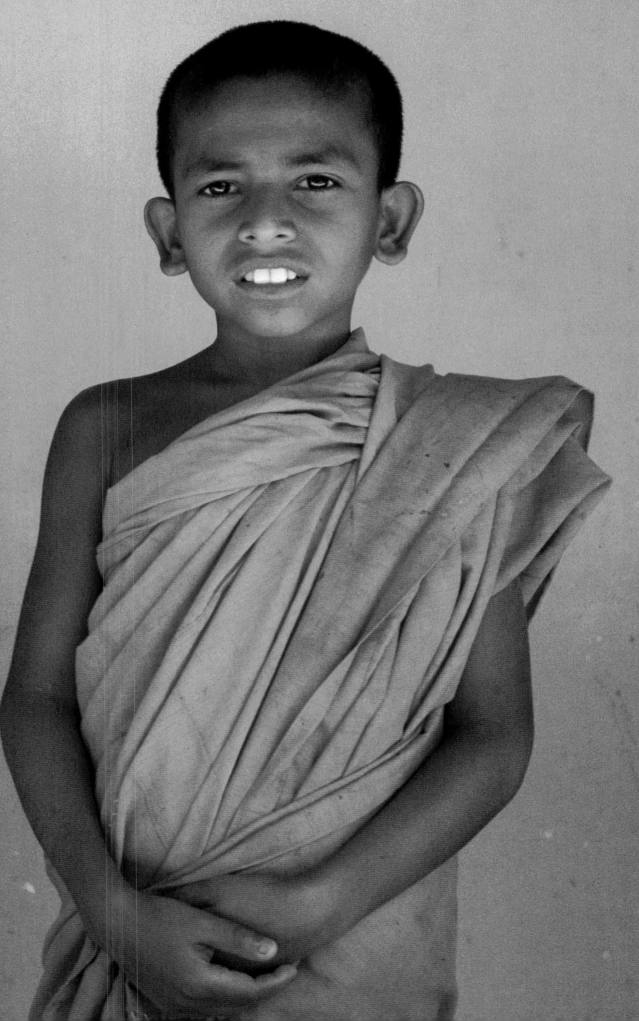

Sri Lanka

CHICKEN CURRY, *recipe page 249*, COCONUT COATED VEGETABLES *(RIGHT), recipe page 250*, CHILI SAMBOL *(LEFT), recipe page 251*, AND COCONUT PUDDING, recipe page 250.

Sri Lanka

GEMS FROM AN ENCHANTED ISLE

Since there is nowhere in Sri Lanka more than 80 miles from the sea, one would assume that seafoods dominate its cuisine. Nothing could be further from the truth. Seafood is important, particularly along the coastal strip, but this tiny island has an astounding diversity of dishes.

Outside influence has been considerable, for throughout her long history, Sri Lanka has been host (willing or not) to people from many different countries and cultures. Naturally there were Indians from across the narrow strait that separates the two countries, but also Malays, who brought with them the rich dishes and exotic seasonings of the Moslems. And the traders – Arabs, Portuguese, Dutch, and finally British – who ruled and dominated, and left their influence on the Sri Lankan way of life, and on her food.

The flat bread, *roti*, of India is now an intrinsic part of Sri Lankan cooking, but they have added their own innovations: *appa* (hoppers), leavened rice flour and coconut milk pancakes baked in little curved cups over hot coals; the indigenous *roti*, which includes grated coconut in its batter; and steamed tubes of *pittu*, grated coconut and flour batter cakes.

The curry is the axis of Sri Lankan foods. The word loosely describes any tasty seasoned dish, and in Sri Lanka curries come in many different styles, classified according to their color. "White" curries, which use coconut milk in the sauce, tend to be reasonably mild in taste with a minimum of seasonings. "Red" curries, brightly stained from chili powder or dried chilies – it is not unheard of to add as many as two dozen chilies to a single dish – can shock the unwary with their intense hotness.

The most typically Sri Lankan dishes, however, do not fall into these two categories, but into that of "brown" curries. The most notable difference between the curries from Sri Lanka and elsewhere is in the treatment of the curry spices. The mixture may well be almost identical to that used in an Indian *garam masala* (curry spice mixture), but before the spices are ground, the coriander, cumin, fennel and maple syrup-flavored fenugreek seeds are first roasted in a hot oven or dry pan until they take on a rich brown hue. This releases a full range of subtle fragrances that proclaim their Sri Lankan origin. To these are added cinnamon bark, cloves, cardamom, dried curry leaves and a handful of roasted rice grains before grinding to a fine powder. Like all curry powder mixtures, they are at their best immediately after being ground, but they can be stored for a short time in an airtight container. Turmeric, that spice which lends its bright yellow tone and a musky, peppery pungence, is not usually added to commercial spice preparations as it quickly overpowers the most subtle sweet fragrances. Sri Lankan cooks add it separately.

Pork, beef and poultry are the meats employed in curry making, and beef is used as well in two quite atypical ways: for the making of Dutch-style *frikkadels*, little meatballs, and for *mas smoore*, in which a large cut of beef is more or less pot-roasted in a spiced coconut milk gravy and served sliced.

Fish and other seafoods are used to make countless different types of curries from mild to super-hot, bland to tart, the sharp sour taste of tamarind being used to make a sauce while simultaneously counteracting any suggestion of fishiness. Crabs abound in the mangrove-fringed shores and, simmered with coconut, herbs and chili powder, they make delicious *kakuluo* (crab) curry.

The island has a bountiful supply of native fruits: the gigantic sweet-fleshed jackfruit, papaya, mangoes, pineapple and bananas. Many of these are used in their unripe state as a vegetable. Vegetables include cabbage, eggplant, cucumber and bean sprouts, with large, tender avocados and fresh cashew nuts as specialty crops. The latter is favored as *kadju kari*, cooked with a hot, creamy curry sauce. *Mallung* (coconut coated vegetables) is an important dish, particularly for the poorer families, for whom it provides much-needed vitamins in an inexpensive form.

Rice is served with most meals, even when bread is included. For special occasions it is made with ghee (clarified butter) or coconut milk, and fragrant with sweet spices. A typical meal will have rice, a curry or two, a soup, some vegetables and several little dishes of *sambola*. Everything is usually served at the same time, with no particular regard to keeping the food hot – a practice common to households throughout Southeast Asia. The dishes are selected to complement each other, and it is acceptable to have a little of each dish on the plate at the same time. Foods are generally eaten with the fingers.

Pickles are just as important to a meal here as they are in India, and come in many forms, but fresh *sambolas* must also be included. *Seeni sambola*, made with chilies, or others of bean sprouts, fried onion, cucumber, coconut and highly spiced seafoods, are made fresh for each meal. Most will only keep for a day or two, but the Sri Lankan housewife would not consider her job complete without taking the trouble to produce at least one at each mealtime.

Sri Lankan sweets range widely, from the rich and buttery concoctions introduced centuries ago by the Dutch, and the sweet pastries popularized by the Portuguese, to delectable local desserts. *Vattalappum* is a pudding made with *jaggery* (palm sugar) and coconut milk, *pol dosi* is a creamy coconut toffee and the Indian-inspired *kusari barth* is a dessert of semolina and cream.

BANANA STALL, COLOMBO

JOHN EVERINGHAM

BOMBAY DUCK *(TOP) recipe page 256,* AND CRISP PEA FLOUR NIBBLES

MURUKKU

Crisp Pea Flour Nibbles

These little crisply fried strips of dough can be served with drinks or eaten as a snack between meals. Murukku *will keep in an airtight jar for several weeks.*

2 cups (1 lb/500 g) chick pea flour, or use finely milled
   all purpose flour
2 teaspoons fine chili powder
1½ teaspoons turmeric
1½ teaspoons salt
½ teaspoon paprika
thin coconut milk or water
oil for deep-frying

Pour the flour into a mixing bowl and add the remaining dry ingredients, mixing thoroughly. Add enough thin coconut milk or water (at least 1 cup) to make a dough that is just slightly firm.

Roll out very thin and then roll the dough into a sausage shape. Use a very sharp knife dipped in flour to cut through the roll making long, noodle-like strands.

Heat the oil to the smoking point, then reduce heat slightly. Deep-fry the *murukku* until crisp and golden. Lift out and drain thoroughly on paper towels. Allow to cool and dry before storing. Extra salt and chili powder can be sprinkled over the *murukku* before serving.

SERVES 10–12

PATTIES

Beef Pastries

Patties, little curried beef pastries, are similar to the Indian samoosa *or the curry puffs of Malaysia. A party in Sri Lanka would not be the same without them. In this recipe coconut milk and finely milled wholewheat flour are used to make the pastry.*

PASTRY

2 cups (8 oz/250 g) finely milled wholewheat flour
½ teaspoon salt
2 tablespoons thick coconut milk
½ cup (4 oz/125g) ghee (clarified butter) or butter, softened
1 egg
cold water
oil or ghee for deep-frying

FILLING

1 slice bacon
4 oz (125 g) finely ground (minced) beef
2 tablespoons ghee
1 small onion
½ teaspoon crushed garlic
2 teaspoons curry powder
1 teaspoon ground coriander
½ teaspoon salt
large pinch each of black pepper and turmeric
1 fresh green chili
2 teaspoons lime or lemon juice
2–3 hard-cooked eggs
1 medium potato, boiled
2 tablespoons thick coconut milk

Pour the flour into a mixing bowl; add the salt, coconut milk, butter and egg. Mix thoroughly with the fingers until smooth, adding just enough cold water to make a very firm dough. Knead lightly, then chill.

Very finely dice the bacon and fry with the beef in the ghee until the beef changes color. Push to one side of the pan. Add the very finely chopped onion and the garlic and fry until soft. Add the curry powder, coriander, salt, pepper and turmeric and fry for 2 minutes. Slit open the chili, scrape out the seeds and chop the flesh very finely. Add to the pan, frying everything together for 2 minutes. Add the lemon or lime juice, the finely chopped eggs and potato and the coconut milk and simmer until the mixture is thick and dry. If it seems too wet, sprinkle a little flour over it and stir. Remove from heat and let cool.

Roll out the pastry very thin, then cut out 36 rounds of about 2½-in (6-cm) diameter. Place a small spoonful of the filling in the center of each, run a wet finger around the edge and fold over, pinching the edges firmly together. Deep-fry in hot oil or ghee, or bake in a preheated 375°F (190°C) oven for about 20 minutes or until the surface is crisp and dry. Serve warm with a sambol.

MAKES ABOUT 36

BEEF PASTRIES

HOT CHILI PRAWNS

Isso Tel Dala

Spicy Dry-Cooked Shrimp

This is one of the Sri Lankan "red" dishes, made searing hot with unlimited amounts of chili. For a milder taste, substitute mild paprika and mashed canned pimiento for some of the chili. Serve either version with white rice.

2 lb (1 kg) medium-sized fresh shrimp (prawns)
½ cup (4 fl oz/125 ml) vegetable oil
2 large onions
4 cloves garlic
1 tablespoon chili powder, or to taste
pinch of turmeric
1 tablespoon ground Bombay duck or dried shrimp
¾ cup (6 fl oz/185 ml) water
1 tablespoon sugar
1½ tablespoons lemon or lime juice
finely chopped fresh cilantro (coriander)

Heat the oil in a large skillet and add the shrimp. Cook the shrimp in their shells or peeled, as preferred. Cooking them in their shells gives them a stronger taste and brighter red color. Sauté, stirring and turning, until they are red, then remove and set aside.

Peel and finely chop one onion; very thinly slice the other. Crush the garlic. Fry the sliced onion in the oil remaining in the pan until very well colored, then remove. Add a little more oil to the pan if needed, and fry the chopped onion with garlic until soft and lightly colored. Add the chili powder (with paprika or pimiento, if used) and the turmeric. Stir in the Bombay duck or dried shrimp and fry lightly. Return the sliced onion to the pan and add the water, sugar and shrimp. Simmer, stirring from time to time, until the liquid has evaporated. Add the lemon or lime juice and the coriander. Stir over high heat until the juice has evaporated and the pan is dry.

The peeled shrimp cooked in this way make a delicious dip. When cooked, purée in a food processor until smooth. Serve warm with fingers of toast.

SERVES 6

Malu Kari

Curried Fish

1 lb (500 g) mackerel steaks, or other oily fish
2 teaspoons ginger juice*
1 teaspoon salt
½ teaspoon turmeric
½ teaspoon cracked black pepper
1 large onion
1 cup (8 fl oz/250 ml) peanut or vegetable oil
1 teaspoon crushed garlic
1 teaspoon grated fresh ginger
2-in (5-cm) cinnamon stick
2 green cardamoms, broken
4 curry leaves
2½ teaspoons coriander seeds
¾ teaspoon cumin seeds
¼ teaspoon fenugreek seeds
¼ teaspoon fennel seeds
1½ teaspoons chili powder
1½ cups (12 fl oz/375 ml) thin coconut milk
juice of 1–2 fresh limes
salt and pepper

Rub the fish with the ginger juice, then with the salt, turmeric and pepper. Peel and thinly slice the onion. Heat the oil in large skillet and fry the fish on both sides until sealed and lightly colored. Lift out and set aside. Pour off half the oil. Add the onion to the pan with the garlic and ginger and fry until well colored. Add the cinnamon, cardamom and curry leaves and fry briefly.

In another pan dry-fry the coriander, cumin, fenugreek and fennel seeds until they are deeply colored and very aromatic. Transfer to a spice grinder and grind to a fine powder. Add to the onion and fry briefly, then add the chili powder and coconut milk and bring to the boil. Return the fish to the pan and simmer gently in the sauce until tender. Stir in lime juice and salt and pepper to taste. Heat again briefly and serve hot.

Made by squeezing grated ginger in a garlic press or small piece of clean cheesecloth.

SERVES 4

CURRIED FISH

APPLES ADD COLOR TO THE MARKETPLACE   JOHN EVERINGHAM

KUKUL MAS KARI

Chicken Curry

2½-lb (1.25-kg) fresh chicken
3 tablespoons ghee (clarified butter)
2 medium onions
5 cloves garlic
4 dried red chilies, soaked
1 teaspoon grated fresh ginger
6 curry leaves
1½ tablespoons ground coriander
2 teaspoons ground cumin
¼ teaspoon lovage seeds
2 teaspoons chili powder, or use less chili powder and add mild paprika or canned pimientos for color
2 large tomatoes
2 teaspoons tamarind pulp
1 stalk lemon grass
1¼ cups (10 fl oz/310 ml) thick coconut milk
salt and cracked black pepper

Cut the chicken in half, then cut away and discard the backbone. Cut each piece in half crosswise to give four large pieces. Heat the ghee in a large saucepan and fry the chicken until evenly colored, then lift out and set aside.

Peel and finely chop the onions and garlic. Drain and crush the chilies. Fry the onions, garlic, chilies, ginger and curry leaves in the remaining ghee until the onions are soft and lightly colored, then add the spices and chili powder and fry again briefly.

Coarsely chop the tomatoes and add to the pan. Dissolve the tamarind in ½ cup boiling water, then strain the liquid into the pan. Trim the lemon grass and bruise with the side of a cleaver or heavy knife to release its flavor. Add to the pan with the coconut milk and bring to the boil. Season to taste with salt and cracked black pepper and simmer for 5 minutes.

Return the chicken to the pan and cook gently, tightly covered, for about 40 minutes, stirring the sauce and basting the chicken from time to time during cooking.

SERVES 4

SPICED EGGS

BITTARA HODHI

Spiced Eggs

8 large eggs
1 small onion
1 clove garlic
2 slices fresh ginger
1–2 fresh red chilies
½ teaspoon turmeric
1 teaspoon salt
oil for deep-frying
1 tablespoon coriander seeds
1 teaspoon cumin seeds
¼ teaspoon fennel seeds
1¼ cups (10 fl oz/310 ml) thick coconut milk
1 small blade mace
1 small cinnamon stick
sprigs of fresh mint

Hard-cook the eggs, then cover with cold water until cool. Very thinly slice the onion and garlic; shred the ginger and chilies. Peel the eggs, wipe dry and prick all over with a fork. Rub with the turmeric and salt.

Heat the oil to medium-hot and place the eggs in a frying basket. Lower into the oil to deep-fry until golden on the surface. Lift out and drain well.

In a medium saucepan dry-fry the coriander, cumin and fennel until lightly colored, then transfer to a spice grinder and grind to a fine powder. Return to the pan with the coconut milk, mace and cinnamon stick, bring to boil and simmer for 2 minutes.

Fry the onion, garlic and ginger until softened and well colored. Add to the coconut milk and simmer a further 5–6 minutes. Cut the eggs in half lengthwise and place in the sauce. Heat through gently for 2–3 minutes. Transfer to a serving dish and garnish with the mint. Serve with rice and a hot sambol.

SERVES 4–6

UMBALAKADA

Bombay Duck

Off to the southeast of Sri Lanka are the Maldives, a group of tiny islands which have become internationally famed for their beautiful beaches and fine tropical climate. In the warm waters here, and northwards along the western coast of India, small herring-like fish proliferate. Affectionately called "Bombay Duck," they can be seen in shining silver schools skipping over the surface of the fierce monsoonal seas that lash the city of Bombay throughout August each year. They are sun-dried, and their pungent taste is enjoyed as a condiment with curry dishes.

6 Bombay duck
12 shallots (or 3 small red/Spanish onions)
lemon or lime juice
1 cup (8 fl oz/250 ml) peanut or vegetable oil
1 teaspoon crushed garlic
1 teaspoon chili flakes
salt

Cut the Bombay duck into small pieces; peel and thinly slice the shallots.

Heat the oil in a skillet and fry the Bombay duck for about 2½ minutes until crisp. Remove with a slotted spoon, then pour off all but about 2½ tablespoons of the oil.

Fry the garlic and shallots in the oil for 4 minutes until well colored and slightly crisp. Add the chili flakes, then return the Bombay duck to the pan and add salt and lemon or lime juice to taste. Cook, stirring, until the juice is absorbed and the Bombay duck is fairly dry again. Serve hot or warm.

SERVES 6–8

MALLUNG

Coconut Coated Vegetables

Shredded fresh leafy vegetables such as spinach and cabbage can replace the local greenery that is used in mallung.

1 lb (500 g) mixed leafy green vegetables (spinach, cabbage, lettuce)
3 tablespoons coconut or vegetable oil
2–4 fresh green chilies
1 tablespoon dried shrimp
½ teaspoon turmeric
6 curry leaves
1 large onion, very thinly sliced
⅔ cup (2 oz/60 g) shredded (desiccated) coconut
salt and lemon or lime juice

Thoroughly wash the vegetables, separating the leaves and cutting away any firm stems. Shred the vegetables coarsely and place in a saucepan. Cover tightly and simmer for 3 minutes.

Heat the oil in a small pan. Slit open the chilies, scrape out the seeds and shred the chilies finely. Fry in the oil for 1 minute. Pound the dried shrimp until they are reduced to filmy strands, then add to the chilies with the turmeric, curry leaves and onion. Fry together for 2–3 minutes, add the coconut and stir in the oil until evenly mixed.

Add the vegetables, toss together thoroughly and heat through, adding salt and lemon juice to taste.

SERVES 4

ROTIS

Sri Lankan-style Flat Breads

Flat coconut-flavored rotis *can be made with several kinds of flour: finely milled wholewheat flour made especially for* rotis; *white self-rising flour; or either of these, mixed with a little rice flour. Unlike similar breads in India, which are merely a mixture of flour and water, Sri Lankan* rotis *have a little finely ground shredded coconut added to the dough.*

2 cups (8 oz/250 g) self-rising flour
½ cup (3 oz/90 g) rice flour
½ cup (2 oz/60 g) finely ground shredded (desiccated) coconut
1 teaspoon salt
1¼ cups (10 fl oz/310 ml) cold water
ghee (clarified butter)

Pour the flours into a mixing bowl, add the coconut and salt and mix together thoroughly.

Make a small well in the center, add most of the water and work in, adding the remaining water if needed. Knead until the dough is soft and smooth and does not stick to the bowl, then place on a work surface and invert the bowl over the ball of dough. Let stand for about 40 minutes for the flour to soften.

Divide into 12–15 pieces and flatten with the fingers into thin round shapes. Heat a *tawa* or heavy iron griddle and spread with a little ghee. When very hot, cook the *rotis* on both sides until golden. Serve hot.

MAKES ABOUT 15

ROTIS, SRI LANKAN STYLE FLAT BREADS

SEENI SAMBOLA

Chili Sambol

Serve as a side dish with meats, seafood and rice dishes.

4 large onions
5 cloves garlic
1-in (2.5-cm) piece fresh ginger
⅔ cup (5½ fl oz/170 ml) coconut oil
3 whole black cardamoms
2-in (5-cm) cinnamon stick
2 teaspoons curry powder*
2 teaspoons chili powder
½ teaspoon turmeric
2 tablespoons ground Bombay duck
2–3 tablespoons ground dried shrimp
1 teaspoon salt
1½ teaspoons sugar
1 tablespoon white vinegar
2 tablespoons tamarind pulp
3 tablespoons boiling water
¼ cup (2 fl oz/60 ml) thick coconut milk
2 fresh green chilies

Peel and very finely chop or grind the onions, garlic and ginger. Heat the oil in a medium saucepan and fry them until the onion is soft and turning brown. Add the crushed cardamom pods, cinnamon stick, powdered spices, Bombay duck and dried shrimp and fry for 2 minutes, stirring constantly.

Add the salt, sugar and vinegar. Mix the tamarind pulp with the boiling water and mash to extract the tamarind essence, then strain into the pan. Add the coconut milk and heat to boiling; simmer until thick. Slit open the chilies, scrape out the seeds and cut the chilies into very fine threads. Stir into the sambol.

Garam masala or Sri Lankan curry spices – a mixture of coriander, cumin, fenugreek and fennel, dry-fried until deeply colored, then ground with cardamom, mace and cinnamon.

VATTALAPPUM

Coconut Pudding

Quite the most luscious pudding imaginable, Vattalappum, although originally from Malaysia, is very popular in Sri Lanka. Milk, thick coconut milk and jaggery *(rich brown palm sugar) combine with eggs in a creamy pudding which can be steamed or baked in the oven.*

4 large eggs, well beaten
1 cup (8 fl oz/250 ml) milk
1½ cups (12 fl oz/375 ml) thick coconut milk
½ teaspoon ground cardamom seeds
¼ teaspoon freshly grated nutmeg
¼ teaspoon ground mace
2 teaspoons rosewater
¾ cup (4 oz/125 g) soft brown sugar or *jaggery*
½ cup grated coconut

Mix the eggs, milk and coconut milk together; stir in the spices and rosewater.

Dissolve the brown sugar in enough hot water to melt it, then pour into the custard. Pour into a heatproof dish and stand in a baking pan half filled with hot water. Bake at 280°F (140°C) for about 1¾ hours or until set. Sprinkle with fresh and toasted grated coconut. Serve warm or cold.

SERVES 6–8

AAMCHUR (India): Powdered dried green (unripe) mango. Substitute lemon juice.

ASAFOETIDA/HING (India): An edible gum used sparingly as a seasoning. Can be omitted.

ASAM (Malaysia), **ASEM** (Indonesia): The tart fruit pods of the tamarind tree. Used to flavor, tenderize and acidulate. Substitute lemon or lime juice or diluted vinegar.

ATTA (India): Finely milled wholewheat flour. Substitute well sifted stone-ground wholewheat flour.

AZUKI BEANS (Japan): Small dried red beans, mostly used in sweet dishes. Available dried and canned.

BANH TRANG (Vietnam): Compressed rice dough wrappers, transparent and require dampening to use. Spring roll wrappers are an acceptable alternative.

BASIL: *Horapa* (Thailand), *Rau Hue* (Vietnam), *Daun-Kemangi* (Malaysia/Indonesia). Sweet basil variations. Substitute common sweet basil.

BEAN CURD: *Dofu* (China), *Tofu* (Japan), *Doobu* (Korea), *Tauhu* (Malaysia/Indonesia): Jelly-like cakes made by coagulating a mixture of ground soybeans and water. Used as a vegetable or a protein-rich meat substitute. Sold fresh in water, or in powdered form. *Taukua* (Malaysia), *Too Hoo* (Thailand) are compressed bean curd cakes. *Yakitofu* (Japan) are grilled cubes of bean curd.

BEAN PASTES AND SAUCES: Seasoning pastes based on fermented soybeans. *Hot Bean Paste*, a mixture of soybeans, salt, spices, garlic and chili, gives a strong hot taste. *Sweet Bean Paste/Hoisin Sauce or Barbecue Sauce* is used as a mild seasoning and as a dip.
Yellow Bean Sauce is made from whole yellow soybeans fermented in brine, usually with chili added.

BESAN (India): A flour made from ground chick peas (garbanzos) used as a thickener and for making certain vegetarian snacks.

BONITO (KATSUOBUSHI) (Japan): a member of the mackerel family. It is dried and shaved into paper-thin flakes as *hana-katsu*. Used to make *dashi*, the basic stock, in conjunction with *kombu* (large-leaf kelp). Sold in packs, or as instant stock granules labelled *hon-dashi* or *dashi-no-moto*.

CARDAMOMS: *Elaichi* (India), *Buah Pelaga* (Malaysia): An aromatic seed pod. Green cardamoms are used whole or lightly crushed in sweet and savory dishes. Black pods should be peeled and the seeds ground finely for curries, sweets, cakes and pickling. Store whole pods in an airtight container and grind just before using.

CHINESE FIVE SPICES (NG HEUNG FUN) (China): Five spice powder, a fragrant blend of star anise, cassia, fennel, cloves and Chinese brown peppercorns (see below).

CHINESE VINEGAR: *Red* vinegar is distilled from rice and has a mild slightly sweet taste. Used mainly as a dip, substitute red wine vinegar. *Black/Brown* vinegar is also mild. Substitute malt vinegar.

CHINESE PARSLEY (FRESH CILANTRO/CORIANDER): *Yin Sai* (China), *Daun Ketumber* (Malaysia/Indonesia), *Hara*

Dhania (India): The aromatic fresh leaves of the coriander plant are indispensable as both herb and garnish. The minced root and stalks feature in Thai curry seasonings.

CHILIES: Hot peppers come in many sizes, shapes, colors and degrees of intensity from mild to searing hot. Use green chilies whole or sliced in curries, soups and dips. Red chilies are used in the same way, but are also dried to make whole dried red chilies, crushed into chili flakes, ground into chili powder or steeped in oil to make a powerful condiment, chili oil, used in Chinese cooking.

COCONUT: Without the ubiquitous coconut, the cuisines of Southeast Asia would have evolved in a quite different way. Coconut oil is used sparingly as a fragrant cooking medium, particularly in Indonesia. Coconut milk, made by processing the fleshy white nutmeat, is used for enriching and thickening curries, in place of cream in desserts, and as a cooling beverage. Readily available in canned, compressed block and powder form, it is easy to use but does not keep well. Store unused portions in the freezer. *Kelapa* (Indonesia) is shredded or grated fresh coconut. Desiccated or dried shredded coconut, moistened with water or milk, are suitable alternatives.

CURRY LEAVES: *Daun Kari Pla* (Malaysia), *Kari Patta* (India): Small aromatic leaves from a native tree, used like bay leaves. Sold fresh or dried, in small packs.

DAIKON (Japan): The giant white radish known as *Loh Buk* to the Chinese. Readily available, but can be substituted by kohlrabi when it is to be cooked, or common red radishes if used raw.

DASHI (Japan): The principal stock used in Japanese cooking. See also notes on *bonito. Ichibandashi* is the first infusion of the two principal ingredients *hana-katsuo* and *kombu*, and is the one generally used. *Niban dashi*, made by infusing the ingredients a second time, produces a weaker stock useful in one-pot dishes, broths and soup noodles. Freshly made is best, but instant granules have a good flavor and are easy to use.

DHANSAK MASALA (India): A blend of spices, primarily coriander and cumin, used to season a traditional Parsi Indian dish, *dhansak*.

DRIED SEAFOODS: FISH: Sun-dried and salted fish are used extensively to flavor soups and stocks and may also be fried to serve as a side dish or crumbled as a condiment. *Ikan Bilis* (Malaysia) are small silver-skinned fish, salt-cured and dried. Readily available, but can be substituted by dried shrimp in most dishes. Dried and/or salt-cured fish can be substituted by dried shrimp (prawns) or by fish bouillon granules or powder.

SHRIMPS (PRAWNS): Small peeled sun-dried shrimp (prawns) give a pungent taste to stocks and are also often used in savory fillings and stuffings. Store indefinitely in an airtight container. Substitute anchovy essence if necessary.

SHRIMP (PRAWN) POWDER/FLOSS: Pulverized dried shrimp (prawns), often combined with chili, used as a seasoning and condiment. Substitute minced dried shrimp and chili powder or flakes.

DRIED TANGERINE/MANDARIN PEEL (China): Sun-dried peel used to give a fresh citrus tang to stocks and braised dishes. Substitute lime or orange peel, or omit.

FENUGREEK *Methi* (India): Fresh leaves are used as a vegetable, dried and crushed as a seasoning for *tandoor* baked foods. The dried seeds are used frequently in curries, pickles and chutneys, having a rich burnt sugar aroma not unlike maple syrup.

FISH SAUCE: *Nam Pla* (Thailand), *Nam Padek* (Laos), *Ngan-pya-ye* (Burma), *Tuk Trey* (Kampuchea), *Nuoc Mam* (Vietnam), *Patis* (Philippines), *Kecap Ikan Petis* (Indonesia). Used like soy sauce as a seasoning and condiment, fish sauce is a thin salty sauce with a strong fish flavor. Readily available. Shrimp (prawn) and squid sauce are similar and are a good alternative, as is a mixture of light soy sauce and anchovy paste.

GAI LARN (China): A stalky green vegetable with sharp flavor. Rape, mustard greens or broccoli can be used instead.

GALANGAL/GALINGALE: *Laos* (Indonesia), *Lengkuas* (Malaysia), *Khaa* (Kampuchea), *Kha* (Thailand). Greater galangal, a rhizome similar to ginger which can be substituted. Most commonly sold as Laos powder.

GARAM MASALA (India): Spice mixture used to flavor curries and occasionally as a condiment. Blends can contain up to 20 different spices, but basics are coriander, cumin, cardamom, cinnamon, pepper and cloves. Commercial curry powders are not used in India, but packaged *garam masala* is available where Indian/Asian spices are sold. Keep fresh by storing in an airtight glass jar.

GINGER: *Geung* (China), *Shoga* (Japan), *Khing* (Thailand): The rhizome *zingiber officinale* is vital to Asian cooking. Always use fresh ginger root, never powdered, and peel before use. Readily available, the young roots with pale cream wrinkle-free skin are best. Store in refrigerator or in a cool area of the kitchen. To make ginger juice, grate ginger and squeeze through a garlic press or square of cheesecloth.

GLUTINOUS RICE: *Ketan* (Indonesia), *Pulut* (Malaysia): Popularly known as "sticky rice" because its high starch content makes it into a thick sticky mass when cooked. It is used often in sweet dishes and also as a savory rice. Readily available, ordinary white rice cannot be substituted.

GULA JAWA/PALM SUGAR: *Gula Jawa* (Indonesia), *Gula Melaka/Malacca* (Malaysia), *Jaggery* (India/Sri Lanka), *Nam Taan Peep* (Thailand): A deep brown compressed sugar obtained from the sap of coconut or palmyrah palms. Substitute dark brown sugar such as turbinado, molasses sugar or soft refined brown sugar.

JIU (China): Distilled rice wine with a strong, dry taste. Substitute Japanese *sake*, or a very dry sherry or vermouth.

KECAP MANIS (Indonesia): A thick sweet seasoning sauce and condiment based on dark soy sauce, sugar and spices. A successful alternative combines dark soy sauce and dark corn syrup.

KEMIRI/CANDLE NUT: *Buah Keras* (Malaysia): A hard, dry, cream colored nut kernel used to thicken and flavor curry sauces. Raw cashews, macadamias or brazil nut kernels can be used.

KESAR (India): Saffron, the world's most expensive spice. The bright red stigmas of a certain crocus grown in Kashmir, it imparts a golden color and subtle flavor. Unless quite expensive, powdered saffron will be adulterated with a filler, but still gives good results. For the best flavor use the whole dried stigmas, lightly crushed. Powdered turmeric can be used instead for savory and rice dishes.

KOMBU (Japan): Wide long leaves of tangle kelp. Used to flavor stock (see *dashi*, above). Sold cut into short lengths, in packs. Wipe with a damp cloth before use; do not wash as this can remove some of the essential flavor. Some cooks score the surface to release extra flavor. Store in an airtight container to keep dry.

KUNYIT (Malaysia), KUNCI (Indonesia): Powdered turmeric, a bright yellow seasoning with a unique and somewhat earthy taste. From a rhizome of the ginger family, it is generally used in powder form and is readily available. *Kunyit Basah*, the fresh turmeric root, when available, should be peeled like ginger before use. Store in the refrigerator.

LEMON GRASS (CITRONELLE, CITRONELLA): *Sereh* (Indonesia), *Serai* (Malaysia), an aromatic leafy herb. The grasslike leaves are infused as a beverage and the tightly packed pale green lower section is used in cooking. Grows readily in hot moist conditions and is best used fresh. Dried chopped and powdered lemon grass are readily available.

LIME LEAVES *Limau Perut Kaffir* (Indonesia), *Makrut* (Thailand), *Daun Keruk Perut* (Malaysia): The dried leaves of a native Asian citrus tree, *citrus hystix* or the Kaffir lime. Substitute strips of lemon or lime peel.

MALI (Thailand): An intensely fragrant flavoring essence made from jasmine. No substitute, but lemon or rose extract/essence can be used.

MIRIN (Japan): A sweet, sherry-like Japanese liquor used in cooking. It should be boiled to remove alcohol and concentrate flavor. Sweet sherry or vermouth are good alternatives.

MISO (Japan): A thick seasoning paste made from mashed soybeans mixed with other grains and injected with a mold to induce fermentation. *Yellow miso* is made with a rice mold and is mild, almost sweet. *Red miso* uses barley mold to produce a stronger taste and color, while bean mold results is an intensely flavored salty dark miso. The texture and flavor of miso are unique so it cannot be effectively substituted. However, most types are now available in Japanese or health food stores.

MUSHROOMS AND EDIBLE FUNGI: Several important types appear in Japanese and Chinese recipes. *Shiitake*, the dried black Japanese mushrooms, are the finest quality, but can be substituted by Chinese dried mushrooms of which the best have a deep brown cap and creamy underside. *Oyster mushrooms* are available canned or fresh. They have a wide, pulpy, pale beige cap and thick edible stems, set off-center to the cap. *Straw mushrooms* are best fresh, but the canned variety has an acceptable taste. *Enokitake* or golden mushrooms have miniscule cream colored caps above long slender stems. Sometimes available fresh, the clump at the end of the stems should be removed. Also in cans. *Wood/cloud ear fungus* is a brownish black crinkly edible fungus with a firm crunchy texture. Sold in small packs, it should be kept dry until used. *Nameko* mushrooms are amber-colored, similar to champignons or button mushrooms in appearance. They have a strong flavor and gelatinous surface. Usually sold canned. Substitute button mushrooms.

NAGANEGI (Japan): This is an onion resembling a small leek or an overgrown green (spring) onion, both of which could be substituted.

NORI (Japan), KEEM (Korea): A type of laver harvested from the sea which is dried, compressed and cut into squares for use as an edible wrapper, or may be finely shredded to use as a garnish or condiment, often in combination with sesame seeds and pepper. It should be toasted to crisp and improve taste before use. It must be kept absolutely dry or it will quickly spoil.

PANDAN/PANDANUS: *Daun Pandan* (Malaysia), *Toey* (Thailand). Its strongly aromatic leaf is used both for bright green color and unique flavor in sweets and occasionally in rice dishes. *Kewra* (India) is a type of pandanus, but with a noticeably different flavor. In essence form it is intensely concentrated, requiring usually one small drop in a dish.

PANEER (India): A homemade curd cheese, produced by coagulating boiled milk and retaining the resultant curds which are pressed into a firm cake. Used in vegetarian and northern Indian cooking, cubes of baked ricotta cheese can be substituted, although *paneer* is easily made at home.

RAU RAM (Vietnam): A pungent herb with peppery/minty characteristics. Tapered green leaves ribbed with purple. Substitute spearmint or common mint.

RICE FLOUR: Very finely ground white rice, used as a thickener and to make many types of sweet dishes. Rice flour dough is steamed to make *rice sheets* which are filled, steamed and served as a savory snack, or cut into strips to become *rice ribbon noodles*; or it may be extruded into thin strands to make *rice vermicelli*.

SESAME: Seeds, both white and black, are used as a garnish, ground and used as a seasoning and thickener, or made into a thick *paste* for use in sauces and dressings. Oil *Ma Yau* (China): extracted from sesame seeds has a strong nutty taste used often in Chinese, Korean and Japanese dishes. Normally used sparingly to flavor, the Koreans and Japanese enjoy the intense flavor it imparts when used in conjunction with other oils for deep-frying.

SHIRITAKE (Japan): The clear noodles used in *Sukiyaki* are extruded from a paste made from the starchy root of the *Amorphophalus konjac*. Clear bean flour vermicelli, as used in Chinese cooking, can be substituted.

SHRIMP PASTE: Known as *Kapi* (Thailand), *Mam Tom* (Kampuchea), *Pazuon-nga-pi* (Burma), *Trassi/Belachan* (Indonesia), *Blacan/Blachan* (Malaysia), this strong-tasting seasoning made from sun-dried, salted and ground shrimp (prawns) is often used to add its unique taste to curries and dipping sauces. Readily available where Oriental foods are sold. It should be stored in a thick, airtight jar as its smell can overpower other spices and seasonings.

SZECHUAN PEPPERCORNS: The berries of the *Xanthoxylum piperitum*, the Chinese peppercorn or Japanese prickly ash. Dried, they are reddish brown, fragrant and intensely flavored but not hot. Known variously as Chinese brown peppercorns, *fagara*, Szechuan (Sichuan) pepper, or by the Japanese name *sansho*, they are readily available.

WASABI (Japan): A powerful pale green powder made from a type of horseradish root. Indispensable when making *sushi* and as a condiment with several important Japanese dishes. Substitute hot mustard powder.

WAKAME (Japan): A type of kale-seaweed which is enjoyed as a vegetable. Sold dried, in small packs, it should be soaked to soften and expand. Requires minimal cooking. Keep very dry in storage.

Acknowledgments

The author wishes to extend her thanks to Mr Ian Thompson of The Decorators Gallery, Red Hill, Brisbane, for the use of many of the beautiful artifacts used in the food photographs. And to Artifacts Gallery, Brisbane, for their similar assistance, a special thank you.

Index

Italic numerals indicate references to photographs.

abalone
  sauteed with lettuce in oyster sauce 76, 76
  steamed in sake 35, 35
almond curd, sweet 85, 85
aubergine, *see* eggplant
azuki paste 45

Balinese skewered pork and chicken in peanut sauce 220, 220
bamboo shoot
  curry, shrimp and 208, 208
  salad 120-1, 129
banana parcels 239, 239
bananas, fried 239, 239
basil and chili, chicken with 106, 108
batter
  besan 180
  pancake 53, 54
  tempura 43, 43
battered foods 43, 43
bean curd
  black mushrooms with 81, 81
  chicken with *laksa* noodles in coconut sauce 169, 169
  grilled, on skewers 21, 31
  Hokkien style noodles 168, 168
  miso-flavored soup with 40, 40
  popiah 148-9, 155
  simmered 31, 31
bean patties 202-3, 207
bean sprouts
  Hokkien style noodles 168, 168
  shredded chicken with bean sprouts 60-1, 74
beef
  and bitter gourd rolls 140, 140
  and kidney bean soup 214-5, 221
  and onion soup, hot chili 10, 55, 55
  and peanuts, shrimp crisps with 137, 137
  aromatic braised beef with noodles in rich broth 144, 144
  balls with cilantro leaves, steamed 67, 68
  barbecued beef salad 132-3, 138
  braised beef with tomatoes 96, 96
  chili beef 112, 113
  dhansak kebabs 174-5, 191
  Japanese barbecue 44, 44
  kebabs 190, 190
  Korean hotpot 55, 56
  pancakes with nine fillings 53, 54
  pastries 247, 247
  rice gruel with shrimp 115, 115
  samoosas 180, 181
  sashimi 39, 39
  skewers with peanut sauce 154, 154
  sliced beef and broccoli stems on flat rice noodles 84, 84
  sour beef stew 95, 95
  spicy braised beef 79, 79
  steamboat 158
  Sumatran beef curry 228, 228
  sun-dried 88-9, 94
  tagalog stew 96, 96
  vindaloo 186, 186
  with vegetables, crisp-fried shredded 78, 78
  with vermicelli 140, 141
Bengal peas 195, 195
bhujia 186, 193
birds' nest soup with lotus seed, sweet 85, 85, 85
bitter gourd rolls, beef and 140, 140
Bombay duck 247, 250
brains in coconut curry 224, 224
bread
  buttered layered flat bread 199
  crisp green onion pastries 83, 83
  fried unleavened bread 198
  griddle-cooked unleavened 185 199
  Indian 198, 198-9
  leavened tandoor bread 198
  rotis 251, 251
broccoli stems on flat rice noodles, sliced beef and 84, 84
buckwheat noodles, chilled 30, 30
besegnek 223, 224
buns, sesame 82
Burmese rice 208, 210

cabbage
  cabbage rolls 181, 181
  chili pickled 48-9, 53, 53, 57
  fried noodles 234, 235
  in a creamy sauce, Chinese 81, 81
  Laotian cabbage soup 120-1, 126
  popiah 148-9, 155
  prawn and cabbage curry 160, 160
  Shanghai dumplings 67, 67
  sour beef stew 95, 95

cake, layered 88-9, 97
calves' liver, curried 224, 224
capsicums *see* peppers
carp
  Westlake fish 73, 73
carrot
  cream dessert 196, 196
  pickled 27
chicken
  and crabmeat rolls with salad 137, 137
  and leeks, clear soup with 40, 40
  and rice pot 30, 30
  and sesame dressed noodles, cold 71, 83
  Balinese skewered pork and chicken with peanut sauce 220, 220
  balls simmered in sauce 21, 37
  balls with quail eggs, *yakitori* 37
  battered deep-fried 185, 185
  curry 208, 209
  curry, Sri Lankan 242-3, 249
  fried noodles 234, 235
  fried spring/egg rolls 66, 66
  grilled 37, 37
  Hainan-style chicken rice 74, 75
  heavenly chicken 100-1, 106
  in coconut and peanut sauce 112, 112
  in the 'Adobo' style (88-9), 93
  Japanese barbecue 44, 44
  nasi goreng 236, 236
  noodles with assorted sliced meats in soup 141, 141
  omelet 71, 83
  onion and peppers, *yakitori* 37
  pancit molo 93, 93
  peppered chicken 113, 113
  rice gruel with shrimp 115, 115
  salad of rose petals and mixed meat 100-1, 113
  shredded with bean sprouts 60-1, 74
  spicy chicken besegnek 223, 224
  steamboat 158
  stuffed with peanuts 127, 128
  tamarind chicken 163, 163
  tender curried chicken 184, 184
  with basil and chili 106, 108
  with *laksa* noodles in coconut sauce 169, 169
  with lemon grass and peanuts 139, 140
  with sesame seed sauce, sake-steamed 38, 38
  wontons 93, 93
chicken 'gizzards' 116
chicken liver
  chicken liver curry 164, 164
  winter melon and ham soup 60-1, 70
chickpeas, spiced 195, 195
chili 233
  beef 112, 113
  beef and onion soup, hot 10, 55, 55
  chicken with basil and 106, 108
  flowers 233, 233
  hot sauce 234
  pickled cabbage 48-9, 57
  sambal 148-9, 167, 235
  sambal balcan 148-9, 167
  sambal cuka 157, 167
  sambol 242-3, 251
  shredded 233, 233
  Singapore chili crab 162, 162
  stuffed chilies 100-1, 108
Chinese vegetable with oyster sauce 60-1, 82
chupatis 185, 199
chutney
  fresh coconut 193, 194
  fresh mint 193, 194
cilantro leaves, steamed beef balls with 67, 68
coconut
  and peanut sauce, chicken in 112, 112
  balls 237, 237
  brains in coconut curry 224, 224
  chicken 'gizzards' 116
  coated vegetables 242-3, 250
  cream, steamed 'sticky' rice in 145, 145
  cream sauce 100-1, 116
  fish moolee 148-9, 160
  fresh coconut chutney 193, 194
  golden yellow rice 214-15, 235
  Laotian noodle soup 128, 128
  layered cake 88-9, 97
  milk dessert 170, 171
  pancakes 117, 117
  pomfret in coconut sauce 183, 183
  pork simmered in 139, 139
  pudding 88-9, 97 242-3, 251
  sauce, chicken with *laksa* noodles in 169, 169
  serundeng 233, 234, 234
  tapioca and rice bean dessert 120-1, 129
  tempe in coconut milk 166, 166
  water chestnuts 116, 117
  yam and coconut pudding 171, 171
coriander, *see* cilantro
crab
  balls with sweet soy sauce, crisp 60-1, 69
  clear soup with crab 21, 40

curried crab 223, 223
  hotpot 41, 41
  noodles with assorted sliced meats in soup 141, 141
  rolls with salad, chicken and 137, 137
  Singapore chili crab 162, 162
cucumber
  cold cucumber soup 10, 54, 55
  cooked cucumber salad 48-9, 57
  pickles 214-15, 232
  pineapple salad 221, 232
  salad, lobe leaf seaweed and 41, 42
  yogurt and cucumber sauce 186, 194
curry
  brains in coconut 224, 224
  chicken 208, 209
  chicken, Sri Lankan 242-3, 249
  chicken liver 164, 164
  curried calves' liver 224, 224
  curried crab 223, 223
  curried fish 248, 249
  devil's 164, 165
  duck 110-1, 112
  eggplant and mutton/lamb 159, 159
  fish *moolee*, a mild 148-9, 160
  hot lentil and vegetable 194, 194
  Kashmiri meat balls 187, 187
  mild curried lamb 214-15, 229
  Moslem 100-1, 110
  pork 209, 209
  prawn and cabbage 160, 160
  pumpkin cream 190, 192
  shrimp and bamboo shoot 208, 208
  shrimp and green mango 182, 182
  Sumatran beef 228, 228
  tender curried chicken 184, 184
  tender lamb 188, 189
  vindaloo 186, 186
dashi 26
  ichiban 26
  niban 26
  stock 26
dhal 195, 195
dhansak 174-5, 190
dip, *see* sauce
doughnuts, Indian 197, 197
dressing, *see* sauce
duck
  and water chestnut soup 109, 109
  curry 110-1, 112
  festive spiced 226, 226
  Peking 77, 77
dumplings
  Shanghai 67, 67
  steamed pork 66, 69

eel, glazed broiled (grilled) 34, 35
eggplant
  and mutton/lamb curry 159, 159
  braised spicy 79, 82
  braised tomato and 186, 193
  in spicy yogurt sauce 192, 192
  puree, fish and 125, 125
eggs
  chicken omelet 71, 83
  egg wrappers 155, 155
  family omelet 156, 156
  fried spring/egg rolls 66, 66
  omelet shreds/strips 233, 233
  pork and mushrooms with egg 78, 78
  spiced eggs 250, 250

fish
  and eggplant puree 125, 125
  baked whole fish 214-15, 222
  ball soup 70, 71
  Bombay duck 247, 250
  chicken balls simmered in sauce 21, 37
  curried fish 248, 249
  fried with ginger sauce 100-1, 110
  grilled/broiled 120-1, 127,
  grilled pomfret 222, 223
  heavenly chicken 100-1, 106
  in hot sauce 221, 221
  in tomato cream sauce, baked 183, 184
  Laotian noodle soup 128, 128
  marinated 109, 109
  mohinga 202-3, 209
  moolee, a mild curry 148-9, 160
  on rice cakes, sizzling 76, 76
  parcels, little roasted 154, 154
  raw fish platter 33
  rice gruel with shrimp 115, 115
  rolled *sushi* 27, 29
  soup 144, 144
  steamboat 158
  steamed whole 60-1, 74
  sweet and sour fish soup 144, 144
  tempura 43, 43
  Westlake fish 73, 73
  with vegetables, sour pickled 94, 94
fruit and vegetable salad, spiced 231, 231

gado gado 230, 230
ginger
  dip 75
  sambal cuka 157, 167
  sauce, fried fish with 100-1, 110
gourd
  rolls, beef and bitter 140, 140

simmered, dried 28
gulab jamons 197, 197

Hainan-style chicken rice 74, 75
ham
  winter melon and ham soup 60-1, 70
  see also pork
Hokkien style noodles 168, 168
hotpot
  crab 41, 41
  Korean 55, 56

ikan bilis, fried 157, 157
Indian doughnuts 197, 197

Japanese barbecue 44, 44
John Dory
  grilled pomfret 222, 223
  pomfret in coconut sauce 183, 183

kachumber 191
Kashmiri curried meat balls 187, 187
kebabs 190, 190
  dhansak 174-5, 191
kim chee 48-9, 57
Korean
  barbecue 48-9, 56
  hotpot 55, 56

lamb
  and lentil casserole, Parsi 174-5, 190
  curry, eggplant and 159, 159
  dhansak kebabs 174-5, 191
  mild curried lamb 214-15, 229
  tender lamb curry 188, 189
  with spinach sauce 188, 188
Laotian noodle soup 128, 128
leeks, clear soup with chicken and 40, 40
lemon grass and peanuts, chicken with 139, 140
lentil
  and vegetable curry, hot 194, 194
  bean patties 202-3, 207
  Parsi lamb and lentil casserole 174-5, 190
  puree 195, 195
lettuce in oyster sauce, sauteed abalone with 76, 76
liver
  curried calves liver 224, 224
  Korean hotpot 55, 56
  see also chicken liver

mango curry, shrimp and green 182, 182
masala, shrimp in green 183
mint chutney, fresh 193, 194
miso-flavored soup with bean curd 40, 40
mohinga 202-3, 209
Moslem curry 100-1, 110
mung bean pancakes 53, 53
mushrooms
  pancakes with nine fillings 53, 54
  pork and mushrooms with egg 78, 78
  rolled sushi 28, 29
  scallops and shrimp with three kinds of mushrooms 72, 72
  with bean curd, black 81, 81
mutton
  curried meat balls 187, 187
  curry, eggplant and 159, 159
  kebabs 190, 190
  soup 158, 158

namprik 104
  rice gruel with shrimp 115, 115
  sauce 107, 107
nasi goreng 236, 236
noodles
  aromatic braised beef with noodles in rich broth 144, 144
  chicken with *laksa* noodles in coconut sauce 169, 169
  chilled buckwheat 30, 30
  cold chicken and sesame dressed noodles 71, 83
  fried noodles 234, 235
  Hokkien style noodles 168, 168
  Laotian noodle soup 128, 128
  sliced beef and broccoli stems on flat rice noodles 84, 84
  with assorted sliced meats in soup 141, 141
nuoc cham 137, 139
omelet
  chicken omelet 71, 83
  family omelet 156, 156
  shreds/strips 233, 233
onion
  crisp green onion pastries 83, 83
  fried flakes 233, 233
  onion *sambal* 148-9, 167
  soup, hot chili beef and 10, 55, 55
oysters
  sauce, Chinese vegetable with 60-1, 82
  sauteed abalone with lettuce in oyster sauce 76, 76
  with garlic and herb sauce 125, 125

pancakes
  coconut 117, 117

filled with red bean *44, 45*
mung bean 53, *53*
Peking duck pancakes 82
popiah 148-9, 155
with nine fillings 53, *54*
pancit molo 93
pastries
  beef pastries *180,* 181
  crisp green onion pastries 83, *83*
  patties 247, *247*
patties
  bean patties *202-3,* 207
  beef pastries 247, *247*
  deep-fried pea flower and vegetable
    patties *180,* 180
  shrimp patties *207,* 207
peanuts
  Balinese skewered pork and chicken
    with peanut sauce 220, *220*
  beef skewers with peanut sauce 154,
    154
  chicken stuffed with 127, *128*
  chicken with lemon grass and 139, *140*
  dressing, salad with 230, *230*
  fried *ikan bilis* 157, *157*
  Laotian noodle soup 128, *128*
  sauce, chicken in coconut and 112, *112*
  sauce for vegetable salad 163, *165*
  serundeng 233, *234,* 234
  shrimp crisps with beef and 137, *137*
  sweet peanut cream 84, *85*
peas
  bean patties *202-3,* 207
  Bengal 195, *195*
  crisp pea flour nibbles 247, *247*
  deep-fried pea flower and vegetable
    patties 180, *180*
  hot lentil and vegetable curry 194, *194*
Peking duck *77, 77*
  pancakes 82
peppers, *yakitori* of chicken, onion and
  37, 37
pickles
  cucumber *214-15,* 232
  sambal 234
  spicy 234
pineapple salad   *221,* 232
pomfret
  grilled *222,* 223
  in coconut sauce 183, *183*
popiah 148-9, 155
pork
  a pork dish from Goa *184,* 189
  and mushrooms with egg *78, 78*
  Balinese skewered pork and chicken
    with peanut sauce 220, *220*
  braised meatballs 80, *81*
  braised with taro 80, *80*
  chicken stuffed with peanuts 127, *128*
  curry 209, *209*
  devil's curry *164, 165*
  fried noodles 234, *235*
  fried spring/egg rolls *66, 66*
  ground pork with roasted rice, in salad
    leaves *126,* 126
  Hokkien style noodles 168, *168*
  in sweet soy sauce 227, *227*
  Korean hotpot 55, *56*
  Laotian noodle soup 128, *128*
  meatballs served in salad rolls 142, *142*
  mold, glutinous rice and 128, *128*
  mung bean pancakes 53, *53*
  nasi goreng 236, *236*
  noodles with assorted sliced meats in
    soup 141, *141*
  pancit molo 93, *93*
  parcels *106,* 106
  rice gruel with shrimp 115, *115*
  roast suckling pig 226, *226*
  salad of rose petals and mixed meat
    100-1, 113
  Shanghai dumplings 67, *67*
  simmered in coconut milk *139,* 139
  sliced with hot sauces 107, *107*
  sour beef stew 95, *95*
  steamboat 158
  steamed pork dumplings *66,* 69
  teriyaki pork rolls 38
  twice-cooked pork 80, *80*
  vindaloo 186, *186*
  wontons 93, *93*
potatoes, savory baked 192, *192*
prawns *see* shrimp
pudding
  coconut *88-9,* 97
  coconut, Sri Lankan *242-3,* 251

yam and coconut 171, *171*
pumpkin cream curry *190,* 192

quail eggs, chicken balls with 37

ras malai 196, *196*
red bean
  glutinous rice balls with red bean
    filling 44, *44*
  pancakes filled with *44, 45*
relishes
  sambal 234
  spicy 234
rice
  and pork mold, glutinous 128, *128*
  brown rice *174-5,* 191
  Burmese rice *208,* 210
  cakes, sizzling seafood on crisp 76, *76*
  chicken and rice pot 30, *30*
  compressed rice 237
  festive rice *148-9,* 169
  for *sushi* 27
  glutinous rice balls with red bean
    filling 44, *44*
  golden yellow rice *214-15,* 235
  ground pork with roasted rice, in salad
    leaves *126,* 126
  Hainan-style chicken rice 74, *75*
  in coconut cream, steamed 'sticky' 145,
    145
  Japanese steamed 28
  nasi goreng 236, *236*
  rice gruel with shrimp 115, *115*
  scattered 28, *29*
  shrimp rice 195, *195*
  Thailand 115
  vinegar flavored 27
  yellow 'sticky' rice *164,* 169
rice flour
  chicken 'gizzards' 116
  coconut pancakes 117, *117*
  coconut pudding *88-9,* 97
  tapioca and rice bean dessert *120-1,*
    129
rice vermicelli
  fried *laksa* 233, *233*
  mohinga 202-3, 209
rose petals and mixed meat, salad of
  100-101, 113
rotis 215, *251*
salad
  bamboo shoot salad *120-1,* 129
  barbecued beef salad *132-3,* 138
  chicken and crabmeat rolls with *137,*
    137
  cooked cucumber *48-9,* 57
  for fish and eggplant puree *125,* 125
  ground pork with roasted rice, in salad
    leaves *126,* 126
  lobe leaf seaweed and cucumber 41, *42*
  pineapple salad *221,* 232
  rolls, pork meatballs served in 142, *142*
  rose petals and mixed meats *100-1,* 113
  spiced fruit and vegetable 231, *231*
  vegetable salad 163, *165*
  with peanut dressing 230, *230*
sambal 233, *234,* 234
  balcan 148-9, 167
  chili *148-9,* 167
  cuka 157, 167
  Malaysian *148-9,* 167
  onion *148-9,* 167
  shrimp paste 234
  soy sauce 235
  tomato 235
sambol, chili *242-3,* 251
samoosas 180, 181
sashimi 21, 32, 33
  beef 39, *39*
  dipping sauce 34
sate 220, *220*
sauce
  dip for grilled/broiled fish *120-1,* 127
  for barbecued beef salad, 1 *132-3,* 138
  for barbecued beef salad, 2 139
  for beef with vermicelli 140, *141*
  for pancakes with nine fillings 54
  for steamboat 15
  for vegetable salad, peanut 163, *165*
  ginger *100-1,* 110
  ginger dip 75
  hot 107, *107*
  Korean barbecue *48-9,* 56
  namprik 107, *107*
  nuoc cham 137, *139*
  peanut 220, *220*

peanut, for *gado gado* 230, *230*
peanut for beef skewers 154, *154*
sashimi dipping sauce 34
sate 220, *220*
sesame soy sauce 34
tempura dipping sauce 43, *43*
teriyaki 38
yakitori 37
yogurt and cucumber sauce *186,* 194
scallops
  and shrimp with three kinds of
    mushrooms 72, *72*
  Japanese barbecue 44, *44*
sea laver *48-9,* 57
seafood
  hand-formed *sushi* 27, *29*
  on crisp rice cakes, sizzling 76, *76*
  platter, raw *21,* 32
  scallops and shrimp with three kinds
    of mushrooms 72, *72*
  squid in hot sauce 110, *110*
seaweed and cucumber salad, lobe leaf
  41, *42*
semolina cake *211,* 211
serundeng 233, *234,* 234
sesame
  cold chicken and sesame dressed
    noodles 71, *83*
  dressing, spinach with *39,* 42
  seed sauce, sake-steamed chicken
    with 38, *38*
  seeds, grilled squid with 34, *34*
  sesame buns 82
  sesame soy sauce 34
  sweet peanut cream 84, *85*
shellfish in vinegar dressing 35, *34*
shrimp
  and bamboo shoot curry *208,* 208
  and green mango curry *182,* 182
  crisps 233, *233*
  crisps with beef and peanuts 137, *137*
  crystal shrimp 72, *75*
  fried noodles 234, *235*
  heavenly chicken *100-1,* 106
  Hokkien style noodles 168, *168*
  in green marsala 183
  in vinegar dressing *34,* 35
  Japanese barbecue 44, *44*
  little shrimp patties *88-9,* 93
  nasi goreng 236, *236*
  noodles with assorted sliced meats in
    soup 141, *141*
  on crisp rice cakes, sizzling 76, *76*
  pancit molo 93, *93*
  paste 234
  paste on sugar cane sticks 138, *138*
  paste relish, dried shrimp and *209,* 210
  patties *207,* 207
  popiah 148-9, 154
  prawn and cabbage curry 160, *160*
  rice 195, *195*
  rice gruel with shrimp 115, *115*
  rolled *sushi* 27, *29*
  salad of rose petals and mixed meat
    100-1, 113
  scallops and shrimp with three kinds
    of mushrooms 72, *72*
  sour and hot shrimp soup 108, *109*
  spicy dry-cooked shrimp 248, *248*
  steamboat 158
  tamarind shrimp *161,* 161
  tempura 43, *43*
  toast *66, 66*
  wontons 93, *93*
Singapore chili crab 162, *162*
soup
  aromatic braised beef with noodles in
    rich broth 144, *144*
  beef and kidney bean *214-5,* 221
  clear soup with crab *21,* 40
  cold cucumber 10, *54,* 55
  duck and water chestnut 109, *109*
  fish 144, *144*
  fish ball 70, *71*
  hot chili beef and onion *10,* 55, 55
  Laotian cabbage *120-1,* 126
  Laotian noodle 128, *128*
  mutton 158, *158*
  noodles with assorted sliced meats in
    141, *141*
  sour and hot shrimp 108, *109*
  sweet and sour fish 144, *144*
  sweet birds' nest soup with lotus seed
    85, *85*
  winter melon and ham *60-1,* 70
  with bean curd, miso-flavored 40, *40*

with chicken and leeks, clear 40, *40*
spinach
  Hokkien style noodles 168, *168*
  lamb with spinach sauce 188, *188*
  with sesame dressing *39,* 42
spring/egg rolls, fried *66, 66*
squid
  in hot sauce 110, *110*
  noodles with assorted sliced meats in
    soup 141, *141*
  on crisp rice cakes, sizzling 76, *76*
  rice gruel with shrimp 115, *115*
  salt and pepper crispy 68, *68*
  spicy squid 162, *162*
  steamboat 158
  stuffed 53, *55*
  with sesame seeds, grilled 34, *34*
steamboat 158
stew
  sour beef 95, *95*
  tagalog 96, *96*
stock
  dashi 26
  Vietnamese fish stock 144, *144*
Sumatran beef curry 228, *228*
supreme creamy dessert 196, *196*
sushi 26
  hand-formed 27, *29*
  rice for 27
  rolled 27, *29*
sweet potato savories 220, *220*

tagalog stew 96, *96*
tamarind
  chicken 163, *163*
  shrimp *161,* 161
tapioca and rice bean dessert *120-1,* 129
taro
  braised pork with taro 80, *80*
  popiah 148-9, 155
tempe in coconut milk 166, *166*
tempura 43, *43*
teppan-yaki 44, *44*
teriyaki pork rolls 38
tomatoes
  and eggplant, braised *186,* 193
  braised beef with 96, *96*
  cream sauce, baked fish in 183, *184*
  sambal 235
  sour beef stew 95, *95*
tuna for rolled *sushi* 27, *29*

vegetables
  coconut coated *242-3,* 250
  crisp-fried shredded beef with
    vegetables 78, *78*
  crisp green onion pastries 83, *83*
  curry, hot lentil and *194,* 194
  deep-fried pea flower and vegetable
    patties 180, *180*
  salad 163, *165*
  salad, spiced fruit and 231, *231*
  simmered 230, *231*
  sliced beef and broccoli stems on flat
    rice noodles *84,* 84
  sour pickled fish with 94, *94*
  with oyster sauce, Chinese *60-1,* 82
vermicelli
  beef with 140, *141*
  dessert *148-9,* 171
Vietnamese fish stock 144, *144*
vindaloo 186, *186*
  paste 186
vinegar dressing, shellfish in *34,* 35
vinegar/soy dip 56

water chestnut
  dessert *100-1* 116
  in coconut milk *116,* 117
  soup, duck and 109, *109*
Westlake fish 73, *73*
whitebait
  spiced *48-9,* 57
winter melon and ham soup *60-1,* 70
wontons
  pancit molo 93, *93*

yakitori 37, *37*
yam
  and coconut pudding 171, *171*
  layered cake *88-9,* 97
  see also taro
yogurt
  and cucumber sauce *186,* 194
  sauce, eggplant in spicy 192, *192*